PRAISE FOR

The
Break
of the
Game

"Mr. Halberstam strides authoritatively through locker room, front office, and network suite and he casts an unsparing wide-angle lens upon the power struggles implicit in this big-money, fierce, TV-dominated enterprise. Big David . . . makes his points."

—The New York Times Book Review

"Halberstam is not afraid to ask much tougher questions than most NBA reporters. And obviously people answer him . . . There are many intriguing people and there is much good stuff in *The Breaks of the Game*."

—Sports Illustrated

"The best book Halberstam has written . . . concerned with people . . . immediate and moving."

—The Washington Post Book World

"Eloquent . . . an impassioned exposition . . . captures the world of professional basketball with passion, intelligence, and exceptional realism."

—San Francisco Chronicle

The
Breaks
of the
Game

The
Breaks
of the
Game

David Halberstam

HYPERION
• • • • •
New York

Originally published by Alfred A. Knopf Copyright © 1981 by David Halberstam

Published in 2009 by Hyperion

Grateful acknowledgment is made to *Sports Illustrated* for permission to reprint from "All Dressed Up, Nowhere to Go," by Paul Zimmerman. Reprinted courtesy of *Sports Illustrated* from the November 26, 1979, issue. © 1979 Time Inc.

Library of Congress Cataloging-in-Publication Data

Halberstam, David.
    The breaks of the game / David Halberstam. — 1st ed.
      p. cm.
    Originally published: New York : Knopf, 1981.
    ISBN: 978-1-4013-0972-5
  1. Portland Trail Blazers (Basketball team) I. Title.
    GV885.52.P67H34   2009
    796.323'640979549—dc22

                                    2008051121

Hyperion books are available for special promotions and premiums. For details contact the HarperCollins Special Markets Department in the New York office at 212-207-7528, fax 212-207-7222, or email spsales@harpercollins.com.

Design by Meryl Sussman Levavi

FIRST PAPERBACK EDITION

7 9 10 8 6

In memory of Dr. Michael Halberstam (1932–1980), who in the last year of his life was fond of sneaking onto Washington, D.C., playgrounds and attaching brand-new nets, which he had just bought, so that he and other playground players could hear their jump shots swish; and for his wife, Elliott Jones, and his sons, Charles Halberstam and Eben Halberstam.

"Fame," O.J. said, walking along, "is a vapor, popularity is an accident, and money takes wings. The only thing that endures is character."

"Where'd you get that from?" Cowlings asked.

"Heard it one night on TV in Buffalo," O.J. said. "I was watching a late hockey game on Canadian TV and all of a sudden a guy just said it. Brought me right up out of my chair. I never forgot it."

—From an article by Paul Zimmerman,
Sports Illustrated, November 26, 1979,
on O. J. Simpson

The Portland Trail Blazers

National Basketball Association franchise established in Portland, Oregon, in the fall of 1970, principal owner Herman Sarkowsky, minority owners Bob Schmertz and Larry Weinberg.

1970–71: Won 29, lost 53. Coach: Rolland Todd. Geoff Petrie is first-round draft choice. Season ticketholders: 1,095.

1971–72: Won 18, lost 64. Coach: Rolland Todd (fired in midseason) 12–44; then Stu Inman (who finishes season) 6–20. Sidney Wicks is first-round draft choice, Larry Steele third-round. Season ticketholders: 2,227.

1972–73: Won 21, lost 61. Coach: Jack McCloskey. LaRue Martin first-round draft choice, Lloyd Neal third-round. Season ticketholders: 2,410.

1973–74: Won 27, lost 55. Coach: Jack McCloskey (let go at end of season). No important draft choices. Season ticketholders: 2,971.

1974–75: Won 38, lost 44. Coach: Lenny Wilkens. Assistant coach: Tom Meschery. Bill Walton first-round draft choice. Season ticketholders: 6,218.

1975–76: Won 37, lost 45. Coach: Lenny Wilkens. Draft choices: Lionel Hollins (first-round), Bobby Gross (second-round). Larry Weinberg becomes principal owner. Season ticketholders: 6,561.

1976–77: Won 49, lost 33. Coach: Jack Ramsay. Assistant coach: Jack McKinney. Maurice Lucas, David Twardzik arrive from ABA. Herm Gilliam arrives in trade. Trail Blazers win NBA championship in six games with Philadelphia. Season ticketholders: 8,103.

1977–78: Won 58, lost 24. Coach: Jack Ramsay. Playing the best basketball in their history, the Blazers are 50–10 when Bill Walton is injured. Partially recovered, he subsequently breaks his foot in the second playoff game with Seattle. Walton then asks to be traded. Tom Owens joins team after trade with Houston Rockets. T. R. Dunn, second-round draft choice, replaces Herm Gilliam. Season ticketholders: 11,500 (ceiling set by club).

1978–79: Won 45, lost 37. Coach: Jack Ramsay. Walton sits out entire season with injured foot. Draft choices: Mychal Thompson and Ron Brewer (both first-round). Season ticketholders: 11,500.

The
Breaks
of the
Game

1

The Game

IN THE WEEK BEFORE THE FIRST PRACTICE THEY BEGAN CHECKING INTO THE small motel near the base of Mount Hood in the small suburban community of Gresham, Oregon. They were rookies and free agents, and the odds were already against them; their motel rooms were paid for, and there was daily meal money, but in a profession where more and more things were guaranteed, they were still at the point in their careers where the only thing guaranteed was a return airplane ticket back home in the likely event they were cut. The veterans, the young princes of the sport, who all owned homes in the swank upper-middle-class sections of Portland, were not required to arrive until the last moment, as befit their superior status. In contrast to the rookies and the free agents, the anxiety level of the veterans was relatively low; they had made the team before, many had even played on a championship team, and most important of all, the money in *their* contracts was guaranteed. For the rookies and the free agents it was another thing. Now, in the fall of 1979, they were at the very brink of their dreams, which was to play under contract in the National Basketball Association.

IT WAS AN odd and unlikely collection. Steve Hayes was white and very tall, 6'11". He also shot well, and once upon a time in this game that had been enough, to be tall and have a light shooting touch; but the game had now become one of speed and muscle, and Steve Hayes was lacking in both categories. He knew the coaches thought he was slow (intelligent but very slow was in fact their precise definition of him) and that in contrast to many of the muscular young blacks with whom he would be competing, his body lacked muscle tone. What he did not know and what would have given him some momentary cause for optimism, was the fact that the team's consulting psychologist, who had just tested him, was very impressed, not by Hayes's jump shot or court intelligence but by his psychological coherence. The shrink had become, because of that, a secret Steve Hayes booster, mentioning Hayes's name frequently to the coaches, prefacing his remarks with the disclaimer that he of course did not know basketball, but then adding very quickly that psychologically Hayes was sturdy, very sturdy indeed, a good bet for the NBA, psychologically speaking.

STEVE HAYES HAD been through all this once before, in 1977, at a preseason camp run by the New York Knicks. Arriving as a fourth-round draft choice, he had been judged too slow and had gone on to play for two years in Italy. He believed he had now spent enough time in the minor leagues. He also knew just how many players there were ahead of him on the Portland roster, and which of them had guaranteed money, and understood that the odds against him were already immense. Coaches who had once coveted bodies like his no longer did. All that made him feel slightly less than sturdy just then.

HAYES's FEELINGS WERE a good deal more tranquil, however, than those of another free agent named Greg Bunch. Bunch, who was black and quick while Hayes was white and slow, was at the moment still in a rage over what had been done to him earlier in the day. Greg Bunch had undergone the same battery of psychological exams that illuminated Steve Hayes's coherence, but, by mistake, had been required to undergo them a second time. That had convinced Bunch, who mistrusted professional basketball management anyway, that they were trying to mess with his head. He had exploded and started screaming at the team trainer, who was administering the test, to *leave his head alone.* Bunch had some reason for grievance in his professional career; a year earlier, as a second-round draft choice with the New York Knicks, he had played well in the preseason camp, had made the team, had even played in twelve regular-season games (averaging roughly eight minutes and two points a game) before being released in what was widely regarded as a racial decision. The Knicks, it appeared, wanted to keep the tail end of their bench a little whiter. Greg Bunch, bruised many times in his brief professional career, was duly sensitive and duly wary of the great white *they* who controlled his athletic destiny.

BUNCH'S ROOMMATE, A young black man from Racine, Wisconsin, named Abdul Jeelani, thought he had never seen anyone so tight. They were competing for the same job, small forward, on a team that already had two small forwards, both white; and it was a mistake, Jeelani thought, for the club to make them roommates. Jeelani had been at rookie camp earlier in the summer with Bunch and Bunch had refused to talk to him; then they had both been in the Los Angeles summer league for a month, and again Bunch had made a point of not speaking to Jeelani. Now here they were on the eve of the start of fall camp, with the veterans arriving the next morning, and they were rooming together. For the first time, Bunch was willing to say a few guarded words to Jeelani, a very few words indeed. They did not go out to eat together; there was too much tension in the air for that. Jeelani preferred in any case to eat out with Steve Hayes, whom he had known and played against in Italy. But he worried about Bunch, who was so tight that he could not sleep at night, always tossing and turning in bed. Jeelani in one sense wanted to befriend Greg Bunch, but he was aware, in the most primitive way possible, that everything good which happened to Bunch was bad for Abdul Jeelani. It was terrible to think that way. So he kept his distance from Bunch. At the same time he couldn't help realizing that the fear and tension in the face of his roommate was the same fear and tension he had seen on his own face during his three previous NBA tryouts, in Detroit, in Cleveland, in New Orleans, when he had looked around him and become convinced that everyone there, rookies, veterans, coaches, scouts, wanted him to fail. At this camp Jeelani felt more confident, more mature. He had three years of European ball behind him and he knew that only one player—Jimmy Paxson, a guard and thus not a competitor—had guaranteed money.

The rookies and free agents were all there; no one had missed his flight to Portland. The coaches were pleased by that. Worn-out by the increasing volatility of the league, they felt as little affection for rookies who missed planes as for rookies who missed jump shots, possibly less. They were exhausted from dealing with talented players of rare skills who were tied up in their own emotional problems—head cases, these players were called. Big talent, the coaches often said of a player like this, bad head. That night, awaiting the start of a new season (Though in fact in the new industrialization of American sports, the season never stopped. It ran from camp in September to playoff games in June, and in the summer there were rookie camps and summer leagues to watch.), the coaches were at once excited and anxious about the new season. The rookies and the free agents looked on the coaches as secure and powerful, men who held the keys to the league in their hands and made the final decisions on their careers. But the coaches and the scouts had their own anxieties and vulnerabilities. It was not a profession or a league to breed confidence in anyone, be he player or coach. The coaches' jobs were never secure. What went up in this league went up very quickly, and often came down just as quickly. Power was for the coaches an illusory thing; the only players to whom they appeared powerful were in fact marginal players, players over whom they could indeed exercise power, but to little purpose. The players over whom they would *like* to exercise their power—that is, the talented players flawed either by attitude or a specific major weakness in their game—more likely than not were completely protected, given the contemporary nature of the league, by no-cut contracts far larger than those of the coaches. It was these players who could, if they listened and obeyed, make the coaches seem more successful and thus more effective, yet it was these players over whom it was impossible to exercise authority directly; instead, unlike players of the past, they had to be stroked and cajoled into doing what the coaches wanted.

That first night the rookies and the free agents straggled into the dining room of the restaurant next to the motel. They were still somewhat wary of each other; for the moment there was too much tension and rivalry for there to be very much friendship.

While the players ate singly, the coaches went out in a group to a fancier restaurant a few miles away. They were all middle-class men, all white, all devoted fathers, but suddenly they had left their civilian incarnations behind. Now they were professionals, among their own kind once again, in a world without women, talking their own special shoptalk. Though the season had not even started, already in the forefront of their minds were the pressures of their game, the difficulties of the year ahead, the injuries and the salary problems.

The conversations between coaches, here in Portland and elsewhere, often possessed a certain melancholy tone these days. Basketball was their lives, they were men still doing what they had done as boys and for that other men envied them, but there was a consensus among them that their game was in trouble, that the real world had invaded their smaller world. There was today too much emphasis on money, on salaries and negotiations and renegotiations. Money now clouded not only the relationships between management and player, but between player and player. One player obsessed with his contract, Stu Inman was sure, inevitably caused all his teammates to be obsessed with theirs. Jack Ramsay tended to agree; when he arrived in Portland as coach three years earlier, the first thing he said was that he wanted no players who were in the option year of their contracts, or involved in any other kind of contractual dispute. This year he had two such players—Maurice Lucas and Lionel Hollins—and possibly a third, Tom Owens.

Inman, the Portland vice president and personnel manager, was depressed by the changes money had wrought, worried about what they meant to his team. His highest enthusiasm was reserved for young, still-innocent college players, preferably from a small college and never before visited by professional scouts; his greatest disdain was for almost any agent or lawyer. He talked a lot these days in an almost mystical way about what was good for basketball and what was bad for basketball, and when he explained why he so greatly admired his colleague Pete Newell, once a preeminent coach and now a scout for Golden State, and a senior statesman of the profession, he used an odd and slightly sad phrase: "Because the game has never ground him down." He spoke as a man who knew and loved basketball, but whose pleasant and private and somewhat sheltered world had been invaded and corrupted by beings from some other planet, richer and more powerful than he. Some fifteen years before, these other beings, powerful and far more commercially minded than the Inmans and Newells, had hit upon basketball as a means for *selling*. Their commercialism now ran through every aspect of the sport, from college to the pros, infecting everyone. One network, showcasing the college games, now competed for national ratings against the pro games on another network. The money pervaded everything: colleges now contended against one another not because they were traditional rivals, but in hopes of getting on national television and making $50,000 for a game. That changed the basketball people, Inman thought;

they became salesmen themselves, recruiters and not coaches. They sold, in his friend Newell's contemptuous phrase, the sizzle not the steak. The mood inevitably affected the players, who arrived at Inman's door complete with agents and lawyers and, he believed, both an exaggerated impression of their own worth and a distorted sense of why they were actually playing the game. Someone suggested to Inman that the answer was to draft in the coming year not the best player from UCLA, but the number one students in their classes from Harvard, Yale and Stanford law schools. Stu Inman was not amused.

Jack Ramsay, the coach, was more accepting of the changes that had taken place, more accepting of the fact that a coach now dealt primarily with spoiled, almost delicate athletes protected by no-cut clauses in their contracts. It was not a state of affairs he wanted, or sought, but he accepted it. After all, as the rewards had become so much larger for the players—not just in terms of salary, but in glory—so too were they larger for the coach; the television eye during playoffs caught not just Bill Walton rebounding, but also Ramsay kneeling, intense, talking to the players during time-outs. As a professional coach, possibly the best professional coach in the country, he had been able to rationalize his own conversion from a successful college coach, working in a world governed by old-fashioned sturdy loyalties, to a big league coach whose world was, in his own description, utterly without loyalty. A college coach, Ramsay believed, was granted authority almost automatically by virtue of his position; a professional coach gained what authority he could by exercise of his intelligence, his subtlety, his very being. He was on his own and Ramsay believed as an article of faith that no loyalty, either from those above who employed you, or those below who played for you, could be expected. Ramsay believed an owner would always fire a coach if he was perceived to be slipping; the players, if it served their purpose, would just as willingly withhold part of their game from a coach. Therefore a coach must learn that loyalty was valueless, and might even work against him, as for example when it encouraged him to keep on an older player, whose skills were diminishing, but whose past heroics he was still grateful for, instead of coldly picking a younger player with potential for the future. For this reason Ramsay rationed his emotions in his personal relations with his players. They might produce this year; he might still have to let them go next year; life was hard. Ramsay devoted his most intense emotion to *winning,* and his connection to the players seemed to end at the locker room door each night; when he and the players departed that room, they departed into very separate lives. Professional basketball was, he thought, a very tough world, a world that by its nature allowed for very few illusions. The question remained whether it was possible to survive and even triumph in such a world, and still exist outside it. Ramsay indeed seemed to be a man within whom the needs of his job and the needs of his humanity were constantly wrestling. "When you are discussing a successful coach," sports psychologist Bruce Ogilvie once said, not of Ramsay but of the entire profession, "you are not necessarily drawing the profile of an entirely healthy person."

Larry Weinberg, the owner of the Portland Trail Blazers, was not with his coaches that night. But their eyes were as much on him as on the players. His friends believed that he too regarded the enterprise with a good deal more skepticism than he had ten years earlier. His player payroll, which in the first season had been some $500,000, was now the fifth highest in the National Basketball Association, $2,228,225. It was the equivalent of running a factory with 7,000 workers, each of whom made $300 a week. Yet no one in his basketball operation seemed very happy. His favorite and most valuable player, Bill Walton, had just left in a flurry of charges and counter-charges, and that had been painful. His second most valuable player, Maurice Lucas, was making $300,000 a year and wanted out unless he got more money; in addition, Lucas's attacks on Weinberg himself were becoming increasingly personal; his third most valuable player, Lionel Hollins, was showing signs of growing disaffection, and probably would be gone next year; and his fourth most valuable player, Bobby Gross, had signed for so much money that his second most valuable player was angrier than ever. Larry Weinberg entered professional basketball thinking it would be fun, and it had instead become, in his own sardonic word, *interesting*.

Nor had the coming of the big money made the players a great deal happier. Like all Americans they welcomed the chance to be paid more rather than less, but in many cases, given their backgrounds of extreme poverty, the instant riches were more than they could deal with; in other cases, the money simply heightened the anxiety that went with any kind of stardom. Now, inevitably, management would eye a player more closely, and veteran players wanting to play one last year could no longer expect to get the benefit of the doubt. This made players more cynical about their future. The increasing preoccupation with money was upsetting, it loomed so large on a team. No matter how much money a player made, and no matter how much more it was than he once expected, there was always going to be someone else, playing somewhere, of lesser ability, who made more. Some former players believed that too much of a player's identity was now tied up in his salary. It touched not only the exterior world of basketball, the world the sportswriters chronicled and fans worried about, but more and more the interior world as well, the secret world that only the players knew and felt. The big salaries, older players believed, had gradually altered the players' self-perception, and gradually made what they did less fun. Rather than diminish grievance, they had in many ways made grievance worse. For whereas fifteen or twenty years ago grievance was genuine—over the lack of a pension plan, for instance—it had unified players by pitting them against management, now grievance had become more subtle, general, amorphous, the grievance of the imagination, of small slights, sometimes real and sometimes completely fictitious, and it often pitted player against teammate. It was now an article of faith among thoughtful former players that the new breed were by far more talented, but that they lacked desperately one key element—a feeling for each other, a sense of community, a loyalty to something besides careers and paychecks. The former players were sure that the game had been more fun in the past. These new players would end their careers with more money, certainly, but their memories would be sour.

Clearly too much had happened to the game, too quickly. Most dangerous of all, the impulse behind the change and expansion, as in so many aspects of modern American life, had not been a natural one. It had not been the gradual and genuine pressure of more fans wanting to pay their way into arenas, bringing the kind of direct and healthy support that might have validated the sport on its own merits. Instead, this was change that had been brought about from outside by powerful new commercial interests that recognized in professional basketball a vehicle to expand markets, *an artificial impulse.* Basketball was a convenience to them; an entertainment medium like any other, though one peculiarly suited to pushing cars and shaving cream and beer; if it served well as a commercial vehicle then everyone might become a good deal richer, including of course the basketball people. In consequence what had been pleasant, exciting, on occasion artistic and above all a *sport,* had become amplified beyond its social and commercial norm. It would be a benefit to some and very much a detriment to others.

For some ten years after the new commerce came to professional basketball, beginning in the mid-sixties, the machinery had worked satisfactorily and basketball had served its new sponsors well. It served them so well, in fact, that those responsible for maintaining the quality of the game—the owners—were suddenly overcome by an unparalleled attack of greed, which distorted and diluted the game, diminishing it artistically even as it was still seemingly on the commercial upswing. It was suddenly a product no longer in harmony with itself. The social consequences of that moment of greed were what everyone, in the league and out—players, coaches, television executives—was struggling with now, to no great success, and with increasing mutual bitterness.

WHAT WAS HAPPENING to basketball was similar to what was happening to a great many products in America. Originally, the impulse behind basketball had been genuine on the part of everyone concerned, the product had been good. And because the product was good all other kinds of people wanted a piece of it, making the value of the product skyrocket. It was rather as it had so often been, in modern America, with so many other producers of good things, bought into and bought up by those wishing to improve their tax position and their rating on Wall Street. A family in the Midwest might for example run a small ma-pa concern making potato chips. Because they loved making potato chips, as their own parents had before them, they did it very well. The potato chips were good, they sold well, and they satisfied a fairly large potato-chip audience. Moreover the company was run well and it made handsome profits. Then a large company that sold tires, and made millions of dollars doing so, decided to buy in to avoid paying huge taxes to the government, and to make its portfolio more attractive to investors. The new owners promptly dispatched the potato-chip king and his wife to Florida for a comfortable and well-deserved retirement and turned the management of the company over to a team of accountants. This was the usual procedure. None of the accountants knew anything about making potato chips, of course, and cared less, but they were skilled at expanding sales while cutting costs. To this end they promoted an expensive though highly successful television advertising campaign and soon many more potato chips of a severely reduced quality were being sold. So much for good potato chips. Now the cause behind this sequence of events was not the potato chips, it was the IRS and Wall Street.

In the same sense movies being made now were not reflecting the tastes and impulses of the moviemakers (or for that matter the audiences—the potato-chip eaters), but the tactics of the financial wizards who ran the studios and spent their time figuring out *what might work;* similarly, huge conglomerates were buying up publishing houses and deliberately setting out to produce not books as they should be—the results of pure creative impulse—but as the accountants liked them—calculated bestsellers lacking commercial risk. The active impulse was never quality of product, but simply bottom line. Nor was there very much risk involved in all this, for the dollars used to buy properties were not real dollars, they were dollars saved from the IRS; even the dollars lost were not real dollars, they were dollars written off against the profits of other subsidiary companies. The phenomenon was not very different in basketball, except here it was more noticeable. And here, of course, the product was human beings.

In sports the crucial change had been caused by the coming of television. Of the major American sports, basketball was perhaps most interesting in this regard because in comparison to football and baseball it had a shorter history and it was less rooted in the national myth. Because its norms were less developed, it was far more vulnerable to the new pressures created by television. As these pressures grew, the guardians of the sport were both less able and less willing to make distinctions between what was good for the sport and what was good for them personally. Many of the new owners came in only because the sport was now on national television. Basketball became overnight not just a game but a show, and overnight it competed not just with other sports (a pleasant, interesting pastime to be watched after the football season ended and before baseball started) but against other television fare—movies, sit-coms, Johnny Carson—sometimes in prime time. Thus it was only logical that when players thought about their salaries and compared them with the salaries of other Americans, they thought not of athletic salaries past and present, nor of steelworker salaries, but of the salaries paid to other entertainers—movie stars, television stars. Very quickly the commercial norms had reached the players themselves and the norms were always for bigger and bigger money. In the evolution of modern sport a league's success was no longer defined by the quality of its play (in this case often phlegmatic during the regular season and brilliant during the playoffs), or by the size of its live attendance (generally disappointing), but by how the networks—or more accurately the great national advertisers—saw it. For in American sports in 1980 there was no God but Madison Avenue and A. C. Nielsen was His prophet.

The first of the great commercial marriages in America in the postwar years had been between advertising and television, as the networks offered national advertisers an extraordinarily attentive national audience; the second great marriage had come in the late fifties and early sixties, as Madison Avenue, seeking ways to reach the American male, discovered live sports as a prime vehicle. Professional football had been the first triumph, with results so exceptional that advertisers immediately began casting about for other sports. Eventually handsome television contracts reached even the fledgling National Basketball Association. The connection gradually changed the nature of NBA ownership, and the structure of its economics. The old owners had been men of limited income, promoters and arena proprietors who stayed one step ahead of the bill collector. Their revenues were what they could draw from live fans. These new owners were primarily young self-made multimillionaires, in it for the connection, for the television money, for the glamour, for the tax writeoffs. Ego gratification was often more important to them than making money. Under these circumstances the economics had gone from real to unreal. Television had changed the nature of the audience too, from a tiny handful of passionate fans who went to live games and paid real money, and insisted on real performances, to millions and millions of *watchers,* loosely connected to the game, who sat in their homes and accepted what a given network offered because it happened at that moment to be somewhat more pleasing (or less displeasing) than what the other networks were showing. The money no longer came directly from the pockets of fans, it came from the projections and expectations of auto companies and breweries. Now when a team lost money, it was rarely real money, for it could be, and usually was, covered by some sleight of hand in an accountant's office.

For all that, the history of professional basketball on national television was short, at first lucrative, and now, increasingly unhappy. The owners and the networks, who as recently as 1978 had embraced each other while signing a seventy-four-million-dollar, four-year contract, were now deeply disenchanted with each other. A period of reckless expansion had damaged the game, the ratings were down, and the owners naturally enough blamed the network, CBS; CBS's executives just as naturally blamed the owners. CBS privately charged the owners with expanding too fast, out of greediness;

the owners in turn thought that CBS had been too greedy, too concerned with ratings, to give their game a fair chance at developing its true constituency.

Few of these owners had been around in the pretelevision days. That earlier generation of basketball franchise-holders had been driven out by the big money of the new bigtime sport. They had no multimillion-dollar businesses against which to write off their basketball losses, thus turning the unprofitable into the profitable; for them, unlike the new owners, losses meant real money. Most of the new owners were vividly aware of what television had done for pro football, and they wanted a piece of the same action.

What happened when Madison Avenue, at the end of the sixties, perceived basketball as a "hot" sport is a fable for our time, a story of instant success and destructive cupidity. For as the ratings went up, revenues went up, and advertisers wanted in; as television made the sport not just successful but glamorous, more owners wanted in; there was now the promise of fame and celebrity, and tax benefits as well. Suddenly all kinds of new American millionaires, most of them young, were clamoring to get in the NBA. This made it possible for the existing owners to charge a premium dollar for membership in this most exclusive club, giving up in return only a few marginal players. In the pretelevision age of the late fifties and early sixties, the price of a club was minimal, something that people won or lost in relatively low-stake poker games; now it began to rise; and this increase became a means of older owners not only recouping their original investments but paying their ongoing debts as well. Both in terms of network payments and of status, ownership became far more attractive. Where once there had been real economics based on real attendance and real payrolls, now there were illusory economics of owner ego and tax writeoffs and television checks and endless new suckers always waiting to get in. In the early sixties a franchise was worth perhaps $200,000; in 1980 Dallas bought in for $12 million. Every time the buy-in rate went up, every other owner could claim that his franchise was worth at least that much, because he of course had a few years of tradition and a few valuable players. It was a dangerous and unreal time. No one could lose. If professional basketball moved into a city which was not ready for it, New Orleans, for example, there were so many others wanting to get in that the present owners, having taken their tax deductions, could always sell at a much higher price to newer owners in another city. There was a goose and it laid golden eggs and every year the eggs would get bigger and the goose would live forever. . . .

In 1967, when television and the league discovered each other, there were ten teams. In that year San Diego (later Houston) and Seattle came in for $1.75 million each with each existing team picking up a neat $350,000 share of it. That made twelve teams. By the time Dallas came in only thirteen years later, those ten early franchises had made roughly $3 million from expansion-club payments alone.

At its best, in the early television years, pro basketball was a sport with relatively shallow roots but exceptional action and intensity and, above all, genuine rivalries. But each new team, and each consequent shift in players, diluted the mix and destroyed team character and identity. The game itself was becoming vulnerable. The problem was not just in the new cities to which basketball had been transplanted, often without much forethought; it was in the old franchises too, whose teams had now begun to age, and who could not—because the draft necessarily spread each year's new players thinner—replenish themselves. Madison Avenue, watching the decline of the traditional powerhouse teams in the early seventies, teams that were located, of course, in the big national markets, became nervous. Because there were more teams, there was now more travel. The players, locked into an endless schedule of eighty-two regular-season games, a schedule which guaranteed a kind of constant fatigue and almost certain minor—if not major—injuries, now faced even greater travel burdens and still more fatigue. Where once it had been only Madison Avenue which had seen the commercial possibilities of the game, and the owners who had seen the chance to make bigger money, now the new money had seeped down to the level of the players, and they were greedy as well, aware of what every other player in the league was making.

Most damaging to the intensity of the game was the arrival of the no-cut contract. Given no-cut contracts, too many games, and a schedule designed to exhaust even the most physically fit young men in America, many players responded by functioning on automatic pilot, coming alive only in the playoff games. Even worse, this had happened as basketball in the early seventies became the blackest of America's major sports. Where in the late sixties there had been some racial balance, the league in the seventies was three-quarters black. Just as the camera had caught and transmitted the true intensity of the old-fashioned rivalries in the earlier days of the league, so it now caught and transmitted with equal fidelity the increasing lethargy and indifference of many players in regular-season games, a lethargy and indifference now seen by a largely white audience as at least partially racial in origin. Those who knew the sport best learned to concentrate on the playoffs, ignoring most of the rest; CBS, frustrated by low ratings in the regular season, seemed bewildered by the difficulties of covering the play-offs adequately, further frustrating genuine fans. With the proliferation of teams, regular-season coverage declined to the point where CBS was ignoring fully two-thirds of them; there were in effect *two* leagues—one consisting of the twenty-two NBA member teams, the other a six- or seven-team league covered by CBS, its version of the NBA.

All this took place in less than a decade—sudden growth, the shift in values from those of pure sports to entertainment and advertising. What had happened to basketball was typical of altogether too much happening in the new American scheme of things: there was more, but it was less.

Yet television remained a seductive force on the game, on the players and on the fans. If it had inflated the sport beyond its proper scale it had also enhanced it, and allowed it to reach millions of serious fans who had never seen a live game. If it had helped make the job of the coach more difficult, it had also made him more famous; if it had made the players in some ways more restless with their station, it had also made them into much bigger heroes and cast their shadow upon the minds of far more young Americans than ever before. The game, for all its troubles, remained in the minds of its most partisan fans the greatest athletic showcase for the rare combination of athletic grace and power. The players, restless, outspoken, contentious, were, many sportswriters believed, the most interesting and often the most honest professional athletes in the country, and the pressures of dealing with such volatile and talented young men meant that the coaching was not just better, but that the coaches were more subtle than ever before. The season was long and difficult but it was not without its rewards, and its glory; nowhere was this more true than in Portland, which in its short ten-year history had known mostly the frustration of defeat and then in one magic year, briefly, the absolute joy of championship. That championship had come, and then had almost as quickly been lost again.

2

Prologue to the Season

THAT SPRING, IN 1977, THEY HAD WON THE CHAMPIONSHIP, THE YOUN-
gest team in history to do so, and the exuberance of their youth and
the profusion and seeming perfection of their many talents, and their
rare ability to control their own egos, had seemed to promise yet more, not
just that something was over and accomplished, but that it had only begun.
The residents of the city, then the smallest in the league, somewhat accustomed to being snubbed and scorned over the lack of size and sophistication of their hometown ("How can I," had said Ned Irish, owner of the then
grand New York Knicks, when it was suggested that the city might receive a
professional franchise, "put the name *Portland* Trail Blazers on the marquee of Madison Square Garden?"), accustomed to losing and accustomed
as well to loving their losers, had seized the moment joyously. On the final
day of the playoffs, the Coliseum had been filled some two hours before the
starting time. The din was both enormous and intimidating to the visiting
players, waiting in their locker room, like lions about to be thrown to the
Christians; with the pregame warmups not yet begun, it sounded like a
crowd in the final hysterical two minutes of an exciting game. The visiting
writers from Philadelphia were appalled by the almost naive enthusiasm of
the crowd, its lack of cool. They did not like the city anyway; there was too

much talk by the residents about being mellow, and the writers were sure that when they went out for dinner the Portland waiters spotted them for what they were, agents of the enemy forces, and deliberately extended them terrible service. When later that afternoon the last game was over, and Portland had in fact won the championship, the Center and Captain, until then the target of more local criticism than praise—for his politics, for the length of his hair, for his culinary preferences, for his medical history (earlier in his career, local fans, annoyed by his recurring record of injuries, had printed up T-shirts saying that he had *brain* spurs, not bone spurs)—had ripped off his shirt and tossed it into the crowd. A young freelance photographer named Barbara Gundle, new to sports, captured the exact moment, the Center adored, people reaching out to touch him, his own elongated arms spread in triumph from a powerful but surprisingly spavined chest. A Christlike image, she thought. The Center said, much later, that if they won again, it would be his pants he would take off and throw into the crowd. The television ratings for the final game in the state of Oregon, an area known for its love of the outdoors rather than for its love of indoor sports such as watching basketball on television, were 96 percent. No one in the history of television had any memory of one event so dominating a single television market.

In the locker room after the game the players poured champagne on each other. The coach said of the Center that he had never known a finer player. Nor, he added, had he ever known a finer competitor. Nor, he added, a finer person. At that point, fortunately, his superlatives gave out. Then the players had thrown the coach into a cold shower and for added good measure had thrown in the Center's best friend, a young man named Jack Scott, who in the past had been described not so much as the Center's friend as his political guru. Though all of this was part of the traditional tribal ritual of bigtime televised American sports, the inherent right of victorious athletes to pour someone else's champagne upon each other and to embrace each other, half-naked, live and in color, none of it made the national airwaves. CBS, the network which broadcast the league, but in larger truth sponsored the league as well, had, the moment the last basket had been shot and the score posted, departed the Portland Coliseum for the green fairways of a new, invented-for-television golf tournament, the Kemper Open. The die-hard basketball fans, perhaps ten million of them, who had stayed the course of a long and laborious twin season of basketball, first the interminable regular season and then the semi-interminable second season of the playoffs, waiting to see what Bill Walton looked like in victory (would he attack the President? the FBI?) and Julius Erving in defeat, saw instead the head of the Kemper Insurance Company welcoming them to a golf course. No one was pouring champagne on his head. Many of them turned off. Many others called CBS to complain irately over this injustice. It was, they knew, a decision which would never have been made at the end of a baseball World Series or a football Super Bowl, where the fans' right to see their winners was inalienable. The decision of CBS to cut away was a reminder that for all of its artistic beauty and its high salaries, and the fact that it might employ more truly brilliant and complete athletes than any other sport, professional basketball had not entered the national psyche or become part of the national myth. It remained, the grace and skill of its athletes notwithstanding, a sport of some isolated urban areas and some rural areas struggling for national acceptance.

The decision at CBS to switch to golf was not made out of malice, but largely out of indifference. The head of CBS Sports, Frank Smith, a man since departed, was a golfer himself and he lived in Greenwich, Connecticut, part of the great upper-middle-class white suburban ring which spanned American cities; it was, by and large, the cities that produced the basketball players, and suburban rings that produced television and advertising executives. Like many another high-level television and advertising executive in Greenwich, Frank Smith not only played a good deal more golf than he did basketball, but he also conducted a fair amount of his business upon the fairways. Thus golf was to him not just a more pleasant athletic and social endeavor than basketball, it was a far more serious one as well. He loaded up the CBS schedule with golf matches, which though they drew low ratings pleased many of his friends and business associates, among them the owners of the affiliate stations. They were the proprietors of television stations in many middling and small towns and cities. Low ratings or not, they *liked* golf, for in those towns and cities, golf was an even more essential part of the social-business fabric than it was in Greenwich, and they and their colleagues from advertising thought that CBS, if anything, did not program *enough* golf.

Still the small slight of CBS in depriving fans of the opportunity to share in the revelry via television was soon forgotten. A few days later the Portland team was honored at a downtown plaza and some 250,000 people turned out, not bad in a city generally estimated to have 365,000 inhabitants all told. No one could remember anything like those days, the victory itself, the celebration, the joy that it produced. Not even the end of World War II seemed to compare. It was a wonderful moment and because they were all so young—Walton the center was only 24, Hollins 23, Lucas 25, Gross 23, Davis 21, and Twardzik, the oldest starter, 26—everyone was sure that it would continue. Everyone spoke of the future and often both average citizens and people on the team used the word *dynasty*. It was not just that they had won, but the *way* that they had won, unselfish in a selfish world and a selfish profession. It had been not just a matter of scoring baskets, but of scoring baskets off the perfect pass. Philadelphia, because of its modified schoolyard play, its one-on-one style, had been cast by the media, by fans, by other coaches, as the bad guys. Philadelphia had paid millions for George McGinnis and some $6 million for Julius Erving. The Philly players were aware of the role chosen for them. "What have we done wrong?" Erving, one of the most intelligent and gracious men in professional sports, had complained after one playoff game. "Why is everyone treating us like outlaws?" When Portland won, the phone rang off the hook in the Portland coach's offices with congratulations from other coaches, professional and college. There were hundreds of telegrams and letters thanking the coach and the players for helping their programs and making it easier to coach basketball the right way. Some people thought there were racial overtones in this, as if white basketball had beaten out black basketball (despite the fact that three and sometimes four of the Portland starters were black). Others saw it differently: the basketball of purity had beaten out the basketball of materialism and selfishness.

That summer was a high for the city of Portland and almost all of the players. The players were champions, so too was the city. It had been made bigtime by the victory. No longer would it be confused, in idle conversations with strangers, with Portland, *Maine*. It had even achieved parity now, in the minds of its residents, with the hated metropolis to the north called Seattle. Jack Ramsay, the Portland coach, was lionized. He had arrived a year earlier and promised a winner, and then had brought the city a championship in his very first season. He was a distinctive figure on the scene, his bald head and his bushy eyebrows appearing countless times on television during the season and the playoffs. There was even one short television commercial shot for Kentucky Fried Chicken in which he volunteered his own autograph to a pretty young waitress who rejected it, prefering instead the autograph of Wally Walker, one of the least used but handsomest and whitest Portland players. "Wally *Who?*" Ramsay had demanded. It was all in all a rare sports euphoria, and unlike most sports highs it did not evaporate in two or three days after the final victory but seemed to go on and on, in part because the fans were so grateful, there being no other big league sport in town, and in part because there was so much promise for the future. What had happened before would happen again. Basketball was a winter sport, but in the sweetness of that summer, Oregonians gathered and talked about the playoffs and about Walton and about how he had changed, how he had become more normal, more like *them,* though of course at Walton's house, his friends gathered and talked about how the *fans* had changed. People's connections to each other seemed to come through basketball; it had become, even more than the rain, their common denominator.

That summer of 1977, amidst all the enthusiasm of the championship, Herm Gilliam, then thirty-one and the oldest player on a very young team, found himself a celebrity. Wherever he went there were people who recognized him and wanted to help him out, and do him favors, and to talk with him about the season and in particular about the great game he had played against Los Angeles. In a city this size, Gilliam thought, fame is even more intense and more lasting. They are shorter on heroes than most cities. Black himself, he was intrigued by the adulation of heroes so black by a community so white. Yet, unlike Maurice Lucas and Bill Walton and his other teammates, his position on the team was tenuous; he was a bench player, he was older, and he was not a particular favorite of the coaches. He knew that in the recent draft of college players Portland had picked up several promising guards who wanted nothing better than to take his place. So that summer he worked harder than he ever had to stay in shape and to keep his eye. He was not a great shooter, he had come in the game as a defensive player and his shot was a manufactured one, part stolen from Rick Mount, a college teammate who was a great pure shooter, and another part from the great Oscar Robertson when Gilliam had played with him at Cincinnati. That summer he had worked on the fingertip action which was crucial to his shot, and he had run and played tennis. His teammates were coasting through the summer; they took their youth for granted. But Gilliam's youth was almost gone. All he wanted was one more season and one more championship.

In the summer, running to keep in shape, he often broke into a sweat and felt the pain in his lungs. He knew it was important to feel that pain. He remembered now preseason camps in his early years in the pros, the veteran players coming back, struggling to stay in shape, having dropped back, over the summer, one crucial level from the season before. How distant their problems had seemed to him then. Herm Gilliam was the senior player on the Portland team, experienced, confident, outspoken, a leader among the blacks. More than the other players, who were young and expected these things, he knew what a championship meant, how rare it was to be the best; he had played on too many teams that had fallen just short. In college his Purdue team had made it to the finals of the NCAA only to be demolished by one of the Lew Alcindor UCLA teams. Perhaps, he had thought at the time, there ought to be two national championships, one awarded to UCLA, and one for every other school to compete for. Later, in the pros, he had played several difficult seasons with good teams that lacked a dominating center, and it struck him that there ought to be a rule permitting every guard in the league to play at least one year with Alcindor—or rather with Kareem Abdul-Jabbar, as his name now was. Gilliam had joined Portland in time for the championship season and he had been excited by the prospect of playing with a talented big man like Bill Walton. Though his role on the Portland team had not at first been a major one, he sensed early on that this team might win everything. Thus in midseason, when Coach Jack Ramsay, knowing that Gilliam was restless with his lack of playing time, said that New Orleans wanted him badly, and that a trade could be worked out, Gilliam had gone home and talked it over with his wife, Betty. "But you told me you had a chance for the championship here and that's what you've always wanted, isn't it?" she said. He had nodded. "Then we ought to stay here," she said. They stayed and he had loved being a part of the championship team. As the season progressed his playing time had increased. In the crucial playoff series against Los Angeles, a team which had beaten Portland all four regular-season games, he played one memorable game. Thereafter his teammates referred to it simply as Herm's Game. Los Angeles was playing at home and playing a strong game, and it led 77–70 going into the fourth quarter. Herm Gilliam started the fourth quarter for Portland and played brilliantly, scoring, stealing the ball, scoring again, hitting difficult off-balance shots, making one particular shot, a falling away jump shot off the wrong foot, with Ramsay, it was said, on the bench shouting as he took the shot, "No, no, *no.* . . . *Yes!*" Portland, largely through his efforts, had gone on to win and Gilliam had scored 24 points on 12 of 18 shooting. Though the general view of the coaching staff was that he was a talented but somewhat erratic player, there was also a feeling that the Los Angeles game had assured his status for one more year.

At the fall training camp Gilliam returned in the best shape of his career. It turned out almost immediately that the main competition was for the job of fourth guard between Gilliam and a rookie from Alabama named T. R. Dunn, whom Portland had chosen on its second pick. Dunn had the strongest body of any guard in the camp and probably in the league; he seemed to be sculpted out of black marble and his physique was the first thing that coaches looked at. To some of the other blacks on the team it was frustrating to see Gilliam and Dunn pitted against each other; they did not think the coaches were being racist, but they also felt that black players were always more vulnerable, their jobs less secure, particularly those of bench players. (On many teams the lower bench positions were often filled by marginal white players, kept aboard principally as a bone to the fans. The blacks resented this and they had a word for it, when a white was kept instead of a black. He's *stealin'*, they would say, just *stealin'* it.) Some of the blacks were bothered by the fact that the competition was restricted to Gilliam and Dunn, and that David Twardzik and Larry Steele, both white, were excluded. To the coaches that was not an issue. Twardzik, they felt, could run the offense as Gilliam could not (no one, thought Stu Inman, the head of player personnel, used other players as intelligently as Twardzik), and Steele, once a guard, had now been switched to the job of backup small forward. The blacks were aware of that, but they also wondered at it—Gross, Walker, Steele, *three* small forwards, all of them white. . . .

Gilliam, arriving in excellent shape, knowing his job was on the line, had been assessed by most players as the best guard in camp. Nevertheless at the last minute he was cut. Inman and Ramsay made the decision. For Inman, who dealt in the future, the decision had not been particularly hard; he thought Gilliam was a good player but erratic (he used the word *streaky*), and he believed that Dunn might develop into one of the premier defensive guards in the league. For Ramsay, a man who had been forced to adapt his emotions to the unsentimental profession he was in, it was a more difficult decision. He was giving up an important player from a championship team, a popular player who had delivered for him, and that meant that he was changing, however peripherally, the texture of that team, and potentially changing the stability of it. There was some emotional reluctance on Ramsay's part, but it was limited—this was professional sports and it was a business. The edge between winning and losing was too thin. Some of the players were upset with the decision. Maurice Lucas, the power forward who was particularly close to Gilliam, stood apart for a time during practice, his arms folded on his chest in a kind of protest. Bill Walton said nothing at the time, though he later called Gilliam and said he thought management had made a mistake. Walton's close friend Jack Scott, the radical sports activist, thought Walton had made a mistake in not protesting the decision. But it was done. The core of the championship team had been changed. Nothing in the NBA stayed the same very long; nothing was that stable.

Soon Herm Gilliam was almost forgotten in Portland. The new season seemed to begin where the last one had left off. The Portland team seemed never to have stopped; if anything it was even better. Walton was playing better than ever. Three-quarters of the way through the season the record was 50 and 10, astonishing in a league so well balanced, where games on the road were unusually hard to win. It was a team of destiny and members of the team began to talk about destiny, about setting a record for the most number of regular-season wins, 70 and 12. Then Walton had been hurt and had missed the last part of the season. His foot bothered him as the playoffs began, but he had with some reluctance taken shots for it, and in the second game of the playoffs he had broken the foot. The season was over for him and, it turned out, for his team as well. There was no championship, no won-lost record. A few months later, denouncing almost all members of the Portland staff, Walton declared that he wanted to be traded, and that if there was to be destiny, he would seek it elsewhere.

The Walton era was over and finished. He was particularly hard in his criticism of the team doctor and trainer, who had been regarded as two of his closest friends in Portland. The next day Bobby Knight, the fiery, intense coach of Indiana University, had called his friend Stu Inman. Usually Knight's calls were as volatile as the man who made them, often coming at 6 a.m. Pacific time, since time differences meant little to Knight; he would demand that Inman share whatever majestic experience Knight had just partaken of (for example Inman *must* see *Patton* since it was the greatest movie in the history of the world). Elinor Inman had long ago decided that any phone call before 7 a.m. was Bobby Knight and she would automatically hand the phone to Stu. That was the price of such an exotic friendship, for Knight was passionate, difficult, arbitrary, often blasphemous, his own worst enemy. Yet he was, Inman thought, a rare contemporary coach, different from many of his modern contemporaries because he was intensely moral and obsessed by the idea of *team*, hating much of what was happening in basketball, the shortcuts taken by other coaches to lure players to their schools, the eventual indifference of these same coaches to the academic progress of their players. Bobby Knight, for all of his histrionics, insisted that his players graduate and deal with life as they dealt with basketball. In 1976 his own Indiana team, devoid of truly great college players, had won the national title and remained undefeated for the entire season. Not surprisingly he was fascinated by the Portland championship team and he often called Inman to talk about it, how well the characters of the players seemed to fit together, how well the team had been isolated from so many of the corrupting pressures of modern athletics. Inman had told Knight that they had been lucky in their mix of both talent and character and that Walton was crucial, his very style of play was essential to keeping the egos of the other players in line. It was as if Knight had a personal stake in the Portland team. On this day when he called he was somber, and he talked sadly with Inman about Walton, about what had happened, the breaking up of a great team, perhaps an ultimate team, when it was still so young. At the end of the conversation he had asked his friend, "Stu, is there any way in this day and age to keep a team together? Can it be done anymore?"

3

The Season

I N LATE SUMMER THE WEATHER IN OREGON IS LOVELY, WARM AND DRY, AS
if conjured up by some Chamber of Commerce to atone for the wetness
past. There is a sense that you can see forever, or failing that, at least, and
with ease, to the awesome mountains that surround Portland. The air is
clear, as if from another, preindustrial, age, since potential polluters fear the
power of Oregon's ecologically alert citizenry, and after the long gray
months so recently past and so soon to return, it seems a special gift. On
days like this it is inconceivable to stay inside, inconceivable to work, and
there is a feeling that no business is being transacted in Portland at this moment, that an entire state may be on vacation. Well, perhaps not an entire
state, for on this late August morning at a motel decidedly unfancy (but
quite pleasant: No, the hostess said to the traveler, there was no place around
for one-day shirt service, but the owner's wife would be glad to wash and
iron the guest's shirts herself), an annual ritual was being enacted. Though
the baseball season still has some two and a half months to run, though
professional football camps have just opened and there are daily stories
about players passing out from heat stroke at the football tryouts, here at
the Coachman Inn near Gresham, at the foot of Mount Hood, a group of
excessively tall young men, most of them black, are walking across the

motel yard to breakfast. Basketball, once a winter game, is now underway. There is in the breakfast room of the motel a quick flash of alien cultures, the grandchildren of early outdoorsmen and loggers, white, often stocky, often bearded, predominating, and then, sprinkled in with them, the grandchildren and sometimes children of sharecroppers from the Deep South—black, tall, elegant, the foremost celebrities of the entire state of Oregon. The cognoscenti of Oregon fans know that the Portland Trail Blazers stay at this motel, and that this is the first day of training. (The interest in this team is so great that a game at rookie camp can draw, if the management chooses to publicize it, some 8,000 people.) So they have just happened to drop by and just happened to bring their children with them, and at this moment a group of young children are surrounding the table of 6'8" Abdul Jeelani (born Gary Cole)—or, more particularly Abdul Qadir Jeelani, the All Powerful Servant of Allah Who by His Own Example Expands the Muslim Flock—himself the son of sharecroppers from west Tennessee. Abdul Jeelani, a gentle shy young man, is a god to these young white children, and he is signing autographs.

In truth, Abdul Jeelani was at that moment a very nervous god, for though he wore the warmup clothes of the Trail Blazers, and though he had signed a contract, he was by no means a member of the team. Though last year he was the highest scorer in the Italian league (the king, one teammate had said, of spaghetti basketball), at $45,000 for the season, and though the Blazers had paid his way out here, he was a forward, and Portland was at that moment said to be very deep in forwards. His status was thus by no means clear. He knew his was not a household name, that in competition with another player of comparable ability he might be at a disadvantage simply because he had tried before and failed before. Still, Allah had given him a fresh spiritual confidence, and he believed that what he was doing was right. That made his way easier. He believed at that moment that he had been cheated in the past not because he was black, but because he was an unknown black from a small unknown school, Wisconsin Parkside at Kenosha. He was glad to be here. This was not to say that Abdul Jeelani preferred Portland to Rome. In fact he loved Rome, loved the whiff of garlic on his teammates' breath, loved the adulation of the crowds and the volatility of the people. But though Rome was, among the benchmarks of Western civilization, perhaps more important than Portland, Portland—as a stop in the National Basketball Association—was more important than Rome.

It was a lovely gentle-clumsy scene. Everyone was awkward. The autograph hunters were timid and shy and the signee was shy. Nevertheless he signed: "Abdul Jeelani." In other times and other places this might have caused a problem, for a black who became a Muslim was automatically suspected of political deviation and embryonic anti-Americanism. (The doubters had included at first his mother, Tennessee sharecropper, worshiper of a good Baptist God herself, who was most uneasy with his conversion and his new name and who for a long time refused to call him Abdul, at all, and then finding after a time that he still loved her and was still a good son, slowly began to come around. Mrs. Cole did this in stages, cheating a little at first, calling him *A-dul* as she edged towards his new name.) But here at the foot of Mount Hood, no one seemed to care that he had changed his name; they did not even know his name. He was tall, he was black, he was wearing a Blazer uniform, and that was enough.

At the far end of the breakfast room there was a table apart, of somewhat older men, all of them white, dressed in the same warmup suits. They were already eating, mostly the new health foods of the modern athlete (Walton, now departed, once scorned for his odd eating habits, had left his mark)—fruit, cottage cheese, the new nonsugared cereals, rather than the ham and eggs of yesteryear. The waitress, young and pretty, knew them; she had served them for several years and, like most of Portland, was a part-owner of a Blazer season ticket. As she served them she was also gossiping; would they introduce her to Jimmy Paxson, the team's first-round draft choice? She had seen his picture and he looked cute. Was he as cute as his photo? Indeed, Paxson, who was white, looked like the star of a new television sit-com about a healthy happy-go-lucky midwestern college student who was always trying to borrow his parents' car and getting into trouble, but the kind of trouble that is easily rectified. (That is, no hard drugs.) Paxson was to become in the year that followed something of a teenage cult figure in Portland, his autographs-signed record bearing a favorable relation to his points-scored record. He had, it seemed, even by opening day of camp, replaced in the hearts of young female fans the now departed Wally Walker, who like Paxson had been young, white, handsome, single and whose departure after one and a half disappointing seasons had caused the coaching staff to wonder whether if he had been a little less handsome (and thus a little less well adjusted in the rest of his daily life) he might have been a hungrier and more passionate basketball player.

At the coach's table Stuart Inman took time from eating his own break-fast to glance around the room. His face, usually animated, showed little emotion. Stu Inman, once shy and now gregarious, given the demands of his profession, not unlike that of a traveling salesman in another age, was fifty-three years old. He had once been, some thirty-two years before, a col-lege star at a small school, San Jose State. He was a center at 6'4" in those days, though in today's game he would be a guard. In those days, when the NBA was very small and very new and very poor, he had been selected as a second-round draft choice, a decision which excited him enormously since he loved basketball. He was told by friends who knew the exotic life in pro-fessional basketball not to expect less than $5,000 for his contract, a good deal of money then. The Stags had instead offered him five months at $700 a month or $3,500; when he had turned that down, they had upped the of-fer to $800 for five months, and with that he had turned down the Stags, who folded the next year anyway, and entered the world of teaching and coaching, starting as a high school coach. At that time playing professional basketball was an act of love. No one was in it for the money. Teams were formed, teams folded, leagues were formed, leagues disappeared. The year that Inman graduated from college, 1950, was the year that two competing leagues merged to form the NBA, the National Basketball Association. The players were still all white (the first blacks arrived the following year), the game was slower; George Mikan at 6'10" was considered a giant, the for-wards were often 6'3" and 6'4". Those who played had to love the game for itself, because there was precious little other reward. By deciding not to play Inman turned down a chance to become a pioneer figure in the league; now just a few years later he was routinely negotiating with college graduates who wanted some $200,000 a year for their services, which was rather more than high school coaches, college professors and even university presidents made. As the man in charge of player personnel it was Inman's responsibil-ity, in a game where player chemistry was crucial, to supply the coach with the right mix of players. There were people in his profession (though not so many in Portland where his mistakes tended to be savored as much as his triumphs) who thought he had become the best of them all, certainly one of the two or three best, and that his was the guiding hand of the delicate bal-ance which formed the 1977 championship team.

Inman's eyes stopped at Jeelani. He was pleased that Jeelani was han-dling himself so well with the civilians; such things mattered to Stu Inman.

But he had his doubts about Jeelani's ability to make the team. He had signed Jeelani to a contract, but no money was guaranteed, and it was the kind of contract that could evaporate the moment Portland wanted it to. He had dealt with Abdul on the basis of a recommendation from an old friend named Jim McGregor, who was coaching and doing some scouting on the side in Italy. Inman liked McGregor, but he also believed that freelance scouts were always trying to sell themselves as well as their products, hoping perhaps for a fulltime job in the NBA. Abdul had arrived amidst a considerable amount of McGregor's hyperbole. As he ate breakfast Inman turned to the table and the other coaches. "This kid is killing people here," he said as if quoting McGregor's letter. *"He's too big for Italy, too big for Rome.* No one can stop him. Forty points a game, seventeen blocked shots a game." Inman imitated McGregor reaching for attention. *"Four hundred and thirty-eight rebounds a game. Sign him now, Stu!"* Portland had signed him and he had played for Portland in a summer league. Inman thought Jeelani a good pure shooter, but he also felt that he was a prisoner of his past, a small school with limited coaching, followed by a freelance situation in Italy; he was thus four or five years behind comparable players, and would have difficulty fitting into a disciplined offense like Portland's.

Inman was a smart, well-educated, well-read man, and he could talk on many subjects, but above all else he loved to talk basketball. When he did, he slipped immediately into scout-talk: A kid had a *good head, bad heart, good hands, long arms, good attitude, small hands, plays small, plays big, good practice player, plays big in important games, disappears in important games.* In Inman's world Jeelani was a good kid, limited background, long arms, good touch, would have trouble playing in a complicated system. In truth, he thought, looking around the room, if Jeelani made Jack Ramsay's team, one of the most disciplined and structured teams in the league, then it would be a sign that the Blazers were in trouble and vulnerable. His eyes left Jeelani and fastened for a minute on Greg Bunch sitting by himself. Bunch was two inches shorter than Jeelani and twenty pounds lighter. Technically he was a better prospect; Bunch in Inman-speak was exceptionally-fast, sound-fundamentals, good-leaper, slim-body-but-long-arms with a-good-concept-of-the-game. But there was something troubling about Bunch. He was a young man, Inman suspected, who was fighting himself, not just in basketball but in other ways, though it showed most clearly on the court.

The waitress interrupted him. She wanted to know where Bruce was.

She was fond of Bruce and knew that this was the time for Bruce's major appearance of the year. Bruce was Bruce Ogilvie, a sports psychologist, a short, powerfully built man who looked something like Jack LaLanne disguised as a shrink. Bruce Ogilvie was a part of the preseason ritual, arriving in time to test the new players on their motivation and psychological soundness. He had been doing this for several years and was now considered a valuable albeit peripheral part of the coaching staff. At first other members of the staff were somewhat skeptical of him. Gradually several cases had turned them into believers. The first was in 1971 when Portland had drafted Sidney Wicks, the most sought-after college player in the country. Wicks had already signed what was considered a near record contract for a rookie, $250,000 a year, when he was sent down to Bruce for testing. Ogilvie finished his tests a few hours later and had rejoined the inner circle which included Inman and Herman Sarkowsky, then the principal owner. They had asked him almost offhandedly what he thought of Sidney Wicks and Ogilvie had said: "That young man is a mass of contradictions—he's charming, he's bright, he's sensitive, but I think he's essentially unmotivated and uncoachable for this team." Sarkowsky, who had just signed Wicks, turned absolutely white, and Ogilvie shortly thereafter had left the room and the others had assured each other that Bruce was, well, a pleasant fellow but he did not know basketball as *they* knew basketball. Wicks was handsome, he was intelligent and he was charming and he had made a great first impression on all of them. By the evening they were even laughing at Ogilvie a little. But Wicks's years in Portland were not happy ones, either for him or for the fans, and most particularly not for a series of coaches who believed their departure from the Pacific Northwest had been hastened by their inability to coach or motivate Sidney Wicks.

Bruce Ogilvie was being taken more seriously when in 1976 Portland drafted in the fifth round a young player out of Auburn named Gary Redding. Usually fifth-round draft choices were training-camp fodder, but Redding played with such intrinsic intelligence and maturity that both Ramsay and Inman were confident that he could make the team, that they had picked the sleeper of the draft. A steal. Nothing pleased a player personnel director more than a steal in the fifth round. At dinner one night Ramsay and Inman were talking about how good Redding was. Ogilvie listened and dissented. "I don't think he's your man," he said. "I don't know what it is, but he's not for you. His heart isn't in basketball." They had scoffed at him, of course. Redding's heart had to be in basketball because *their* hearts were in basketball. The next morning Gary Redding knocked on Jack Ramsay's door, handed in his playbook and said that he wanted to thank them for the opportunity they had shown him but that he was unhappy and that he wanted to study medicine.

With Redding's departure Ogilvie took on yet greater stature among the coaches, though many of the players were still uneasy about the idea of someone trying to peer into their heads. Bill Walton had not allowed Ogilvie to test him. Another player, Larry Steele, was particularly wary of Bruce. Steele, an intense, highly aggressive young man, had played at Kentucky during the latter years of Adolph Rupp when the great man, the legend of college basketball, was becoming more than a little senile and was in fact something of a figurehead, with his assistant coaches actually running the team. Steele, singularly straight, uniquely devoid of guile, had responded directly to Ogilvie's questionnaire, and when the questions had focused as they often did on his attitude to coaching ("Do you listen to your coach: all of the time? Most of the time? Some of the time? Never?"), he had thought of Adolph Rupp, who was *the* coach. The fact was that he had paid very little attention to Rupp, and he had answered truthfully that he almost never listened. Thereupon Bruce Ogilvie had reported that Larry Steele, perhaps the most straightforward young man ever to play for Portland, was uncoachable, and Steele, enraged, refused to take the second part of the test, harboring little affection for Bruce Ogilvie or for shrinks in general.

Still, the coaches liked Bruce Ogilvie. They were impressed by what he could tell them about the essential psychological coherence of a player, and of a player's athletic instinct—his desire to impose his will on other athletes. He was also good at exposing myth. It was part of the American myth of the fifties and even the sixties that blacks were quitters, a myth born of an age when blacks had little chance to succeed and were most certainly encouraged to quit. Ogilvie had found the reverse, that blacks tended to have more dedication in professional sports than whites, that the game meant more to them. That was an important point, for much of black passion in pro basketball was concealed; and there were constant debates among the whites who ran the league over the question of why black athletes were so dominant.

FOR RACE OF course touched everything. It was not that the NBA was a racist place—quite the contrary. In contrast with the rest of American life there was more real contact and friendship between blacks and whites than almost anywhere else, barring perhaps the armed forces. It was simply that the NBA was a showplace for American racial tension; no matter how successful the black athlete, and no matter well paid he now was, he brought to the game a complicated assortment of anxieties about growing up black in a white nation. For all of his success, he played in a league where the owner was always white, the coaches were usually white, the sportswriters were almost always white, the referees were almost always white, and the fans were almost always white.

Yet this was the blackest of the major sports. If the first part of the history of the league had been given over to its formation and the stardom of athletes like Mikan and Joe Fulks and Max Zaslofsky, then the second part began with the arrival of the black athletes. The first of them had played in 1951; in 1956, with the coming of Bill Russell, the game itself had begun to change, turning into a sport of jumping and speed. The rapidity with which black athletes took over the league was astonishing. In the 1961–62 season, with no more than two or three blacks on most teams, seven out of the league's top ten rebounders were black; three years later, with perhaps three or at most four blacks on each roster (which as a rule consisted of eleven men), *nine* of the top ten rebounders, and six of the seven top assist leaders (where, again, speed was crucial) were black. Nor was basketball the only sport; in football and baseball too, blacks added a dimension of speed.

Why this had happened was a delicate question. There seemed to be a prototype black body in basketball, long leg bones, slim calves tapering up to powerful upper thighs and powerful chests; blacks, O. J. Simpson once said, referring to the legs of many black running backs, were built for speed. Many black athletes themselves believed there were physiological differences. Yet sociologists and black leaders were reluctant to accept such explanations. Not only did it tend to diminish the achievement of the athlete himself, but it opened the door to other arguments of genetic difference. Black sociologists preferred instead to point out that athletes were the only obvious role models for millions of ghetto youths, and that perhaps as many as one million black high school students wanted to play in the NBA. Trying to change that, to explain what other career possibilities existed, was like trying (said black sociologist Harry Edwards) to fight CBS, NBC, ABC and *Sports Illustrated*. Blacks dominated basketball, these black intellectuals believed, because so much of their potential had been funneled into so narrow an outlet. Others thought this was true, but the real explanation was more complicated. Many NBA coaches were struck by the differences they saw between the black bodies (created for the most part without the help of weight machines and often on limited diets) and the far frailer and softer white bodies of basketball players. Some coaches thought it an odd and ironic genetic legacy of slavery; slave hunters, they believed, had picked out the best physical specimens possible, and then bred them for even greater physical excellence. Only the strong had been able to survive the hard labor of slavery, creating in the end a generation of very powerful young men and women in the postslavery South. In any event the black players, when they spoke among themselves, often laughed about white bodies; if a black player was a weak jumper he was said to have white legs. Someone black or white who was a step and a half slow was said by the blacks to have "white man's disease." Almost all of the great jumpers in the league were black. It was, black players believed, an advantage given them, and in a country like this any advantage was rare enough.

THE BREAKFAST WAS soon over and most of the coaches drove the few miles to Mount Hood Junior College. Ramsay, the coach, biked it; he had a passion for physical fitness and he had earlier that day biked the twenty-five miles from his home in the Lake Oswego section of Portland to the motel, in part because he loved biking, in part because it made him feel better and in part because his excellent condition commanded extra respect from his players. He did not just preach condition to them, he was season in and season out in better shape than they were, at times seemingly married to the Nautilus machine. Ramsay was typically intense about his body-conditioning. Several years earlier, when he had been coaching in Buffalo, he had decided that his players should jump rope, that it was a good and necessary part of their daily stretching and limbering-up exercise. The trouble was that Ramsay himself had not been very good at it, and the Buffalo players had been somewhat amused by the sight of a balding, red-faced man in his late forties struggling awkwardly with the jump rope. They were sure he wouldn't make them do it. But in the middle of the summer, trainer Ray Melchiorre received a phone call from Ramsay. "I'd like you to add the jump rope," the coach said, "say, three hundred jumps in two minutes."

"You've got it down, don't you?" Melchiorre said.

"Yes," said Ramsay, "I've been doing it five or six times a day and I finally have it." Melchiorre had never heard the coach's voice sound so happy, almost smug.

While Ramsay biked over, Stuart Inman, once a better basketball player than the coach but now in not as good condition, drove over. He was also (a mild offense in front of the coach) a chain-smoker. Unlike Ramsay, Inman did not have to meet with the players on a daily basis. Inman nevertheless had a special power over the players: he dealt with some of their contracts, and he had a large say in whether or not they were cut or traded. Thus though he did not attend many Portland games—he was usually busy scouting in distant gyms—the occasions when he did show up made them extremely nervous. He just seemed to materialize before a game, and then vanish equally rapidly. For that reason the players had a nickname for him—the Shadow. Sometimes shortened (by the blacks) to the Shad. Inman's trademark was to sidle over to a player, loop an arm around his shoulder, deliver a fast one-liner about someone the player knew that Inman had just seen—a college coach, a former teammate—and then Inman was gone. It was the word among the players never to let the Shadow get his arm around you, it was said to be a sure sign that a trade was in the works, and there were players who, seeing Inman's arrival, tried to move to the far end of the court. Inman was aware of this reputation and he would in good moods tease the players he was comfortable with: The worst thing they could do was buy a house in Oregon. The next worst was to register to vote in Oregon. One day he walked through the parking lot outside the arena and he saw the fancy new car of Mychal Thompson. The license plate bore no number but simply announced MYCHAL. "That's the cardinal sin," Inman said. "I'm going back to the office to see if I can work out a trade."

On this day Inman's usual good nature was absent. He was tense and nervous and chain-smoking. He was apprehensive about this day and apprehensive about the season, more so than Ramsay. Hard days had come upon the Portland team in the two years since they had been champions and had dreamed of a long reign at the top. A series of disasters, some involuntary, some self-inflicted, had struck the Portland franchise. All of it reflected the volatility of professional sport in the modern, highly commercial television age. First Bill Walton, the star of the 1977 and 1978 teams, and perhaps when healthy (no small qualification) the greatest overall player to play at center, had left the team for San Diego, charging medical malpractice and suggesting that most of the front office be fired. The loss of any player with Walton's unique skills would have been shattering; that he left while attacking the careers of various members of the staff was particularly damning. In addition, the commissioner had not yet awarded Portland the players from San Diego who were to be exchanged as part of the compensation for signing Walton.

In the season just past, the team had adjusted surprisingly well to the loss of Walton. It was by no means the classically beautiful team of those two rare seasons, the championship team of 1976–77, and the even better team of 1977–78, 50 and 10 until Walton was injured, but it was a strong team which had grown more confident as the season went along, and it had pushed a very strong Phoenix team to a close three-game playoff series. One of the keys had been the play of Mychal Thompson, then a rookie forward from Minnesota, a player of unusual quickness. He was big, strong and colorful, and said to be a cousin of David Thompson, the great leaper from Denver. This rumor, invented and spread by Mychal himself, turned out not to be true—they were in fact not related at all—but Mychal, coming into the college and professional game after David, decided that it would help his image and his reputation if people thought he was part of the same bloodline. Mychal entered the University of Minnesota as Michael, but had decided his name was too prosaic; he after all considered himself quite colorful as a personality, and his name should be colorful as well, and so he legally changed the spelling to *Mychal,* becoming a Michael of greater distinction. Mychal, by whatever name, enjoyed a superlative rookie season, growing stronger as it went along, and becoming more confident as well. (It was said that he showed great courage and confidence not only on the court but off it. Late in the season, after a tough loss in Chicago that had enraged Ramsay, Mychal had nevertheless—his audacity had impressed his older teammates—smuggled not one but two lady friends aboard the bus back to the hotel.) It had been, all in all, a wonderful rookie year and the trade that brought him to Portland was now regarded as one of Inman's best. But then during the off-season Mychal had returned home to the Bahamas where he was something of a national hero and where all other activities stopped during nationally televised Portland games. There, during a summer pickup game, he tripped and landed badly and in the process snapped his leg and broke the femur, a clean break, unusual for basketball. In this game injuries abounded, of course, but they were of a different nature, reflecting systematic stress upon the knee, or the tendons in the leg.

The last comparable break Ron Culp, the trainer, had observed was some fourteen years earlier. In the absence of Walton, Mychal Thompson's presence had been crucial and he was expected to compensate for the loss in both speed and power. Now he was out until February or March at the earliest. He had arrived at practice that day, his entire leg in a huge cast, on which was written "God: Superstar," and "Jesus Loves Me and I *Know* It." Morris Buckwalter, the assistant coach, looked on the cast and the accompanying graffiti and he had thought for a moment that if there were that much heavenly concern for Mychal Thompson he might not have broken his leg in the first place. For his loss was exactly what Portland did not need. The loss first of Walton, then of Thompson, was difficult enough, but on this opening day, Inman was in addition upset over the organization's frustrating relationship with Maurice Lucas, the team's remaining big man and star.

Lucas, playing alongside Walton, had been almost as much a symbol of the championship season as the center himself and as much a key to the team's success. He was big and strong and competitive, and a surprisingly good shooter; indeed Luke, never short of ego, believed that *he* rather than Bill Walton had been the most valuable player in the championship series with Philadelphia, and that what was more, *Bill Walton knew this* and that his way of acknowledging it was a postseason gift of a huge photo showing Luke stuffing a basket over Kareem Abdul-Jabbar. Maurice Lucas had, for several years and with considerable justification, been unhappy with the size of his contract, and over the preceding summer, completely frustrated, had asked to renegotiate it. Portland had as a matter of policy refused. The refusal of the team to renegotiate with him festered over the summer— though for the first time in this coming season Lucas was making big money, $300,000. That money had not eased his anger; on the contrary he had become obsessed with how long it had taken him to reach this level, and how much more other power forwards of lesser accomplishment were getting. He believed the Portland organization was making millions of dollars, much of it off his skills, and believed also that other organizations had been willing to renegotiate with *their* stars. During the summer he asked to be traded, and Portland came very close to sending him to Chicago, but it had not worked out and now he was arriving at camp, the most influential player on the team, distinctly unhappy and discontented.

He was not the only one unhappy. Stu Inman was unhappy with both

Maurice Lucas and with Larry Weinberg, the owner, for failing to resolve the Lucas issue. Inman would have been delighted to oblige Lucas and trade him to another club. He was not, in his own words, a great Maurice Lucas fan. He had never been one. Even on the eve of the ABA dispersal draft, when the remaining players from the collapsing league were in effect auctioned off to the NBA, Inman had given what was considered a fairly cold-blooded evaluation of Lucas, one of the prime players coming out of the old league: Lucas, he said, was a strong player, a good competitor, more of a one-on-one player than Jack Ramsay liked. But he had, Inman cautioned, a considerable ego and could become a problem in later years. "Have no illusion," he said, "this is what you are getting—a strong player and a potentially difficult one." Inman checked first with Hubie Brown, a coach known for his brutal, often blasphemous tirades against his players. Hubie Brown, who had coached Lucas in Kentucky, was precisely the wrong kind of coach for Luke, a man who did not like to be insulted in front of teammates and friends and did not lightly forgive; Brown reported to Inman as negatively as he could on Lucas. Inman then called Bob MacKinnon, who had coached Luke in St. Louis, and received exactly the opposite report. MacKinnon thought Lucas an easy player to work with and a strong competitor. Inman decided to seek a third opinion, that of Al McGuire, Lucas's sometime college coach, now a broadcaster, a bright glib verbal man who was regarded by players and coaches alike as something of a flake. Inman called him and McGuire had said, "No, Lucas never played very well for me, I don't think he'll make it in the pros." But, insisted Inman, Luke had been virtually an all-star in the ABA. "Is that right?" said McGuire. "I didn't know that—that's terrific. In that case I'd go for him."

That Hubie Brown hated Lucas came as no surprise. There had been one terrible moment when Brown yanked Luke from a game and dressed him down. Luke had walked away and sat down at the end of the bench. Brown had come over and continued the tirade in front of teammates and thousands of fans, voice loud, words harsh, fingers moving. Luke had sat there for a moment and then followed Brown to the team huddle, grabbed him, spun him around, taken him by the jacket and told him never to talk to him again that way. Never. So it was not surprising that when the two leagues merged in the following year and Hubie Brown, by now coaching at Atlanta, with a chance to pick Maurice Lucas from the dispersal pool, had instead passed on that opportunity and quite gladly traded his rights to Portland.

What was surprising was that Bob MacKinnon had so enthusiastically recommended Luke to Portland—game, comportment and all. Some of Luke's teammates on the St. Louis Spirits thought that he had been on the very edge of civil disobedience in St. Louis, always seeking the edge against opponents, teammates, coach and management. Steve Jones, now a Portland announcer and then a player in St. Louis, had watched a memorable scene in Luke's rookie year. Jones, after many years in the league, was both aficionado and practitioner of what he called the bust. That was his word for confrontation, either unavoidable or, in his favored style, deliberate and mocking. Light busting meant going after a teammate or sportswriter, catching him off-guard and immediately going on the assault, as publicly as possible, homing in on the other's most vulnerable point. Hard busting was true confrontation, two men jostling for authority over the same piece of turf. Busting, as Jones understood and practiced it, was restricted to veterans. Rookies were not permitted to participate. On the St. Louis Spirits, however, Jones had watched Luke as a rookie in a hard bust scene. The Spirits, in their expensive but short-lived career, had played in San Antonio and were on their way back home. Luke, as was his wont, had overslept and had missed the team bus, joining the rest of the team at the last second at the airport. That meant a sure fine of perhaps $100, particularly since MacKinnon was supposed to be a tough coach, a disciplinarian of the old school. Jones, a lover of the theater of basketball, had positioned himself so he could watch the entire scene, wondering how Lucas would react to a bust from so tough a coach. But no, to Jones's amazement, Luke came in steaming, not about to let this coach bust him. MacKinnon was moving towards Luke. But Luke was waving him away. "No, goddamn it, get away from me, goddamn it," he was saying. "I didn't get any goddamn wakeup call and you can damn well keep away from me. I'm tired of all this crap, *a team run this poorly, no wakeup calls ever.*" Luke, Jones saw, had pulled himself up to his fullest height. His finger was jabbing at MacKinnon. His indignation was righteous. The coach, Jones realized, was not going to bust Luke, but *Luke was going to bust the coach.* Jones looked at MacKinnon and saw the surprise on his face, could see MacKinnon thinking and could read his thoughts: I'm the coach and he's a rookie, I'm supposed to discipline him and he's busting me. "Luke," MacKinnon was saying but his heart was no longer in it, "you know the rules." "Shit, goddamn it," Luke was saying, "I don't want to hear it. Just get away from me, you hear, I don't want to hear it. You can't run this team right, can't even wake a man up." That, thought Jones, is some rookie. Put the burden right back on the Man. Seize the moment, seize the turf.

With Luke it was that way, turf, always turf. He had learned that on the streets of the Hill section, the ghetto of Pittsburgh. Set the rules or someone you don't like will set them for you. It was the way he had grown up, and it was the law of the streets, on the court or in life, dominate or be dominated. For Luke was always testing people, challenging them and challenging rules, not so much, one sensed, to break the rules, but to show that he was different, that he did not just accept things—blind acceptance was no longer in the cards. There was always a thin sharp edge to things. If he had not been a professional basketball player, he once told friends, he could just as easily have stayed in Pittsburgh and been a pimp. Things had worked out for him; they had not worked out for most of the kids he had grown up with; the area was very rough, you did not really understand how rough, he thought, until you went away and found there were other places and other ways to live, places where people were not always trying you, testing you. In his neighborhood that was the law: someone was trying you or you were trying someone else. You always had to be very careful, you did not want to be alone on certain occasions. But it was always territorial. If you did not try to intimidate others—and you did that mostly out of fear—they would surely try to intimidate you. That was particularly true if you were a big man. If you had that size you simply had to use it. Otherwise people would lose their respect for you.

His professional career had been a reflection of that. He arrived in the NBA with a full-fledged reputation as an enforcer, made when he was in the ABA and had taken out Artis Gilmore, perhaps the strongest man in basketball, with one quick shot. That fight had started because Luke, struggling for position near the basket, had used his hands trying to move Artis, there being no other way to play a man that strong, and Artis, regarded by other players as far too gentle for his own good, a 6'2" soul in a 7'2" body, had finally become enraged, and chased Luke downcourt. Gilmore caught up with Luke near the midcourt circle and Luke had immediately begun backing away. Artis, absolutely furious, dukes up, was screaming at Luke and Luke had *his* dukes up, though in as friendly a manner as possible, ready, should Artis change his mood, to become friends instantly. Artis continued advancing and Luke continued retreating until he was under his own basket and there was no more room to retreat and he had decided that this was as good a place as any to test or be tested. If the game was territory he was almost out of it, and he had given Artis two quick rights smack on the chin, and Artis crumpled to the floor. At that point Luke, who had clearly been very scared, began to enjoy the fight and puffed out his chest and began to shout at Artis, "You want some of me, big fella, you can come after me." He was yelling at Artis and Artis was there sprawled out on the floor, and Luke, encouraged by this, began to parade around the arena, still pointing at Artis. He was Luke the conqueror. That secured his reputation as an enforcer. There were those who thought that Artis Gilmore's standard of play seemed to decline for a time.

Lucas's first year in the NBA had been remarkable. He was a constant physical presence with a light and almost delicate scoring touch and he brought Portland a sense of physical protection that Walton, somewhat intimidated by more physical NBA players in his first two years, badly needed. Luke's ability to intimidate other players had been important that year. Walton, in fact, believed he had witnessed the single most intimidating act in NBA history, the intimidation, not of an opposing player, but of a referee. It was in the first game of the miniseries against Chicago, a very physical team then on a prolonged hot streak. The game was in Portland, the regular referees were on strike and the game was being refereed by scab refs, men accustomed to handling high school games of smaller, slower, less powerful players. In the third quarter, with the game close, one of the refs, angry at Luke's performance, had called a technical foul on him. Luke had shouted back his disagreement and stormed towards the referee. The referee had reached for his whistle, about to call the second technical, which meant automatic ejection, just as Luke arrived. The whistle was poised there in the ref's mouth, ready for blowing. Luke's hand touched the chain. Luke shook his head, very gently. But his eyes were burning. "You don't want to do that," he said. Their eyes met. The referee was 5'10" and Luke was 6'9". Luke held the referee's eyes. The referee slowly took the whistle out of his mouth. Amazing, Walton thought, Luke had backed a referee down. It was pure theatrical instinct.

But if Luke was a presence during a game, he was also a presence among his teammates—sometimes, as in the championship season, an immensely positive presence but sometimes, Stu Inman believed, more dubious. There was, Inman felt, too much dissent, too much ego and too great a taste for challenge in Lucas. Inman was sure that he was bound to bring problems to something as delicate as a basketball team. Where the black players on the team—particularly those who played with Walton before the championship season—believed that Luke had breathed confidence and zest back into Walton's attitude towards the game, Inman believed that Walton had made Luke look better, particularly on defense, and equally important had helped control Luke's ego. Perhaps they were both right.

At the end of the 1977–78 season Inman suggested to Ramsay that they trade Lucas, that their problems with him were about to increase, and that it was probably wiser to move him when his trade value was high, before he became—as Inman was convinced he would—a team problem. Inman had been through the entire Sidney Wicks episode at Portland and that had been a difficult time for everyone involved—management, the player himself, teammates. Wicks, a great college player at UCLA, had been the college player of the year, and was drafted by Portland as the number one player in the country. Expectations for his pro career were high; some scouts perceived him as potentially the greatest power forward to enter the game since Elgin Baylor. He was quick, smart, had a strong body, passed well, and had played a disciplined game in college. Though he was chosen rookie of the year in Portland, his years there were in the end disappointing. Perhaps it was the wrong setting for him: coming from all-powerful UCLA teams to a weak expansion franchise, he had difficulty adjusting to constant defeat. Perhaps too much was expected of him: he might after all not be a true power forward able by himself to turn around a weak franchise, but rather more of a finesse player, his quickness more exceptional than his strength. Perhaps he was a victim of the new world of guaranteed contracts which deprived young players of adequate motivation. But for whatever reason, Wicks was never the player Portland hoped for. He clashed with teammates, he clashed with coaches. Yet the Portland management always hesitated about dealing him, lulled by the idea of what he still might be, while at the same time his trade value inexorably declined.

Because of the Wicks case, Inman considered himself a combat veteran of one of the most difficult and turbulent periods in professional sports, a period when the coming of bigtime television and its accompanying money and new labor laws had dramatically changed sports salaries in general and basketball salaries in particular. Other sports salaries had risen significantly in the very brief period from the late sixties to the middle of the seventies, but in that seven years basketball salaries had gone up some *700 percent*. In the process, the money had frequently changed a player's attitude towards the game, towards his coach and towards his teammates. The explosion of the sport, the coming of television and its extraordinary social amplification system, dovetailed almost exactly with the coming of a rival league (there was a rival league in football too, but it had been incorporated *before* money in sports became really big). Unlike football and baseball, basketball, with so few players, presented the illusion that a single superstar could transform a loser into a winner. There had been a rush by new owners—often unaware of the complexity of the game, anxious to be winners, anxious to be celebrities themselves (one became a celebrity in sports by paying celebrity wages)—to endow young gifted players with huge salaries and make them superstars. Bidding wars took place over players like Spencer Haywood, Bob McAdoo, George McGinnis, and even Wicks, driving the salaries from an average of $75,000 in the late sixties to $500,000 and $600,000 for a superstar by the late seventies.

This explosion of salary, sudden and overnight (owners for the first time, proud capitalists that they are, being forced to pay the market value in what had been the hitherto conservative sanctuary of sports), had changed not just the financial structure of the game but, more significantly, the political structure as well. In the past coaches had been the figures of authority, as a rule paid more than players. They moreover had the power to withhold playing time (and thus statistical production) from players and thus determine to no small degree the course of a player's career. A coach could determine whether a player had a good year, and if the player had a good year he might be able to sign again, perhaps for $5,000 more. The choice was management's. Overnight the pay scale changed, superstars—some of them mere rookies—were now being paid four and five times as much as the coaches. Even more important, they had guaranteed, no-cut, long-term contracts. How they performed on the court in the future no longer mattered; at least in financial terms, the future was already theirs. The leverage of the coach and of management to control players dropped accordingly. Since the ownership was now deeply committed to the superstar, if a problem developed (as it often did) it was not the superstar who departed. The superstar was the key to the gate, to season-ticket sales. It was the coach who departed.

Portland had been through this in various forms with Sidney Wicks.

There had been ugly scenes between Wicks and two of his coaches, first Rolland Todd then Jack McCloskey. The one with McCloskey, chosen as coach because he was said to be a strict disciplinarian and would bring order to a chaotic clubhouse, involved Wicks announcing to his coach: "I've checked you out and you're nothing but a *loser*. You've been a loser every place you coached, and I've been a *winner* everywhere I played," and McCloskey (soon, of course, to depart) answering in turn, "All-star? Sidney Wicks an all-star? The only all-star team you could make is the all-*dog* team."

Perhaps the money and the no-cuts had come too quickly to players who were not yet ready for it, whose value systems were not yet complete; or perhaps it was the stress of being the star player on an otherwise weak team. For whatever reason things had worked out poorly for many of those instant superstars of the early seventies—Haywood, McAdoo, McGinnis, Wicks—all of whose value in the league seemed to plummet year after year. Soon many of them were almost unmovable in the league.

Then there was the team itself. The arrival of a high-salaried superstar, Inman believed, threatened the fabric of a basketball team far more than that of a football or baseball team. All three, of course, were team sports. But baseball was highly idiosyncratic and egocentric. Baseball players brought their highly specialized skills to a team, but remained singular. They did not have to blend their skills or sacrifice their talents to enhance each other as basketball players did, nor did they even have to get on particularly well with each other. ("What's the best thing about playing for the Yankees?" Graig Nettles was once asked. "Getting to play with Reggie Jackson every day." "And the worst thing about playing for New York?" he was asked. "Playing with Reggie Jackson every day.") Football, more than baseball, was a team sport, but again on every play the role of every player was clearly defined: an offensive lineman blocked as well as he could, a runner ran as hard as he could. But basketball was far more vulnerable to the change caused by the arrival of big money, Inman and his colleagues thought. For basketball demanded that though the players be talented, they also subordinate their individual talents to the idea of team and to each other. A truly great basketball player was not necessarily someone who scored a lot of points; a truly great basketball player was someone of exceptional talent and self-discipline who could make his teammates better. Basketball was a sport where under optimal conditions a great player with considerable ego disciplined himself and became unselfish. But big money, creating the idea of the basketball player as superstar, militated against sacrifice in sports. The super salaries went by and large to those with impressive statistics, and big statistics usually came at the expense of team. No one in the two years of great Portland teams had exceptional statistics, most of the rare things they had done on the court never showed up in the box score. The entire Wicks episode had taught Inman, in addition, how fragile the idea of team was, how quickly one player could throw it off. Now that Walton was gone, he believed that Lucas wanted out, that his ego had probably changed and that there was no way he was likely to remain happy and valuable in Portland.

In the summer of 1978 Inman had not been able to convince Jack Ramsay to move Lucas. Ramsay understood the volatility and passion of his player, genuinely liked him, liked his toughness and his competitive instinct, sympathized with his complaints about money and in fact felt that some of them were quite legitimate. Lucas was, by the league's standards, badly underpaid. But the 1978–79 season had been more troubling, there had been more friction. At the end of the season, during the Phoenix playoffs, Lucas was nursing a bad hand. Reporters asked Ramsay whether Luke would be ready for an important game, and Ramsay shook his head and answered, "I don't know, you'll have to ask him." Clearly Ramsay was annoyed with Lucas's playoff performance. During the off-season, having tried and failed to renegotiate, Lucas had come to Ramsay and asked to be traded. He did this because he believed that there were only three times when a player had any real leverage in the sport. The first was when he first came in the league, and he, Maurice Lucas, had blown that. Second, when a player became a free agent, and he had blown that too, signing at the beginning such a long contract that the only way he could get a commensurate NBA salary was to extend the contract even further, which made his free agency a distant question. And third, when a player was traded and a new team was anxious to keep him happy and thus meet his demands. So Lucas's only hope, given a salary he did not particularly like, was to be traded. His request had insulted Ramsay, who believed that his players should want to play for him, that it was something of a privilege to play on a Ramsay team, particularly for a player like Maurice Lucas whose overall game, Ramsay and his assistant Jack McKinney believed, they had greatly improved. Ramsay had turned to his assistant Jack McKinney and said: "Fuck him. He wants to play someplace else. We'll oblige him."

Earlier in the summer, there had almost been a trade with Chicago—Artis Gilmore, the huge but aging Chicago center, for both Lucas and Lionel Hollins, the talented Portland guard. At the last minute Portland backed out, somewhat dubious of Gilmore. McKinney objected to the fact that Gilmore was not a good passer, and a center who could pass was essential to the Ramsay offense. "Jack, he can't pass," McKinney had said. "I'll teach him to," Ramsay had answered. In the end McKinney had asked for permission to make one phone call, this to a man named Ed Badger, who had once coached Gilmore at Chicago. Badger over the phone confirmed McKinney's impressions if a good deal more forcefully, and the deal had been canceled.

A little later Inman thought he had managed to work out a trade for Lucas that in his opinion bordered on a steal. On the eve of the college draft he had worked out a deal with Chicago. The draft was an annual league event in which the professional teams chose out-coming college players. The weakest team, that is the team with the worst record, selected what it considered the best available college player in the country. Then the other teams would pick, in inverse pattern to the quality of their season. According to the deal Inman worked out, Portland would deal Lucas to Chicago for its first pick, number two overall in the draft, and take David Greenwood, a UCLA player that Inman coveted. Greenwood was a well-coached intelligent player, not as physical as Lucas, but like many UCLA men a finesse player. Inman saw Greenwood as a good and potentially *very* good NBA player who would add versatility to Portland's front line.

He could not believe his good luck. There were other players in the draft that Inman would like to have had, most particularly a player named Calvin Natt, later drafted by New Jersey, but Greenwood was the player who most suited Portland's post-Walton needs.

Inman believed he had snookered the Chicago front office, and he was appalled when the trade was vetoed by Larry Weinberg, a successful Los Angeles home builder and real estate man who was also the principal owner of the Portland team. Weinberg was considered around the league a very shrewd businessman, and a very tough man to make a deal with, both at the level of other owners, who felt what he wanted for his players was very high, and from the level of his players and their agents, who felt that what he offered was generally very low. Weinberg, it turned out, was far more enamored of Lucas's play and his statistics than Inman was. The owner, said one member of the Portland front office, was "willing to trade Luke to New

York for the Statue of Liberty, the Empire State Building, three starting players, and either a draft choice or La Guardia Airport. With Washington all he wants is the Capitol and the White House and Elvin Hayes. But Ramsay won't go for it—he hates Elvin Hayes." Inman had explained the deal carefully to Weinberg—in Lucas they had a player with a powerful personality showing increasing signs of being disaffected, whose value might drop very quickly if he had a bad year. He told Weinberg that Greenwood would fit readily into the Ramsay system. Ramsay himself, Inman emphasized, was completely behind the deal. Weinberg listened and then rejected the proposal. He thought they should get a good deal more for Lucas.

Inman was furious, he hated the lack of professionalism of it. He had after all spent the previous season in a hundred small motels in a hundred tiny towns watching a hundred college games, rushing for the next airport, flying by some tiny airline into another small college town, and then returning later in the year over the same route because he had learned the hard way that one look was not enough. All that work was down the drain. Now, over the telephone, he began to shout at the owner, the angriest he had ever been with Weinberg: "Are you really telling me that you are rejecting what I recommend and all your coaches recommend, and that you know more than us?" The Lucas problem would undoubtedly get worse. It was, he said, unfair to the team and unfair to Lucas. Unable to control himself anymore he had handed the phone to Ramsay and stormed out of the room.

A few weeks later Inman thought he had worked out the possibility of another trade to New Jersey, Lucas for Calvin Natt, but that too had fallen through. So nothing had been done about Lucas, and Inman was upset, he thought there were too many uncertainties on this team, too much baggage from the past.

AT THE MOMENT that Stu Inman was arriving at the first practice, Maurice Lucas, the body in question, was already there, having his picture taken. The photographer, a somewhat fey Oriental, was trying to tease and charm Luke into smiling. But Luke did not like to smile, or at least not at the command of others. He liked to scowl. It was part of his role as the team's intimidator to scowl, both in basketball and in life. Even the commercials he had done for a local auto company reflected this. "My friends buy their cars at John Lucas Chevrolet," he said in the commercial, looking somewhat angrily into the camera, his face becoming a little harder. "Are you my friend?" His body was impressive, powerful, well muscled, and the scowl, almost imperial in style, seemed an extension of it, suggesting a certain dark black anger towards white authority. His look was as much a part of his game as his elbows. Bill Walton used to tell friends that he loved to look out of the corner of his eye during a game and catch Luke giving an occasional elbow to some opponent, preferably younger. Luke threw an elbow and scowled, and the scowl was a warning. An elbow today, something worse tomorrow. He clearly did not like the photographer pushing him for a smile. His smiles were rationed, not handed out to strangers in public, much less in full view of his teammates who were now laughing and teasing him. Lucas could in private be very funny and very charming, but he liked to choose the moment, not let some young photographer do it for him.

"Come on, Luke," Lionel Hollins said, "*do what the man says.* It don't hurt a bit." Luke frowned even more. The photo session finally over, he grabbed Steve Kelley, a bright irreverent young reporter for the Portland *Oregonian.* "I want to talk to you, Kelley," he said. Kelley and Lucas had an odd love-hate relationship. Lucas took what Kelley did seriously (he read the paper carefully, he loved what he called the *pub,* or the *ink,* and he often hoped to be traded to New York, a city of far more and far greater purveyors of pub than Portland). Kelley was of the new breed of writers and talked as much about issues of contract and grievance with players and agents as he did with management. Indeed, one Blazer official accused Kelley of being "in Luke's pocket." Still Kelley's relations with Maurice Lucas were erratic. At one point in the previous season, after a mention of how many points his opponent had scored against him, Luke cut the writer off. "I'm not talking to you anymore," he said, "you're a fly-by-night reporter. Write that down, fly-by-night." "What'd I do wrong?" Kelley asked. "You're the writer, you're so smart, you figure it out," Luke answered. They had stopped talking for a while, and there had been little Lucas pub, until finally Luke took him aside. "Kelley, you got anything against me personally?" No, Kelley had answered. So they had spoken again. But it was always risky, and Kelley never knew when he would get the charm and when he would get the scowl. One night after Luke cut him off again, Kelley had gone to dinner with some colleagues from his paper, including the music critic. The music critic complained about the difficulties inherent in writing critically about such sensitive people as professional musicians. "I don't want to hear it," Kelley had said, thinking of Luke, "I'm just not sympathetic. Your timpani player is 5'8", maybe 5'9". He weighs maybe 155 pounds. Make it 160. The people that I get angry are 6'9" and they weigh 220. Don't tell me about your timpani players."

At this first practice Lucas called Kelley over. "I've got a bomb for you," he said. "What is it?" Kelley asked. "A blockbuster," said Luke. "I'll tell you when I'm ready. Stay tuned." A long season, Kelley thought, a long season.

Lucas was also the most openly political member of the team, particularly with Walton gone, acutely conscious of race and the double standards in both American life and his chosen profession. He did not believe that Portland would ever pay a black star as much as it paid a white star and a large part of his proof lay in the difference between his salary and that of Bill Walton. His coaches thought that though he had legitimate salary grievances, he should not confuse race with ability, that the difference between him and Walton was not necessarily one of skin color, but of overall value to the team. But what bothered Lucas was his belief that while the coaches spoke of him as the best power forward in the league he was not paid as such, and even now, when the owner was trying to trade him, he was offering Lucas to other teams at one level of value, and paying him at another. Not everyone connected with the Portland front office thought his logic poor. After five years as a professional, four of them as one of the top players in the league, he was only now coming into big money, but even that money wasn't as big as that paid to other players. George McGinnis was paid more, and Luke was proud of his ability to inhale George McGinnis; his best games were almost invariably against McGinnis or other power forwards he considered to be (unjustly) paid more than he was. Now with five years to run on his contract and in a time of rising inflation the figure of $300,000 no longer seemed big enough. His friend Walton had signed with San Diego for some $700,000 a year whether he could play or not. Weinberg, he thought, was always talking about how he would not renegotiate with any player, but Lucas was absolutely convinced, when Bill Walton criticized the team's medical practices, that Weinberg would have renegotiated Walton's contract in order to keep him.

The first day of practice was supposed to be light. Photo sessions for local photographers, media interviews. Then, just as a reminder that Jack Ramsay ran a tight ship, and that Ramsay teams were in the best of condition, a two-mile run, known as the Ramsay Two Mile. On this day the players were somewhat resentful because in the past they had only had to deal with the Ramsay Mile, to be run in under six minutes. Now it had been doubled. Two miles. That was too much. One mile was too much. Off they went, at once trying to pace themselves, impress the coach, and yet manage to finish the race.

In the middle of the race, Maurice Lucas pulled up and walked his way home. Ramsay and the other coaches were furious. A few minutes later, going to lunch, Bruce Ogilvie asked the others, "Did you believe that you would ever see the day that a player making $300,000 a year would want to renegotiate his contract?" At lunch Ramsay was still furious. "Do you know who led the team in fines last year?" he asked as if of himself. "Lucas." Those at lunch included Ramsay, Morris Buckwalter, the new assistant coach who had once been a scout, Ed Gregory, the new scout, Inman and Ogilvie. Ramsay wanted to unload Lucas right then and there, make a deal whether Weinberg liked it or not. This was a challenge to him and more, a challenge to the idea of team. The only question now was which player they would go after, David Greenwood or Calvin Natt. Ramsay turned towards Gregory, who had seen more of their games than anyone else. Natt was a small forward from a small school in Louisiana whose team had not played in high-level competition; he was 6'6", ruggedly built, relentless if not stylish in his game. Greenwood, 6'10", was the product of the ultimate college program, UCLA.

"Which one did you like better?" Ramsay asked.

"Well," said Gregory, "I think Natt can be a good NBA player and Greenwood a great one. Natt has a good attitude, a very good one. He's not that big."

"How often did you see Natt play?" Ramsay asked.

"Three or four times." Greenwood? "Fifteen times."

"Did you ever see Greenwood have a bad game?"

"No," said Gregory, "not really."

"I saw him play on television three or four times," Ramsay said, "and I never saw him have a good game. He had some good moments, but mostly it looked like he wasn't out there." Around the league Ramsay was regarded as an excellent coach and a relatively weak judge of college talent, almost inevitably too negative in his assessment of players. When he was first hired in Portland, Inman, whose specialty was player evaluation and who had great faith in Ramsay's ability to do more than anyone else with talent already assembled, had asked Ramsay if he minded not being part of the player personnel process. Not at all, Ramsay had said, and that was the way it remained.

"No," Gregory was saying, "I don't agree with that. I saw him mostly in the second half of the season and he was very good." Gregory switched then to his scout-talk. "Greenwood's got good reach. Good long arms. 6'9", 6'10", but seems taller because those arms are so long. He can play backup center. Likes the ball in the clutch. Carried a weak UCLA team in the second half of the season. In the NCAA semifinal against DePaul he simply took over and kept them in the game by himself. Good kid, good student."

Someone asked Gregory to compare Greenwood with Mychal Thompson, last year's first-round pick. "Well, right now he's ahead of where Mychal was at this point because he's used to playing facing the basket, whereas Mychal had his back to the basket when he was in college. Listen, this is the best kid I saw all last year. Smart, good attitude. History major. His body is not quite as good as Mychal's but he's got that extra reach, maybe a longer reach than Mychal."

"Get him," Ramsay said, and Inman separated himself from the table to call management in Chicago about Greenwood and Kevin Loughery in New Jersey about Natt. Inman was melancholy. He thought the time for the trade had already come and gone, that it would be harder for a team to pick up a player of Greenwood's quality once he had arrived in the league. The original deal with Chicago had been premised on its being completed before the draft. "Look, if we draft Greenwood and then ten hours later trade him, the people here will kill us," Jonathan Kovler, the Chicago managing partner, had said. Similarly, Inman believed that once New Jersey's coaching staff discovered how physical and tough Natt was, that they would probably want to keep him. He was already angry about the whole business. A little later he returned, dejected. "This is the worst time of the year to deal—everyone is saying this is the best camp they've ever had." Chicago, he said, was probably out. New Jersey might be interested. He doubted that their interest would last very long, that each day that they saw Natt in practice the deal would become less likely.

That night at dinner the coaches met again. One thing they were pleased about was that Bobby Gross, the small forward who had been threatening to sign with another team, at the last minute agreed to terms and came into camp at a good weight, seemingly in good physical and mental condition. Right through the summer it had been unclear where Gross, who had been a crucial player in the championship season, might go. That he had returned removed at least one question mark. His new salary with Portland was staggering for a small forward of exceptional if often underutilized gifts; he had come in at $300,000 a year. Some of the coaches were afraid that much money and its implied security would affect his game. Ramsay, a great Gross fan, was confident that it would not.

The signing of Gross had been a particularly clumsy piece of work, and it underlined some of the imbalances of the league with its new high salary and high entertainment pressures. Gross's skills were unusual, but they were not dramatic or fancy, nor did they necessarily show up in the statistics. In an age where sport was seen mainly through television and the camera was always fixed on the ball, Bobby Gross made most of his contributions elsewhere on the court. He moved well without the ball, thus setting up opportunities for other players, he saw the court structure instants before other players (Ramsay thought his court vision was second only to Walton's), he passed well, and he played good smart team defense. In that championship season he had been a connoisseur's player. Always, by NBA standards, he was dramatically underpaid; the championship season was his second year in the league, and he had signed as second-round draft choice for a four-year contract that averaged around $50,000, far below his worth and his contribution. Ramsay, realizing this and sensing eventual difficulty in the future, had suggested that Weinberg tear up Gross's contract and give him a new fairer one, perhaps averaging $125,000 a year. Even at that figure he was a bargain. Ramsay made this suggestion on behalf of a number of players who were, because of contract flukes, being paid well below their market value, but for no player did he make the case as strenuously as for Gross. But Larry Weinberg refused to bend. He was not, the coaches thought, a particular fan of Gross's game, Gross did not have good statistics and besides, as a flat policy rule, Weinberg did not renegotiate contracts. He did not do this in his other businesses and he would not do it in basketball. That other businesses more truly reflected the free market did not matter, a rule was a rule. If a player signed for a high salary and proved, as some had, a disappointment, Weinberg met every payday.

As the contractual problems mounted, Weinberg's inflexibility took on a significance central to the problems of the team. But Ramsay's arguments—that voluntary salary adjustments now would reduce bitterness and save trouble down the road—made no headway with the owner. Ramsay had crossed a line, becoming the basketball coach talking about business. The owner knew more about business, he was sure, than the coach did. Weinberg told Ramsay that if you renegotiated with one player, you renegotiated with them all, and that they would all take advantage of you. Ramsay did not agree. He did not believe that was an acceptable way to view the professional athlete; he felt that there were good people and some bad people in this business, as in others, and that you could base these decisions on merit and character. Those who played within the idea of team should be rewarded, and those who played outside it should not. To disregard this principle diminished his own leverage with the players, since he was constantly asking them to be unselfish. Yet the salary standards of the modern league had been set more by television and its norms—flashiness, points, excitement—than by coaches' norms. Two of the least selfish players on the team were Gross and Twardzik, and they were, regrettably, among the two most poorly paid. But he could not budge Weinberg. Ramsay thought Weinberg an honorable man, perhaps far more honorable than the average NBA owner, but regrettably far more rigid as well. He thought Weinberg desperately wrong on this policy; it was much too rigid for a business as emotional as sports. He and Jack McKinney had begun arguing with Weinberg some two years earlier, at the time of the championship, telling him that he must change his policy or there was going to be trouble further down the line. Now they were further down the line, and there was, as he had feared, trouble.

The Gross negotiations had gone on for almost two years. They pitted two of the toughest and most relentless men in the business of sports against each other: Weinberg, the Portland owner, rich, smart, very tough, and Howard Slusher, a sports agent–attorney, not so rich, tough and very smart. They were well matched. Weinberg was the bane of existence for most sports agents, since in their opinion he did not really negotiate, he would simply make an offer and then sit back and wait. More often than not that first offer seemed to be the last one. He used silence and his own patience as negotiating tools; Weinberg negotiated, one agent said, by exhausting you. Emotionally he, like other owners, had a distinct advantage. The game of basketball was rarely their principal business, as it was that of the player; the careers of the owners in their main businesses usually lasted for some forty years, whereas the player, limited to seven or eight years in his career, was more desperate to sign. Not only sports agents disliked dealing

with Weinberg, other owners found it difficult as well; they thought he always seemed to need some sort of advantage at the end, not so much to save
money—he was far too rich for that—as for reasons of ego and self-esteem.
He would not be made a fool, and no one would put anything over on Larry
Weinberg. If anything, he would put one over on someone else. Agents
came in with their demands, blustered to the press, and then as the start of
the season neared, as their athletes become nervous about missing the
season—for not playing was like not living—they gave in, and came down
in price and delivered their athlete, usually on terms favorable to Weinberg.

Not Howard Slusher. Slusher was like Weinberg. He did not necessarily
call back, he made an offer and he stayed with it, and he was capable of
holding an athlete out not just for a game or two but for an entire season if
necessary. Indeed, there were owners who, in the draft of college seniors,
wanting and needing a particular player, would now bypass that player if he
was represented by Slusher. To owners Slusher was a fearful figure, blunt,
unbending, willing to cast himself in local newspapers as the devil incarnate if it helped his clients. In his negotiations he was like a very good battle
commander who knows that in order to take an objective he must accept
some casualties, that the end eventually justifies the sacrifice. By holding
out a few of his athletes for very long periods he had made credible his
threats not just on them but on other clients, as other agents had not. He
was smart and quick, he held both a Ph.D. and a law degree, and he had in
fact taught a full course load at USC while attending law school there.
Slusher was philosopher turned jock representative, a man who loved Martin Buber. One of the most important moments in his life was his visit to
Buber himself, in Jerusalem, at his home on Love of Zion Street. As an academic, Slusher had written a highly esoteric Buberesque book on sport entitled *Man, Sport and Existence.* "Man lives in order to develop his *I,*"
Slusher had written, talking of the individual and the team. "However the
I can only exist as it relates *with* another being *(Thou).* The word *with* is
crucial at this point for it means a community of living rather than the
encounter of two isolated individuals in a society. Life therefore and all
that is real is essentially a series of *intimate relationships.* One can only
develop his *I* by relating to a *Thou.* . . ." That book, highly regarded in college philosophy departments, had been published in 1967 and sold some
4,500 copies—none of them, it was believed, to owners of professional
sports teams—and there were some owners who later wished that it had

been far more successful, in which case Howard Slusher might have remained in academe, closer to Martin Buber and Paul Tillich than to Paul Westphal, Sam "Bam" Cunningham and Gus Williams, to name a few. Slusher philosophy in some ways still applied to the people he dealt with in sports. He broke it down now into simpler categories. Some owners and coaches, he believed, were real, and some were not. To Slusher, Art Rooney of the Pittsburgh Steelers was real, Sam Schulman of the Seattle Sonics was not, Red Auerbach of the Boston Celtics was a bully but he was real. To the surprise of many who knew both men, Howard Slusher believed that Larry Weinberg was real. In Slusher's view, the key to dealing with Weinberg was in understanding that he was a real estate man, and that a real estate man waits and waits for the *closing*, and if he doesn't close on the house he wants, he closes on the next-best house. That was a technique which served Weinberg well in his principal business though, Slusher suspected, not so well in sports, where emotion and personal chemistry were more important than in real estate.

Bobby Gross was by chance a basketball player in search of Martin Buber, a connoisseur's player, a young man in a sport increasingly given over to *I*, who was truly a child of sports as *Thou*. His game exemplified team play, he looked always to pass rather than to score himself, and he seemed embarrassed if he scored more than fourteen points in a game. His own statistics were never impressive, but what he did for his teammates always was. Yet in the championship series against Philadelphia, it was Gross's singular play against Julius Erving, perhaps the most exciting and talented player in the game, that had captivated professional basketball men. Gross maximized his more limited physical skills against the man that other players considered the single greatest *athlete* in the game. Out of that series had come Gross's new reputation as a special player, and Ramsay thought of him as perhaps the best small forward in the game. The refusal to renegotiate was still another wound to Gross's pride. At the end of his first year there had been a very ugly difference of opinion over whether or not he was entitled to a bonus performance clause of $10,000. According to the clause he was supposed to average 24 minutes of play in 60 games and if he did, he received the $10,000. Since he was then playing for $40,000, the bonus bulked very large. There was some difference of opinion over whether all his games, or only his best 60 games, should be averaged. The Portland management claimed that he had averaged only 22.75 minutes and thus was not entitled to his bonus. Appalled by this behavior, and almost unable to comprehend the mentality behind the decision—these were people he had played *for*, not *against*—Gross called a lawyer he had once met named Howard Slusher and asked him to intervene. That was how Howard Slusher had entered Bobby Gross's life. They settled on a figure of $7,500 for the bonus but Slusher, not unduly modest, decided years later that the issue had cost Portland some $500,000 over the next five years, since he represented Bobby Gross, and then, doing so well with him, he came to represent other Portland players as well.

Before negotiating Gross's new contract, the first thing Slusher did was to call a former student at USC, Paul Westphal, who was also the first player he had ever represented. How good is Gross? Slusher had asked. "He's the best," Westphal had answered, "the player's player. Everyone in the league wants to play with him. The ball goes in to him and it always comes back." That was good enough for Slusher. Several years earlier he had represented Lynn Swann, an exquisitely talented wide receiver then drafted by the football Pittsburgh Steelers. Slusher had been very pleased by the contract Swann had signed. Though drafted number seventeen in the first round by Pittsburgh, Slusher had gotten Swann the number two amount of money among rookies, a measuring scale of great importance for agents. At the press conference called to announce the signing, Art Rooney, the owner of the Steelers, had taken Slusher aside and said in a very pleasant manner, "You think you screwed us, don't you?" Slusher had not answered, though in fact he *did* think he had screwed the Steelers. "You're wrong," Rooney said. "We got you. My son says he's not a good football player, he's a *great* football player. Probably the best draft we've ever had. Maybe better than Bradshaw or Joe Greene." Still Slusher said nothing, because in some way Rooney was clearly trying to tell him something. "Let me teach you a lesson, young man," Rooney had said. "You can never overpay a *good* player. You can only overpay a bad one. I don't mind paying a good player $200,000. What I mind is paying a $20,000 ballplayer $22,000." That had taught Slusher a very good lesson and he had henceforth always prepared for his negotiations by checking out the strengths and weaknesses of his clients.

Weinberg had not been very admiring of Gross's game, Slusher thought, and judged him in the worst way possible on the basis of his statistics. Weinberg of course knew exactly what all the small forwards in the league were making. Scott Wedman, he said, mentioning a very muscular small forward for Kansas City with far nobler statistics, Scott Wedman only makes about $150,000. "That's what small forwards make," he added. "Larry," said Slusher, "Bobby Gross is not a small forward, he's a *basketball* player. He's a very important part of a team. The other players need him." Weinberg reiterated the going price for small forwards, even good ones, and Slusher said that made no difference, if he accepted that rate then he was allowing someone else to negotiate for his client.

So they went back and forth. Slusher had prepared himself well. He had earlier taken Gross aside and said that he thought they could get nearly $325,000 a year, that his payday was finally coming. But the key in dealing with Weinberg, he emphasized, was patience. There would be moments when it all seemed hopeless and that a contract could not be arranged. There would be other times when Weinberg's offers would seem good enough to call off the bargaining and sign for. But if they were willing to be patient, he was sure he could win. Bobby Gross, angry over the way he had been treated in the past, turned out to be very patient. That was vital. To win in negotiations like this the client had to have both skill and nerves. A lot of kids, aware of how brief their careers were, sensitive to the derogatory public remarks management often made in the heat of negotiations, lacked the nerve. But Gross was very tough. He trusted Slusher completely. The key, Slusher suspected, was how poorly Portland had treated him in the past. The grievance over money was in his case quite genuine.

In the end Howard Slusher and Bobby Gross won. They were helped, Slusher was quite aware, by two factors. The first was that with Walton gone and Maurice Lucas's status uncertain, the team desperately needed Gross. Portland was shaky enough with him; without him it would be like starting a new team. The other factor was that Gross had a potentially very damaging medical grievance against the club. In the spring of 1978 he had felt pain, mentioned it to others and, because Dr. Cook had been absent, had been allowed to continue playing without being X-rayed. He had subsequently broken his ankle. He was prepared, if need be, to sue the team, though not Dr. Cook. Portland, Slusher was sure, was aware of this. In the end he had signed for $303,000 a year, making him the highest-paid player on the team. The salary included his membership fee of some $10,000 in an expensive golf club and annual golf fees. They had come to the end of the negotiations, and Slusher had asked Gross if, for icing on his cake, there was anything he wanted out of life that was special, a fancy car, a gift for his parents. Gross had pondered the question and had answered that he loved golf, and golf memberships were very expensive. So it was that Bobby Gross got his golf fees paid, and though golf was clearly unlike basketball, a sport of *I* rather than *Thou*, Slusher was sure that Martin Buber would have approved.

Though Howard Slusher had gotten for Bobby Gross roughly twice what he would have been paid had Portland been willing to renegotiate with him earlier, the irony of that prolonged, difficult bargaining was that Howard Slusher and Larry Weinberg, instead of becoming bitter enemies, as was often the case after Slusher contract battles, had become quite fond of each other. Each had come to respect and admire qualities in his adversary. Slusher believed that Weinberg was truly an exceptional man, very tough and very smart, but above all ethical, perhaps ethical to a fault. If he tripped on anything in something as emotional as sports, it was his own righteousness. Slusher regarded him as a very compassionate man, but unlike many other sports owners who had a flair for dramatizing a fake compassion, Weinberg was not very skilled at showing his decency. But he was, the ultimate Slusher accolade, very real. Slusher began to seek Weinberg out for advice, not in sports but in personal areas, talked to friends about Weinberg as if he were a father, and often told other friends that he was for Larry Weinberg for President of the United States because he was the toughest, smartest man he knew.

IF EVENTS WERE somewhat somber in Portland, whence Bill Walton had departed, in San Diego where he arrived everyone seemed optimistic. Season-ticket sales, stimulated by the word that the Redhead was back, were booming. It had been a good team the year before, and now with Walton it might be a great team. Walton, who had not played basketball in well over a year, said he was feeling well. He seemed optimistic about the 1979–80 season and his return to the game. Old friends marveled at how strong his body looked, toned by hundreds of visits to local Nautilus machines. The Clipper management, Beverly Hills in its essential orientation, was already preparing a new and more stylish incarnation for him. Though Walton had in the past been given to wearing rough backcountry clothes, though he had shown up by chance at a ceremony to receive the Sullivan Award as the nation's outstanding athlete in a dirty flannel shirt and blue jeans streaked with grease from repairing a bicycle, though the Portland *Oregonian* had once called him the best center who ever came out of the *Whole Earth Catalogue,* he was now, at the behest of Irv Levin, the mod owner of the Clippers, being outfitted in Beverly Hills's most expensive stores. Jeans and flannel shirts were being replaced by three-piece suits which cost as much as $1,400. It was typical of Walton and his troubled NBA career that even his clothes were an issue. He had, at Levin's direction, been taken around Beverly Hills by a man named Hal Kolker who once represented Neil Diamond. All really the same business. Kolker was selling the new Bill Walton, better in dress and thus better (this was the implication) in attitude. Kolker even wangled Walton an appearance (this after all was a new and far less threatening Bill Walton) on the *Hollywood Squares* where, as he walked in, he was welcomed by Peter Marshall. Peter Marshall was very excited about meeting Bill Walton, though Bill Walton, insufficiently acquainted with game shows, was somewhat less excited about meeting Peter Marshall ("Who *is* that guy?" he asked). He did not do badly on the show. Marshall asked him if it was true that Louis Leakey, the great anthropologist, had said that one reason that man survived in early days was because other animals thought he smelled so bad that they wanted no part of him. For Walton, a vegetarian who had, in his early years in Portland, consistently complained to his teammates about how bad they smelled—"meat eaters," he would say in the locker room, "you stink"—it was an easy question. Back in San Diego, Walton was also making the rounds of civic luncheon clubs to talk to businessmen about the coming season. That too, like his clothes, was news. In general, the mood in San Diego was high.

Only one player at the San Diego camp seemed uneasy about the coming season. That was Kermit Washington, the power forward, a young man who had gone in one year from being something of a social outcast in basketball because of a nearly fatal fistfight with another player, to a far happier year as a Clipper starter, where at the end of the year he was voted by fans as the most popular player on the team. Washington, who had never enjoyed a very easy or pleasant professional career, had always been aware of the rootlessness of the professional athletic life and how hard it was not just on the athlete himself, but even more on his wife and children. But in San Diego his wife had finally found, he believed, not just a residence, something bought at one price, inhabited superficially, and sold later at a higher one, but a genuine home, a place where they would always live. It was, he thought, the easiest city in America to live in, with a climate even better than Los

Angeles because there was less smog, and where the beaches were less crowded and more accessible. For Pat Washington, who (given the traveling schedules of NBA athletes) often served her children as both mother and father, a special plus was that every other couple in San Diego seemed to have children the exact same ages as the Washington children.

Their summer had been easy and pleasant; they seemed surrounded by new friends. Kermit Washington liked his new teammates. During the summer many of them had stayed in shape by practicing together, something he had never seen on any team before, and they had even come over to his court and basket and practiced outdoors. Swen Nater, the giant center, usually brought the basketball. Nater was so strong and so physical that in pickup games like this it was impossible to stop his moves to the basket without fouling him, and so they fouled him, much to his genuine anger, and he would warn them once, and warn them twice, and finally, since no one seemed to pay any attention, he would take his basketball and go home. It made basketball fun, it was like being boys again and it seemed to reflect the happiness of his new life. In San Diego, Kermit Washington had found an ease of living and an acceptance as a man that had eluded him for much of his life.

His career before the fight had been difficult enough, and he had fashioned himself into a high-level professional athlete against the odds, mostly by personal determination. There was a particular irony about the stigma of the fight, for Kermit Washington seemed by his very game and his attitude to want social acceptance more than almost any other player. His face reflected his emotions: if he had made a mistake the pain and guilt always showed on his face and as he ran upcourt past his coach his expression at once showed apology and responsibility; he would, his face seemed to promise, not repeat the error. But the fight had made him an outcast. The film clip showing Washington smashing Rudy Tomjanovich in the face as Tomjanovich ran at Washington, a double force of collision because both principals—Washington black, Tomjanovich white—were moving, had been featured mercilessly on television sports shows, whose newscasters had piously attacked the violence of the moment, and whose executive producers had relentlessly rerun it because it was such rare footage, such good *television*. Washington had hated that time, the fear of what he had done to Tomjanovich, the knowledge that he had almost killed a man, and he had hated as well the fact that an entire (white) nation, a jury of millions and millions of people, had judged him and found him guilty, not of being in a fight during a heated moment in a game, but rather of premeditated assault on another player. That moment, which was alien to the rest of his career, had stamped him indelibly in the eyes of most American sports fans. He was not the player from the ghetto who had pushed himself to become a scholastic all-American, or the player who, having failed pitifully in his early years with the Los Angeles Lakers, forced himself by special coaching tutorial to become a quality basketball player. He had instead become the villain. Without any hearing, he had been immediately suspended from basketball; he had been fined $10,000 and the suspension cost him another $50,000.

AMERICA BELIEVED THAT its athletes were heroes and, being highly skilled at something so exemplary as a sport, were by nature also immensely self-confident; after all, their own high school heroes of yesteryear, now older and balder and heavier, had been confident and secure and had always won, as the fairy tale demanded, the best-looking girl. But the new American athlete, particularly the modern American professional basketball player, was very different. He was rarely confident about anything save his own sport, he had rarely as a young boy been garlanded by his peers and by beautiful cheerleaders. Instead he was more often than not black, often came from pathetic economic and psychological circumstances, was a basketball player out of desperation as much as anything else. Despite both athletic and financial success, his status in the greater society remained shaky. He remained as aware of where he had started as where he had ended, and how easily he might return.

Kermit Washington had come from such circumstances and though he had by dint of hard work created a far sounder environment than many of his professional peers, still the vulnerability was always there, and the reaction following the Tomjanovich fight had underscored it for him. He had remained in isolation and under suspension until rescued by Irv Levin, then owner of the Boston Celtics. A deal had been arranged. He would be traded to the Celtics by the Lakers and thereafter reinstated. Because he was saved by Irv Levin, Washington felt a special gratitude to the owner. A few months later, when his contract expired and he became a free agent, suddenly other teams were pursuing him actively, power forwards of his attitude and character being extremely scarce. Denver had been unusually anxious to sign him and had offered, over four years, some $200,000 more than Levin. But in a show of loyalty rare in professional sports, Washington turned down Denver and signed with Levin. Shortly after that Levin, a man of the West Coast, had, by sleight of hand and with the consent of his owner colleagues (who might after all want to pull off such a move themselves one day), switched franchises, taking the virtually defunct Buffalo team to San Diego, giving up the Celtics to the former Buffalo owner, and taking with him from the Celtics a number of their more valuable players, including Kermit Washington.

Washington became one of the few beneficiaries of the trade, winding up in San Diego. He liked the city, he liked the climate and he even liked his teammates, many of whom were considered like himself social rejects by other NBA teams. He enjoyed Lloyd Free, the great shooter, a Philly reject ("I'm so good, even I couldn't stop me"), who would on the day of a game often eat no more than a candy bar and yet play brilliantly; he enjoyed Sidney Wicks, the Portland-Boston reject who, as on his previous teams, was always talking but who had come finally to the right team because *here everyone else was always talking,* and no one was listening; he liked Nick Weatherspoon, Washington-Seattle-Chicago reject who, arriving in San Diego, had also become a born-again Christian (upset with an article written about him in a local paper, he had turned to the sportswriter and had said, "May the Lord forgive you for what you've done"); and, above all, he liked Swen Nater, the huge white center, a seriously religious young man who upon the occasion of any important decision (buying a new car or a new house, signing a contract) kept a Bible at hand so that he could open the Good Book to find, with any luck, from the randomly opened page, the proper prophetic guidance. It was fun playing for San Diego, Lloyd Free had said, because *everyone* was a little crazy.

Washington had thought it a mistake in June when Irv Levin signed Bill Walton. In the previous season the Clippers gained strength as they went along and had in the end barely missed the playoffs. Considering the compensation inevitably due Portland for a player of Walton's caliber, signing him meant mortgaging much of San Diego's future for a gifted but physically troubled player who might or might not be able to play. Washington was also aware, from the moment he heard the news, that given Walton's exceptional value and San Diego's limited roster and previous rulings by Commissioner Larry O'Brien, Washington himself was almost certain to go to Portland. That would not just mean four cities in three years but worse, having to prove himself yet again. He had sent O'Brien a handwritten letter, pleading for permission to stay in San Diego, telling of how difficult his readjustment had been after the turmoil caused by the fight, how hard he had worked to "rebuild my confidence as an individual. It was hard enough the first time getting rid of my negative image. Proving myself all over again would be even harder. . . ." He did not expect the commissioner to take any letter from him seriously but he felt he ought to write it anyway. Every day Bill Walton went out of his way to be particularly courteous to Kermit Washington. Walton was even quoted by reporters as saying that Kermit was stronger, perhaps even better, than Maurice Lucas, Walton's old running mate (a comment which irritated Lucas a good deal), and that the one player San Diego could not afford to give up in the compensation was Washington, the most physical forward on the team. Commissioner O'Brien, Kermit Washington thought, was not likely to take the words of Bill Walton any more seriously than he took the words of Kermit Washington. He was almost sure he was gone.

Still, Washington spent that summer as he had spent previous ones, building up his body on weights every day, and twice a week getting up at 6 a.m. to drive the two hours to Los Angeles and practice under Coach Pete Newell's harsh and unsparing eye. This year he received permission from Newell to take a young center-forward named Jerome Whitehead with him, in no small part because Whitehead, so frustrated after his rookie year, in many ways reminded him of himself. The Clipper organization had very quickly given up on Whitehead, saying behind his back that he was not smart enough to play forward. That reminded Kermit very much of the Lakers talking about the young Kermit Washington. So he talked Newell into letting Whitehead join the class, where in fact Whitehead had done quite well. Whitehead loved the tutorial even if it meant getting up so early because Newell seemed to care about him as a player, and seemed to have time for him.

One day they were driving back from Los Angeles to San Diego.

"Kermit," Jerome Whitehead said. "Mister Newell is the best coach you know, isn't he?"

Washington agreed that he was.

"Well, Kermit, why can't Coach Newell just come down to San Diego and coach the team there?"

"Because that's just not the way things work in the NBA, Jerome," Washington had said.

A WEEK INTO the Portland fall camp the coaches went out to dinner together. They were wondering whether the new contract would affect Gross's game, what the incentive would be now that so much money was guaranteed. Gross was a quality person, they thought, but it was simply harder to be eager when everything was settled, and your future was guaranteed. Well, Ramsay said, good athletes are good athletes. Then they talked about the compensation from San Diego. It was still on hold, and they wondered who they would get. Inman in particular coveted Kermit Washington.

"You know," Ramsay said, as if brought back from a darker reverie, of players gone, players injured, agents hovering nearby, contracts unsigned, all those things which were now outside a coach's control but which haunted a coach, especially now, with the 1979–80 season looming, "when I was in college I didn't want to be a basketball player. I wanted to be a baseball player. I thought I was pretty good."

"You probably didn't care enough about winning," said Inman. "Probably not competitive enough."

"No," said Ramsay, "I went out for the baseball team. At St. Joe's. The coach was Pep Young. Used to play in that million-dollar infield for the Tigers. I remember that he had an old Detroit Tigers warmup jacket on. Made us feel bigtime. Anyway, I was going to be a pitcher and I thought I could really throw the ball and I went out there and I reared back and I threw as hard as I could. I mean I thought I threw smoke. So I finished and I was feeling pretty good and I thought maybe he would tell me that I had a pro career ahead and he was going to call some of his old friends in Detroit. So I turn to him and he doesn't say anything. *Nothing.* So I finally waited and then I asked him what he thought and he stood there looking at me a long time and he said, 'Put more ass in it, kid.' That was my career as a baseball player."

OF THE ROOKIES and free agents, they were still uncertain. They all liked Steve Hayes, he was a nice kid, with a light shooting touch. He was slow and awkward, and it would be hard for faster teammates to work with him and through him on offense. But a lovely young man, they thought. The problem was that body. By contemporary basketball standards it was soft. It meant, they decided, that Hayes had never spent much time in the weight room. Was that a lack of commitment? Still, they were confident they would get one of the two San Diego centers, Swen Nater or Kevin Kunnert. Hayes, nice young man that he was, would have to go. The question of Bunch or Jeelani was more intriguing. Bunch was a better player technically, more fluid, more graceful, and he would fit more naturally into the patterned Ramsay offense. But something was missing with him; he was playing below his expected level and he was tentative, not getting the tough rebounds, the ones that came down into a crowd of people. He did not, in Inman's expression, "stick his nose into the ball." Jeelani by contrast was a constant surprise. He was not a graceful player, he had a great deal of trouble with the patterned offense, but there was something exuberant about him; he was always around the ball, always scoring when it seemed he shouldn't score. He seemed hungrier than the others and he had an instinct for scoring, if not for the game. The Portland players, rookies and veterans alike, all seemed to be playing tight and Abdul more than anyone else contributed an extra joyous energy. Every time they watched him they saw a little more and were more impressed. He had a genuine chance of making the club, they decided to their surprise.

It was no surprise to Abdul. Every day he arrived at practice and sat by himself for a few moments; in that time he thought about how much making this team meant to him. In particular he remembered how, as a seventh grader in Racine, Wisconsin, he had begun to realize that he had a talent for basketball, and how suddenly everything depended upon it; without basketball, he had no status and no friends. With basketball he became a person whom others were nice to. In those days the only place to play during the winter was in the YMCA league. But that cost $24, a lot of money in the Cole household. The Y sponsored a cookie sale; the cookies were taken on consignment and sold for $1 a box. That winter Gary Cole sold 30 boxes of chocolate chip cookies. It was hard work and he was often scared to knock on the doors of strangers but he wanted to play so badly that he stayed with it. Many of his buddies got bored and took to sitting on doorsteps and eating the cookies themselves. But not Gary Cole. Now, trying out for the Blazers, he often thought of his cold winter as a cookie salesman. It made him play harder.

Abdul stayed. Both Hayes and Bunch were soon gone, to colder climes— Hayes to play in the Continental league in Alaska, Bunch to play in Helsinki.

* * *

THEY TALKED A little more about their own team, and then they went on, as basketball people often do, to talk about players of the past. Players I Would Pay to See, Inman called the game. "Bill Russell," Inman began it. "I remember the first time I saw him play and he couldn't even sink a free throw and he was skinny too and I thought, turkey, turkey. Then there was a fast break, a sure basket and at the last second Russell had raced the length of the court and swooped down and blocked the shot. It wasn't just the block, it was the psychological destruction that went with it. I remember," Inman continued, "when the Celtics would play the Lakers in championship games and the Laker crowd would be noisy, and they would introduce the players before the game and they would come out, one by one, and slap hands, and then they would introduce Russell and he would come out, and stand apart, absolutely motionless, his face scornful, and the crowd noise would just stop. He didn't just intimidate other players, he demoralized the home crowd."

"Oscar Robertson and Jerry West," Buckwalter was saying. "I would pay to see them both. Jerry had those hands. Greatest hands I ever saw. They should bronze his hands. He would come up the court, give that fake, and then the last bounce on the dribble would be extra hard so that the ball would come higher and easier to shoot. Oscar was so complete and so economical. You'd watch him before a game in warmup and he was so methodical, working the perimeter of the shots he was going to take during the game. During the game he could always get to the exact place where he wanted to be. Big men, you know, can back in on their opponents like that, but Oscar was the only guard who could do it so well. And he had the moves. They tell the story, I'm sure it happened, of Oscar going for the basket, making a move, putting a head fake on his man, and then spinning for the basket. He gets by and scores and Earl Strom calls it walking. 'How can it be walking when you've never even seen that move before?' Oscar asks Earl."

"Bradley," Ramsay said. "He made that Knick team go. The smartest player on it. Saw everything before it happened. I'd pay to see him." What about Walt Frazier? someone asked, knowing that Ramsay did not like Frazier, that to Ramsay, Frazier was a symbol for all the things in the modern athlete that Ramsay did not like but would not discuss in his own players. "Too egocentric," Ramsay said, "slowed down that team. The others carried him. He was a creation of the New York media." So much for Walt Frazier.

There was a pause in the conversation; they had named Russell, West, Robertson and Bradley. They all pondered the question for a moment.

"Walton," Inman finally said. "I would pay to see Bill Walton. A great shot blocker, a great concept of the game, great intelligence and he brought a special tempo to the game, there was a *rhythm* to his game and it was always the right rhythm. Most of all," he paused, "his effect on his teammates. As long as he was there they all knew they would be in every game and they controlled their own egos. With him they always knew they could do it as a team." As he talked, Ramsay seemed far away, as if for a moment he were still the coach and Walton were still the star and this was still the championship season, and he was still there at courtside on one knee, seeing the same opportunity at the same moment that Walton did, knowing that he did not even have to shout it out, that Walton had seen it too, at the same moment. "He was so competitive," Ramsay said. "The bigger the game, the better he played. Once we were playing Milwaukee and he had made a couple of bad plays, and I called time, and the other players came over to the bench and he just stood there under the basket shouting at himself. 'Just don't throw me the fucking ball. Just pass it to anyone else.' Great competitor." Just then the waiter came over bringing free drinks, reminding them that they were back in Portland and no longer living in their imaginations. "I just want to say one thing, Coach Ramsay," the waiter said. "I hope you get what you want in the compensation."

Three days later the commissioner awarded the compensation. Portland received Kermit Washington and Kevin Kunnert, two draft choices and either (it was up to San Diego) guard Randy Smith or cash. In San Diego, Bill Walton, sitting at practice as assistant coach Bob Weiss read off the names of the soon to be departed, felt terrible. It seemed to go on and on. "I couldn't look at anyone," he said later. "I wondered if he was ever going to stop reading off names." He was angry at what O'Brien had done. Because of the ruling, "the Trail Blazers are not the bad guys. They're the good guys. *I'm* the bad guy." He sat and watched a team being torn apart and men who had made their homes in San Diego having to pick up their families and leave. He felt that he could not face some of the men who had just been his teammates.

In Portland the coaching staff was pleased. They had gotten the players they wanted plus the two first-round draft choices, and those choices, considering the damage their loss might do to San Diego, could prove very valuable to Portland. Weinberg officially complained that Portland had not been made whole, that there was in fact no way to compensate for a player of Walton's rare quality, and the front office suggested again that Portland would be glad to match San Diego's offer in order to have him back. Inman and Ramsay, however, were quite pleased. "Maybe it's just as well this way," Ramsay said.

Inman immediately called the homes of the two players, finding both out, but the wives at home. Both wives were very emotional. Kunnert had moved around the league a good deal, being just strong and rough enough for other teams to covet, and never quite attractive enough for his own team to keep. Inman thought of him as the classic backup center, which was a good thing: backup centers in the NBA were extremely marketable. Front-line centers were always getting hurt, and no team could afford to be without a strong backup. There was no telling, once the season started, how good a deal they might make for Kunnert if the opportunity arose. Kunnert might help Portland, which needed some muscle. "Mister Inman," asked Mary Kunnert, who had learned the hard way about the marketability of backup centers, "will this be our last move?" Inman thought he heard tears at the other end of the phone. He thought for a second before he answered because he was not entirely sure and he did not want to lie. "I hope so," he finally answered. Pat Washington was a little easier. Inman was absolutely sure there was a place for Kermit in Portland and when Pat had asked, "Are we going to stay in Portland or are we going to move again?" he said, "I can guarantee that you'll stay here." The connection to Kermit had already been made. Pete Newell, the former Cal coach who gave Kermit and some of his friends special summer tutorial, was Inman's closest friend in sports, and Inman had worked diligently through Pete Newell to let Kermit know how badly Portland wanted him, how appreciative the fans would be, and how well he would fit into the Ramsay system. Inman was almost gleeful about the prospect of adding Washington to his roster. "An NBA starter who took lessons every summer on his own," Inman kept repeating to any-one who would listen. He was pleased that Pat Washington seemed to take the news so well.

All she was thinking was that it would be another move, and another house and new friends. Being in the NBA was like being a kid and always having to have to go to a new school. She wondered about Portland and all that rain. In San Diego it was so easy. The sun came out every day. San

Diego, she thought, was a city designed for the mothers of young children whose husbands traveled more than they should. Kermit would have to go up and find the house. He was the real estate man in the family. She wondered what the city would be like and whether Kermit would be able to win fan approval again as he had in San Diego or whether the Tomjanovich fight would be held against him. She wondered what the other wives would be like.

Nothing in the NBA had been easy. When they first arrived in Los Angeles, newly married, Kermit a first-round draft choice, she had expected to find camaraderie among the fellow players and their wives, but she found instead a caste system. The Washingtons were new and they were young, and if they were successful they might take away some older player's job. So they had been isolated. No one had been very warm. The wife of another black player, a veteran, had taken her aside and explained that while they might sit together at games they could not socialize. Why not? a puzzled Pat Washington asked. "Because my husband's a starter and your husband sits on the bench," the woman answered. "After all, does the bank president socialize with the tellers?" Then there had been a severe injury for Kermit and after that the Tomjanovich incident and the isolation and the terrible public disapproval. When Kermit had finally been traded to Boston she stayed behind with the two tiny children, feeling terribly lonely. David Cowens's wife, Deby, understood her problems right away and since one of the airline companies was offering passengers bonus tickets, Deby Cowens had gone out on her own and collected as many tickets as she could for Pat Washington to visit her husband in Boston.

She had a sudden vision of a long rainy winter in Portland with Kermit on the road most of the time, while she lived among people she had never met before. Later that afternoon, some of the neighborhood kids, aged thirteen and fourteen, came by. They played basketball with Kermit on his own home court in the backyard almost every day and had come to regard him less as a distant professional star than a neighborhood playmate. When they knocked on the door, Pat Washington answered it. "Can Kermit come out and play?" one of the kids asked. "He can't," she said. "He's been traded to Portland. He's already gone." "But he didn't say goodbye," one of the kids protested. "How could he do that?" I don't know how he could do that, she thought, that's the NBA. The boy, she noticed, seemed near tears. So was she.

* * *

WHILE KUNNERT AND Washington were working out their travel plans, Larry Steele was trying to hold on to his job as backup small forward. He knew that his job was vulnerable because it was *always* vulnerable. His talents could never secure him a position; he depended on attitude. He had worked out all summer on the Nautilus machine, and because he was bothered by chronic bad knees, he had also put in a hot tub at his house so that he could soothe the pain in his legs. He was the senior member of the team; if he made it this year, it would be his ninth year in Portland, an unusually long career by contemporary standards. Steele was white. His size, 6′5″, made him a swing man, but he was really not quick enough to play guard. He was not that big, he did not have particularly remarkable court vision, nor was he an exceptional shooter. Yet he survived. He was, by his own admission, a survivor and adapter. None of the four coaches he had played for in Portland, including the present one, had really admired his game, yet except for Ramsay the coaches were all gone and he was still there. There was always talk of trade; he was just well enough known around the league as a utility man to be of considerable trade value and he knew that on several occasions trades including him had been virtually consummated only to be unconsummated at the last minute. Three years ago, at the beginning of the championship season, he knew that Ramsay did not want him at guard and that even at backup small forward, the coach probably preferred that year's first-round draft choice, Wally Walker. Since Bobby Gross was already playing small forward and since clubs did not like to cut their first-round picks because it showed a weakness in their scouting system, it appeared that Steele might be gone. But he was tougher and more combative than Wally Walker and he beat Walker out for the backup job. A year later Walker had been traded and Larry Steele remained. He did this by sticking relentlessly to his game, playing aggressively, diving for loose balls, all of which made him immensely popular in Portland. There were black players who were resentful of his longevity, not resentful of him personally, but convinced he survived where black players of comparable ability might have departed. When this was mentioned, someone defending the Portland organization would say yes—but Larry also *knew the system,* which was true. To which the blacks would respond that he knew the system only because he had been around for a long time, whereas a black might not stay around long enough to learn it.

None of this bothered Steele very much. He knew his limits quite well and he knew what he could contribute. Abdul Jeelani was playing well and Abdul could play at both big and small forward. But Portland could market Steele where it could not market Jeelani—who knew Jeelani's name and value? That was a sound business perception on the part of Portland's management. Steele thought the greatest mistake an athlete could make was to regard professional basketball as a sport, not a business. It was, he was sure, not only a business but a fairly harsh one. He was a survivor; if necessary he would survive somewhere else. In the meantime he and trainer Ron Culp were worried about his knees. Over the years, by scraping his knees on countless floors, he had sandpapered them down to a dangerous fragility. He worried now not just whether he could play one more season but whether he might have knee damage that would bother him for the rest of his life.

One more season. He knew that Jack Ramsay did not think very highly of his game, but he had his own reservations about Ramsay. He thought him a good coach, but he also thought that Ramsay had coddled Bill Walton, that there had been in that championship season a double standard, however slight. Too many small privileges had been dispensed to Walton, at practice, on the road; there had been too many quotes in the paper about Jack having consulted with Bill before deciding what to do next. The coaches had bent to Walton's will, Steele believed, and they had in return won the championship, and so everyone had been happy and Ramsay had been lauded.

But he did not think you bent to a player's will without losing something. The coach that he liked best had been an assistant coach at the University of Kentucky named Harry Lancaster who was, in Steele's words, the meanest coach he had ever met. When Steele was a freshman at Kentucky, Lancaster had once stopped him and asked, "How are things going?" "Okay," Steele had answered. *"How?"* Lancaster said, flashing a little anger, and Steele had answered again, "Okay." Then Lancaster grabbed him and shook him and said, "What's this okay shit? From this day on it's 'Yes sir, No sir.'" That was the way things had been at Kentucky in the old days—no coddling, no one with no-cut contracts. Because of that Steele had beaten out high school All-Americans. Like the Marine Corps, he supposed, it either made you or broke you.

Steele was an unabashed square. When Tom Meschery was assistant coach, there had been a team party, and Meschery, Portland management's link to the counterculture, offered Vicki Steele a marijuana cigarette. She, being from the same small town in Indiana as Larry, had been appalled. Coaches did not smoke pot where she came from and they most assuredly did not offer joints to players' wives. Steele had never been caught up in the madness of the championship season and his Portland friends thought there was a certain irony bordering on sadness in his Portland career. His best years, when he played the most minutes, and scrambled after the most loose balls, and the crowd loved him the most, had come before Portland's great team jelled. With the coming of the championship team his role had been reduced, from starting guard to reserve small forward. The central player on that team, Walton, looked down on his skills. When, in the middle of the playoffs against Denver, starting guard Dave Twardzik had been hurt, Ramsay thought momentarily of starting the more experienced Steele against Denver. But Walton had gone to Ramsay and lobbied for a rookie named Johnny Davis, a young black of explosive speed, a player who with his quickness was far better suited than Steele to Walton's special talents. Ramsay listened to Walton, and the move had been widely applauded; some people thought Portland was even tougher with Johnny Davis in the lineup than with Twardzik. But that had not been pleasant, having a teammate denigrate your talents, being forced to play a smaller role on a great team. Still, he made it through eight seasons in Portland. He held two Portland records, one for the most games played, 594, and the other for the most fouls, 1,779. On the second record, no one else was even close. With a little luck, and if his knees lasted, he might make 2,000. It was no small thing to accumulate 2,000 fouls in the NBA.

Kermit Washington and Kevin Kunnert finally arrived from San Diego. They were immediately initiated into the madness of Blazermania. A motel put a sign on its marquee: A KERMIT AND A KUNNERT ARE BETTER THAN A PAIN IN THE FOOT. Kermit Washington could not believe the instant celebrity. Though he had not yet played a single game, people competed to give him things. He went to buy some shrimp and the woman insisted that he take them free. Others called, volunteering to be babysitters. There was a free leased car. Kunnert, somewhat shaken at the prospect of joining his third team in three years, uncertain whether he might soon become trade bait for a fourth, was delighted to find at least one old friend in Portland, Tom Owens.

Owens was equally happy. Now Owens had a friend, someone equally tall to talk to; in addition, Kunnert was almost a perfect partner for Owens's conversation, in that he almost never talked back. They seemed as if chosen from central casting for a World War II movie: Owens, the New York city slicker, loquacious, funny, knowing all the angles and none of the angles; Kunnert, the farm boy from Iowa, given to few words but lots of folksy nods of the head. Kunnert did not exactly say "aw shucks," but he looked like he should say "aw shucks" and that was good enough. Besides, as one of the least physical centers in the league, Owens was delighted by the arrival of Kunnert, one of the most physical centers. On the first day of practice Owens introduced Kunnert. "If games get rough, Bub here is going to come and save my ass, right, Bub?" Kunnert nodded. "Bub's strong and no one pushes Bub around, right, Bub?" Another nod. "Bub got all those country boy muscles down on the farm, plowing up those leaves there, right, Bub—they just fix a plow to you." Again Kunnert nodded. "Right, T.O., we plow a lot of leaves back home."

There was, one sensed, a secret pleasure for Owens in his new status as starting center. The last time they had been together, Kunnert had been the starter for much of the season and Owens the dispensable third-team center, averaging some ten minutes a game. Now that was reversed. Portland, needing a backup center for Walton, had picked up Owens in 1977 after the championship season. Robin Jones, then backup center, had been heard in the victory celebration grumbling, "I don't feel a part of this—I didn't get my minutes." Shortly after, the deal had been arranged. Houston was anxious to move Owens, not so much to get rid of him as to avoid paying his guaranteed $145,000 salary, excessive, it believed, for a man now playing third-string center. Knowing the avarice that burned in the hearts of the Houston owners, Inman had arranged a deal in advance: Jones for Owens, but only if Houston paid $45,000 of Owens's salary. Otherwise, Inman said, his owner would not go for it, for Larry Weinberg—who had shied away from the huge salary of Moses Malone (by then the *first*-string Houston center)—was not a man to pay $145,000 for a much traveled backup center. Inman called in Ramsay and explained his game plan. He would present it to Weinberg as a potential coup, something which, with a little luck, he might be able to pull off. Thus Weinberg would feel a part of it. So they went into the meeting; there Inman explained the deal and told the owner he thought he could talk Houston into it. "Well, all right," Weinberg said somewhat reluctantly. "But only if they pick up that much of the salary."

"Hey, I thought it was already arranged . . ." said Jack McKinney, the assistant coach, who had clearly not been brought in on the scam. Inman quickly kicked him under the table. Weinberg, who wore a hearing aid, did not notice the comment. The deal was done and Owens had fitted into the Ramsay system, and had played the best professional basketball of his career.

On the third day that Kunnert came to practice, Owens took Ramsay aside. "Hey, Coach, I think Bub's really glad to be up here with us." Why was that, asked Ramsay, pleased but not surprised that a veteran player liked being on his team. "Well, because yesterday after practice I said to him, 'Hey, Bub, you were really putting the ball up a lot yesterday in practice,' and he said, 'You better believe it, T.O.—the way they play down there, I haven't seen the ball in two years.'"

IN THE EARLY days of the 1979 preseason camp, the Blazer officials were at first worried and then gradually reassured by the attitude of Lionel Hollins, one of the key veterans from the championship season. Though he made noises during the summer that had been critical of Ramsay and some of his methods, and though there were contract problems with him as well as with Lucas, Hollins arrived in excellent condition. He won the Ramsay Two Mile on opening day and that had brought a sigh of relief. For Lionel Hollins was in many ways the prototype of the best of modern professional athletes, more talented, more creative, better educated and, at the same time, more sensitive and delicate emotionally, than an older generation. The normal wounds of professional athletic life—those incurred on the court, those caused by what the coach did or did not do, or by that which was published—lingered long with Hollins. It had, for example, taken him longer to adjust to Portland and its fans than it did other players. When he first arrived, black, aloof, proud, he had been pressed into immediate action by Lenny Wilkens, then the coach, one of the league's great guards himself, who saw in Hollins the backcourt man for Portland's future. But his early years on that team were not easy, he was too quick for some of his teammates, his style of play too complicated for some of the Portland fans, still new to the professional game, to appreciate. He had also taken some playing time away from Larry Steele and there had been residual resentment over that. The crowd rode him hard, and Hollins responded to it. There had been one memorable night when the crowd booed him—there had been several turnovers—and Lionel had pranced gracefully in front of the bench, pirouetting the full three hundred sixty degrees in light ballet, raising aloft his hands and his middle finger in an age-old symbol of defiance. Hollins thought that some of the crowd's resentment of him was racial; soon after his arrival in Portland he had been interviewed on local television in the company of his then wife, who was white. Wilkens worried in those days whether he was pushing Hollins too quickly, subjecting him to too much pressure—Hollins, after all, was his man. He thought that the main problem was that Hollins was a better player than the fans were as yet prepared for. He did things on the court that they were not yet able to see. Later, after the championship year, Lenny Wilkens was amused when the Portland fans talked of how Lionel Hollins had improved; in his view it was the crowd which had improved in its appreciation of the essence of basketball.

Portland was a difficult city for Lionel Hollins. He was shy and he soon went through a divorce. He did not make friends easily outside basketball and yet he did not want to be known primarily as a basketball player, he wanted people to know him as a complete person. But that was hard. Besides, it was cold and rainy during the winter and Hollins, who had grown up in Las Vegas and Arizona, did not like cold weather. In Portland he had to wear Oregon-style clothes, heavy down parkas, thick formless pants. He hated clothes like that; he was slim and elegant and everything about him seemed stylish, his clothes, his manner, his girlfriend. He hated being bundled up like some Eskimo. Why take care of yourself if you were going to look like some blimp, he thought. You might as well eat too much and put on weight and be fat. Still, he made his adjustment and bought a house there and moved his grandmother and several of his cousins in to live with him. But the 1978–79 season had been a difficult one. There had been personal problems, a sister had died of a drug overdose. Then he hurt his knee badly, and it had overnight changed and limited his game. He was afraid to cut, and even more afraid to try a full jump. He could no longer leap and stuff the ball. When he went for an open basket, unlike every other back-court man in the league, he had been forced, at the last moment, to lay the ball up. That, for a professional basketball player, was terribly threatening. If he could not stuff, was he truly a professional player?

Hollins had been injured for a significant part of that season and he had tried to come back, he later decided, too quickly. His physical skills had not entirely returned by the tail end of the season and the three brief playoff games that Portland played. Ramsay used him as a third and fourth guard.

Hollins resented this, believing that he had made a sacrifice in trying to come back after an injury and that the appreciation shown for it had been marginal. His pride had been severely wounded. It had not been a happy year.

Though he was a particular favorite of the reporters covering the team, being intelligent, thoughtful and fair, and more aware than most professional athletes of a world beyond sports, he turned moody and introspective in that year. One day he came into the locker room and saw a writer whom he liked and who was wearing by chance a green sports jacket; and he had brushed the writer aside rudely, saying only, "Get out of my way, green jacket." It had been that kind of year. He decided at the end that in the coming season he would not play at all unless he felt in perfect condition. What made all of this even more complicated was the fact that Hollins was entering the last, or option, year of his contract. At the end of the year he would be free to sign with any team he wanted, though that team still would be forced to pay Portland compensation. If there was anything professional coaches and general managers hated it was a player in his option year, even a quality player like Hollins. In the option year players always seemed distracted. They were inevitably pitted—by their agents and their wives—against the ownership of the team, and thus potentially the team itself. They tended to think too much about statistics which could be used the following spring in negotiation. Even a player like Hollins might be just sufficiently out of sync to throw the rest of the mechanism off. Ramsay felt that the one weakness in Hollins was a tendency to try to do too much, and in an option year that might be a problem.

What made the case of Lionel Hollins even more interesting was that in the off-season he had learned something of his real market value. Portland, anxious to close up the gap created by Walton's departure, had come very close to making a package deal for Artis Gilmore, the Chicago center, and part of the package had been Hollins. But because his contract with Portland had a clause against his being traded to certain cold-weather cities, Chicago included, the Bulls's management had called Hollins to ask whether he would be willing to waive the clause and accept the trade. That had given him some additional leverage and he had mentioned the figure he wanted, something close to $300,000. (He was then making $150,000 and he knew Portland would pay $200,000 a year, but after that things got sticky.) The Chicago people had readily acceded, so readily in fact that Hollins wondered if perhaps he should have asked for even more. The deal subsequently fell through but Lionel Hollins had learned two things from it: first, that there was a very real limit to Portland's loyalty to him—if the management could help itself by trading him it would, so loyalty meant nothing; and second, that his market value was a good deal more than Portland might be willing to pay. Ramsay and Inman also knew what Hollins knew, what his worth was, and they also knew that, given Weinberg's salary policies, the figure might be too high. Thus the potential for a trade remained.

During the off-season Hollins had given a long interview to Steve Kelley of the *Oregonian* in which he had been critical of Blazer management, and critical of some of Jack Ramsay's coaching practices. That of itself was something relatively new in sports generally, and particularly so in Portland. The tendency in the past had been for reporters on the one hand to glamorize the athletes and the sport, but on the other hand, on all economic and social issues to go automatically to *management* for any statement. Gradually during the new iconoclasm of the mid-sixties, journalism had become more irreverent and more willing to challenge authority in the society in general, and finally, somewhat later, in sports as well, to hear athletes talk about not just how they felt on the Day of the Game but how they felt on a wide range of social, political and financial matters, some related to sports, some unrelated. That had been an important part of the larger revolution taking place in sports, bringing it out of the toy-department isolation that American myth had created for it into inevitable contact with the furor and volatility of the larger society. Portland, with only one professional sports franchise, and that so recently acquired, was hardly a center of sportswriting activism, and a large part of Bill Walton's grievance against the city consisted of his belief that in his early conflicts with management, some local sportswriters had automatically taken management's positions. Kelley was however of the new tradition; he talked not just to management, which regarded him warily, but to the players as well, who also regarded him warily. In Kelley's story Hollins was quoted as saying that on many occasions players tired during games because Ramsay held too many morning practices. He also said that he did not expect that he and Lucas would be members of the team that year because clearly Ramsay wanted a new center and the two of them were likely to be part of the price. But the most important thing he said was about Ramsay and his system. While Ramsay was a very good coach, he said, and should be praised both for the high-level professional caliber of his work and his success in bringing a winning atmosphere to Portland, there was a serious danger in the way the Portland media deified him. Hollins did not think that Ramsay had adapted particularly well to the post-Walton era. His interview was a reflection of the fact that some of the Portland team members saw Ramsay as a man who believed more strongly in his system than in his players, and thus perhaps more in the coach than his material. The system came first. If you stayed within the system and ran the plays right, you won. Ramsay, Hollins said in the interview, was stubborn about making changes.

It was an important criticism even if no one but Hollins made it, but there were others on the team who agreed, and it suggested what might cause a split in this team. Steve Jones, a former player and now an announcer, agreed with it, so did Herm Gilliam (who was also now an announcer), and so did Lucas. It was an odd thing, racial without being racist. The quality of coaching in the NBA, by agreement of almost everyone concerned, had in the past decade gone up dramatically; where in the past there had been a belief in the NBA that because the players were professionals they did not really need coaching, now there was an awareness that many of them, no matter how great their talent, had never been coached sufficiently—or at all. Ramsay by all accounts was at the top of his profession; a recent poll by *Sport* magazine of general managers on coaches and their ability had named him the best coach in the league, well above anyone else. But it was also true that the coaches who liked their systems the most, and who were most effective in employing them, were, to a man, white and the players who were on occasion most restless with the lack of freedom in these systems were by and large black. It often boiled down to a question of who dominated, player or coach; some of the players felt that the coaches so wanted to control a game that, however involuntarily, they took something away from the creativity of their players. The game was in part knowing the plays and in part trusting your instincts; Herm Gilliam thought that one problem with the Ramsay-Inman team was that in the fourth quarter there were too many players looking constantly at Ramsay on the sidelines as they brought the ball up, instead of watching the court and making their own decisions. Lenny Wilkens, an ex-player of distinction himself, by contrast was regarded by the players as someone who prepared his team, had his requisite plays but let his players play and did not overcoach. All in all, Hollins's statements amounted to a surprisingly candid interview with an intelligent professional athlete. Ramsay was not bothered by it, he had always admired Hollins's intelligence and his independence (and the fact that though Hollins and Luke were friends, he was the only member of the current team who was independent enough to stand up to Luke). He thought some of what Hollins said quite legitimate. That did not mean he agreed with him, but it *was* legitimate.

Yet at the camp Hollins seemed in good spirits. The darkness from the previous year seemed to have disappeared. He was close to Lucas but seemed to have none of the anger that Lucas harbored. He advised his teammates and Ramsay that Luke's problems were far more serious than anyone realized, that the contractual problem seemed to hang on him, that Luke would try to remove it from his mind, and then a few hours later he would be back, talking about it, how they were making millions off him and paying him a pittance. Hollins would tell Luke to put it aside, to concentrate on playing basketball, and the money would take care of itself. Luke would agree, and then he would start up again. It was really festering with Luke, Hollins said.

Hollins himself seemed almost eager to play. He seemed to want to establish an identity apart from Walton and the Walton team. The media's fascination with Walton had, in the aftermath of the championship, bothered many of the players, and they often talked about how, when they had won the title, the *Oregonian* ran a banner headline BILL AND COMPANY WIN. *Bill and Company,* that stuck in some of their throats, the way it had always been Bill Walton *and* the Portland Trail Blazers. Walton himself added to that feeling. When he had announced that he was leaving Portland and joining San Diego, he had given a press conference and at that press conference he said that before his injury, "I was fifty and ten." Coming from so dedicated a team player, that had stung his former teammates. *I was fifty and ten.* A few months before, a writer named John Strawn had approached Hollins about doing a profile on him for a national magazine. "It's not going to be another of those Bill Walton pieces, is it?" Hollins had asked. The big guy, he said, was gone and everyone had to learn that. That was a fact. Walton played for San Diego now. Still, he was excited about the new season; he felt healthier. He could not stuff a basketball yet. Even on layups he used the backboard. But his body felt more like it belonged to him and not to someone else. He was glad to be back playing basketball.

Just before the season started Ramsay and Inman went down to Los Angeles to watch a doubleheader and saw Bill Walton play for the first time in more than a year. Both of them had been impressed. It was vintage Walton, Inman thought, he was filling the lane, blocking shots, throwing the outlet pass, playing with exceptional enthusiasm. For whatever pain Inman had felt over Walton's angry departure from Portland, he was glad to see him playing again. Walton was, in that Inmanesque phrase, good for basketball. Ramsay had agreed. Walton looked to him to be completely back. Ramsay found that he was glad; he could think of Walton without bitterness and wanted him to play, and play well. The next day there had been a small story out of San Diego saying that Walton's foot was bothering him and that he might be out for a few more exhibition games. The story was small and no one took it very seriously. Still, for someone with Walton's history of foot ailments, it was a melancholy note.

A FEW DAYS after that the San Diego team had gone up to Los Angeles by bus for an exhibition game. Walton accompanied the team but had not played. After the game he sat in the bus and looked at the stat sheet and finally turned to a fringe player named Bob Carrington, who was desperately trying to make the team and had shot poorly that night. "Carrington," he said, reading the sheet, "you shot three of twelve." Carrington nodded. "Carrington, didn't you make two dunks?" Carrington had nodded again. "Carrington, that means you shot only one of ten from more than one foot away from the basket." It was an unkind moment, cruel to a player just barely holding on, and probably soon to be cut. Bill Walton, some of those who knew him thought, was a different man when injured and deprived of doing the thing he loved most, playing basketball.

IF THERE WAS one thing which buoyed the Portland coaches, it was the knowledge that whatever afflicted their team afflicted any team that had been successful. It was the special burden of success in the NBA. The moment a team reached the top, the very mechanism that had worked to pull the players together began to work to pull them apart. Watch out, Red Auerbach of the Celtics had warned Harry Glickman, the Trail Blazers' general manager, after the Blazers won the 1977 championship, now your troubles begin—they'll think they're All-Stars now.

Players were willing to sacrifice on the way to a championship, but once there, once at the top, it was a different matter. Agents and wives spoke of bigger salaries and of greater recognition, and of how much rival players, of lesser talent and playing on losing teams, were making. In Washington, runner-up the previous year, Bob Dandridge was said to be sulking; there was also dissidence from other players and Dick Motta, the coach, was reported to want out. In Seattle, which had finally won the championship, Dennis Johnson, the most valuable player in the championship playoffs and signer of a huge contract at $400,000 a year, was already said to be dissatisfied. He was, a friend had told Ramsay, acting petulant, disregarding his coaches. A Seattle sportswriter had told Steve Kelley that Johnson was disaffected because, though he had signed for $400,000, he knew that his teammate Gus Williams, now in *his* option year, was going to get *$700,000* or more. Johnson figured he had asked for, and received, too little.

Nor was it just the players who changed after victory. Sam Schulman, the Seattle owner, having finally won his championship, had chosen the night of the victory party to inform Paul Silas that his salary, if he intended to return the following year, would have to be cut in half. Silas, then thirty-six years old, fifteen years in the league, his skills clearly eroding, was considered around the league to be the ultimate team player and leader, a man who cared about winning and who brought to whatever team he was with a sense of tradition and integrity that was badly lacking in pro basketball. He was considered a link between the young Sonics, struggling to establish a team tradition, and the old Boston Celtics, the only team in the league rich in tradition and character. Though his skills were clearly beginning to diminish, his value was greater than his performance on court, if only as a link between past and present, players and coaches. During the previous year's playoff series against Phoenix, with Dennis Johnson going into a childish funk during a crucial game, Silas had sat next to him on the bench and lectured him in harsh terms about how much was at stake and how much he was costing his teammates. Johnson had gone back in the game, played better, and hit the last-second shot which allowed Seattle to win. After the game, a reporter had approached Silas. "Good game to win, Paul," he had said. "Yeah," Silas agreed, "too bad an asshole had to win it for us."

Now, with the championship achieved, Silas had become a luxury again. Even Silas, a rare expert on the lack of sentiment in the NBA, had been surprised by Schulman's way of rewarding him, of breaking the news. Three hundred fifty thousand dollars a year was clearly too much for tradition. For a time it appeared that Silas might be traded to New York, and he liked that idea, but Red Holzman wanted no part of him. Finally Lenny Wilkens had intervened, telling Schulman that the Seattle team needed him, and Silas had come down a little on salary and Schulman had gone up a good deal and he had been signed. But it was one more lesson on the fragility of loyalty in the NBA. Steve Kelley, writing about the Seattle problem in the Portland paper, saw it as endemic in the league. "In the NBA," he wrote, "nothing recedes like success."

Lionel Hollins, reading about Dennis Johnson's contract, was not displeased. Dennis Johnson was making $400,000 a year and he was not a great scorer, he was instead a fine defensive guard and team player. Four hundred thousand dollars a year, he thought, a lot of money for bouncing a basketball. Lionel Hollins, not a particularly good scorer, was an equally fine defensive guard and team player, and perhaps a better ballhandler. It boded well for the season and the contract ahead. The odd thing about this, about all the contracts and agents and the huge salaries was that Hollins had never thought as a boy that he wanted to be a basketball player and he had never dreamed of making big money. But if the big money was available, then he wanted his share. As a boy he had wanted to be a baseball player. He actually would have preferred playing baseball. It was simply harder for a black boy to play baseball than basketball where he grew up. He had tried to play baseball but it was difficult, partly because he could not afford a glove. His first glove was homemade, fashioned of tin from a dog food can and bent into a vague replica of a first baseman's mitt. He had managed to put two fingers inside it, just as he imagined bigtime pros doing. He had scrounged up an old tennis ball and he would bounce the ball against his house, and then catch it in his glove. He did this thousands of times and became expert in the tricky bounces that a dying tennis ball could produce. This was in Las Vegas where he had grown up. As he bounced the ball, he broadcast to himself the exploits of Lionel Hollins playing in the big leagues. When he was twelve he had tried out for a Little League baseball team and made it; the coach gave him a real glove, made of leather, and took it right back at the end of the season. Finally Lionel Hollins had gone out for the high school baseball team, convinced that he would make it. He knew he had the speed and the good eye. But there had been so many kids that first day that he spent most of the time shagging balls in the outfield and there was virtually no time for him to bat. Finally, near the end of the day, he came up to bat and the pitcher threw four pitches, all of them balls, and the coach said for him to take his base. Hollins had protested that he wanted to hit one, so the pitcher delivered one more pitch, a ball which bounced before it reached the plate. He had been walked to first base and he did not make the baseball team. That was the end of his baseball career, and the beginning of his basketball career. It was a metaphor for black life, he thought. In baseball, as in so many other aspects of American life, it was just so much harder for a black to show what he could do. But in basketball the skills were so readily visible. He always wondered whether he could have made a professional baseball player. There was a part of him that remained confident that he could have. Of course he had never seen a major league curveball. Or a minor league one either.

So basketball had become his sport and he played it every day. The weather was good for that. Lionel Hollins did not believe that he had had an unhappy childhood. His parents had split up before he could remember and he had grown up in Vegas with his mother and grandmother and aunts and cousins. Some of his professional teammates had grown up with a feeling that no one really wanted them. The phrase that Kermit Washington used was being *passed around*. Kermit and many others he had known had been passed around a lot as children. But Lionel had a different feeling, one of all the women in his family fighting over who was to have him. His memory was of always being wanted. Still, there were no male role models. Once, when he was about fourteen, he had gone back to Ark City, Kansas, where he had been born and where his father had stayed when the family split up, to see him for the first time in his grown life. His father worked for an outfit doing auto body work and Lionel walked into the body shop that day wondering whether he could pick his father out from among his fellow workers. He had been told that he looked a good deal like his father. He wanted him to be very tall and slim and handsome, perhaps 6'5". He was quite nervous as he entered and looked around and saw five black men, all of them wearing grease-monkey outfits. Hollins picked out the tallest, best-looking man and decided *he* was the senior Hollins. His father, by chance, had not shown up for work that day. When they later met, he found that his father was in fact only 6'1", and not nearly as slim as Lionel had willed, and clearly losing his hair. Still, he was Lionel's father. It had been an uncomfortable moment, meeting his father for the first time at age fourteen. At the crucial moment, he hesitated, not knowing what to do. Do you kiss your father? he had wondered. Finally, stiffly and awkwardly, he had stepped forward and shaken hands.

Still, he did not think it had been a bad boyhood. Not like those of a lot of players he knew, who had had *bad* times, growing up. He wondered how some of them had ever gotten out. He thought about his origins now a lot, especially after seeing the television series *Roots*. He even followed up a small advertisement in an airline magazine which claimed that it would trace his family for him (and find his family coat of arms, if possible—he had smiled at that—the Hollins coat of arms), but the attempt had not worked out. The Hollinses had turned out to be more anonymous than the company deemed worthy of its time and investigators. Still, he would have liked to know more.

UTAH, NEW TO the league, displaced from New Orleans, came to Portland for the opening game. The Blazers were still shaky, still—as in the previous season—the walking wounded. "When we walk onto the floor before the game," trainer Ron Culp had once said, "the organist should play the theme from *M.A.S.H.*" Walton was gone. Mychal Thompson was out for at least two-thirds of the season. Lucas was out, still favoring a finger (and sulking, Ramsay thought). Bobby Gross was favoring his back. David Twardzik had a bad leg and a bad back. This was a far different team from the championship and post-championship seasons. The starting center was Tom Owens, slow, subtle, smart, a player who maximized a limited body in the most physical position in the game. At forward Kermit Washington would start, new to the team, new to the system, with Larry Steele, whom Inman and Ramsay had often thought of trading. At one guard was Ron Brewer, in his second year out of Arkansas, a wondrous jumper, and fine pure shooter, but not a particularly good ballhandler. Brewer played what was now called the off-guard position, that is, he shot the ball but did not handle it if possible. He was a player of exceptional talent, who seemed to move in and out of focus in games. There were wonderful games in which he would go up to shoot and the defensive player would go up with him, and it appeared to be a bad shot, and then as gravity summoned the two men, the defensive player would start to descend, and Brewer seemed to hang in the air an added split second for an open shot. On days like that he seemed absolutely unstoppable. But then there were days when he simply disappeared from view, a phenomenon as puzzling to his teammates as to his coach and probably to himself. With most players with that fine a touch, the problem for the coach was telling them to shoot less; with Ron Brewer, it was trying to get him to shoot more. At the other guard was Lionel Hollins, the only starter from the championship team, somewhat unsure now of his own ability, coming back from an injury, and unsure of his new teammates. Would they mesh with him as their predecessors had? If he gave up the basketball would he get it back? Was this a group of five basketball players or was it a team?

Jack Ramsay, in the final days of the exhibition season, had been enormously frustrated. The players were inconsistent, they had not run his plays, and he was scratchy with them. He seemed irritable about little things. Too many players out injured, too many players like Washington, a quick learner, and Kunnert, a slow learner, new to the team. He was not happy beginning another season with Tom Owens as the starting center. He had done it once before, and Portland had gone further than anyone expected, and Owens had played the best basketball of his career, but Ramsay was still not convinced Owens was physical enough to be a starting center on a winning NBA team. It meant that in every major game Portland started at a disadvantage, with no physical edge at the central position. Still, by the opening game, Ramsay was ready and, if anything, optimistic. It was impossible for him not to be optimistic. Of course they could do it, of course they were good enough. If they stayed within the system, if they ran their plays. They could do it because *he* could do it. He absolutely believed in himself and thus in his players; no team over a period of time would be better than a Ramsay team. A Ramsay team would play harder, play better defense, be in better shape in the fourth quarter. It would do these things because in the most literal sense imaginable it was an extension of Jack Ramsay. Since basketball and winning meant that much to him, it would mean that much to them. He was the invincible man.

His friend and colleague Stu Inman was more vincible. Inman was in fact somewhat pessimistic about the team. The Lucas thing, he was sure, was far from over and would haunt the team. In addition, he was unhappy about the other players. He felt that he was more objective than Ramsay. Ramsay's emotions were mandatory; he believed in the team because he had to believe; he could not coach if he did not. The one player Inman was pleased with was Kermit Washington, perfect for this team, perfect for

Ramsay, good for the younger players. He saw the team as being in transition from the Walton team to something as yet undefined. Perhaps Kermit Washington was the first piece in the new team. Inman still coveted Calvin Natt, now solidly in New Jersey, as a second piece. Right now he had a feeling that this might be a very long season. There were players possessing individual talent who might not fit well into a system. Abdul Jeelani, for example, played well in the exhibition season, scoring more than most of the older players; he would make the team. There was no doubt of his ability to score, he was an exceptional freelance player. But at heart Inman did not think him right for the more disciplined Portland system. Still, they would keep him behind Bobby Gross at small forward, and they might deal Larry Steele, a move that he knew would not be popular in Portland.

Portland would also keep, for a time, Jim Brewer, a veteran player who had played most of his career in Cleveland, and who was then twenty-seven, with his career at the crossroads. He had come to Portland in a preseason trade, anxious to stay in professional basketball, aware that he might not make it and wondering whether he should try law school instead. He was there not so much out of economic need, but out of wanting to play basketball a bit longer. His career had been an odd one. He had been a high first-round pick for Cleveland, drafted off a strong Minnesota team. Cleveland, which was not known in those days for scouting particularly well, picked him to play center, a physical place in a physical league. Brewer was indeed burly, but on the first day of Cleveland's practice, Ron Culp, then the Cleveland trainer, had on orders from Bill Fitch, the Cavaliers' coach, measured Brewer and found him only 6'7", extremely small for an NBA center. "How tall is he?" Fitch had asked. "Six-seven," Culp answered. "List him at six-nine," Fitch had said, "he's playing center." So his career had developed, always out of position, not quite physical enough to dominate by sheer size the other immense centers he played against, and lacking the finesse to play forward, a position he had the perfect body for but which he had never been taught. Kermit Washington, who had been with Brewer at the 1972 Olympic camp where Brewer was a big star, thought that Brewer had once been a far better shooter than he was now, that the years in Cleveland—where he had been virtually under orders not to shoot—had robbed him of confidence. In any event, he arrived in the Portland camp with less offensive ability than almost anyone else. But he had intelligence, strength of character, and a strong sense of what life in the NBA was like. His teammates were fond of him and teased him about shooting bricks, the league word for a shot that went nowhere near the basket. There must be some cement in his blood somewhere, they said. Brewer was acutely aware of his vulnerability on this team, that the moment Maurice Lucas had recovered from his injury and was able to play, he might be gone, not just from Portland but from the league. Still, he was glad to be there.

If Portland was shaky on opening day, then Utah, the Utah *Jazz*, was even shakier, a reminder of the lack of professionalism at the managerial level in the league. Utah was new this year; the previous year the same team had been the New Orleans *Jazz*, and having failed gloriously there, it had been moved, lock, stock and nickname, to Salt Lake City (the name a rare contradiction in terms, given the Mormon beliefs on race, though it suggested other possible misnomers in the league: the Los Angeles Nordiques, the Atlanta Yankees). Basketball failed in New Orleans for a number of reasons. It had been poorly thought out there from the start, and the management, fearful of developing a black-dominated sport in so southern a city, had decided to build the franchise around Pete Maravich, a white player of exceptional skills, though skills rarely disciplined. Because Maravich was white, a local hero, and so flashy a player, the ownership had traded away the future of the franchise—two first-round draft choices, two seconds, and two roster players—to pry Maravich away from Atlanta, where he had already worn out his welcome, and where a comparable management, anxious not to offend *its* white fans (or, more accurately, hoping to locate them), had broken up a very successful, virtually all-black team, and drafted Maravich out of college. In New Orleans Maravich had signed a long-term contract for some $700,000 a year, more money, it was said, than the other players put together. There had been, not surprisingly, tensions between Maravich and many of his teammates throughout his career (there were similar salary discrepancies everywhere he went), since in order to justify that much money he had to handle and shoot the ball all the time. But fans, particularly fans new to the game, loved him, he was exciting and wonderful at the theater of basketball. Weak management, worried about finding fans, loved him in the early years because it could hype him. More than any other athlete in basketball he dramatized the conflict between pure sports as they should have been and sports in the modern televised era. He always landed in situations where a nervous management was anxious to hype, not the quality of the game but a show, Pistol Pete, the flashy scorer with the fancy moves. He had been handsomely rewarded for his service, not merely in terms of salary but in publicity; there had been magazine covers to pose for and television commercials to shoot. But at the same time something happened that was terrible for a fine athlete. His essential covenant had always been with the hype instead of with his teammates and the game. Every move—and there were many—to sell him and make *him* the show had pulled him that much further away from his teammates and the idea of basketball. Now, in his tenth year of the professional game, one of the two or three highest-paid players in the league, he had a reputation in some quarters of being a loser. Even those sympathetic to him did not really know if he could play team basketball. His career was almost over and no one really knew how good he was.

Not surprisingly, though the return of Maravich to New Orleans had been much heralded, the Jazz had never played particularly well, nor had they drawn well. Part of this was due to the size of the arena: the New Orleans Superdome could seat, if necessary, 46,000. That was precisely the problem. Because there were so many seats available, no one in New Orleans felt any real need to become a season ticketholder. Yet the key to NBA economics (or at least one key, for the most important was the league's network television contract) was season tickets. If a franchise could sell 7,000 or 8,000 season tickets, then it could usually produce the upfront money needed for the new high salaries. Without season tickets, management always lagged behind. Inevitably managements in weak franchises sought big star names, like Maravich or David Thompson, to boost preseason ticket sales. Now, when the league looked at a prospective city anxious to become a member of this chosen fraternity, it decided accordingly. White collar cities were in, blue collar cities were out. It was believed, for example, that one reason Buffalo had failed as a franchise was that it was a blue collar town, and while blue collar workers were good season-ticket candidates for football, this was not true for basketball where there were so many more games. Blue collar workers might be good basketball fans but they got no tax deduction for their outlay on season tickets. Cleveland and Detroit, for example, were considered shaky. Dallas, at that moment applying for membership in the league, was considered by contrast to be an excellent possibility despite the fact that Texas was known for neither its high school nor its college basketball teams. It was a football state. But Dallas was a city filled with new successful service industries, good clean white collar companies (American Airlines was one company that had fled the grime—and taxes—of New York for the good air and tax benefits of Dallas). These companies, the NBA's computer showed, were likely sources of season ticketholders, since the tickets could be written off. Given America's industrial decline and its shifting economic strength, Dallas, with no basketball tradition, was a much better bet than many eastern and northern cities rich in basketball history.

It was not by chance that the league was schizophrenic; its players to a large degree came from the blighted ghettos of an older, more tired America, industrial cities undergoing urban decay in the beginning of a postindustrial age; but its new markets—for that was the league word, *market,* television worked not cities, but markets—were in the West and Southwest. Professional basketball was moving in some curious way away from the roots and natural habitat of many of its players. In its western and southwestern migration, the league had recently entered San Diego, Denver, Portland, Seattle, Phoenix, Salt Lake City, San Antonio, Houston, and now, potentially, a third city in Texas, Dallas.

Basketball had come to Portland in 1970, and the franchise soon developed into one of the league's strongest. Opening home game at the Memorial Coliseum was a major social occasion, for in Portland it was *the* ticket. There was nothing else competing with it during those long winter months, except of course the rain. Joe Gushue, the referee, once asked by a fan the toughest city to referee in, had immediately answered, "Portland—they've got nothing else to do all winter." It was classically the Green Bay syndrome, the bigtime sport in a very small city that had become the focal point of much of community life. Seattle had a professional football team and baseball team as well, but Portland had only basketball. In the summer the Portland newspapers chronicled the doings of Oregon natives playing minor league baseball. If, during the season, one sportswriter new to the scene seemed too critical of the Blazers' performance, another older sportswriter might caution him in print that this was not Seattle, where there were other teams. The Blazers were all Portland had and a Portland writer's job was to be supportive. In the personal columns of the *Willamette Week,* the counterculture's weekly newspaper, where lonely men and women sought other lonely men and women, a man was sure to list all his principal assets:

> 50-year-old very, very well-to-do, tall, divorced male seeks "Dolly Parton-type" to share Trail Blazer season tickets, theater, music, dinners, travel, etc. Would like to meet lady 35–50, that's not tied down in any way and is free to have fun with a fun-loving, sincere person that's no phony. Reply to Box 175 c/o Willamette Week.

Anything to be part of the 12,666. That was the magic figure. Against the Utah Jazz, despite their own weaknesses, despite the frailty of the Jazz, the Blazers had their 102nd consecutive sellout, and automatically now, after every home game, in the box score the management listed the paid attendance, the magic figure 12,666.

During the great years, when Walton had been at his best, marriages where couples shared one ticket had hung in the balance over which partner would get the family seat for a particularly important game. One of the things that grated on Maurice Lucas was the automatic nature of the sellout. He thought part of the problem with the management was that it had such a lock on this town that it did not have to compete with other sports and other forms of entertainment. During the championship year the number of season tickets had been limited to 11,500 in order to permit a few tickets to be sold for each game. In addition, an average of nearly 2,000 more fans watched the game on a large-screen closed-circuit television hookup at the downtown Paramount theater. Given that intensity of feeling, it was not surprising that the Blazers were gods in Portland. Now that Walton was gone, Ramsay, a familiar figure during games, his bald dome making him easily identifiable, was the most recognizable man in the entire city. It was a city in love with its basketball players, most of whom were black.

This meant that the relationship between player and city was not without a certain irony. Many of the black players, drafted involuntarily to this distant and alien timberland, populated as it was primarily by white people, came to love it. They loved Oregon because of its natural beauty, because life was easier here, because the people were so pleasant, because it was an easy place to raise children and because they remained well known long after they played their last game. Several years later they were still *Blazers*, and still a mark for autograph hunters. They stayed on after their careers were done, heroes of the past, beneficiaries of the civic madness. Greg Smith was selling space for a radio station. Herm Gilliam was editing a magazine about basketball and doing some announcing. Lloyd Neal was still there, his wife was going to law school, and he was thinking of opening a men's clothing store.

Those who were black and who stayed on knew there was something of a trade-off. They were the favorite sons of a white city. They were away from their own people, from the sounds and the laughter and the music—they often complained about how hard it was to hear on Portland radio the soul music they wanted. The rhythms of life were different here, white middle-class, and they lived as part of that community. Sometimes, Herm Gilliam thought, there was a price for that cultural isolation: Jai, his four-year-old son, for example, thought that because his father often revisited Atlanta, where he had once played and where most of his friends were black, all the black people in the world lived in Atlanta and all the white people in the world lived in Portland. But the balance was still in favor of Portland; some of them were wary of returning to the places whence they had come. They had seen what happened to so many of their friends who never left. So there was a certain ambivalence: they were at once protecting their children from something and at the same time cutting them off from something. But there was something else they loved about Portland and that was the sheer physical beauty of the place. Many of the blacks had never seen anything like it before—the mountains, the forests, the rivers—they had heard of land like this but it always seemed to be something that would belong to white people. Here they had a share of it. Once in the early days of the Portland franchise there had been an ebullient player named Charlie Yelverton, a sweet and talented young man from the Bronx who, though heavily recruited for college, had stayed home in order to take care of his mother and had played at Fordham. Thus Portland represented a double culture shock, since Yelverton had never been through a transitional period at college. He had fallen in love at once with the sheer beauty of Oregon, the stunning sight of those mountains, the trees, the endless sense of space and the quiet that seemed to go with the land. Once he had told Wayne Thompson, who covered the Blazers in the early years, that he wanted to buy a tree.

"A tree," Thompson had said. "You mean a small seedling? You'll carry it back to New York City?"

"No," said Yelverton, absolutely sure of what he wanted. "One of those big ones. You know, a redwood. I want to buy it and leave it here and then come back and visit it all the time."

The opening game was an event. Season ticketholders communing with other season ticketholders. Fans dressed up, if not for the season, for the opening game. The 12,666 were there (at least 70 percent of Blazer tickets, one office official estimated, were written off on expense accounts or as tax deductions), an estimated 4,000 more were waiting for season's tickets, and 1,805 were watching at the Paramount. Throughout the country other basketball teams, many of them better and many of them in far, far bigger cities, were playing their opening games to smaller crowds. The opener was not only a social occasion but a form of homecoming as well, in particular for a very tall, very handsome black man occupying a very good seat near the Utah basket. He was surrounded by dozens of fans, all of them friendly and admiring, and he was signing autographs, giving prognostications on the game to come. The black man was dazzlingly handsome, with a smile so quick and all-encompassing that for a brief instant one sensed he was a man from a toothpaste commercial. He looked tall enough to play basketball, which he was, 6'11"; young enough to play basketball, which he was, twenty-nine years old; and certainly popular enough to be a star, which, given the nature of the crowd, he also was. The problem was that he was not good enough to be a professional basketball player. This had been a traumatic problem at one time for the Portland front office, which had invested heavily in him, and even more for himself. His name was LaRue Martin, Jr. Only a few years ago he had been picked not just in the first round, but the first pick in the first round, number one in the entire country. It was a rare honor indeed, and an even rarer honor for a player of such limited gifts. Indeed, in 1980, an article in *Inside Sports* by Bob Ryan, a noted basketball writer, on the worst first-round picks in basketball history, singled out *LaRue Martin* as the all-time worst decision in the NBA, Stuart Inman's tallest albatross. In Inman's defense it had been a difficult year for him: the team had collapsed of internal dissension between Sidney Wicks, Geoff Petrie and other players; in the final weeks of the season the coach, Rolland Todd, had been fired; and at the crucial moment for a professional scout, Inman had been pulled away from his real work to coach the team. It had not been a good year for a very high pick anyway; there were not many sure quality big men coming out. Bob McAdoo was coming out hardship and

Portland was interested in him but then when the deal was cut, a large one, McAdoo's agent had added new requirements about a car and tickets, and that had blown it. Inman had seen LaRue Martin of Loyola of Chicago playing two games back to back against Bill Walton of UCLA and Jim Chones of Marquette, the other big man who was coming out that year. By chance, those were Martin's two best games of the year. Checking with Chones's coach, Al McGuire, Inman was surprised to hear McGuire tell him to take Martin over Chones. Reluctantly Inman had decided that Martin was the best available big man in the draft, a "project" whose skills would take some time to develop. But Portland, a young team and a young franchise, could afford a project, Inman believed. Martin would never be an offensive threat—the offense would have to be run around him rather than through him—but with guidance he could play strong defense and become a shot-blocker. So Portland chose LaRue Martin, and it turned out to be a disaster for everyone involved, particularly for Martin, a quiet, vulnerable youngster who had not asked to be number one in the country, who had no illusions about his ability, and who was crushed by the fact that he had never lived up to other people's expectations. Even in rookie camp he had been pushed around by Lloyd Neal, four inches shorter, fifteen pounds heavier, taken in the third round, hungry to succeed and make a career. Martin worked hard to develop, but the NBA was not a good place for on-the-job training. It was an impatient harsh world where the stakes were high and the difference between winning and losing was all-important, and also surprisingly thin. LaRue Martin was not by nature aggressive, nor strong or agile. His early years in Portland were murderous. The fans had expected a savior and he had signed for a savior's salary. He became almost immediately an object of scorn, from the fans, from the media. When he was cheered, there had been a sardonic quality to the cheering, as if cheering the clown, applauding equally his baskets and his turnovers. Then slowly, subtly, it had changed, with a growing sympathy for what was so evidently a nice young man desperately over his head. By fan-sign day, at the end of the first season, when fans could sport their own homemade signs, Wayne Thompson discovered half a dozen signs attacking him for criticizing LaRue Martin, which he had frequently done. Nowhere else in the basketball world but Portland, he thought, could that have happened.

LaRue Martin had hated those years, the constant sense of failure. Every day he felt he was letting people down and letting himself down. Every day he read in the papers what a failure LaRue Martin was and what he had done wrong that day. If other people failed, they failed in private. He failed in public. Worse, in Portland there was no place to hide. He was tall and black. Everyone knew who he was. Every time he went out he expected people to make fun of him. Often, to his surprise, they were quite polite and kind. Still, by the end of his second year he wished it all had never happened, that he had never been picked number one, and that all those eyes were on someone else, waiting for someone else to make a mistake.

His career did not last long. Four years. Bill Walton arrived and Martin was traded to Seattle. That pleased him. He would get a chance to play for the great Bill Russell, then coaching Seattle, who would be able to help his game. Besides, *Bill Russell had wanted him,* that was important. He never played a regular-season game in Seattle. He was cut before the season started. He had just turned twenty-six. He drove back from Seattle to Portland where his family had remained and the trip seemed to take twenty hours. He remembered every sign, every rock on the highway. He wondered if he had gotten a fair shake. Would Bill Russell have been unfair to him? But then Russell had not seemed very interested in him after the first few days. It was a difficult question for him because if he had gotten a fair shake then it meant he was a failure in both Portland and Seattle, and that there was something seriously wrong with him. He had not wanted to stay in Portland after that; the city was a symbol of his failure. One good thing was that he was in excellent financial shape. His agent had put most of his money in real estate. His problem was not money, it was himself. He moved around for a time, first to Los Angeles, then to Chicago, where he worked as an assistant coach and finished his college education at Loyola. He was surprised to find out how much a college education cost, how much the books alone added up to. No one had ever mentioned that before, it had all been done for him. When he received his degree he thought about where to live. The Chicago he knew only too well was a city of tenements with broken glass in the playgrounds and the rims of the baskets always bent and the smell of urine in the stairwells. He knew he had been lucky to get out of there, that it had been a fluke of his height, and luck and a mother willing to save up the money, $50 a pair he remembered, to buy the outsized sneakers he needed as a boy. There was a white Chicago standing there along the lake shore, in new glassed-in high-rises, but he had never dared enter it. It was a world apart. He did not want LaRue III to live in the kind of jungle he had come from. He knew about Portland and he remembered that the people, despite his failures, had always been surprisingly kind. (He thought he knew the reason: when he failed, it wasn't so bad, because they could see themselves failing too; it simply made him more human.) He wanted his son to grow up in a place where there were mountains and cows and chickens. So he returned to Portland and became, to his surprise, an immensely popular figure, a kind of living historical monument. He bought season tickets and went to every game, and often took LaRue III to the games, and people always clustered around him and talked about the good old days, which of course were, so far as he was concerned, the bad old days.

THEY BEAT UTAH that night. Utah was a genuinely bad team, with a lot of one-on-one players. Maravich was nearing the end of his career, struggling with his body and his coach. Bernard King, a talented but troubled young man, had a drinking and drug problem. Utah was a team that the Blazers had to beat, and yet winning with this lineup was pleasing. No one expected it. Portland had won with defense. T. R. Dunn, the young guard who had taken Herm Gilliam's place, had limited Maravich to only 9 shots attempted. Usually an NBA team takes about 95 to 100 shots a game. In this slow, inartistic game Portland had limited Utah to only 67 attempts. Part of the reason was that Portland itself, far from deliberately limiting the pace of Utah, lacked the speed to accelerate the game. That was a startling reversal from the Walton years. With Walton, the very essence of Portland's game had been speed.

But they won. Then in the second game they beat Denver, another weak and troubled team, also at home. The schedule-maker had been generous— the early season games were with soft touches, at home. After the Denver game, all the former players—LaRue Martin, Greg Smith, Geoff Petrie—had come by the locker room. Everyone was talking about the way T. R. Dunn had stopped David Thompson, taking away his natural moves, pushing him to the right. Ramsay was ebullient, holding the stat sheet. "Ron Brewer," he was saying, "*Ron Brewer* . . . eleven of fifteen . . . not bad." His old assistant, Jack McKinney, a slightly sunnier Ramsay clone now coaching Los Angeles, came in. McKinney had played for Ramsay in high school and in college and had remained a lifelong friend. He had been Ramsay's assistant in the championship year and had taken the Los Angeles job, a choice one, just before the start of the season. McKinney was ebullient about his new job and his new owner, a high roller named Jerry Buss. "Jack, he's never with the same girl twice," McKinney was saying. "None of them over twenty-five. Hard to remember their names because they're never back. You see one and try and figure out the name, and then she's gone. Hard on my wife. She's stopped trying to get the names right." "Sounds like it's harder on you," Ramsay said. "Jack," McKinney continued, "you've just never *seen* an owner like that. All he wants to do is spend money. Wants all the players in the league to know how much he's going to spend, so that when compensation ends next year they'll all end up in Los Angeles." Ramsay listened, his face changing as McKinney talked, first a look of pleasure and approval. Then a look of disapproval. Then another smile. It was hard to tell which words caused which reaction, whether it was his pleasure in McKinney's success, or the idea of an owner who spent money (perhaps disapproval), or the idea of an owner who traded in girls every week (possible approval).

Across the room Dr. Robert Cook, the Portland doctor, was coming out of the therapy room with an immense black man. It was in the nature of Cook's work as medical consultant to a professional basketball team that he was always destined to look small. The name of the black man was Lloyd Neal and he was 6'7" or 6'9" depending on the momentary enthusiasm of the public relations people who listed his height, and he weighed 230 pounds, depending on whether or not he could keep his weight down, which was not easy. He was at that moment twenty-nine years old, he had not played in two years, having retired prematurely because of chronic knee problems, and at the moment he and Dr. Cook were still discussing, some two years after his retirement, whether or not he should have yet another knee operation, his fourth. In the 1978 season Lloyd Neal had bumped into Maurice Lucas under the backboard; it had been like a football clip and his knee had gone. At the time he had been playing the best basketball of his career. It was his third and final knee injury. He tried desperately that summer to come back, played in four early season games and then retired. Among the Portland players, Neal was a legendary figure for his courage. His teammates had nicknamed him Ice, in honor of the fact that he was always encased in ice packs after a game. Cook thought he was the single most courageous athlete he had ever seen. No one ever worked at rehabilitation like Lloyd Neal. If Cook suggested sixty repetitions of a particular exercise, Ice would do six hundred. Everyone liked him. Management liked him because he was a throwback to an older generation of athletes who seemed not to worry about pain; he accepted it as part of the professional life, and he gave off no smell of agent or lawyer. His teammates liked him for his courage, not just in recuperating from injury, but for the fearless way he stood up to much bigger and more intimidating players. Because he was black and from a small town and because he often seemed to use the wrong words, there were those who knew him only peripherally who thought he was dumb and treated him as such. Those who knew him better thought he was quite possibly the shrewdest man on the team. Once during a prolonged painful recuperation from an injury he had told Cook, "Maybe I should have been a chess player, it would just be a lot easier." But even as he said it, he caught himself. "But then it would probably be my brain that hurt all the time." He was, in truth, a kind man, a mark for others; his teammates liked to tell of Lloyd Neal taking a phone call from his wife in the locker room after a particularly tough practice, "No, Marcia, no . . . I can't do the shopping . . . no, goddamnit, Marcia, I'm a professional athlete, and I've been busting my ass up and down this court for two hours and I can't move and I'm exhausted and I've got to go to the exercise room and I can't shop . . . No, Marcia, I refuse to . . . two quarts of milk, a pound of butter, three boxes of diapers, sugar, two pounds of hamburger . . . All right, Marcia. . . ."

With the coming of the championship team Neal's role diminished almost overnight. Maurice Lucas arrived, a player as strong and yet more gifted, a better shooter and passer for the Ramsay system. In October 1976, just before the season started, Neal reinjured a knee and, fearing Luke's presence, tried to come back too quickly. He was limited in what he could do for much of the year. The next year, later in the season, he collided with Luke and his career came to an end. As he quite precisely pointed out, the damaged object was a posterior cruciate ligament. ("I'm an expert on the knee now.") That injury had cost him stabilization in his knee, which wobbled back and forth. As he came out of the therapy room he and Dr. Cook were continuing their endless dialogue over whether or not Neal should have his fourth knee operation. The knee sometimes seemed to float, not an unbearable problem on an average day—simply walking was not too hard. But Neal loved exercise and he wanted to play tennis or bike every day of his life. When he did, or when the rain came, the pain was often severe. Neal himself was ready for the operation; he did not want to be hobbled for the rest of his life, particularly with young children growing up. He did not want his legs to turn him into an old man. Cook was wary about cutting. He was not sure it would help. He had shopped Neal to several other doctors who preferred to see first whether the knee could be rebuilt through exercise. It was clear that this was not the answer Neal wanted. The postoperative pain was terrible, he had been through it twice before, it was unlike anything he had ever known, but the uncertainty was worse and he was willing to put up with the pain in exchange for a sound knee. He wished he knew what the right thing to do was. He seemed in a dark mood.

He looked across the room and saw McKinney, a favorite among the players.

"Hey, Coach, how you doin' now? I hear you're down there with The Cuckoo Man."

"That's right," McKinney said, "we've got him. I just talked to him. He wants me to trade for you. The Cuckoo Man wants you, Ice."

The Cuckoo Man was Jack Nicholson, the movie star, a devoted follower of Laker basketball who had a seat right next to the Laker bench. In the championship season, when Portland had played Los Angeles, Nicholson had thus sat only about three feet away from the last man on the Portland bench who, in this case, happened to be Lloyd Neal, and everything that Nicholson said, every cry praising Kareem or belittling Walton, thundered in the ears of the Portland players. It was as if he had been chosen by the gods to bedevil them. At the halftime the Portland players had filed into the dressing room and one of the other players, impressed that so famous and yet now so manic a presence was seated so close to them, asked Ice if he knew who his neighbor was. No, he said, who? "Jack Nicholson, Ice," someone had answered. "You mean the little fellow, not much hair?" Neal asked. "Yes." "Who's he?" "A movie star. Did a picture *One Flew Over the Cuckoo's Nest*." "Oh yeah," said Ice, "I know who he is, that guy." The others were not so sure whether Neal had seen the movie or not, they could never tell about Ice, whether he was smarter than they thought but playing dumb, or dumber than they thought but playing smart. In the second half Nicholson had kept up his cheering, loud, partisan, a noise which fell relentlessly upon the Portland bench. Then, late in the game, at a crucial moment, the game hanging in the balance, the Lakers had made a run and Kareem had gone out for a shot and as he did, Walton had gone up too and he had blocked it, and even as Walton reached the apex of his jump, his hand outstretched, the entire Portland bench had been aware of an even more dramatic moment: Lloyd Neal rising up out of his seat, huge now, intimidating, a great dark-visaged figure pointing a massive and threatening finger in a massive threatening hand at the suddenly tiny Nicholson. The others had watched this tableau, it seemed frozen in time for them, as if to symbolize the team's new invincibility, that they would not be beaten, not by Kareem, not by Los Angeles, not even by rich and celebrated actors, for there was Ice screaming at Nicholson, "Take that, *mother-fucking cuckoo!*" The moment had become part of the unofficial team history, a symbol of its triumph, and Nicholson, star of *Chinatown, Five Easy Pieces* and other great American films, had become simply The Cuckoo Man.

"You tell The Cuckoo Man," Ice told McKinney, "they going to cut me one more time. Then I'm going to heal, get it all better, and then I'm going to come down there and get his ass."

Still, the team had won against Denver. Lionel Hollins had gone down during the game, his knee hurting, which was bad news; he was the one player the Blazers could not afford to lose. Nevertheless, they won. Maurice Lucas was out, he was to miss the first eight games with a bad hand (Ramsay was convinced he was sulking and fighting a guerrilla war against management), Bob Gross was to miss the first thirteen games, David Twardzik the first five games—but still they won. The team played very tough defense, it fought for loose balls, as a Ramsay team was supposed to, and walking wounded or no, it went on to win its first nine games. Everyone in Portland was first stunned and then excited by this prospect: if the team could do this well, with its long injury list, imagine what would happen when the injured players returned! The one exception to the euphoria was Stu Inman. He was absolutely unmoved by the surprising success of the team. It was, he thought, the worst 9–0 team in NBA history. He was waiting for the other shoe to fall.

They beat Los Angeles, in Los Angeles. Tom Owens, to the surprise of many of the fans and some of his teammates, had played particularly well against Kareem. After the game Steve Jones, the black Portland broadcaster and former player who devoted much of his season alternately to playing cards with Owens and then teasing him, had teased Owens, who was white, that he could never get up against *white centers*. Only the black ones. "Absolutely disappears against the whiteys," Jones was saying. "You never see this tall, skinny, undernourished—what you eat all the time, T.O., Big Mac's, Little Mac's? You never see him have a good game against any other tall, skinny, white boy. Of course to T.O., all white centers look alike." It was winner talk. They were playing well, they were surprising themselves. It was not just the players. It was Ramsay too. A few weeks earlier he had been discouraged about the prospects for both of his centers. Owens was not physical enough and Kunnert, more than adequate physically, seemed too clumsy, had trouble grasping the plays and seemed to lack the attention span to learn them. Now he was talking almost as high himself. Kunnert? Kunnert lacked confidence, but then so had Tom Owens at a comparable moment the year before. Kunnert would come around. Kunnert had surprised him with his strength. Now he was saying that with the Owens and Kunnert combination they might be stronger at center than any other team in the league. Individually neither was that strong, but together they were impressive and they complemented each other.

KERMIT WASHINGTON AND Jim Brewer were both staying at a small motel near the Blazer offices in Portland where Stu Inman booked new players. The Stu Inman Sheraton some players called it. They often had breakfast together. Washington, whose status on the team was secure, usually dressed in jacket and tie, ready to do battle with real estate agents, homeowners and banks. Brewer, his status marginal, was not in the house-buying market. He was there to play basketball, one day at a time. He wore his warmup jacket and pants to the coffee shop, even though practice was several hours away. The two men were friends from 1972 when they had been at the Olympic tryouts together. Then Brewer had been the star, a major player from a major school, Minnesota, and Washington, his records gathered against comparatively weak opposition, was the hopeful. Now their fortunes had changed. Washington, two months older, was a certified star, and Brewer was barely holding on. Portland was permitted to keep eleven players and Jim Brewer might well be the twelfth. He knew that Portland might be playing the numbers game with him, and he accepted that, it was part of the sport. He might stay around and he might be gone, depending on who was healthy and who was injured. Appropriately, the two men studied different sections of the paper. Washington read the real estate section. Brewer examined the sports page carefully, particularly a small listing under the title TRANSACTIONS. This was a brief listing in agate type which told what had happened the previous day in all professional leagues, who had been signed, cut, placed on an injured list or traded. At that moment, Jim Brewer was waiting for Maurice Lucas's finger to heal. If Luke returned to active duty then Brewer might make the agate type: PORTLAND TRAIL BLAZERS. WAIVED JIM BREWER, SEVEN-YEAR VETERAN it would say. Then he would be gone. So he read carefully, looking for potential openings on other teams.

"These real estate people up here are funny," Washington told Brewer one morning. "They think they're in California. I try to explain to them that they're in Oregon, and California is somewhat south of here. I told the woman, 'You're selling an Oregon house at a *California* price.'" "Probably," Brewer said, "they see someone very tall and very black and up here they think he's rich. You can't hide too well here, Kerm. You don't exactly look like a native son."

This morning at breakfast they were talking about the possibility that President Carter might boycott the 1980 Olympic Games. They were both somewhat dubious about the pleasures of international experience. The 1972 camp had not been fun. It had been run by a coach named Hank Iba, a conservative old-style coach who had practiced old-fashioned slowdown basketball which some players and some pro scouts believed canceled out the strengths of much of the raw American talent, particularly black talent. Iba had done his best coaching in an age where the players were white and slow, and the scores were lower.

It had been a conservatively run camp in terms of style and political outlook. The other coaches were Don Haskins of Texas–El Paso, Joe Hall of Kentucky and Bobby Knight of Indiana. The coaches had been very physical with the players during the camp. "I couldn't take it," Washington was saying, "those coaches were always grabbing you, putting their hands on you, shouting at you. I *never* had that done to me before. I guess when I was at American with Coach Young I had been sheltered. I hated being there. I was never so unhappy. They made you feel so stupid." (Hall of Kentucky, it was said, had been particularly physical with him. When Washington went home to Washington he mentioned this to Adrian Dantley, his close friend, and then one of the most highly recruited high school players in America. Dantley, who had been said to be leaning towards Kentucky, ended up at Notre Dame.)

"They were funny about the blacks," Brewer was saying. "Iba, *Mister* Iba [Brewer smiled every time he said Mister], said right at the beginning that they weren't going to have any of this dipsy-do stuff. I think that meant the blacks and Ernie Di. [Ernie DiGregorio, a white player whose flashy style was more in the tradition of black basketball than of white.] Iba couldn't remember anyone's name. He certainly didn't remember mine. The fifteen best basketball players in America and none of us seemed to have names. 'Young-uns,' he called us. I don't think he much liked the way we dressed, and he hated the stereos. A lot of blacks arrived with stereos." Brewer did an imitation of Mister Iba shrieking and sticking his fingers in his ears and jumping up and down. " 'Stop that, young-uns! Stop that infernal noise! Turn that terrible machine off! Right now. You do it right now, *hear!* Why do you have to have that ugly noise!' I don't think he liked our shot selection too much either. Remember Ed Ratleff?" He named a black player who had played at Cal–Long Beach. "Ratleff liked to shoot. Had good range, thought he had better range. So one time we'd been working the ball a little too long, and Mister Iba is yelling 'Shoot, shoot,' and the ball comes to Ratleff and he is *way out there,* and he lets go, *maybe thirty feet away* and Mister Iba is jumping up and down on the sidelines, hands back in his ears like he can hear Ratleff's stereo, shouting 'Shoot, shoot . . . *No, no, no, not* from there.' "

"I think there was a quota there," Washington said. "So many whites. So many blacks. They kept some good blacks off that team."

Brewer agreed. "They kept Marvin off." Marvin was Marvin Barnes, a black player of legendary talent and regrettably even more legendary ability to waste it. "Marvin tore that camp apart. The best player in the entire place. He was quick and strong. They thought he was too physical in practice. He beat up Tommy McMillen a lot and they didn't like that because Tommy was white and very young and a big hero in the press and the press wanted Tommy to make the team. They did not like Marvin. He had all that ability and he knew he had all that ability and he didn't pay too much attention to giving the coaches a lot of *respect* and they were coaches who put a lot of value on getting *respect* from players. Marvin was never very big on respect. He always figured the person he would respect was the person who could stop his game."

"Marvin," Washington said, "was not too respectful about curfews. No one was sure he knew what the word meant. His watch was always different from everyone else's. Me, I was a scared kid. I paid attention to all those rules but I couldn't take it. I just wanted to get back home. When I got back home there was a story in the *Washington Post* about my not liking it there. Made it sound like I was anti-American or something."

"You didn't miss anything," Brewer said. "They tell you it's all about brotherhood. Then you play a game against the Japanese and all you hear from some of your coaches is 'Get the slants, get the slants.' What kind of brotherhood is that? I thought all that stuff was over in 1945. We're winning big against them and the coaches are talking about running it up. All they talk about is get the slants, get the commies. You begin to worry a little, the next thing you know maybe they'll use *the word*." The two of them nodded. The word of course was *nigger*. Now forbidden, still sometimes hanging out there. "Remember that team from Texas–El Paso that won the NCAA championship?" Brewer asked. Washington nodded. No black player ever forgot that team: in 1966 five blacks starting for an unheralded small school had beaten an all-white team from Adolph Rupp's Kentucky. It was a symbolic moment of great meaning for blacks and for whites alike. "Well, that was big for all of us. A little hard on some of the players on that team. Big Daddy Lattin who was on it told me one of the coaches kept using the word all the time. 'You niggers' this and 'you niggers' that. So finally they got together a committee to see him and make a protest, and he seemed genuinely surprised. 'Hey,' he told them, 'I didn't mean anything bad by that, I don't know any better. That's just the way I was raised. Don't take it personal, okay?' "

"I don't know about coaches like that," Washington said. "They just don't know any better. They're always trying to make you be like they were. They were all small and tough and maybe not that talented, so they're always trying to get these very talented players to be like them. Hard to do."

"Can you imagine keeping Marvin off the team?" Brewer said. He paused and came back to the present day, the world of agate type that told of sports transactions. "Marvin's supposed to be down at San Diego getting a tryout. He showed up, and then disappeared. Just like Marvin to do that."

Three days later Jim Brewer was in agate type. Lucas had come back and they had to make room on the roster. He went back to Cleveland where he owned part of a foreign auto company and he waited for the phone to ring and he watched the agate type in the Cleveland papers.

ON THE TENTH game the winning streak ended. They played Phoenix at home. It was a sentimental night. Portland, ten years in the league, was commemorating the occasion by inviting back all the members of that first year's team. They came back, heavier, balder, and bringing with them memories, now pleasurable, of those often bitter early days when Portland seemed forever an expansion team stocked with other people's rejects. Victories had been rare, Portland had always been behind, its players had played out of their offense most of the time, simply hoisting shots up. When they won, they won against other expansion teams which was only like half winning. Wayne Thompson of the *Oregonian* covered the team in those days and this night he was talking about his favorite game in the first year. It had been against Philadelphia in Portland. Portland was ahead by one point with one second left, and Philadelphia had the ball, when time was called. It was a big moment: if the Blazers won, it would be their first victory against a nonexpansion team. At this point in any game, the role of the timer becomes crucial; the home team supplies him, and a smart timer with deft fingers can stretch one second into nearly three seconds, or cut four seconds down to under two seconds. So with one second left Philly took the ball out, and it went in to Archie Clark. He dribbled right. No buzzer. He dribbled left. No buzzer. The Blazer coach, Thompson recalled, is dying. Clark faked right. No buzzer. Clark pumped and shot. The buzzer sounded as the ball went through the hoop. Philly wins. After the game, Jack Kaiser of the *Philadelphia Daily News* rushed over to Thompson. "Where's the timer, where's the timer?" he shouted. "I want to see him. I've got to see him!" "He's gone," Thompson answered. "Besides, you can't interview him anyway." "I don't want to interview him," Kaiser said. "I just want him to time the rest of my life."

IT HAD BEEN a warm night filled with nostalgia for most of the players and writers from the old days. But among those who had come back was a young black man named Shaler Halimon. He had played 79 games in Portland that first year, averaging 8.8 points, his best NBA season in a brief career which had barely lasted four years. Then he departed, first to the ABA, and then into the nonbasketball world, a civilian. Like many of the Blazer players he stayed on in the Portland area after his career was finished; unlike many of the others he had not done very well. He was driving a city bus at the time of the reunion. He was then thirty-four years old and he had not played for six years. Before the game he approached Bucky Buckwalter, the Blazer assistant coach who had once tried to recruit Halimon when he was a coach at the University of Utah. "Coach," Halimon said, "it's bad about you having all these injuries. Hard on everyone." Buckwalter agreed that it was. "Coach," Halimon said, "can you talk to Coach Ramsay about a try-out? I've stayed in shape. I'm still playing ball. I know I can do it. I know he can use me, especially with all these injuries." Buckwalter was shaken. A few minutes later one of his friends looked at him. "Buck, you look funny. Anything wrong?"

THE GAME ITSELF was not a happy occasion for Portland. Phoenix had one of the best organizations in the league. It had continuity. It scouted well—its third and fourth draft choices consistently surprised other general managers by their ability and their capacity to meld into the Phoenix system. It played consistently smart, well-integrated, if marginally physical, basketball. John MacLeod was like Ramsay; in the *Sport* magazine poll which had measured the coaches, Ramsay received the highest rating according to his peers, but MacLeod had been second. Like Ramsay his presence on the sideline was obvious during a game. A Ramsay-MacLeod game, players on both sides sometimes complained, was like watching a chess match between coaches: moves, countermoves, players with one eye on the bench. The Blazers trailed through most of the game and then went ahead by one point. With three seconds left, there was a Phoenix time-out. Then the ball, just as MacLeod wanted, went to Walter Davis, one of the fastest and most exciting players in the game. Two players covered Davis, just as Ramsay wanted. Davis, with no shot, had taken the shot anyway, off-balance, falling away. The ball went in. The winning streak was over, mortality had descended.

THEY LOST AGAIN three days later to Golden State, and then they flew to San Diego. The game had been ballyhooed as Bill Walton against his former teammates, but now it was twelve games into the season and Walton had missed all twelve games. His foot was hurting once more and no one could determine what the exact problem was. Yet everyone in basketball was ready for his return. *Sports Illustrated* had commemorated the arrival of the new season by putting Walton on the cover, complete in San Diego model three-piece suit and hair at acceptable length, and a coverline reading, "Is *this* Bill Walton?" (with the answer: "You better believe it, and he's rarin' to play center for San Diego"). CBS, anxious for a white superstar, had decided to televise the San Diego opening game against Los Angeles, the better to exploit not just the arrival of the black and infectiously joyous Magic Johnson, but the return of Walton. Jack Scott, the radical sports activist who had once been one of Walton's closest friends and was now somewhat alienated from him, thought there was a certain sadness as well as irony in what was happening to Walton. The NBA, Scott thought, had finally discovered the one simple truth about Bill Walton, that his great love and great enthusiasm was above all else for basketball. Other preferences, choices, styles came and went but his devotion to basketball was unshakable, which made him on the court a happy figure in an often dour and envious world. Sadly, Scott thought, the league was only now willing to sell and push him when his ability to play at a top level was more and more in doubt. Scott was bemused by Walton's appearances at San Diego civic clubs in his suits, and his statements about being born again as a capitalist. He suspected that Walton, after a difficult and frustrating career in which his injuries had made his politics more of an issue than they should have been, was simply tired of the hassle, and wanted to get along, make as few waves as possible and play basketball. Scott and Walton had once been so close and had shared so much politically that it was difficult for him to accept Walton's new incarnation; it was so alien to Scott that he assumed it must be alien to Walton as well.

In the past he had regarded the league officials and the network officials as so obsessed by Walton's politics that they had failed to appreciate the purity of his love for the game. Very sad, he thought. Scott called the Clipper front office a week into the season and asked about Walton's condition. A day-to-day thing, a Clipper official had answered. *That's it,* Scott had thought, *nothing ever changes,* for if there was one thing Walton had hated while he was in Portland it was management's habit of telling reporters that Walton's condition was "a day-to-day thing." That, Walton accurately believed, put all the burden for playing or not playing on the player. Because of Walton's uncertain condition, the Clippers were playing poorly; there was talk of Coach Gene Shue's job being in jeopardy. Seasoned Walton-watchers had noticed how at the very beginning of the season he had been very prominent on the bench, arriving in one of the celebrated suits, actively drawing plays for his teammates, and then gradually moving to the end of the bench, no longer diagraming. Subsequently, Walton moved to a seat behind the bench, then began sitting high up in the stands in owner Irv Levin's private box. Already some of his new teammates, particularly black ones, were privately telling reporters that they had played in pain for a lot less money and that everyone in this league played in pain.

Jack Ramsay came out of the visiting team locker room in San Diego to meet local reporters. The questions of course were about Walton. Subdued and cautious around reporters anyway, his answers generally carefully prefabricated and sanitized, Ramsay was more cautious than ever. This was a sensitive subject, where every word could open a still-fresh wound. No, he had not seen Walton but he had heard that the medical news was not good. He hoped that was not true and that Walton would soon be able to play again, a great player should always be able to play. Do you feel any bitterness? a reporter asked. No, he said, there was no bitterness, there had been a great season, two great seasons really, and then the injury. Was there a slight hesitation in the cadence of Ramsay's reply? Perhaps there was.

Ramsay walked away and caught up with the team. He would not see Walton socially in San Diego, though once they had been very close. Walton, he told friends, was one person when he was healthy and playing, exuberant and positive; and he was another person when he was injured, erratic, susceptible to other influences. Ramsay still remained ambivalent on the subject of Bill Walton, hurt by what had happened, by Walton's accusations against the Portland medical staff and management (and by implication, against Ramsay as well), and by the fact that Ramsay's finest moment in professional sports had come with Walton, when he had seen not just his plays but his dreams executed on the court, the game as if in some extraterrestrial form. Ramsay did not like to talk about what had happened. Sometimes when friends questioned him he answered rather limply that he thought Walton had been injured so much that he was wary of being hurt again and once again disappointing the Portland fans. No one who knew Ramsay well accepted that explanation. There were still too many unresolved conflicts in their relationship, too much pain.

Ramsay had come to Portland in the first place because of Walton, all that potential as yet untapped; he had considered it for that reason the best job in basketball. He had come there from Buffalo after being virtually fired after a year marked by increasing friction between himself and the owner. When the news of his new job was announced during an NBA meeting, Bob Ryan, the *Boston Globe* basketball writer, had said, "Jack, that's great news, but how are you going to stand all that rain in Portland?" "In the basketball season," he had answered, "I don't have time for the weather."

He had gone into Portland on the run, had met immediately with the local media and had promised them that his Blazer team, unlike any of its predecessors, would make the playoffs. Then he had rushed out to the house where Walton lived, to pay his ceremonial call, charming him and courting him, spending some three hours there, asking Walton's advice on various problems, which the center, intelligent and highly opinionated, readily supplied. They, of course, agreed on the style of play—aggressive, fast-breaking basketball, Walton to rebound, immediately throwing outlet passes to speedy guards. Walton had not liked many of his Portland teammates, and especially he was not admiring of the Portland guards, since they did not complement his particular game, which was speed. The basketball, he told Ramsay, never touched Larry Steele's left hand. No way, Ramsay had said, that Larry Steele was going to play guard for him. Maybe some small forward, but not guard. What about Petrie? Ramsay had asked. Walton and Petrie were close personally, they did outdoor things together, camping, backpacking, white-water canoeing, but Walton was not an admirer of Petrie's game, which was slower than the one he preferred. Petrie was a very good shooter, but there was a tendency when he was in the game for the team to depend on his long jump shots and for other players to stop moving. In any case, Petrie was in the midst of a contract dispute and he was soon dispatched to Atlanta. What about Sidney Wicks? Ramsay had asked, for Wicks had by then become a symbol of Portland's dissension and frustration, a player of great potential skills who seemed to play beneath his level and was regarded as a source of dissidence. Wicks, Walton thought, had been a problem, but he also considered him a victim of unfair fan pressure and expectations, and that the negative feeling about him in Portland was at least partly racist. Ramsay had listened and had decided to take Sidney Wicks a little more seriously, but a few days later Wicks, whose capacity to win friends and influence coaches had steadily declined over the years, had come to see Ramsay to complain about the amount of money he was making, which was in fact more than Ramsay was making. He had, even worse, added: "Coach, I don't want you to take it personally, but there's a salary they're paying you, and a full salary they're still paying Lenny Wilkens and a lot of that is money that could be going to Sidney Wicks." Ramsay, much to Wicks's surprise, *had* taken that seriously and shortly thereafter Wicks was traded to New Orleans, where, after a very brief visit in which the New Orleans general manager expressed his extreme displeasure over Wicks and his personality, he was returned to Portland. From there in October of that year he was finally traded for marginal value to Boston, a city where his years were said to be even less happy for all concerned than in Portland.

RAMSAY HAD ARRIVED in Portland at precisely the right moment for Walton. After two frustrating years in the league, where he had been constantly bothered by injuries, by the style of many of his teammates, and by the physical quality of the professional game, he was desperate to play winning team basketball. The one thing basketball had always been to him in the past, spiritual liberation, had been missing, and his paycheck, no matter how big, therefore, provided him with little sense of accomplishment. Unlike many of his teammates in basketball, who often came from broken homes, Walton was a somewhat sheltered young man from a secure middle-class background. Basketball was not for him an economic passport from one America to another, as it was for so many teammates, as it was a spiritual pursuit. It gave him not money but status and happiness. He loved the game and he sought a sense of purity from it. But he had soon become disillusioned with the professional game. Part of the fault, Tom Meschery thought, was that he and Lenny Wilkens had led Walton to believe that they too were into more than just winning, that they sought what Walton sought, not just victory but a larger goal. That, Meschery thought, had been a mistake; he and Wilkens were classic NBA products, tough men in a tough business who struggled to hang on to some measure of idealism, while at the same time surviving and winning.

But Ramsay might be different. Meschery was a published poet and Ramsay was not, but there was a part of Ramsay, for all his toughness and his obsession with winning, that believed there was poetry in the game, that it was connected to ballet, and that there was beauty and truth in it, the right movement of the right body flashing by another body to score. Ballet with a scoreboard. Ramsay, like Walton, seemed to love practice as much as games, seemed sometimes to believe that the execution was as important as the result. In this case the coach and the player had been seeking each other. Later, after the championship season, in a book on basketball that he wrote with John Strawn called, not surprisingly, *The Coach's Art*, he said:

What is this game that runs through my mind? It is a ballet, a graceful sweep and flow of patterned movement, counterpointed by daring and imaginative flights of solitary brilliance. It is a dance which begins with opposition contesting every move. But in the exhilaration of a great performance, the opposition vanishes. The dancer does as he pleases. The game is unified action up and down the floor. It is quickness, it is strength; it is skill, it is stamina, it is five men playing as one. . . . It is winning; it is winning; it is winning!

So coach and great player were well suited, each apparently in search of the other. They were, it seemed, ordained by some larger spirit, not just committed to quick tempo basketball, believers not just in winning, but in basketball as a spiritual experience. They were both reasonably liberal products of serious Catholic homes, and they shared not just a view of basketball but similar diets. No longer was Walton the lone vegetarian among savorers of flesh, complaining, much to their annoyance, of their stench. His coach shared not just his vision of basketball, but his exceptional attitude towards food.

Now, when the Portland team arrived in San Diego, Steve Kelley asked the other vegetarian of that group, Maurice Lucas, if he was going to get together with his old friend Bill Walton. "No," Luke said, "I've got no reason to see him." Then he cut Kelley off.

If Walton's first two years in Portland had been unhappy, then the arrival of Maurice Lucas had had an immediate effect. Walton liked Luke right away; he was so smart, so funny, so shrewd—a curious blend of street-smarts and genuine raw intellect. Lucas in turn was attracted because Walton, a white player of rare ability in a predominantly black sport, had refused to accept the role that the American sports world wanted him to fill, that of a great white hope, and he had deliberately isolated himself from those who most wanted him to be so enthroned. He did not, Luke thought, just talk his politics but in an admirable way tried to live them, while at the same time trying to limit his personal publicity. When Lucas came to Portland he had gone out for dinner with Walton the first night, and they decided that they both could be winners. Luke promised that he would take the physical pressure off Walton—he would love banging bodies. They had agreed, in addition, and this was crucial for two big men, that they would not let their egos get in the way, they would not be jealous of each other; they were the big men, they would run this team and they would from the outset be friends. So that first night they had done something that no coach could do for them, they had divided turf, accepting their limits, with Luke, given the nature of the game, accepting more limits than Walton. To a considerable degree in the two years that followed, they kept to their promise. It was like the friendship of many forceful and egocentric men, tinged with admiration and some rivalry. When Walton, just before a game, indulged in the prerogative of *the* big man, having himself taped last, no small perk, Luke would on occasion try to sneak back and have himself taped after Walton. Boys, after all, will be boys. But they had strengthened each other. Luke's very physical presence had given Walton an instant confidence he had not felt during his two earlier seasons of pro ball. When Luke talked about banging bodies, he seemed to mean it; bodies most certainly would now be banged. When Walton returned home from dinner with Lucas that first night he was almost ecstatic. "I'm pumped!" he told his friend and roommate Jack Scott. "Luke is great! Basketball is going to be fun again! Just like it was in college!"

After the San Diego practice Steve Kelley ran into Walton wearing civvies outside the locker room.

"Is Luke with the team?" he asked.

"Yeah, Bill, he is," said Kelley.

"It's funny," Walton said, "I haven't heard from him yet."

"I'm not sure he wants to see you, Bill," said Kelley. "The salary thing is really eating him up."

Tom Owens, arriving in San Diego to play against his former teammate, was stung by what Walton had said in remarks to a magazine reporter and on his own radio show, that the way to beat the Blazers was to take it right to their center. Tom Owens, he had said, did not play strong defense. That was a touchy point with Owens. By contemporary NBA standards he did not have a strong body but an angular white body like the big men of the fifties, and he consequently struggled his entire career against the judgments of fellow players, scouts, coaches, that he was not built like a modern basketball player, and therefore was not a modern basketball player. When Owens was a teenager he had grown quickly, almost as if overnight, 6′5″, 6′7″, 6′9″, 6′10″, but his coordination had not accompanied that burst and he had felt himself awkward and slow and, playing against stronger men of his age, weak. Though he was the best player in his Bronx neighborhood, he was hesitant to play kids from other neighborhoods. A friend named Bobby Cremins insisted that if he wanted basketball to be his ticket out of the

Bronx, if he wanted to get to college on the strength of basketball, he had to play against tougher competition. Owens was shy and uneasy about going outside his neighborhood, but Cremins, who was street-smart and seemed to know everyone in the subculture of New York playground basketball, made him leave the Bronx. The uncertain and somewhat reluctant, gangly Owens would find himself playing in Harlem, Lenox Avenue and 145th Street, and the blacks—faster, more muscular, they had come into their bodies younger than the whites and they had come into better bodies—immediately seized on him. They had muscles and he did not, he was very tall and they were not, he was white and they were not. He was, in sum, the ideal mark. They singled him out. They loved to dunk on him and then taunt him, *"In your face, whitey."* Some of it was very ugly, there were near-fights, and Cremins thought Owens was often on the edge of tears. He expected, each time he called for his friend, to hear Tommy Owens say no, he had had it, it wasn't worth it, it was too painful. Instead, agonizing as all of this was for a shy young man, Owens kept coming back for more and never complained. He's a survivor, Cremins thought, he's going to make it somehow. Slowly, almost imperceptibly, Owens got better, his coordination and his sense of the game improved, and he learned how to take stronger players and use their strength and their quickness against them, to give little head fakes that drew them off-balance. He was heavily recruited by various colleges but even then he was acutely aware that his body was against him. Though basketball coaches traditionally listed their players as being taller than they actually were, when Owens finally decided to go to South Carolina, he insisted to the head recruiter that South Carolina list him as 6'9" instead of 6'11". If he was 6'9", he thought, the pro scouts would see him and be impressed by his performance and think forward. But if he was listed at 6'11" they would think center, and all they would see was his accursed body.

His body continued to haunt him during his pro career. It stood there, as if in judgment against him and his skills, hindering him, limiting his recognition. He knew that coaches—even Ramsay—doubted his body. But for Walton to say it in public like that was doubly painful. (Walton, of course, had been stung earlier in the year when Owens publicly backed the Blazer medical people in their dispute with him.) He thought Walton was his friend; he had loved playing backup to Walton in the season after the championship, the year in which the players thought the team was even better than the year before. His own game improved dramatically that season, in large part because of those two rare coaches, Jack Ramsay and Bill Walton. Not only had Ramsay worked with him patiently every day, coaching him personally as no one had ever done before in the pros, explaining precisely what he wanted, but Owens had the opportunity to play against Walton every day in practice, and Walton's excellence and love of basketball were contagious. A team's big man could set a tone and Walton set an unusually positive tone. That in itself was unusual. It was almost an NBA rule that being the Big Guy gave you the right to hold back in practice. This had been particularly true of Wilt Chamberlain. When Bill Sharman first became the Lakers' coach, with Jerry West, Gail Goodrich and Wilt on his team, he had called West and Goodrich into his office to explain his system. On nongame days, he said, they would always practice for one hour starting at 10 a.m. "Terrific," West had said, "and then what do we do?" "We go back to the motel and wake up Wilt," Goodrich had answered.

Walton had taught Owens that there was a right way and a wrong way to do everything on the court, and he had seemed to Owens to do everything right, as if by instinct. His feet were always in the right place, his body always in the right place turned at the right angle, hands always in the right position. He also did it *effortlessly,* Owens observed. Owens did not begrudge Walton his skills because it was so marvelous to be with an athlete who was so good and who also took so much pleasure from what he did. Owens loved the season so much, the artistry of the basketball that the Blazers had played, that he had taped many of the games, and was immensely proud of the fact that he had been part of it, perhaps only fifteen or twenty minutes a game, but still part of it. He wanted those tapes, not so much to study as to *have,* as a small connection to history, and it was said that during his current divorce proceedings, which were not pleasant, his estranged wife had taken some of his precious tapes, erased the great moments in Blazer history and replaced them with cartoons.

Before the Portland–San Diego game, Ramsay, wanting to fire up Owens, had repeated Walton's judgment in the locker room. Then Portland had proceeded to blow San Diego out. The Clippers looked lost, unsure of themselves. They had been waiting for Walton and he never came. Nor did many of the fans. Only 7,300 showed up, a far cry from the automatic 12,666 Portland faithful. A basketball team in a city like this, with such fine weather and so many other activities, had *better* win. At halftime, with

Portland ahead by seventeen points, Walton went on the Bill Schonely radio show, beamed back to Portland. He seemed quite sad. He was just waiting for the pain to go away, he said. He had no idea when that would happen. Schonely asked him about an article in *Sports Illustrated* in which he had criticized the good Portland fans. In Portland, Walton answered, he was tolerated but not accepted. That was all right. "I get all the credit if we win and all the blame if we lose. . . . I like it that way. I like it tough, I like the pressure." Anything else he wanted to say back to Portland, Schonely asked. "Hello, everybody up there in Oregon. Hang in there. I'm okay. I've got a smile on my face." Hearing it there seemed some kind of image warp: this was Bill Walton, a celebrity, a great powerful athlete, about whom much was written and much was debated. He sounded in that moment like a kid, a somewhat nervous kid.

The second half was even worse. At the end of the third quarter Portland led by 28. Abdul Jeelani came in for 14 minutes, made 9 of 12 shots and scored 19 points. After the game, Irv Levin, the owner, dressed as the archetype of the Beverly Hills swinger, world-class tan, shirt open two-thirds to the navel, gold chain at half chest, was furious. Irv Levin clearly did not like to lose. Stars, he said, he was sick of *stars.* He had signed all these stars, he told reporters, and they weren't winning. "Look at Portland," he told reporters, "they don't have any stars. Look at Owens. Owens is no star, and look at how he played." Over in the Blazer locker room at that moment, Owens was shouting at Ramsay, "Hey, Coach, I told you to stop relying so much on Walton's scouting reports." But he was still angry at Walton. "He only signed with San Diego because he wanted to come home. That's okay, but he didn't have to blame it on the medical staff."

If Walton had sounded lost on the Schonely broadcast, he was. It was a bleak time. He was back home in San Diego, a city he loved and where he could be outdoors every day, but he was dealing once again with the private terror of his career, with the ever increasing fear that he might not be able to play again, or more precisely, that he would never be able to play again at his special level of intensity and enthusiasm. His foot was not responding. It was as if there were hidden devils in there working against him. The pain, as often in the past, remained mysterious, and no one seemed able to locate it. He could sense that the doubts of his new teammates were vastly increased by the size and nature of his contract. "I play hurt," Lloyd Free had told a reporter a few days earlier, "why can't he?" Walton was aware that the clock ticked faster for a professional athlete, particularly a basketball player, than for other mortals. A doctor or a lawyer had a forty-year career, but an athlete in this league now had a career no more than seven or eight years long. When he missed a season or a large part of a season he was losing a surprisingly large slice of not just his career, but of his life. Bill Walton had just missed one season, 1978–79, now he might miss another. Those two seasons could constitute a third or fourth of his entire career. His financial position was secured. He had signed, it was said, with a then eager Irv Levin for seven years at $700,000 a year, five years guaranteed hard clean cash whether he played or not. Reportedly he made another $200,000 if the Clippers averaged more than ten thousand fans per game at home, and *another* $100,000 if he played in sixty games per season. But the very nature of the contract, of those built-in guarantees, reduced sympathy for him among teammates and fans, and it made other players, mostly black, aware again that the league seemed to have a double standard. If Walton had been meticulous in the past about avoiding the white-hope role, still, in the eyes of his peers, this contract was a great white hope's contract. There was no way in the world, they thought, that even a player as great as Kareem, with his remarkable ability, had he had anything approximating Walton's injury record, could have secured a contract like that. The irony of it all was that big money still meant very little to Walton; he would have been delighted to play more for less money. A big salary was important to him only in terms of status within the sports hierarchy—it proved his worth and his standing. A big salary was not goods, it was ego. He had never liked the link between sports and capitalism and early in his career he had been a vocal critic of it. All things considered he would have preferred a different kind of league—a shorter schedule, fewer teams, fewer games and, necessarily, smaller salaries. But the NBA as it stood was the premier league, the only place, he once said, where at his level of play he could, in the most basic playground vernacular, "get a game." When, just before the signing, Larry Weinberg had asked him what he wanted from life, Walton had answered that if he had a thousand dollars a month for the rest of his life, that would be very nice; the answer had struck Weinberg as both touching and exceptionally innocent. He drove a wagon instead of a Mercedes in his early days in Portland because it was easier on the mind; if you had a Mercedes, he explained, you worried about it and it distracted you from other things. At Portland his clothes were as simple as an Army-Navy store could provide and the only restaurants he frequented were health food places. Now in San Diego in his new character as an allegedly born-again three-piece-suit capitalist, he and Susan Guth, finally married, lived in a very nice pleasant house, largely devoid of physical possessions except for a vast assortment of Grateful Dead tapes and children's toys. His closest friend was not from the upper-crust world of San Diego sports or sports followers, but a funky young man named Arthur Hartfelt, who shared Walton's passion for the Grateful Dead, and who taught English to prisoners in a local prison for a salary that amounted, in a year, to about what Bill Walton made for playing in (or rather being willing, if not able, to play in) one basketball game, a fact which seemed to bother neither of them. Even in his new incarnation some of his old friends thought he had not really changed dramatically in his politics. It was more that, given his injuries, given the hassle that his political preferences *plus* his injuries had caused him in the past, he simply found it easier not to contest the society on so many fronts at once. What he wanted, they suspected, was not so much to replace Cesar Chavez with Ronald Reagan, but to be left alone.

So in the fall of 1979 he waited for the foot to heal or, at least, for the doctors to find out what was wrong. He got up very early every morning to work out on the Nautilus equipment at a local health club so that his body remained in condition. At the same time he waited while his lawyer friend in Portland, John Bassett, quietly prepared a malpractice suit against the Blazer medical staff, including Dr. Robert Cook, the team doctor who had once been Bill Walton's closest friend in Portland.

His former friend and coach, Jack Ramsay, was not overly sympathetic to Walton's plight. Certainly sympathetic with the sadness of so great and passionate an athlete whose career is made vulnerable by so rare and yet fickle a body, but not sympathetic to the way that Walton had handled the case, absolving himself of responsibility and blaming others including Dr. Cook and, implicitly at least, Ramsay himself. The NBA, Ramsay had replied, when Walton had made his charges, was not without its rewards, nor its risks.

THAT LAST WAS vintage Ramsay. His appearance was deceptive. Viewed from afar, he was almost a caricature of the coach as primitive, kneeling on the sidelines, face red, veins seemingly about to pop through, intense, as much a part of his game as his players, gesturing, imploring, yelling, pleading with referees. His clothes were loud, the sports jackets more than sporty, the pants—there seemed to be hundreds of different selections—shouted for attention. No golf course would, with those pants, dare turn him down. There at the sidelines, concentrating on the game, working the referees, he was a wondrous magnet for opposition fans; they yelled at him more than they did his players. Often their taunts were mean and personal and, in his early years as a professional coach, he had responded: a fan in Cleveland had gone too far once and Ramsay had barged into the crowd, grabbed the fan, and in full view of everyone else, had calmly and with the utmost contempt, flipped the man's tie over his shoulder, turned and walked away. Yet he was a surprisingly supple man, very tough, very sensitive, almost delicate. For all the fury he unleashed during a game, the frustration with the play, the anger at a referee, when a time-out came he was absolutely in control, restrained, calm with his players, his voice never raised. In those moments he was always understated. He did not let his fury interfere with his sensitivity, nor his sensitivity interfere with his toughness. Everything about him marked his determination. "Jack," a smart young woman in the Blazer front office named Gail Miller had once chided him, "have you been out yelling at the players again?" "I never yell at the players," he had answered. "Jack," she said, "you have the quietest yell of any man I've ever known."

Ramsay's roots were in a very different era from those of his players. Harder times and smaller salaries had stamped him indelibly. Though he rarely voiced this opinion openly and was careful in his public criticism of players, his own and those belonging to other teams, there was a part of him which clearly felt that most contemporary players were coddled and semispoiled, and he never found it easy to muster sympathy for their financial and social problems. He considered them insulated from the real world outside. That many of them had been driven by their backgrounds, so destitute and deprived, to practice long hours and become, by force of will, exceptional players, seemed somehow remote from his thinking. He appreciated their talents, but they were different; their passion was often hidden, as his was not; their style was often cool, his was not. Only with the rare player like David Twardzik or David Cowens, whose value systems were so obviously close to his own, did he seem completely in tune. Cowens had always played for other teams and his intensity had hurt Ramsay teams in many a game, but on the days when Portland played Boston and the two men shared for a moment the same gym, their affinity for each other was striking. Watching them together, seeing their instantaneous mutual affection, one had an immediate insight: if Jack Ramsay had been 6'9" and still a player, he would have been David Cowens.

He was an absolutely driven man. Every minute had to be used, everything was part of a search for excellence and for victory. He wanted above all to win. In the NBA, where the very existence of so long a schedule—eighty-two games—meant that players lived on carefully contrived and controlled emotional plateaus, where it was important that defeat in a single game dare not mean too much, Ramsay's great challenge was at once to be himself, to deal with the totality of each defeat, no matter how much it shook him, and yet not infect his players with his own dismay. That had been his most difficult adjustment in the professional game, to control his own emotions. In college, where the season was shorter, the players more malleable and passionate, they suffered as the coach suffered. But the professional game was different. In his early years there had been a danger that Ramsay's moods might infect his players.

There had been, in his early years of professional coaching, endless demonic postgame, postdefeat midnight walks from arena to hotel through the darker side of ghettos, as if deliberately inviting conflict. When he made his move to Buffalo, Billy Cunningham, one of his favorite Philadelphia players, had taken his new trainer, Ray Melchiorre, aside. "I want you to be sure," Cunningham told him, "that when this man loses a tough game, he is never left alone, and I mean *never* left alone, afterwards." His players appreciated him, his dedication, his intelligence, his careful preparation before a game, his essential fairness, which was far above the norm in the league. But even now, in his twenty-third season as a coach, twelve of them in the professional game, there was something unnerving about his single-mindedness, about how much basketball seemed to matter to him, and how much he was torn apart by defeat. The season was simply too long, many of them thought, too many early planes and different hotels and missed meals and early morning wakeups, for anybody to take defeat so seriously and to hold on so tightly afterwards. They were bothered by his singularity of purpose. He in turn was bothered by the fact that so many players lacked his focus, that in too many cases basketball did not seem to mean quite so much to them, that there were other pulls—wives and children, money. In season he wanted them thinking basketball and nothing else. That was one of the things that had drawn him to Walton.

In this season, however, Ramsay's obsessive focus made a difference. Given the Walton defection, the Mychal Thompson injury and the other assorted injuries, physical and psychological, another team would have come apart. Portland might easily have started out by losing a few games and immediately easing into a semipermanent state of psychological defeat. Not a Ramsay team. He willed them to win; as he was not defeatist, they would not be. If the championship team, in its style, its speed and its vision, had been more classically a Ramsay team, this team seemed at the beginning to be a Ramsay team in emotional terms: a few good players, a few manufactured players, and a few marginal players, all of them working harder than anyone expected, beating better teams and, of course, sticking to the system. It was an article of absolute faith with Ramsay that if his players followed his system, stayed within its limits, ran their plays, that the system would inevitably deliver the right basket at the right moment.

To Ramsay coaching was virtually an end in itself, a profession with a special sweetness all its own. He saw it as a drama of one man, standing out there alone, his job always on the line, players ready to disappoint, fans ready to be fickle, owners ready to tear up contracts, the coach nevertheless doggedly building, creating, taking one player of considerable gift but limited vision and breaking the game down piece by piece so that finally the player could see what the coach saw and become just that much better, just enough to give the Jack Ramsay team a slight edge. That was all it took, the slight edge. He loved that, a triumph for the player, a triumph for the coach, a small added dimension that only he and perhaps one other person, another *coach* sitting on the other team's bench, could appreciate. There had been a moment, early in the championship season, that he was still proud of; his own team was still not the power that it was to become, and Philadelphia, with McGinnis and Erving and Doug Collins, was, for fans who liked pure talent, a dream team. Portland was to face Philadelphia at home and Ramsay had gone down to Golden State to scout Philly. He had seen a powerful team filled with barely visible vulnerabilities, and the next night he had with great precision described to his own team how to beat the Sixers. They were, he said, prisoners of their power and their reputations; they were lazy and did not get back quickly on defense; in effect they were tailor-made for the Blazer fast break. Everything he had said had been true, that which he had seen in his imagination a day earlier took place on the court, and that night the Blazers came of age; they had simply blown

Philadelphia out; the final score was 146–104. After the game, Ramsay had savored the victory with his team, then walked out alone in the night, thinking to himself again and again, *I coach a team that could beat any team in the world.* What more could a coach ask? It was a brief moment of nirvana; it wiped the slate clean of so many other problems he had to face.

Indeed he liked coaching in the NBA because it was the highest level of the sport, and because the extra-athletic, societal stress on the coach was so much greater than in the college game. But his friends thought there was a part of him that would be just as happy coaching a girls' or boys' junior high school team, pushing his players to one more level of excellence and, of course, one more victory. "Jack," Bill Walton once said admiringly, "simply won't believe that he can't win, can't believe that he can be outcoached. If he's behind eight points with ten seconds to play, Jack is there on the bench figuring out a nine-point play."

His real link was not so much to the players as to the coaches. It was his club, his calling. The dues were serious, years coaching in small programs in small schools with unheated gyms, training small, marginally talented kids who had walked in off the street. It was not a place for amateurs. He simply hated the fact that some former NBA star, because he had played well and had a big name, would on occasion be named to coach an NBA team. That was trespassing. He bristled at people like this who had not paid their dues. Just tourists. One of his rare expressions of public joy had come in Madison Square Garden in early 1979 before a game between the Blazers and the Knicks. Red Holzman, the Knick coach, had previously been forcibly retired by management in favor of Willis Reed, a valued local star of heroic proportion. Now, as a result of Reed's troubles with the same team, Holzman had just been reinstated in midseason. As Holzman walked out on the court before the game, Ramsay rushed out to the center of the court to embrace him, his face beaming, his pleasure evident. Score one for the coaches' club.

If there was a flaw to him as a coach, his friends thought, it was a tendency to denigrate the abilities of players. When players were mentioned to him he rarely seemed enthusiastic about them. On one occasion in Philadelphia, he was talking with Billy Cunningham and Matty Guokas, two of his favorite players. "I don't see why everyone makes such a big thing about Willis Reed."

"Jack," said Guokas, "he's a moose. He plays hurt. He beats you to death. He's got a great shot. No one in the league has more courage."

There was a long silence and then Ramsay asked, "Okay, but what about Bradley? What does he do?"

Cunningham had looked at Ramsay a bit oddly and said, "Jack, he knows the game like a coach."

He was also *Dr.* Jack Ramsay. There was a Ph.D. in his background (in education, University of Pennsylvania, 1963, dissertation a study of the role of intercollegiate athletics in the liberal arts college) and he was known around the league, to other coaches and to players, as Doctor Jack, a measure of added prestige and respect. The Ph.D. was important, for there was a suggestion, given Ramsay's intelligence, subtlety and his drive, that at times he, and his wife as well, were bothered by the fact that perhaps coaching was somehow not quite serious enough a course for so talented a man. The title brought added respect. There were after all so many other things such a gifted man might have chosen. His friend Bruce Ogilvie, the sports psychologist, thought that with his absolute courage, his strength of character and instinct to lead, plus his exceptional attention to detail, Ramsay might have made a brilliant battalion commander. Stu Inman, a coach who had chosen not to coach in the NBA because the odds were so much against doing it with any real degree of success ("You ask," Inman once told a friend, "why anyone would want to be a referee. The real question is why anyone would want to be a coach in this league. You're always on the road, the pressure to win is terrible, the players are not conditioned by salaries to listen, and there's simply no time to teach the kids in practice."), thought that Ramsay closely resembled the very successful professional football coaches: great attention to detail, great sense of organization and planning, great awareness of the individual needs of his players. Like Vince Lombardi he was intensely emotional about winning, and he was shattered by defeat, yet he was essentially unlike Lombardi, whose relationships with his players were so emotional, kinetic and direct. The emotional tissue was different. Perhaps it was the difference in the length of the seasons, Lombardi's teams had played in a twelve-game season and he could orchestrate each game to a high, whereas Ramsay's teams played eight and nine times more games, and the emotional relationships could not be so long sustained.

In an era of explosive change in sports caused by the arrival of big new money, there was something about Ramsay that was a throwback to another America, an older, poorer world of blue collar people given one chance to escape small towns and harsh jobs through their ability to play sports. Those men had seized on that one chance, they felt gratitude to sports for their escape, and a comparable awareness that it all could be taken away again, the athlete returned to the mine or the factory. Jack Ramsay came from that era, but not from that background. He had known the Great Depression and the hard times it had produced, but he had not been affected by it. He came instead from distinctly middle-class circumstances. He was born in Philadelphia, but he grew up on the Connecticut shore. His father was in the mortgage and loan business. Ramsay was not driven by an urge for money; it was more personal, about proving himself. All his life he had been doing that, most notably as a grown man, through sports. He had not, as a boy, been a very good athlete, but he had been obsessed by sports. In high school he had been a skinny, gangly kid; his own memories of himself were of lying on the floor at time-outs during high school games, a frail kid, unable even to stand up, gasping for breath. That was not an image the later Ramsay, finely muscled, king of the Nautilus, purveyor of team health, liked to recall. Later when he went to high school the family had moved back to Philadelphia and Jack Ramsay had gone to St. Joseph's, a small Catholic college in Philly. Along with twenty-five other kids he tried out for a basketball scholarship and, much to his own surprise, had won one. He entered St. Joe's intending to be a doctor and tried premed studies, but the hours were long and they cut into basketball practice, which was the thing he loved most. Though he was not a particularly good player, basketball had come first and he gave up the idea of being a doctor. The coach was Bill Ferguson, a straightlaced, rigid man in a black suit, starched collar and black tie, in the style then made fashionable in Philly by Connie Mack. Ferguson's dress and manner advertised to all concerned that he was not just the coach but coach and disciplinarian, a source of complete authority to these eager and nervous young men, products themselves of strict authoritarian homes. Ferguson was, in Ramsay's own recollection, a righteous man, a teetotaler who imposed rigid standards on himself as well as others. The players would be in top condition, they would not smoke, and of course they would not drink, nor would they hang out with what were called loose women. If the players violated these precepts they would be cut. That was the power of a coach in those days, particularly a coach in a black suit and a stiff collar.

The war had interrupted his college career, and he went into the Navy, eventually, in typical Ramsay fashion, still testing himself, volunteering for underwater demolition duty. He was training for the invasion of Japan when the war ended and, feeling only partially cheated, he returned to college. The Navy changed him. He had entered as a slim intense boy, passionate to excel but unsure of himself, and the Navy had toughened him; he had endured the most physically demanding duty the service had, and he survived and excelled and gained a new confidence in himself. He was tougher now, more sure of his territory. He finished his college career a good college player, hardly a great one. But he loved the game and the feeling of unity that it created, young men come together, caring about a single shared goal. There was in those days, immediately after the war, a fledgling NBA, hardly celebrated, which offered poorly paying jobs to young white athletes. Ramsay thought for a time of trying out, but the NBA was insecure, the salaries were around $3,000 a year, and he already had obligations, a wife, one child, soon another child. So he had taken a job coaching in Chester, Pennsylvania, knowing nothing about coaching but never doubting his capacity to do it. This was in 1949 and he was paid $2,400 a year with a $100 bonus if his school made the playoffs, which in his third year it did. (Some twenty years later many professional players made $2,400 a *game*.) In those days economic problems seemed very immediate; he worried every day whether he could support a wife and an expanding family on his salary.

But there was no end to his ambition. He was also taking graduate courses at the University of Pennsylvania for his doctorate and playing at night in first one and then two semipro leagues. The principal league was the Eastern, a notch under the embryonic NBA, a place for players who were either too small, not quite good enough for the NBA, too burdened with family responsibility, or too frightened of air travel. In those days Ramsay was always tantalized by the idea of playing in the NBA. It was the best. Players were under *contract*, paid a year's salary to do what they loved best. But it was also risky, and no one was really pushing him to give up teaching and turn pro. He was sure he was good enough to play in the NBA; he knew many of the players, he had played against them in school and they were good, but not *that* good. His own semipro team scrimmaged against

NBA teams and played against them in exhibitions and every time it did, he became more sure he could make the grade. There had been a game in Wilmington with the Philadelphia Warriors where Ramsay played well, and afterwards a local reporter asked Eddie Gottlieb, the owner of the Warriors, about him. "Ramsay?" Gottlieb answered. "Ramsay? Listen, we'd love to have Ramsay. He's a hell of a player. But he wants to be a teacher and he won't play for us." Won't I, Ramsay had thought, reading the paper the next day, oh, just ask me, please just ask me. But it had never gone beyond that and he was sure it was just smart old Eddie Gottlieb trying to make a local boy look good in front of the home folks. (Thirty years later, he could remember the exact quote: *Ramsay, we'd love to have him.*)

So it was grungy nighttime basketball with a ragtag collection of semi-pro teams (including, among others, Block's Department Store of Norristown for the princely total of $5.00 a game). For two years he played with a team in Harrisburg, and then when that team folded, he played with the Sunbury Mercuries. (Stu Inman, who had a special love of exotic team nicknames and rare college fight songs, had fastened on that, and at tense Blazer management meetings he might ask Ramsay if they had done it that way on the old *Sunbury Mercuries.*) They played two or three times a week, all men with other jobs, car-pooling to save on expenses, and they talked basketball incessantly. The car pool was an ongoing basketball clinic. Jack McCloskey, who preceded Ramsay as a coach in Portland, was a teammate. They would play thirty-five games a year and perhaps in a good year they made $1,500 apiece. At home they got a share of the gate and they were always sure to count the house. It was a very tough league, no one was there on talent, they were all there because they loved to play and because they desperately needed the money. During one game Ramsay dived for a loose ball, cracked his head open and had to be taken to the dressing room. About an hour later he came to. "What happened?" he asked his teammate McCloskey. "You got knocked out and the game's over," McCloskey answered. There was a brief pause, the cobwebs still clearing, then Ramsay asked: "You get my money?"

Yet he had never been a real professional player, and this seemed to leave him with something to prove. His players in later years became extensions of himself; they would prove it for him. He drove them and demanded the highest levels of performance from them. Billy Cunningham, a four-year Philadelphia veteran when Jack Ramsay first came into the NBA, could remember an exhibition game in that first year, just before the season started. As befitted a veteran and all-star, Cunningham was not yet in top shape. They were playing in the second half and the game was, like all exhibition games, meaningless to everyone in the arena, with the exception perhaps of a few rookies and, of course, Jack Ramsay. Cunningham, exhausted by the pace, ran down the court and yelled to Ramsay, "Coach, Coach, take me out! I need a blow. I can't do it anymore!" Ramsay had heard him and had known even before Cunningham had asked for it that he wanted a rest, and Cunningham had heard Ramsay's voice following him down the court, "Just two minutes, Billy. Just give me two minutes more." The amazing thing about it, Cunningham thought later, was that he gave Ramsay the two minutes. It seemed so natural to give Jack Ramsay what he wanted. After all, he gave so much of himself.

Some ten years later, Ramsay, by then at the pinnacle of his career, one championship in his pocket, another barely snatched away by injury to a great player, stood at the airport in Los Angeles with Bill Walton. Not long before, Walton had announced that he intended to leave the Blazers, and on this occasion Ramsay and Walton had just come from a meeting at Larry Weinberg's house where Weinberg and Ramsay had tried, unsuccessfully, to change Walton's mind. Now, at the airport, Walton had tried in a more personal way (the only person at the meeting he really cared about was Ramsay) to explain to the coach why he was leaving, that he liked him and respected him and that, in spite of everything, he had learned more basketball from Ramsay than from anyone else. But, he said, he could not come back and play anymore. Ramsay was puzzled, they had been so good together. It had been more than a complete professional association, coach and player absolutely tuned to each other by mind and by instinct; they had also been friends, had never in any real sense disagreed. Ramsay pointed this out. It was hard to imagine a more complete relationship. But Walton had responded that he could not go back, that Ramsay was too intense, too consumed with winning.

That, for a time, deeply wounded Jack Ramsay. Yes, he was passionate about winning, but he was considered by his peers and rightfully so, to be one of the most ethical and principled men in professional sports, driven and single-minded, but honorable and responsible as well. He subjected no player to greater stress than he subjected himself. He lived within a certain harsh and unsparing code but there was nothing cheap or duplicitous or covert about him. So Walton's accusation was painful, and for anyone who knew both men, it was as if Walton was talking not just about Ramsay but about himself as well, player in search of coach, coach in search of player. If Ramsay was too intense, so was he; if Ramsay was too competitive, so was he; if Ramsay was consumed by winning, so was he. They were, their mutual friends thought, far too much alike.

FOR WILLIAM THEODORE Walton liked to win at everything. *Everything.* If there was a Ramsay mile run at the beginning of the season, he liked to fake out Lionel Hollins, hanging back for the first two-thirds of the race as if in poor condition, and then come roaring up at the end. If he was at a pickup picnic soccer game with women and children and dogs, he liked to smash through and score the winning goal, bodies, if need be, sprawling to left and right. When his team had won the NBA championship, Walton had, to his credit, avoided all the normal national media hoopla, the repeated coronation of the supreme athlete by magazines, organizations and other groups as anxious to crown themselves as the athlete, and had quietly gone instead, by himself, with no media contingent, to an Indian reservation in the Dakotas where Phil Jackson, another professional player, ran a camp for Indian kids. There, on his first day, just a few hours after winning the basketball championship in front of the entire nation, he and Jackson chose up sides with a few Indian boys on each team and played playground basketball until within moments it dawned on Jackson that to Walton this was no little playground game. *My God,* thought Jackson to his amazement, *Walton wants to win.* A moment later Jackson amended that: *He has to win.* With the Blazers during practice, in simulated games, if his team lost he was always complaining about foul calls and, on occasion, he would refuse to leave the court, maintaining, in all seriousness, that his team would have won if it hadn't been for the bad calls. Once, just when his complaints were becoming a little shrill, Luke had yelled, "Come on, big fella, quit acting like a baby," and they had all fired basketballs at him and it had ended as fun, everyone laughing, the game of hit-the-big-red-head-with-a-round-ball. But there was a thin line in this, a love of basketball that edged on obsession, of pushing himself and thus everyone around him to the sharpest point, more practice, always more practice. If the team arrived in a town and everyone was tired, Ramsay might ask Walton whether they should practice or not, and Walton would say yes, of course. He was, in the black vernacular, a genuine Basketball Jones, a player who cannot let go, who even after 110 games has to play more, who, even in the off-season, seems to gravitate towards a playground. He loved every victory, he loved every challenge and it was not necessarily for show; there was nothing in the *Guinness Book of World Records,* after all, about how many times the Red Shirts beat the White Shirts in Portland practices.

No one can ever decide who is the greatest player ever to play a particular game. To an uncommon degree Babe Ruth's records dominate those of his contemporaries, but then of course Ruth played in an era when black athletes were not allowed to compete. (Perhaps there should be an asterisk after the record of every athlete who competed before 1946, before Jackie Robinson.) One player rarely dominates in baseball—perhaps a pitcher, but a pitcher works only once every four days. Football records are harder to calibrate, the game changes more regularly than baseball, and there are more players on a team than there are on a baseball team, 22 to 9, and it is therefore much harder for one player to dominate a particular game or a season. But basketball is different from either: there are only five men on the court and one great player, particularly a great center, can make a decisive difference, imposing himself on both offense and defense, changing patterns of the opposing team and changing the roles of his teammates. Thus Bill Russell was the single most dominating team athlete of the modern big-sports era. He changed the flow and tempo of every game he participated in. He took away from opposing teams that which was central to their game, and systematically made his own teammates better. He transformed players of more limited gifts, protecting them from their weaknesses and enhancing their skills. Kareem Abdul-Jabbar is likewise a dominating player. He is not the defensive force that Russell or Walton was, but he is so consistently good on offense that he changes the texture of every game he plays. Whether he affects the strengths and weaknesses of his teammates as much as Russell did is doubtful.

On this scale it is hard to measure Walton because his career as a professional has been so marked by injuries. Unlike Kareem he simply lacked the plateau of a career. In his first two professional seasons he was beset by a variety of personal and physical problems. In his third and fourth seasons, when he was free of injury, he surely ranked with Russell. He was perhaps not quite the overwhelming defensive player that Russell was (though he played in a more physical league against more big powerful opponents than

Russell did); on offense he was by no means the offensive threat that Kareem is. Kareem essentially looks to shoot and passes when he cannot shoot; Walton looked to pass and he shot when he could not pass. But it was Walton's total ability, both on offense and defense, his competitive zeal, and, above all, his brilliant passing that made his game so distinctive and made him such a force. Walton, Inman thought, might at his best have an advantage over Russell; given the exact same cast of players, Walton might have a greater effect upon them.

He loved *competing*. The more intense the competition the better. Graduating from UCLA, he turned down an offer from the ABA worth perhaps twice as much as he received from Portland, because he thought the quality of its play inadequate. In his early years at Portland, unhappy with the city, the rain, his teammates, the league, perhaps even himself, he seriously considered for a time leaving the professional game, starting his own team and playing in a high-level semipro circuit. But that meant that he would not play against the best, and that was unthinkable. He loved, unlike most professional basketball players, playing on the road, because he was able to focus his entire day on basketball, with fewer distractions. In addition he liked the *theater* of the road game, the enemy arena, the way the opposing crowd focused all of its emotions and hostility on him—their antagonism made his adrenaline flow. His favorite games were the close games with great rivals on the road, the noise of the opposing crowd rising in crescendo as the game progressed and then (in his own words) the silence at the very end. The silence was his own personal reward. He hated playing against second-rate teams and inferior centers and it was hard to motivate him on these occasions; his performances were almost uniformly subpar.

He loved the day of a game, particularly an important game. It was a time which belonged completely to him, a time pure in its purpose. On the day itself he did not analyze the game, he had done that the night before, thought about the team and the player he was going against in the most clinical way possible. The night before was the analytical time. The day of the game was different, it was an emotional time. He always took a nap on the day of a game, waking up two and a half hours before the game. Later, as his career progressed, he increased it to two and three-quarters. This was the time in which he felt the rhythm and tempo of the game, almost like feeling a dance of his own. He played his own music, from the Grateful Dead, a rock band of which he was virtually a member, and the music helped, it flowed through him and he thought about the tempo he wanted to set and how he could move. He would sit in his home or his hotel room in those hours and actually see the game and feel the movement of it. Sometimes he did it with such accuracy that a few hours later when he was on the court and the same players made the same moves, it was easy for him because he had already seen it all, had made that move or blocked that shot. He loved that time, he had it all to himself, he was absorbed in his *feel* for basketball. He was amazed in those moments at how clearly he could see the game, see the spin on the ball and the angles from which different players were coming. Moment by moment in that time he became more confident until when he arrived at the locker room he was absolutely ready, pumped in his word. There he stayed by himself, breathing deeply, psyching himself. Lionel Hollins had loved watching him in those moments, knowing he was ready, the deeper the breathing the better the omen. Walton would flex his hands and bounce on the balls of his feet, like a boxer getting ready for a match. The tempo was important, for he intended to impose his tempo on the opponents lest they do the same to him.

Basketball had given him his particular niche in life. He had been a tall spindly boy with a terrible stutter, almost pathologically shy with strangers. His nickname in high school, not sought but perhaps inevitable, was Spider Walton, though he had never thought of himself as the Spider. From a very early age basketball was the activity he felt most comfortable with, where it was always easy for him to tell right from wrong. From his earliest childhood days he was tall and that helped, and he was quick, and that helped even more. His high school coach, Gordon Nash, aware of both the boy's intelligence and his painful shyness, believed that one reason that the young Walton had become so superb a passer was that while he loved to play the game and loved to win, he did not relish being the center of attention. By passing the ball to others, he helped his team to win and yet did not make himself the focus of the crowd. In time, as basketball preeminence and success came to him, he became more confident and the stutter seemed to diminish, although the sensitivity about his height was always there. In the Portland program and then the San Diego program, his height was always listed as six-eleven. Never seven feet. Six-eleven, he explained to friends, was tall, but seven feet was a freak. So Bill Walton was six feet eleven. When a reporter brought this up and suggested that he might in fact be seven feet tall, Walton had laughed and said, no, as far as he knew he was six feet eleven. At least he was the last time he was measured. Which was, he added, in his junior year in college.

In a sport populated by young black men, most of them from deprived circumstances, few of them with fathers around as they grew up, Bill Walton was different. Few of the blacks would have left their northern ghettos or their small southern towns were it not for basketball. For Bill Walton a college education was a natural assumption and basketball simply made it easier. He came from an incredibly secure middle-class home. Both parents were college-educated. It had been a warm close American home, built around family, all its limited resources poured into the children, four of them, all large and, it seemed, noisy, who ate immense amounts of food. His parents were old-fashioned liberals. Ted Walton was a social worker. His anger, Bill Walton remembered, seemed reserved for those contemptuous of the poor, and for television channels which were forever showing old World War II movies which, he believed, glorified war and killing. If much of the corruption in bigtime American sports began with the recruiting of high school stars, then the Walton children were well immunized against it. Ted and Gloria Walton had heard many stories about recruiters and their sweet songs, and cars and cash and fancy dinners, and they had decided most vehemently that they would not let this happen to their children, who would go to college, either with athletic scholarships or by paying for it themselves. If colleges wanted to recruit their children, they would not take the Waltons, father, mother and star son, to the fanciest steak house in San Diego. Bruce Walton, who was a year older than Bill and a high school football star (and later captain of the defensive team at UCLA), had decided first that he did not like the idea of the recruiters taking them all out, it had made him feel indebted, and his parents readily agreed. Instead, starting with Bruce, selected recruiters, cleared in advance through the high school coach, came to *their* house for dinner. The Waltons liked it better that way, they were not on the recruiters' turf, eating food they did not really want, in a restaurant they felt uncomfortable in, with an invisible price tag on everything. The recruiters liked it better that way, or at least the smarter ones had the good sense to say they did, and they would flatter Gloria Walton about how good it was to have a solid home-cooked meal after so many nights on the road.

On the fabled night when John Wooden came for dinner—John Wooden, who prided himself that he never personally recruited his players (he had not, he boasted, gone after Lewis Alcindor, which was at once true, and untrue)—he had played the role not of the famed national figure from Westwood, but the simple God-fearing country boy from Martinsville, Indiana. He endeared himself by asking for a second helping of Gloria Walton's potatoes. The national figure as country slicker. By contrast, another college recruiter, one never to be named in the Walton household, had come to eat dinner one night in that sturdy if not very fancy house and afterwards, misreading the signals as completely as a man can do, had talked about jobs for *everyone*, parents, brothers. The recruiter was asked to leave, and the children were sworn never to talk about the incident again, as if the very mention of it was contaminating.

Ted Walton was a big strapping man, 6'4". He had gone to Cal-Berkeley, where he had hardly been an athlete (in high school, he once said, "I played on the thirteenth team, and we always lost to the girls"). After graduation he met Gloria, a handsome woman six feet tall, at a club for exceptionally tall people called The Tiptoppers. In terms of size Bill Walton was virtually bred for the role; his brother Bruce was big enough to be a football star at UCLA and to play in the pros for a time, while Andy, who chose not to compete in intercollegiate athletics, was 6'6".

Theirs was an old-fashioned American home. Bill Walton, often a social-cultural contradiction to his friends, was a son of that strong, caring, Catholic couple, and a child of modern, liberated Southern California as well. The home was based on the strength of the family unit, strong and coherent, and made even more remarkable by the fact that it was rooted in San Diego where, unlike the American centers of novelists past, the sun almost always shone, the rain never fell, and whatever it was that the children wanted to do, swim, climb mountains, play basketball, they could do it outdoors and almost every day of the year. It was a land governed by the assumption that life, like the weather itself, would always be good. In later years Walton's friend Jack Scott, a product of Scranton, Pennsylvania, pointed out this difference between them—in Scranton you took life and the weather for what it was (and what it was not), and in San Diego the weather and life was expected to be a high. Bill, Scott reflected, felt a personal crisis if it rained, and was upset on the days when his car would not start. The Portland weather, Walton once told Lenny Wilkens, was robbing his body of strength.

Bill Walton, shy about his height, had started playing basketball in the

fourth grade, though he often played with sixth-grade kids lest he dominate boys his own age. Soon, because he felt comfortable playing basketball
and did virtually nothing else except perhaps hike, he was playing almost
all the time, in five or six different school and recreational leagues, his father and mother chauffeuring him from game to game on Saturdays. He
was in such demand that he usually played only half of each game, adapting
his schedule somewhat if a game was unusually close. This did not please all
his coaches or teammates but that was too bad, it was the way things had to
be. He had become, at an early age, a basketball junkie. He loved basketball
because each play was different, nothing was ever quite the same, and because there was, nevertheless, a strict sense of order on a basketball court
that had eluded him in real life. No one ever made fun of his height on a
basketball court.

By the time he was in the sixth grade he was not only tall and skinny,
but—and this was to be a Walton trademark separating him from so many
other tall white kids—he was surprisingly well coordinated. Playing against
boys two, three and four years older than himself, and hence a little bigger
than he was, he did not play center, he played guard, and this was crucial to
the breadth, depth and originality of his eventual style; he became the
quick little man who brought the ball up. Most big men in basketball have
always been big, which means they have always played as big men and seen
the court as big men. Conscious of their own roles but not those of other
players, they understood the end of a play, not the beginning. Walton, by
contrast, developed a guard's view of the entire court, and he could, as few
centers could, see an entire series of moves even before they developed. He
not only improved his ability to handle the ball (Red Holzman of the Knicks
once said that Walton, were he smaller, could play guard in the NBA), but
far more important he could *see* the court. He was growing up in the game
he loved, depending not on his size, which was to be quite special, but on
his vision and his quickness. He learned, and learned well, that basketball
was not a game of height but of quickness, of using speed to set up an intri-
cate series of moves so that one player would end up with a one-step advantage on his opponent.

As he entered high school his growth seemed momentarily to have
slowed. He chose Helix High in the San Diego suburb of La Mesa where the
Waltons lived because it was a good school with a good athletic program.
Then between eighth and ninth grades he began to grow again—two inches,

until he was 6'1". As a sophomore he hurt his knee and played very little, but in one three-month period in his sophomore year he grew at a startling rate, becoming, as if overnight, 6'7½", and gaining in the process only five pounds. He was by his own admission appallingly skinny and desperately self-conscious about himself. But as he was becoming more awkward with kids his own age he was becoming far more valuable as a basketball player. Now for the first time he played in the forecourt, at forward. What amazed Gordon Nash, his high school coach, was that during that stretch of such sudden and remarkable growth, Bill Walton did not lose his coordination. Most young men growing so quickly would have become gangly and awkward, all hands and feet. For a time it puzzled Nash, but he finally decided that this was simply a case of rare natural ability. Walton was even then an astonishing player; usually kids that young can do one thing well—shoot or pass or rebound—but Bill Walton already had the makings of a complete game. Shorter, older, more mature players did not have his quickness. In his junior year he grew again, he was now a little over 6'9" and weighed 170 pounds, and Nash knew he was going to be a great player.

The first letter had come in his sophomore year. It was from Denny Crum, an assistant to John Wooden at UCLA, who was Wooden's chief recruiter. Was young William interested in going to college? If he was, might there be something the good people at UCLA could do for him, help him plan his curriculum? They certainly would be interested in helping out. They kept in touch. Tuesday was usually basketball night in San Diego so, as if by clockwork, on Tuesday nights Denny Crum would call Ted and Gloria Walton asking how the dinner was, and how Helix had done that night. All of that was electrifying to young Bill Walton, the idea that a college cared, and above all *UCLA*, for UCLA was John Wooden and the then Lew Alcindor, and every basketball player in the West grew up watching UCLA basketball and dreaming about playing for Wooden. Alcindor had been Walton's particular idol. He could remember Alcindor's first varsity game, in which he scored fifty-six points. Soon almost every college in the country seemed in pursuit of young Bill Walton, who was widely considered the best high school basketball player in the country. There were scouts calling the house, old friends with connections to Ted Walton reopening friendships.

Coach Gordon Nash, who was also a biology teacher, screened his young player from this as much as he could. Nash was determined that basketball be fun. No scouts or coaches were allowed in the locker room—to reach Walton they first had to see Nash. The young man himself felt uneasy with all this attention. People were no longer content to watch him play, they now wanted to know more about him, share, it seemed, the secret parts of him. Most other players might revel in the hoopla that attended Walton's senior year, but not this private young man. The publicity, the off-the-court pressure, unlike the pressure on the court, seemed to cut to the heart of his shyness, making him feel more vulnerable than ever.

Yet for all Walton's shyness there was, Nash thought, a certain maturity to him that went beyond his years. At the beginning of his senior year he had gone to Nash and said that that year he wanted very badly only to rebound and play defense. He would get the ball out to his teammates as quickly as possible and they would do the scoring. It was, Nash thought, a remarkable gesture; almost any other seventeen-year-old already besieged by scouts would have wanted to use that year to make his mark, shoot for the record book, catching the eye not just of college scouts, but of the pro scouts who were already beginning to watch him as well. But Walton, Nash realized, knew that there was a lot of bigtime basketball ahead of him, while for most of his teammates this was their last chance to play in organized games. It was not, Nash thought, that Walton lacked ego (his ego, the coach suspected, was immense, no one could compete at that level of athletics without a big ego), it was that he was more in control of his ego and knew how to funnel it into the game itself, the better to help his teammates and in the process the better to exhibit his own unusual talents. He understood very early that shooting and scoring points did not separate him from the crowd, or make him a world-class player, but taking his speed and intelligence and using it to heighten the skills of his teammates did. If Nash had any problem with Walton in his senior year, it was getting him to shoot. The ball would come in to him, he was open and he would send it back out. Nash would call a time-out, instruct Walton to shoot, they would resume play and the same thing would happen. Those were glory days; he was 6'11", already the best passing center that many pro and college scouts had ever seen. Helix was undefeated, and everything seemed so natural, basketball was a complete and wonderful universe, everyone was in the right place and the right things happened, it was a world so much better ordered than the other world he was a part of.

They got up early in the morning in San Diego and flew back to Portland

```
        #10   02-08-2016 12:00AM
    Item(s) checked out to p2638071.

TITLE: INTERLIBRARY LOAN MATERIAL
BAR#: C117747634
DUE: 02-23-16


        Main Library  955-6785
```

just in time to play San Antonio that night. They were all exhausted. The San Antonio game was exceptional. With twenty-nine seconds left San Antonio led 116–109. Then Ron Brewer hit a three-point shot, and Portland managed to force the Spurs into two turnovers. The second of them with ten seconds left was a steal and a basket by Lucas which tied the score. In the overtime, with Luke scoring six points, Portland won. The locker room was the noisiest it had been all season. Larry Steele sat by himself, putting ice on his knees. He had played 35 minutes, scored 18 points and his knees hurt. They always hurt now, it seemed. He had tendinitis—now known, because it is so endemic in basketball, as "jumper's knees"—and he had it in both knees. He was taking painkillers but had not yet been operated on. There was nothing, Steele thought, that could be done about it. The knee was the basketball player's great nemesis, now that the game had gone into the air. The knee is a delicate piece of equipment, a fragile human hinge whose architect had never suspected that its proprietor might spend some fifteen years in a profession where the principal act was jumping as high as possible some seventy or eighty times a night.

Bobby Gross, whose substitute Steele was, was still out with back pains. That meant that Steele was playing more than anyone had expected, placing more and more stress on his knees. He sat in the locker room after the San Antonio game and knew the next day was going to be painful. The pain had begun in both knees last March, the result of another long season, of a body he knew was gradually wearing down. He had worked over the summer to build the knees up. But despite the use of his hot tub, as the summer progressed he had felt nothing but a constant nagging ache in both knees; it was often hard to tell which of them was the worst, the pain seemed so steady and relentless. He knew his wife, Vicki, was worried about his health and worried that the disability might become permanent. He himself worried about the future; he had seen too many former players whose injuries were permanent. He had a seven-year-old son and he wanted to be active with him, not be some older man who was more like a grandfather than father. In the summer it was all right when he was just walking, but the pain was real whenever he exercised.

But then the season began and all that care simply disappeared under the steady strain. He was amused to hear the commissioner of basketball, Larry O'Brien, go on television and say in defense of basketball that this was the only league which had made its schedule shorter. "That's not true,"

Steele was saying, "they didn't make the season shorter. They made it tighter. And not because of the players. Because of television. They just didn't want it going into baseball season at playoff time. It hurt the ratings. So they tightened it, which makes it harder. There's less time to rest between games." He was, he said, lucky nevertheless. At least he had had a full career. "My knees weren't burned out when I came in. But they've got kids, rookies coming in the league, and their knees are already gone. Playing too much in junior high on these hard surfaces, playing too much in high school on hard surfaces, playing too much on playgrounds, coming down on these hard surfaces. They come in the pros and their knees are already gone." He pointed across the locker room to Ron Brewer, who was icing his knees. Brewer was, in player vernacular, a jumper, one of the best in the league; his high school and college coaches had tried to tempt him to come out for track and become a national high jump champion. Leaping was the center of his game. Now he sat there icing his knees. "Look, he's maybe twenty-four years old and his knees hurt and he's icing them," Steele said. He yelled across the room to Brewer, "Boot—how do those knees feel?"

"Twenty-five-year-old body," Brewer said, laughing, "sixty-year-old knees."

THE TEAM WAS supposed to fly to Indiana twenty-four hours later but Steele had flown ahead on an earlier plane. Other players now on occasion broke from the team schedule for business reasons, a commercial to tape, an agent to meet, but Steele had requested the day off—and Ramsay had given it to him—so he could go home and help his father and uncle shell corn on the family farm. A country boy he had come into the league, a country boy at heart he remained. The Steeles had always been farmers and Larry Steele had grown up near Bainbridge, Indiana. It was a rural area, dotted with small towns and people linked by the land and not by factories. The towns were simple. They featured feed stores, small grocery stores and banks which carefully watched the harvests and the level of rainfall. It was in terms of American sports a rare rural area where basketball was as important as in the great urban centers of the Northeast. In the thirties and forties, when the state's athletic traditions and psyche were set, before the coming of good rural roads and consolidated school systems, there were some nine hundred high schools in the state and only about a third of them had enough boys to play football. Very early, before other states followed suit, Indiana had a state basketball tournament, in which every school, large or small, competed against every other, and that had helped fix basketball as the focal point of athletic and, even more important, social achievement in the state. Everyone still remembered how little Milan, with only fourteen boys enrolled, won the state tournament in 1954. Scattered throughout rural Indiana were tiny towns, often with under one thousand people in them, which had gyms that could seat five thousand or more. Season tickets for the high school games were hard to get. Families passed them on, member to member, and sometimes they appeared in wills. Not surprisingly, just as a town's identity came from basketball so too did a boy's.

Larry Steele was certifiably rural. He went to school in Bainbridge, his family banked in Danville, the postal address was Coatesville, and the phone listing was Amo (which of course Stu Inman had loved, the fact that to call Steele he had had to go through the *Amo*, Indiana, telephone switchboard, and he had teased Steele about Amo for ten years). His life as a boy had been built around basketball. He and his brother had shared a rollaway bed in their tiny three-room house but even in their bedroom they had played basketball with a small brown ball and a rim fashioned out of a wire clothes hanger. Later their father had built a basket for them on a nearby plot, a dirt court prescribed by nature (the dirt, Larry Steele decided later, had prolonged his career—while other kids were having their knees worn down by playing on concrete in cities, the dirt had a built-in cushion). If you drove too far to the left you went into the bordering creek; if you drove too far to the right you went up a hill. The net (it was an old country trick) had been dipped in wax to make it last longer. They practiced all day long. Bainbridge had a grand total of four hundred fifty people and the school serviced part of the region. All twelve grades were housed in one building. Because his class was a little larger than most, he was part of the postwar baby boom, the authorities had been forced to whitewash the coal room and make it a classroom. In his sophomore year Bainbridge had been weak, but in his junior and senior years it had a very good team, the record was 23 and 3 and the team had gone to the state tournament and done well, and the entire town had followed it there. Among those who went was the cheerleader who was Larry Steele's girlfriend, later his wife. He had known her since the second grade. It was that kind of boyhood, scarcely a step removed from an old *Saturday Evening Post* cover.

More than one hundred colleges were interested in him; he narrowed the choice to Indiana, Purdue and Kentucky. Indiana seemed the most likely, but when he visited there someone broke into his car. Then there was Purdue but in the end he decided he was a limited student at best—he was going to college not for an education but to play basketball, and in that case there was no real choice. Kentucky in those days stood above everyone else. In college basketball there were the good eastern teams at one end of the continent, UCLA at the other and Kentucky in the middle. It was bigtime, high recruiting, highly mechanized basketball, with Adolph Rupp dominating the culture and politics of the region as Bear Bryant later dominated the politics and athletics of Alabama. What Rupp wanted he got. Steele, upon arrival, felt dwarfed by the number of other, bigger, more highly sought-after stars who arrived with him, and the number of already legendary red-shirted players, that is, players sitting out a year without losing their eligibility, who were available. But their stars descended and his ascended; for many of them, flattered by recruiters and the talk of bigtime athletes and coaches who had coddled them, Kentucky with its disciplined, almost harsh program had proven too difficult, and they disappeared. In Bainbridge-Amo, Indiana, no one was ever coddled and, thus stronger than he had thought, Steele survived. His college life was basketball. That was all he thought about because that was all there was time to think about. In the first year he got good grades; they went down steadily from then on. Practice started every day at 3:15. The moment the second hand hit twelve you were shooting. The curtain around the basketball gym came down and for two hours you went all-out. That was the center of your life. His game in those years was much as it became in the professional ranks—scrappy, aggressive, doing just enough to win, sacrificing himself just enough for the common cause. He did not think in those days of a professional career, he believed his talent too limited. In his senior year, he was nevertheless disappointed when the Indiana franchise in the ABA picked him in the seventh round. So much for being a local hero. Portland picked him in the third round (though he was the fourth player the Blazers took). That did not impress him very much either. He thought of going on to graduate school and becoming a CPA. A friend of the Kentucky basketball program would finance it. But Stu Inman called. Inman was more enthusiastic than the draft position implied. "I've picked a kid in the third round you're going to love," he had told Harry Glickman, the general manager, since Glickman was fond of scrappy players. Steele flew out to Portland where he was offered a three-year contract at $25,000 a year with a $5,000 bonus. But none of the salary was guaranteed. He thanked them but pointed out that if he was going to walk into a rookie camp without any protection, he might as well do it closer to home. At that point Portland offered to guarantee one year. So he signed. As four years earlier at Kentucky, he arrived with no illusions about his talent. He knew he did not have good statistics or a great shot. Nor, for that matter, great speed. But there were always loose balls to be dived after. That had been nine years ago and he was still there and coaches had come and gone, stars had come and gone, most of the first-round draft choices had come and gone. He had never gotten the big money; his current salary, about $105,000, was his best. The next year he would make a little more but then, of course, like ten years ago, it was not guaranteed. His position would be fragile. And now his knees hurt worse than ever. Even being back working on the farm in Indiana did not bring that much pleasure. It was all so mechanized now; working in the cabin of the combine, big, air-conditioned, was like working in an office.

THEY LEFT EARLY in the morning for the flight to Indianapolis, Milwaukee, Chicago and Kansas City. Four games in five days. The very prospect of the trip, the road, the plane trips, the early wakeup calls, the missed meals, the hostile crowds, seemed to cast a pall over them. The myth of the professional basketball player was that he drove a Mercedes or, failing that, something grander. Not in Portland; perhaps it was the contagious quality of the outdoor life and what the locals drove, perhaps it was the fact that they could lease cars like these free for a year, but for whatever reason, most of them seemed to drive vans and wagons. Few shared rides to the airport. They were not that close. The moment the home game or the practice was over, they disappeared into their own many little worlds of Portland. On the road, the very nature of their profession, the isolation of it, funneled them together; they could not be apart from each other because there was no time. At home it was different. They saw little of each other socially because they saw so much of each other during the season. But then, few basketball players were close with each other anymore. The old-time players, from the fifties and sixties, had often been closer. They had shared, it seemed, more off-court experiences, going out drinking and carousing after a game. But those days were different: the money had been smaller, vast differentials in salaries were uncommon, careers were longer, teams more stable and players tended to stay with one team for several years. Besides the game was less demanding physically; there was—with the exception of a team like the Celtics—less running and jumping, the bodies were less sore. Most modern basketball players did not carouse. They did not go out drinking because they were too tired and because they knew drinking and smoking cut into their wind. Ten years earlier most members of a team smoked; now almost no one smoked (Tom Meschery as assistant coach had, when he visited Bill Walton at his home, felt terribly embarrassed about bringing in his pack of cigarettes; he had felt as though he were toting some kind of pistol). They might smoke some dope later; it was a relaxant, it was said not to hurt your condition. There were some of them, the wealthier ones, who used cocaine (that was a great league concern), though this Portland team was squarer than most and its use of drugs was thought to be marginal.

But it was probably the coming of the harsher schedule, more travel to more teams in more cities, coupled with the big new money and the exigencies of contracts and trading practices and legal rights, that had changed the relationships. The older players had drawn less money, and they had played at least in large part for the fun of it. It was hardly, at those old salaries, a profession. The modern players of the seventies were different. Big money and superstar status made camaraderie more difficult; it was hard for a player making $60,000 a year to pal around with one making $500,000. In the old days teams remained teams. Now there were more trades and more dealing. It was no longer just owners who dealt players, but for the first time players dealing themselves. Teams did not remain teams very long; it did not pay to bring permanent emotion to so transitory a relationship. A good team was simply a group of very disparate athletes who assembled each day from radically different lives and—with luck—for one shared moment put aside their differences, their dislikes, their egos and their rivalries, harnessing their energies towards a common goal. Even that was rare enough.

The new salaries had made it all more difficult. It had heightened natural tensions between teammates as it increased the differences in status that always existed. Nor did the pressure come from the players alone. Much of it came from wives and girlfriends. Even when the players were reasonably casual about the differences, wives and girlfriends often were not. Their status was derivative and usually had no actual achievement to support it.

In their own minds, they were stars as well, celebrities to their neighbors by virtue of their relationships with these heroes. It was, Pat Washington thought, as if the wives thought that *they* shot the fouls and got the rebounds and made the key baskets. They conceived their own pecking order: the wife of the superstar was the queen bee, and she set the tone; then there were the wives of the starters and, lower down, the wives of the substitutes. This was true on all teams. All general managers were made nervous by the wives, by the tensions they could create, knowing that they could easily hound their husbands to ask for more money, to push for greater statistics. Even on the Boston Celtics, the classic team in terms of sharing, it was believed by connoisseurs that some of the tensions which began to sap the strength of the team came not from the players but from the wives, most particularly because national television always seemed to fix its camera on Beth Havlicek, the wife of John, pert blonde, the cheerleader incarnate, with the kind of face that sports cameras loved (they would have picked her out of the crowd even if she had not been his wife), and there would be the voice of Brent Musburger, just as John was about to shoot a foul, saying "There's his lovely wife, Beth." That would provoke a groan from the other wives, mostly black. "*She's* on television again," one would say to the other.

If there was real friendship, it had been back in college. Still, when times were good, during the championship season and the season after it, some of the Portland players had been closer. The very act of winning helped bind them, basketball had been more fun and because it was more fun, it was more central to their lives. In those years there had been the Walton group—Walton, Lucas, Hollins—looser, more hip, all single or semisingle, and the squares—Twardzik, Steele and Neal. Johnny Davis was apart from everyone and most people associated Bobby Gross with the Walton group because he played so well with them, but he was mostly off by himself. Twardzik had not very much liked Walton, even in the good years; he thought him spoiled and he believed that on occasion Walton had, with the lightest touch imaginable, tested Ramsay and gotten away with it. Walton for that matter had not much liked Twardzik. The differences were social and cultural as much as anything else. Walton was the child of the freedom of Southern California of the seventies and of athletic gifts so immense that great personal leverage went with them; Twardzik was the descendant of Polish immigrants, a child of poverty-stricken Pennsylvania, his physical abilities so limited that it was almost an accident that he was in the pro game, blue collar in his politics as well as his game. Where a few other players resented Walton's status and his willingness to use it (and, in their minds, abuse it), Twardzik was willing to stand up to him and challenge him. But in the flush of victory those tensions had not mattered, they mattered only when you were losing.

On this team, like most others, there was a breakdown by race, by status, by geography, by levels of sophistication, even, it sometimes seemed, by height. Guards with guards, tall white centers with tall white centers. Luke and Lionel were still close, but it was a friendship not without its rivalries. Steele and Twardzik, both white, both straight, still roomed with each other though they were not particularly close. Ron Brewer and T. R. Dunn, both southern blacks, were often together. Kermit Washington and Jim Brewer, both blacks, both big men, both products of similar environment, got on well, and Kermit and Bobby Gross often went out together on the road. Tom Owens and Kevin Kunnert, both white centers, both near seven feet tall, were inseparable, always together, always talking, with Owens doing 98 percent of the talking and Kunnert assigned to the listening. ("We got Kevin Kunnert," Bucky Buckwalter had told the team's Christmas party, "so Tom Owens could have someone to talk to.") Race was always there, blacks tending by and large to go off with one another and whites with each other; on the plane blacks sat with blacks, whites with whites; but it was not as sharp a division as it had been twenty years ago. Most of the contemporary players had grown up playing in a sport that was dominated by blacks. They got along. They accepted each other. Usually they were not close. That was good enough. Jim Brewer had played basketball at Minnesota with Dave Winfield, who had gone on to become one of the preeminent baseball stars of a generation. A few weeks earlier, Winfield had called him. "You just don't know how lucky you are," Winfield told Brewer. "You've got nothing there but people that went to college and you have all those people to talk to. You just don't know what it's like being on a baseball team. Loneliest thing you can imagine."

They walked through Indianapolis Airport on their way to their bus. It was an aspect of their profession that always made them uneasy. Each of them was tall, and each was used to some stares, but together, a team, all of them tall, they stood out. Everyone turned around, everyone gawked, people felt free to come up and ask if they were basketball players, to ask how the weather up there was ("Raining," Wilt Chamberlain was said to have once replied and then spit down on the civilian). They were, in that one moment, passing through the airport, no longer just athletes, they were close to being freaks. ("Are you basketball players?" a middle-aged lady had asked Swen Nater as the San Diego Clippers went through an airport and the 6'11" Nater had said as politely as he could, "No, ma'am, we're not basketball players, we're gay ice skaters." At which point Sidney Wicks, standing next to Nater, had pointed to him and added, "And, lady, this big guy really wears me out." The woman fled.) The older generation of players, who had traveled in whatever was available, old planes, coach seats, and had stayed in terrible hotels, thought the new generation had it easy. The players now flew first class, there were private buses at every airport to take them into town, they stayed at good hotels, and they never touched their luggage except when they left and they had to bring it down to the lobby. The per diem for everyone was twenty-six dollars. (Three years before, during the championship season, one rookie had eaten Big Macs every day and banked 80 percent of his per diem money, to pay his rent.) The older generation thought them rich and spoiled. But for all of that, little of it was fun. Their body clocks were always slightly off. They were always trying to adjust their eating habits to the clock, trying to find meals after games, which was not easy, hotel room service usually closing much earlier, and plainly America did not much fancy serving meals at 11:30 p.m. There was always, somehow, a practice the next day. Ramsay liked his practices, and they were rarely light ones.

By the time they reached Indiana, Maurice Lucas was playing again, but it was still a constant struggle between him and management and thus between him and Ramsay. He had missed the first eight games. Ramsay thought Luke's reasons, bronchial problems and a sprained finger, were not the kind of reasons that ought to keep professional athletes out. Ramsay had been even more angered when Luke had failed to show for practices (Mychal Thompson with a badly broken leg had shown but Luke had not). That was bad enough; what was worse was that Ramsay found out he could fine Luke no more than $125 a practice. One hundred and twenty-five dollars, Ramsay thought. What does that mean to an athlete making $300,000 a year?

It was, Ramsay knew, always going to be a test of wills with Luke. Of the blacks on the team, he was by far the most political and also the most anxious to test authority, any authority. Some of the other blacks, Ron Brewer and T. R. Dunn, for example, had grown up in the South and had gone to southern schools; there was, some coaches thought, a lack of assertiveness to their play, something the coaches suspected could be traced back to their childhoods, to that region where, despite significant social change, authority still belonged to whites and blacks remained tentative about expressing their feelings openly, whether in politics or sports. But there was no problem like that with Maurice Lucas, of Pittsburgh, Pennsylvania, late of the Hill district of the ghetto. Sometimes the Portland front office, talking about a particular player in college or on another team, used the phrase, and to them it was positive: obedient kid. *Obedient kid.* Maurice Lucas was most demonstrably not an obedient kid. He was very black, very articulate, very political, a strong and independent man sprung from circumstances that could also create great insecurity. There was about him a constant sense of challenge; everything was a struggle, and everything was a potential confrontation, a struggle for turf and position. It was in part what had made him at his best so exceptional an athlete. He liked the clash of will. He was at once an intensely proud black man, justifiably angry about the injustice around him, and a superb and subtle con artist, a man who had in effect invented himself and his persona—Luke the Intimidator. When he was making demands, when he talked about race being an issue at point, it was sometimes hard to tell which Maurice Lucas was talking—the Lucas who genuinely believed that he was a victim of such obvious American racism, or the Lucas who knew that his cause was more dramatic if he deliberately cloaked himself in it. Indeed, it was not possible at certain times to tell whether he himself knew. (He was capable of complaining that Portland would never pay a black superstar what it would pay a white superstar, which was possibly correct, and, in the next breath, of complaining about the fact that Mychal Thompson, a rookie, who was also, it happened, black, had made twice as much in his rookie year as Luke made, then in his third year in Portland.)

When Lucas first came to Portland, Ramsay, aware of his reputation elsewhere as a difficult player, went to him and tried to start the relationship as candidly as he could. "Listen," Ramsay said, "we may disagree, but I intend to treat you like a man with full respect and I expect to be treated in the same way in return. I don't intend to embarrass you, and I don't expect you to embarrass me." Where other coaches sometimes developed their ego at the expense of their players, Ramsay was better. He was confident and passionate but solid in his sense of self. He and Luke got along fairly well, given how strong-minded both men were. There had been challenges even in the championship year, quick flashes of Luke's anger, followed by truce and friendship. But the edge was always there, Luke was always testing. In 1978 the team had been at practice doing the stretching exercises which were a reasonably sacred part of the Ramsay routine. Luke went on talking during the stretching and Ramsay had been angry. Talking was forbidden, the exercises were a deadly serious matter designed to prevent hamstrings and nothing should make them seem frivolous. Ramsay began to stare at Luke. But Luke kept talking. Finally Ramsay's voice was heard, brisk, authoritative: "No talking during stretching exercises." There had been a moment of silence, and then Luke's voice was heard, not quite a challenge, more a light probe. "Jack LaLanne talks during *his* stretching exercises," he had answered. Score one for Luke. But this year was different, there was less fun in it for either of them, both were locked into something they wanted out of. Ramsay kept telling Luke that they were trying to deal him and that the best thing for him was to play as hard as he could to send his market value up.

But that had proven difficult. Luke's mind was elsewhere, obsessed with his contract. He wanted to be traded, he said, and Portland continued to try to oblige him. The trouble of course was that what Stu Inman had feared might happen *was* happening. Because he was not playing well, his value had very quickly gone down; similarly because the word was out that Portland wanted to unload him there was a new wariness among other clubs. If a player of that caliber was available it was a sign he must be a troublemaker. Chicago, once desperate for him, was now cool. New Jersey, owner of the greatly desired Calvin Natt, had backed off. Inman, working the phone banks in Portland, could feel Lucas's value going down almost daily, like a hot stock suddenly cooling off. He had called Red Auerbach. "We're interested in Rick Robey," Inman said, mentioning the Boston backup center. "That's just fine," Auerbach said, "because I'm very interested in Kermit Washington." "So is Jack Ramsay," said Inman.

All of this affected Lucas and affected the team. He was the team's leader and he was the disaffected man. He was also bothered by the arrival of Kermit Washington, who was playing Luke's own position and, because of the winning streak, had become an immediate crowd favorite. Now, going into the Indiana game, he had missed nine games and been back for four. "How's Luke doing?" Stu Inman asked Ramsay in a phone call before the game. "He tantalizes you," Ramsay answered. "Sometimes he's very good, and sometimes he's not there at all." The Indiana game turned out to be a bad one. Indiana was a weak team, struggling itself, the kind of team that Portland had to beat on the road if it was to make the playoffs. The Blazers had taken a sixteen-point lead early in the second quarter and then proceeded to blow both the lead and the game. Late in the game, frustrated with the way Luke was playing, Ramsay pulled him, and Luke walked back to the bench in his best imperial style, as slowly and as regally as he could, as if demonstrating a policy of nonrecognition towards all authority. Ramsay-watchers on the bench, knowing how frustrated he already was with Luke, knowing how angry he was about this particular game, watched him, waiting for the explosion. The face tightened. The brow furrowed. (Luke, an expert on Ramsay's facial expression, especially his use of those thick eyebrows, called it "laying on the brow." "Man," he would say of Ramsay, "he was really laying the brow on me today.") The veins stood out. Luke seemed to half turn, as if waiting for the explosion and ready to respond. Instead the moment passed. Indiana won. To be continued, thought Bucky Buckwalter, the assistant coach.

THREE NIGHTS LATER they played in Chicago. Larry Steele's knees were hurting more and more. The right knee had gotten worse game by game and now the left was beginning to hurt. It was all right when the knees were warmed up but the pain after the game, as they cooled down, was becoming more than he could handle. It was also affecting his game. In the Indiana game he could not jump and when he ran down the court his knees were always in pain when he reached the other end. Knee bends were becoming harder and harder. He was losing increments of flex every day. By the middle of the Chicago game he could no longer bend. That meant he was a standup basketball player. After the Chicago game he told Ron Culp that he did not think he could play against Kansas City the next night. He needed to rest. He would return, he suggested, when he could do a full knee bend. He had already played six hundred eleven regular-season games for Portland, more than anyone else in team history. He had also, as it turned out, played his last game.

They came into Phoenix limping. Larry Steele hoped he might return in a few weeks; Ron Culp, working with him, was far less sanguine about his prospects. Lionel Hollins was also favoring his knee. After playing in the first three games he reinjured it and had sat out every game since then, sixteen in all. Ramsay was bothered by Hollins's absence and though he was particularly fond of him as a player and a person, he was not so sure that the injury was as serious as Hollins seemed to think. Just possibly the injury was in some way connected to option year and contract problems, if not consciously, then at least unconsciously. A player with so much at stake, contract unsigned, big dollars just waiting, would be particularly cautious about jeopardizing his career. Bobby Gross, the small forward whose absence had forced Larry Steele into more minutes, had finally returned, after missing the first thirteen games with a bad back. But his return had not been easy, he was not yet in shape, and his confidence seemed shaky. His game was more tentative, in part because he himself was not ready and in part because these players were not as deft and sophisticated in their command of the Ramsay system as he was. Ramsay had been desperate to have Gross back. He was the best passer on the team and his sense of movement, of when to cut and go against the flow in order to create opportunities, not so much for himself but for his teammates, was crucial to the system. It was more often than not Gross's movement and passing, a connection between the guards and the slower big men, which created the slight angle of advantage that led to a basket. It was an anticipatory sense, absolutely instinctive, something difficult to teach. Gross had it. Few others did. Gross could sense the flow of the play towards one side of the court and, even as the ball was moving that way, he could cut in the other direction. Then, if the ball came to him, the defense had to shift radically to catch up with the ball. Because of his movement and sense of angles, it meant that the defense was often a split second behind Ramsay's offense. That was all it took to free a player. If not every fan was aware of what he meant to the team with his exceptional eyesight, his teammates were, and his coach was.

Ramsay badly needed Gross in general and especially needed him against Phoenix for Phoenix had Walter Davis, a talented joyous player who was probably the quickest small forward in the league ("not the league," amended Bucky Buckwalter, "the world"). It was Davis who had ended the nine-game winning streak with his off-balance shot, and the Blazers had to stop him in order to win. Lucas, who had missed the first eight games and then had played a bit, was out again. His finger this time. ("How's Luke?" a reporter asked Ramsay. "Luke," he said, "is giving us the finger.") The medical list was so long that Portland had only nine players dressed. At practice that day, in order to have two teams, they had drafted Herm Gilliam, he of the championship season and now a broadcaster, to round out the roster. Since all the injuries, beginning with Walton and Gross and continuing over the last two years, had taken place after Gilliam was cut, he had constantly been teased about putting a hex on the team. "Didn't do it," he had protested. "Took my departure like a man. No voodoo, no hexes." But all of these injuries had not deterred Ramsay. On the day of the game, they had gone to the Phoenix arena, absolutely empty, filled, it seemed, with ghosts—no lights, no janitors, no bodies, no souls—and Ramsay, sensing that his team was listless, was already pushing them. "Come on, get moving, one hour in the gym, that's all. We don't waste it." That was typical Ramsay. Everything was done the right way, and the railroads ran on time. (During the championship season the Portland team had shown up at the Philly arena for its two-hour practice at 1 p.m. right on the dot. Because Philly was running off schedule, its practices were always lax, players always late, they asked to extend for fifteen minutes. No way, Ramsay said. "But it's our arena," one of the Philadelphia assistants had said. "Not for two hours it isn't," Ramsay had answered.)

Ramsay wanted to win this game. Phoenix was an important team to beat. Last year it had eliminated Portland in the miniseries and had come very close to eliminating Seattle in a seven-game series, which featured better basketball than the eventual championship games between Seattle and Washington. Besides, Ramsay and MacLeod were extraordinarily similar as coaches: each had a system and each used his system, and the players stayed within that system or they were gone. Just as there was some resentment in Portland now about Ramsay's dependence on the system, some of the Phoenix players were now restless with MacLeod's system. Most notable among them was Paul Westphal, the all-star guard who was already talking about wanting to be traded. If in Portland it was primarily the black players who were restless with the system, then there was no contradiction in Westphal, who was white, sharing some of their feelings. For he was a white player that the blacks greatly admired. In their view he played *black,* that is, he could freelance, he could drive and he could dunk like a black player. So Phoenix-Portland games were very good ones but they were also very controlled, and there was a constant awareness, not just of the ten men on the court but of the two older men sitting and kneeling at courtside.

It was an evening of Walter Davis. His game was a rare pleasure to watch, not just his speed and talent, but his boyishness which cut through so much of an often dour atmosphere. Sometimes he played a little out of control, and even he couldn't keep up with his speed. But mostly the speed was exciting, he could dribble faster than other men could run, and when he scored on a drive, a sudden burst of speed accelerating past other players who had always thought of themselves as the fastest players around until they met Walter Davis, he would turn around with a look of unconcealed delight. No twelve-year-old, making his first basket in a junior high game, could have matched it. If Phoenix lost in close competition and Walter Davis missed the final shot, he became inconsolable; he would remain in the locker room long after everyone else had left, weeping by himself. The tears were genuine and had nothing to do with money. That night Walter Davis scored, in a low scoring game, thirty-two points.

It was a terrible night for Bobby Gross. It was not just that Davis was too quick for Gross, he was too quick for everyone and it was not just that his points came off Gross, they could have come off any quality player. What was worse was that Gross, so graceful and artful a player, seemed disconnected not just from his teammates but from himself. He was the best passer on the team and yet his passes this night were out of control. He had ten turnovers for the night, which meant that on ten occasions when he had the ball it had gone over to Phoenix without a Portland shot; normally he committed ten turnovers in a total of four games. In the end it had come down to the last ten seconds, Portland ahead 97–96 and Phoenix with the ball. Instead of doubling Davis, Portland had gone to single coverage and Davis had scored on an eight-foot shot. Portland rushed the ball up-court, T. R. Dunn took a long shot, far outside his range, and missed. Kevin Kunnert had gone up for the rebound, over a Phoenix player, and as he did someone cracked him hard from behind. Kunnert went down as if shot. The whistle blew. Kunnert was writhing on the floor in terrible pain. The whistle blew again. The referee pointed a menacing finger at Kunnert's writhing body. The Phoenix crowd, realizing that the foul was on Kunnert, that the victory was secure, began to cheer wildly. "Loose ball foul on number forty-four, *Kevin Kunnert*," the p.a. system announced gleefully. An even greater Phoenix cheer went up. Kunnert was still rolling back and forth on the floor, a man turned into a child in his pain. Teammates were gathered around him and doctors and trainers were rushing to his side.

"That is *Kevin Kunnert's* sixth personal foul and he *leaves the game,*" the p.a. system said. An even louder cheer swelled up, and the crowd stood and continued cheering. Kunnert, still unable to move, was now trying to cover his face with his hands. He had to be carried off by two players, the crowd cheering as he left.

The Portland locker room was like a morgue. Ramsay was off by himself, unreachable. He no longer fired empty beer cans against the wall as he had earlier in his pro career, but the intensity was there. It was as if he were wearing a sign which said DO NOT DISTURB, DO NOT APPROACH. Reporters walking into the locker room for the ritual post-game interview took a step or two, saw his face and turned away. Gross was in another corner, his head bowed, covered by both hands. It was impossible to tell whether or not he was crying. It had been one of the worst nights of his pro career. His body was not yet ready and it was as if now, after two frustrating years of injuries and changes in team style, he was searching for the player he had been. David Twardzik, whose body was now in perpetual pain, was applying an ice pack to one of his knees. Both Owens and Kunnert, the two big men, were lying on the floor, ice packs on both knees. Culp, having sent out for more ice, was now applying medication to Owens's wrist because he had been cut during the game, probably by a fingernail. Finally Owens was able to get up. Kunnert seemed immobilized. Two Phoenix doctors came in and gave Kunnert a quick examination. It did not seem so bad, one of them said. Kunnert looked unconvinced. Finally, with the help of teammates they managed to prop him up and Culp helped him on with his pants. He looked like a man who had frozen both his legs. There was some question of which knee hurt most. It was a bad night. Portland had come into the game with too many injuries and now there were even more injuries. The euphoria of the winning streak was fading fast.

The next morning Ron Culp, who worked the longest hours of anyone on the team, got up at 4 a.m. The wakeup for the players was at 5:15, the bus was at 5:45. He got up earlier because he had to pack his own gear and get upstairs and begin the clumsy process of helping Kevin Kunnert dress. After getting Kunnert ready, he helped him to the lobby, went back and made a second phone check of the players and coaches and writers, then made sure that all his equipment, physical therapy machines, uniforms, basketballs, were packed, that the bus driver for the chartered bus actually knew the route to the airport. You could never, he had learned the hard way, be too sure. No one, save an early morning bellboy, helped with all this. Culp loaded most of the suitcases on the bus himself. In the contract of the players' union was a clause which said that the players had to carry their luggage only to and from the hotel lobby and their rooms. The trainer did all the rest. Once upon a time, in the medieval days of professional basketball, rookies had helped trainers with their more menial tasks; that was no longer true. Jimmy Paxson, who was a rookie on this team, made roughly six times what Ron Culp did, and though Paxson had exceptionally good manners, he did not load or unload bags.

This time the bus driver knew the way. At the airport the players, coaches and writers all headed to the restaurant to have the traditional American airport breakfast of eggs congealed in light plastic, chilled with the ice which was intended for the lukewarm fruit juice. While they ate, Culp, now team travel agent, stood at the departure gate making sure that all the players were in first class, as their union's contract demanded, and that the coaches, announcers and writers at least managed to get on board. Culp as trainer was part doctor, part therapist, part traveling sports information officer, part travel agent, part historian and part nursemaid. (A few months later, dealing with a rookie named Michael Harper who seemed vague about how to furnish his new Portland apartment with such necessities as sheets and dishes, Culp had said, "Michael, do you know who we're going to draft next year?" "No," said Harper. "Who?" "In the second round we're going to draft your mother," Culp said.) As a boy Culp had suffered from a rheumatic heart condition and had been unable to participate in organized athletics and had learned to take pleasure in the role of athlete by association. He had a degree in physical therapy and was a bright, hardworking man with a sharp, caustic sense of humor. Early in his career he had come to dislike the league for what on occasion it did to young, enthusiastic players, making them more cynical; now, he realized, among those who had changed the most was himself. When he had first come into the league, with Cleveland in 1970, and still when he joined Portland in the summer of 1974, he had believed in the idea of loyalty and the idea of team, that the players were connected to each other as part of something larger and there was a spiritual unity to sports, which he shared in. That belief had been strengthened by the championship season in which he, as trainer to the team and as Bill Walton's close friend, played a major part. Culp regarded the championship season as nothing less than—in his own words—a spiritual crusade, unselfish players playing with great generosity and moral conviction, who were close off the court as well as on and who, in the Lucas-Walton-Hollins friendship, seemed to symbolize athletic and racial togetherness. He did not merely minister to these athletes, he *believed* in them, not just in their victories but in their larger purpose.

Not everyone in the Portland organization felt as he did about loyalty. Jack Ramsay had come to Portland a year after Culp and Ramsay argued constantly with Culp that there was absolutely no loyalty in professional sports, that any management would inevitably let go of a once popular player the minute it thought he was fading, that it would fire a coach even more quickly and that the only change in the equation was that the new generation of players, unlike the old, understood this and now had the means and power to retaliate. Ramsay and Culp argued about this constantly, and Culp was sure that while Ramsay was generally right, there were exceptions to the rule; the Portland team, he felt, was such an exception, especially in the championship season.

Then in the spring of 1978 Culp's world had collapsed. First there had been the Walton injury, which knocked Portland out of the playoffs and which was eventually to have serious ramifications for everyone involved, terminating friendship with lawsuit. But more immediately painful for Culp had been what happened when the players met to vote shares of the playoff money. Since, by NBA standards, trainers were unusually poorly paid, their salaries in those days averaging some $22,000 a year, a share of the playoff money was important. It was, too, a way of the players tipping the trainers who had taped them dozens, perhaps a hundred or more times during the season, and performed countless other services, many of them menial. That day the players, with Maurice Lucas the dominating voice, voted not to give Ron Culp his expected share of the playoff money, roughly $2,500, though finally they gave him—it was as big a slap in the face—a quarter share. At first the players claimed that the vote was unanimous. In fact, as was soon evident, the vote had broken down along racial lines: the white players—Steele, Twardzik, Owens, Gross—had voted for him, the blacks against him. Clearly, Culp's sense of humor, which was often sharp, had stung blacks in some way that had not affected the whites, clearly also the blacks perceived him as being closer to the whites. That was certainly part of it. As he pieced them together later, some of the complaints voiced against him both in that meeting, and later when he sought out some of the players himself, were appallingly petty. Lionel Hollins had not liked the way he dressed, for Culp dressed in a suit or sports jacket, unlike other trainers who usually dressed in warmup clothes. Johnny Davis had resented the fact that when sportswriters came into the locker room after the game they often went to Culp before they talked to the players. Lloyd Neal, whom Culp had taped and taped until he was virtually a walking mummy, had resented the fact that the Christmas party had been held for the last two years at Culp's house, which he interpreted as Culp trying to show off his house. But the central complaint was his relationship with Walton: the black players had come to regard him as Bill Walton's private trainer, one more reflection of Walton's (white) superstar status. Culp, they claimed, had been too close to Bill Walton and spent too much time ministering to him instead of to the others. In retrospect Culp believed that there was considerable legitimacy to this viewpoint, though he wished they had come to him beforehand and warned him of how they felt. He *was* close to Walton; it was not just a professional relationship but a friendship and there were things done for Walton that were not done for anyone else. On the road all of Walton's incoming phone calls were funneled through Culp's room to protect Walton's privacy, and if Walton was going out to dinner, Culp often called ahead to secure a table in an uncrowded area so Walton could eat in relative peace, without having to deal with gawkers and autograph hounds.

At first Culp felt humiliated; he felt like the one kid at the playground who was not chosen in the pickup game. He had not been part of that specially blessed and unselfish community after all. But, gradually, as time passed and his personal wounds began to heal, he realized that he had been wrong—that what he thought he had been a part of, and had not, simply did not exist. This was a team of good basketball players who combined their talents well, that and apparently nothing more. The unselfishness was of only human proportions. The vote, he came to believe, had been aimed not so much at him but at *Walton*. Luke and Walton were supposed to be the best of friends and by the prevailing standards and mores of white stars and black stars in the contemporary professional league they were indeed friends. But the vote made plain the sort of latent resentments which Luke and the other players harbored towards Walton and towards his special status and salary. There was loyalty in sports, Culp decided, as long as the stakes were very small. Walton, stung by what happened, had thereupon gone to management and offered to make up the difference to Culp out of his own pocket. Harry Glickman said not to worry, that management would pay for it, though in fact it never did.

Shortly after that Walton made his own charges of improper medical care against both Dr. Cook and Culp. A little regretfully Culp told Ramsay that he had been right in maintaining that there were no real loyalties in professional sports. From then on he controlled his loyalty and never fully committed it again. He was not, as he had once believed, part of some spiritual community. Nor did he work as slavishly as he had previously. When players called in the middle of the night to complain about their (or their wives') minor aches, he found himself telling them where the nearest drugstore was. What he had was a job, a job he liked, but certainly nothing more. Actually, he thought, it was one of the best 5 a.m. to 11 p.m. nonexecutive jobs in the country.

BEFORE THE CLEVELAND game John White, the Blazer publicity man, was sitting in the pressroom handing out the historical minutiae of Cleveland-Portland games. White had held his job since the franchise began, and he was delighted that Bill Walton had gone to San Diego. John White did not like Bill Walton. "Best thing that ever happened, him going down there," he was saying. "He took years off my life. *Years* off it." The particular offense that Walton had committed against White was the most grievous that a professional athlete can inflict upon a publicity man—he had refused to give him his home phone number. That meant, in those days, whenever Walton was in the headlines either for a new injury or for assaults upon such American institutions as the FBI or the Presidency, there would be hundreds of phone calls from reporters all over the country. They would all be trying to reach Bill Walton, to get a statement from him or, best of all, get his home phone number so they could call him direct. That number was of course the one phone number in Oregon which John White was unable to procure. In time this became quite humiliating. White would be forced to say that he did not have the number. Not everyone believed him, and nearly everyone found it hard to accept the fact that White frequently was in no position to give them a statement from Walton because he hadn't been able to reach the great man himself. Often, given the time differences between the two coasts, he was awakened at 5 a.m. in order to supply what he could not produce. Old friends who had known White for twenty years, unable to reach Walton, took out their anger on White, and accused him of lying to them. Every radical and semisubversive in America, thought White, knows how to reach Bill Walton and I don't. Nor did White like Jack Scott, Walton's radical friend, who, he believed, superseded him and acted as Walton's personal publicity man, giving out his number to selected reporters, probably of the leftish persuasion. Scott of course knew the number because it was his *own* number, living over there in the same house, eating god knows what vegetables and herbs and roots, and smoking god knows what leaves and herbs and roots. This night, as White dispensed stat sheets, he was playing a guessing game with reporters. "I have something here which is going to be a very valuable piece of sports memorabilia in about ten years," he said. "Guess what it is." Most of the speculation centered around Inman. Perhaps, guessed one reporter, it was Inman's college uniform. Perhaps, said another, a photo of Inman playing for Alameda High School. No, said White, it's better and more valuable than that. Finally he unveiled it, a photo of a San Diego Clipper preseason game. "It's a picture of Bill Walton playing basketball for San Diego. Going to be worth a lot someday," he said.

Steve Kelley, diligent reporter, went to the Cleveland locker room to talk to Randy Smith, the Cleveland guard. Jack Ramsay was only three games away from winning his five hundredth pro game, a landmark event in the professional world, and Kelley planned a major piece about it. Since Smith had played for Ramsay for several years when they were both in Buffalo, Kelley was anxious to find out if it was true, as alleged, that Ramsay had mellowed since those days.

"Oh, yeah, man," said Randy, "it was rich. I mean Doctor Jack would get angry in those days, and that team was hard to coach and Jack did not like to lose and there'd be scenes, *great* scenes, man. Jack saying anyone who wanted to do it another way or wanted to challenge him could step out in the hallway. Great show. Doctor Jack is all right. Great coach. Got to do it his way, though."

Later that day Kelley asked Ramsay about the confrontations in Buffalo. "No, no, no," he said, "that stuff's all overblown. Nothing like that at all. You know how something small happens and then it gets exaggerated. There's nothing to it."

"But Jack," said Kelley, "I was just talking to Randy and he said there was a lot of it."

"Well," said Ramsay, beginning to laugh, "in that case, if he says so, I guess there was. Who remembers stuff like that anyway? That wasn't an easy team to coach. Those were not the players I wanted and we had to change a lot of them. . . ."

LENNY WILKENS, WHO had once been the Portland coach, walked through the Portland pressroom and everyone greeted him like the old friend he was. Stu Inman put a quick Inman special move on him, one reminiscent of Lyndon Johnson in his prime, left arm around the Wilkens right shoulder, right arm flexing and pumping the left Wilkens elbow, as if it were in dire need of more blood. "A good coach," Inman was saying to a passerby, "but he lacked the credentials as a player. But not a bad coach." Wilkens, the Seattle coach, smiled his smile, which was carefully circumscribed, not too big, not of course too small, the smile of a man who was always courteous and graceful, but who did not under any circumstances encourage intimacy. Lenny Wilkens was a finely controlled man. He did nothing to excess. He did not even curse. In the two frustrating years during which he had coached in Portland, years to try the soul of the strongest man, he had not blasphemed. Tom Meschery, his assistant, was his designated curser. One of their players might, at an important moment in a game, offer up a long hopeless jump shot, thus taking the team out of its patterned offense, and Meschery would burst into the requisite coaching blasphemy: "Jesus Christ, Lenny—did you see that shit?" Wilkens would then quickly nod his assent. *"I agree, I agree,"* he would say. Wilkens was a black man who had triumphed against great odds in a white world, the second black ever to coach in the league, and a man who always carried his own distance with him, and especially when he visited Portland. The two years he had coached in Portland had been the most frustrating in the franchise's history. They were the early Walton years, when the local expectations of fans, players and management were at their highest. At the end of the second year, just when Lenny Wilkens thought he had begun to put together the nucleus of a winning team, he had been fired by Larry Weinberg. Though Lenny Wilkens coached out of love for basketball—it was a sport he knew and cared about—he was also a very proud man and he regarded his coaching position as part of an ongoing demonstration of racial dignity. He was, in the best sense imaginable, an advertisement for what might be. Therefore to be fired in a profession he knew and loved by a man who, in his opinion, knew virtually nothing about basketball and who, even worse, had constantly frustrated his attempts to improve the team by trading Sidney Wicks—whom Wilkens considered the most disruptive force on the team—was especially painful. So far as Wilkens was concerned, Weinberg was an amateur with only the vaguest insight into the sport. He loved players with bloated statistics, he had little sense of the less visible actions by which players could positively (or negatively) affect a team, and he had, by refusing to trade Wicks, seriously limited Wilkens's options in that year. To be fired by such a man was a painful reminder that in twenty years some things had not changed.

On the day of the firing, Bill Walton had driven out to Lenny Wilkens's house and abjectly apologized for his own failures and ailments. The blame for the firing, he said, belonged to him. Wilkens had told him not to worry—that the best thing he could do was stay healthy and Portland would win the championship. As a matter of fact, that is precisely what had happened: Jack Ramsay had promptly arrived, Walton had stayed remarkably healthy and Portland had won the championship. In some ways Wilkens felt vindicated; the team that won was the team he had been trying to put together. As often happens in situations like this, Larry Weinberg also felt vindicated, absolutely convinced that a major share of the credit for the championship was his, because he had seen fit to make the coaching change.

For so proud a man, the pain of the firing had not soon gone away. Wilkens was one of the pioneer blacks in professional basketball, a man who spanned several generations in terms of the sport's racial history. All his life he had contested the racial stereotypes of American life. One of the main reasons he had decided to coach was to show, by his own personal example and conduct, the difference between stereotype and reality, what a black was and what he could do. In his twenty-five years in bigtime sports the American myths of black capability (and incapability) had gradually become more sophisticated. The early ones had been remarkably crude. In the forties, whites, having legally excluded blacks from professional competition, went to bigtime sports events and, failing to see any blacks, concluded that this proved them inferior athletes. (Track and field was of course different—being amateur instead of professional, it was open to blacks and everyone always knew *they* could *run* fast.) As segregation in sports broke down the myth refined itself. Soon there was a more subtle one, proclaiming that blacks lacked guts and were never tough in the clutch. That particular myth had fallen a little more slowly (in part because a great black pitcher named Don Newcombe, having pitched an otherwise superb game against the Yankees in the World Series, gave up a late-inning home run and lost) but gradually in the mid-sixties a generation of black cleanup hitters, sure-handed pass catchers and basketball players who always seemed to hit the last-second shot had gradually dispelled it. The latest incarnation of the black incapability myth was far more insidious. It acknowledged that blacks were *superb* natural athletes—if anything, some mythologists whispered, they might even be better than whites—but they were supposed to lack the capacity to think and make instantaneous judgments in the heat of battle. This was especially true, it was said, in football. Some twenty years after great black athletes like Jim Brown had helped break down stereotypes about black skills and black courage, that sport, a greater bastion of myth and superstition than either baseball or basketball, demonstrated its superstition by reserving the position of quarterback for whites. The implication was clear: blacks might have great natural ability and speed and balance, and even perhaps strong throwing arms, but they lacked the intelligence which that most sacred position demanded. Yet, in basketball, ironically, in terms of on-court performance, that particular myth had already fallen precisely because of the performances, starting early in the sixties, of men like Wilkens and Oscar Robertson who, in effect, played the role of quarterbacks. They ran their teams, controlled the action, and made under intense pressure the split-second decisions necessary to hold a team together. Often, with the clock running out, they took the last shot themselves. Leading a basketball team required no less skill or intelligence than leading a football team. The idea that Oscar Robertson could not, had he so chosen, become a great professional quarterback, was laughable, but in football the myth held.

In basketball another version of the myth survived. Could blacks coach? Could they handle players, including black players? They could, everyone now admitted, play with intelligence, but wasn't that really a natural gift? Didn't that instinct just come to them? Could they really sit down like a white coach and draw on a blackboard the X's and O's that defined the analytical game and distinguished it from the free-flow game that was native to the black? It was in that particular context, and Lenny Wilkens's own career-long personal campaign against stereotyping, that his firing in Portland had to be weighed. He was an early black coach, in a profession which had become black at the bottom but remained white in its hierarchy. By being fired he had been told that something larger had failed. He had deeply resented it.

When Wilkens had left Portland therefore, he had done so with a considerable amount of concealed resentment. He had gone north to Seattle where he became director of player personnel. Then in 1977, with a dismal 5 and 17 at the start of the season, he had taken over as coach, changed the lineup dramatically and turned Seattle into a powerful, winning team. He had very quickly gained a reputation as a skilled coach, regarded by his players as a man unusually sensitive to their anxieties who, because of his own long career, understood what bothered players and scared them. He was known for being very good with his men, telling them what he expected of them, what their role would be, and then sticking to that.

Seattle in the spring of 1978 had returned to Portland for a Western conference playoff series against the Blazers. It was a severe test for Wilkens's emotions. Preparing his team he had begun to harp so much on the advantages Portland had at home, the big intensely partisan crowd, the constant noise, the intimidation of referees—the referees always let the Portland players hold their opponents—that finally his assistant, Les Habegger, had taken him aside. "Lenny," Habegger had said, "we've got to do certain things to win these games and we've got to think of them as *basketball* games. It can't be personal. That hurts us. You've got to forget about beating Portland. We're going to win *basketball* games, not get revenge on Portland." "Yeah," said Wilkens, "I know, but sometimes it's hard."

IN THE SECOND game of the playoffs in 1978, Walton broke his foot and Seattle won the series. In Portland the loss magnified the frustration caused by Walton's injury: Seattle, the hated rival to the north, had won with a lesser team and had *usurped* Portland's rightful longterm glory. Portland-Seattle games, always intense rivalries, had become more so. In 1978 Seattle had gone on to the finals before losing to Washington. The following year, 1979, it won the championship. Now Seattle arrived in town, a troubled team, trying to cope with the problems of success. In the 1979 championship series, Dennis Johnson, known as DJ, a Seattle guard, had been named the most valuable player in the series. This year his photo was on the cover of the official NBA guidebook. But winning the championship had not made Seattle a stronger or happier team, rather it magnified existing problems, especially those of Dennis Johnson. Even in the championship season he had been something of an erratic player in the view of some teammates, given over to more than occasional moodiness and sulking. On a team where the roles of the players were very carefully prescribed, rather like the old Celtics, DJ more than any other Sonic player had slipped out of his role. The post-championship renegotiation of his salary, from $75,000 to $400,000, had not made him happier; rather, he had become, if anything, moodier. In addition, some teammates thought it had changed his own perception of his game and his role. Now he saw himself not just as a great defensive player and jumper, but as a scorer. He seemed to resent the fact that in the Seattle system Gus Williams, the other guard, was permitted to take long shots and he was not. When Wilkens tried to guide DJ back into his system and to his proper role, he became resentful. He complained that the coach was critical only of him, never of the other players, never of Gus. He was, this early in the season, already beginning to challenge Wilkens's authority in little ways, showing up late for practice, loafing in practice, looking the other way when Wilkens was talking or, more and more, talking back to him. Silas, like Wilkens a veteran of many years in the NBA, was disturbed about what was happening. He believed that Wilkens was letting the problem get out of hand, and that it would only get worse. But Wilkens, with only a quarter of the season gone, believed that he would be able to handle DJ. He was proud of his reputation as a coach who could understand and relate to his players and yet at the same time summon their best efforts on the court. Their problems, he felt, were so similar to problems he himself had experienced. Silas accepted that, but he also believed that this time Wilkens's magic was not working, that quite steadily Dennis Johnson was becoming more and more resentful, not just of Wilkens, but of Silas, and even John Johnson, another veteran, who up until then had been Dennis's best friend on the team.

Silas thought of himself and Wilkens as survivors of another era in the NBA. They were among the early blacks to play and their careers ran from that time of overt prejudice and smaller salaries to the modern era of huge salaries and more subtle racial frustrations and anxieties. He regarded Dennis Johnson as typical of many of the new players now entering the league, far more talented than their predecessors of fifteen years ago, but with their

raw talent far outstripping their capacity to deal with the immensely complex social situations into which their ability and affluence had catapulted
them. Silas had been, over his long career, one of the prime movers in creating a players' union, and he was proud of the great gains that the union had
made in advancing players' salaries, including his own. But he also believed
that many players were now coming into big money far too soon for their
own good. Superstars in high school, coveted by college recruiters, always
stroked and coddled and catered to, they could not deal well with reality or
adversity, either on or off the basketball court.

Many of the new young stars were black, and Silas considered himself in
a better position to say these things to them than a white player or coach
would be. He and Wilkens had discussed Dennis Johnson, and Silas allowed the justice of Wilkens's position, that you had to give a player as talented and sensitive as Dennis Johnson room to grow, you could not make
him conform. But Silas saw the drawbacks too. First, the more flexibility
Wilkens showed, the less respect Johnson had for him. Second, DJ's behavior was tearing Seattle apart. It was not playing like a championship team;
nor did it *feel* like a championship team. A championship team, he believed,
had a certain respect of coach for players and players for coach, and, above
all, of players for each other. A respect that had its own built-in discipline.
Silas had played for the Boston Celtics, and he had not at first believed the
myth of the Celtics as being special. But very soon he became a convert, and
one of the things he admired most was the way in which Red Auerbach
made the players themselves the keepers of the tradition, and thus the en-
forcers of their own discipline. He sensed that on this team Dennis Johnson
was now a threat to the entire delicate mechanism. Perhaps, thought Lenny
Wilkens, perhaps Silas was right, but for the moment he was trying desperately to reach his talented young player, trying to excuse the rudeness and
the rebuffs he was receiving. He was convinced that if any coach in professional basketball could understand Dennis Johnson, could identify with his
problems and the complexity of his world, it was Lenny Wilkens. He saw
himself, quite rightly, as a pioneer both in race relations and in changing
the labor laws that made it possible for young players to negotiate huge salaries. It was odd to deal with a young man who had so little respect for what
had gone before, so little appreciation of the past.

When Lenny Wilkens was a young player, after several years as a premier guard in the NBA, slowly edging his salary up to the grand figure of $14,000 a year, he had found that he and Ben Kerner, one of the last of the old-style owners, were still $2,000 apart. Then it was only $1,000.

"Are you going to let a thousand dollars stand between us?" Kerner had asked.

"No," said Wilkens.

"Good," said Kerner, handing over the contract, "sign this."

And Lenny Wilkens had signed.

It was as if much of the racial history of the sport could be summed up in his life. Wilkens had entered the league in 1960 when blacks were still very much a *they*. He was the second black player on a great team (the St. Louis Hawks) where blacks were not terribly well received, either by fans or for that matter teammates; by the time he played his last game in 1975, the NBA was a predominantly black league; eighteen of the twenty-four players on the all-star team were black. He had lived through all that and yet stereotypes remained; there were basketball people who still felt that blacks could not really think on the court, and there appeared to be a double standard in coaching. White coaches, Wilkens knew, could year after year have records that were dangerously close to .500 and still be regarded as valuable. The axe would fall more quickly on a black, he suspected.

In 1960, when he arrived in St. Louis to join the Hawks, they had a single black player, Sihugo Green, who had played there only one full season. Three seasons earlier an all-white Hawks team had won the NBA championship and that nucleus remained. The big star was Bob Pettit, one of the truly great players in the league's history, and there were two other popular players, Clyde Lovellette and Cliff Hagan. The Big Three, they were called, and it was the job of the other players to make sure they remained stars. Si Green had found, joining the team, that he was under orders to rebound and play defense; he was supposed to make sure that the ball went to the Big Three and to take as few shots as possible himself. It was still a primitive league with players who were not only white, but who—unlike the white players in generations to come—had almost never even played with blacks in school or college. The nation in the fifties had been segregated far more completely than it realized. The outstanding black athlete was still an exception.

There were subtle tensions on a team like this. The veterans dressed at one end of the locker room, the rookies at the other. The veterans were almost all white, the rookies more and more black. St. Louis was still a southern town, not yet ready for integration. There were restaurants and hotels the whites could go to and places—other places—that the blacks could go to. Not only were the team's stars white, but so too were the fans, which made management nervous about promoting the new black players. Wilkens once got what was for him a rare promotional appearance at a department store. His pleasure in the $25 he received dimmed when he found out that Pettit and Hagan had each received $75. That was St. Louis, and probably the other cities too. White players got the good things, the points in the stat sheet, the promotional appearances and the tips for the stock market that eager businessmen, anxious to include famed athletes in their entourages, were on occasion willing to hand out.

In the beginning there was a joking but real racism to the team: Lovellette sometimes teased Si Green, when they arrived at airports, by saying, "Bwana, get my bag," jokes that were often not jokes. There were words, Wilkens believed, thought but never spoken, and he knew that when Si Green was playing and would make a turnover, the whites would not say anything, they would simply raise their eyebrows as if to say, *what can you expect, that's the way they are.* In the beginning it was a loneliness the like of which the young Lenny Wilkens, late of Brooklyn and Boys High, then of Providence College, had never known before and for which he had not been prepared. It was as if he was always being tested: by his opponents who were white, by the referees who were white, by the fans who were white, by the owners of restaurants who were white, and even by his teammates who were white. He felt himself a man without a real community; in the beginning most of his own teammates simply tolerated him. There was one major exception to all of this, Cliff Hagan, once of Kentucky, who seemed to know no racial prejudice. In a quiet understated way Hagan befriended the young Wilkens, and they ate together on the road; they even went out together with their wives which, given the times, was even more delicate. Acceptance came more slowly with Pettit, who had played in Louisiana in the early fifties, and whose mores were set in a very different time. Professional acceptance came quickly, as Wilkens was by far the best guard the Hawks had, a superb playmaker and passer. He could feed Pettit the ball where and when he wanted it. Wilkens felt that it took several years for Pettit to accept him as a man, though that too eventually came. But the early years were very hard on him. He had never in his life been around so much prejudice and in the off-season he could not wait to return to New York.

In the sixties the league and the team changed quickly. More and more blacks arrived. Eyebrows were no longer raised over black mistakes. Now more and more the jokes were about whether white centers could dunk the ball. By 1968, when Wilkens finally left, the Hawks—now in Atlanta—were on their way to becoming one of the first great black basketball teams in the league. The old white stars had gradually moved on, to be replaced by talented blacks like Wilkens, Zelmo Beaty, Bill Bridges, Paul Silas, Joe Caldwell, Lou Hudson, all exceptional players and role players as well. For a time, five blacks started; then a white player was obtained so that at least one white could start at home, and Joe Caldwell, averaging nearly twenty points a game, went, much to his displeasure, to the bench. What was happening in St. Louis was typical of what was happening around the league: as the game became more exciting, faster, blacker, it was moving ahead of the fans' capacity to accept it, to accept both the new level of play and the blackness of the players who exemplified it. There was a certain shakiness to many of the franchises, and yet, because of the coming of television, because owners had realized that television was bound to change professional sports, make them bigtime and almost certainly profitable, the league was expanding. New franchises appeared, owners and cities anxious to get in, and salaries, with the arrival of a rival league, rose. Wilkens had signed in 1960 for $8,000 a year with a $1,500 bonus. Now, ten years later, sports had access to a new larger entertainment dollar and the money was there for salaries. Wilkens could sense the change in Ben Kerner, the owner of the Hawks, who seemed to have less taste for the job. Kerner was different from the new owners, young self-made millionaires who, having conquered their own professions at a young age, were now looking around for something to relieve the boredom and anonymity of life—owning a sports franchise, running for the U.S. Senate. For Kerner, professional basketball was a business. Every dollar in it was his own. One year he boasted to Wilkens that he had run the entire club for $100,000. Now, as the team became blacker, fan acceptance diminished, and Wilkens sensed that the management seemed hesitant to promote the new players. St. Louis was in the process of getting a professional hockey team, a decidedly whiter sport with great appeal to blue collar whites, which would play in a new arena. An agreement to share the premises failed. Kerner could see the handwriting on the wall; he was the poor boy in the new rich man's poker game. Other teams were now routinely signing players for more than $100,000 a year. His time had clearly passed. So he sold the club to owners in Atlanta where, primarily for racial reasons, it remained a troubled franchise for a decade to come. Lenny Wilkens, unable to come to terms with the new owners, was traded to Seattle and moved to the Northwest, first playing and then becoming a player-coach, before being traded once more to Cleveland and at last ending up in Portland, first as player-coach (anxious to play with Bill Walton) and finally as coach.

A Seattle-Portland game was always special. There was a natural rivalry between the two cities, particularly as far as Portland was concerned. Besides, though it was never spoken and never admitted, both coaches liked to beat each other. Wilkens liked to beat Portland, particularly *in* Portland; even for a man with a limited sense of vengeance it was a natural thing to do. Ramsay equally wanted to beat Wilkens, partly because as an ex-jock Wilkens was to a degree an outsider in the coaching club and partly because he wanted to demonstrate that it was not just luck and not just a healthy Walton that had produced those two great teams in 1977 and 1978. All of this was without rancor, no angry words were ever spoken, but the feeling before a Portland-Seattle game was special.

Nor could the two men have been more different in their styles and attitudes. Among players Ramsay was the ultimate coach's coach, a man of consummate discipline who believed above all in his system, and seemed to have more confidence in it, the players sometimes believed, than he did in them. Everything about him was professional. Nothing was left to chance. His scouting and his breakdowns of opponents before a game were acute, complete and prophetic. He expected certain things to happen on the court and they almost always did. In his world the coach was important, very important. By contrast Wilkens was now known in the league as a players' coach, a coach who used certain plays but was willing to let his players follow their natural instincts, make their own adjustments on the court. Some of his players believed that he had more trust in them and their natural ability than did coaches like Ramsay or John MacLeod of Phoenix. In addition the courtside manner of the two men seemed to reflect their different personalities. Ramsay, to the average fan, seemed on occasion almost out of control, so intense was he during a game. He quite deliberately fought with officials, contesting and challenging them, raging against the injustice of bad calls. Sometimes he did this because he wanted to change the tempo of a game, sometimes because he wanted to affect the way his own players played, but mostly because he hoped to invade the minds of the referees themselves, to make them think twice before they reached for the whistle again, to say to themselves no, no, if I do that I have to deal with Ramsay and I don't want the hassle, particularly here in Portland with 12,666 people ready to follow his charge. Ramsay, one of the most theatrical of coaches, always aware of the crowd, had his various roles down pat. Sometimes it was just pure visceral anger, visible even in the cheaper seats. Sometimes (a friend called it his away-game move, for opposing crowds) when he wanted to be a little more subtle, to reach the referee without inciting the enemy crowd, he would do it with light body language—Jack Ramsay as the pilgrim at Lourdes, face in slight pain, hands extended in the time-honored stance of the supplicant seeking help: I want, if not your mercy (he seemed to say), at least your earnest consideration. Early in the season, when he had worked a referee named Tommy Nunes a little too hard, Nunes had walked over to Ramsay and yelled at him, "Jack, you've been having at me for seven years. Why don't you come and get me?" Then Nunes had begun to shake his body like a disco dancer who believed her belly was the most seductive offering imaginable. Ramsay had not taunted Nunes for the rest of the evening or, for that matter, for the rest of the season.

Wilkens, by contrast, rationed his emotions. He did not want to lose his own dignity and he did not want his players losing theirs. We will not, his face, his style, always so cool, seemed to say, be pulled down to your level. During a game, no matter how important, he never raged. He would, provoked by a call of the most dubious origin at the most vital moment, show a slight condescension, his eyes rising to the ceiling, his face going into the basic Wilkens pose, worthy of the family album: abiding, stoic, patient. Sometimes the silent ceiling gaze could strike doubt into the heart of those refereeing: was Lenny, already widely regarded as the closest thing in the league to a saint, actually communing with God?

This time, in 1979, Portland looked stronger, though both teams were absolutely exhausted. Each was playing its third game in three nights. Portland could dress only eight players. But somehow playing Seattle seemed to make a difference. Kermit Washington seemed stronger than ever. He had played 44 minutes the night before and tonight he played 38. Against this very physical team he had 15 rebounds. Dennis Johnson, by contrast, seemed to be playing in a funk. He hoisted up long jump shots, and often when they failed to go in, Portland started a fast break. Midway in the third quarter Portland had a 17-point lead. When Wilkens took Dennis Johnson out, he seemed not to see the player. They did not talk and Wilkens's eyes appeared to be searching a distant corner of the Coliseum, as if someone seated there might hold up a sign on which would be written the secret of how to deal with so talented and so troubled a young man. Portland eventually won by 5 points. Dennis Johnson went 5 for 16.

Later, in the locker room, a Seattle sportswriter approached him.

"Dennis, about those jump shots . . ." he began.

"What jump shots?" DJ said. "I didn't see any jump shots." He turned to John Johnson near him. "You see any jump shots? Were any out there? Not that I saw." He seemed to be smiling.

KAREEM ABDUL-JABBAR, ONE of the great players in the game of basketball, sat in the lobby of the Benson Hotel, then Portland's finest, at midmorning in a bizarre costume of lavish purple pants and lavish purple jacket. On the back of the jacket it said, to no one's surprise, *Lakers*. It was the costume of his trade. Seated around him were white American businessmen also wearing the costumes of their trades, gray suits, blue shirts, striped ties; there was an almost physical collision of different men and different worlds. They had stared at him and he had looked at them and through them—his look had simply obliterated them, it was one of the most powerful looks of nonrecognition imaginable. Some of them quickly turned and looked away and others busied themselves with their newspapers. He was, like them, a businessman among businessmen, and he was there to ply his trade that night in the Portland Coliseum. Like other businessmen, he had his expenses paid, room and meal money, and like them he was dealing as best he could with inflation; that season his new owner (he had an owner and they did not) had raised his salary from something like $600,000 a year to $1 million a year. He was exceptionally well paid for his primary role, that of the most valuable player in the league, and his secondary role, which was to play in the twenty-one other cities which the Lakers visited that year, the part of the villain. His main predecessor in that role, Wilt Chamberlain, had once said that no one cheers for Goliath. Kareem could have added the Abdul-Jabbar corollary: Goliaths do not come cheap.

He was very tall and his height was a matter of some conjecture. He listed his height as 7′2″. Other very tall young men, seven feet even, who had played against him, swore he was at least 7′4″. Some, not given to exaggeration, said he was surely 7'6". What most people did not see was the grace, the agility so rare in any man, but truly astonishing in a man of his height; they saw only the height, which was greater than their own. Failing to see the grace, they also failed to see the passion, which was brilliantly concealed, hidden behind two layers of masks, first a protective eyepiece which was a mask to the face, and then the face itself which was a mask to the soul. They saw the lack of emotion and decided that Kareem did not care as they cared. In a comic movie he appeared in as, of all things, an airline pilot, a young boy accused him of loafing on the court. Not only little boys in movies, or fans, did this—sometimes it was professional basketball men. Players never did. They revered him as they did few others—perhaps Julius Erving for his natural ability and Paul Silas for his intelligence and character. But they were in genuine awe of Kareem and what he did every night, and the burden which, as so great a player, he brought to every game. Nor did the black players like it when white media people talked of Kareem and Bill Walton in the same breath; Walton to them was a special talent, but he was only a flash, a season and a half, while Kareem was a *career*. Others in the game were not so sure. A previous Laker coach, Jerry West, frustrated on one occasion with a season that had gone sour, betrayed his attitude by turning to near-strangers after a game and saying of Kareem, "Did you see that? *I mean did you see that? Is that a joke or is that a joke?*"

His play had, if anything, too much consistency to it. His good games were forgotten, his bad ones remembered. He had played for much of his career on weak teams or on teams poorly designed for him. Often too much depended on him, and because he was so dominating a force, opposing teams always knew that the key to stopping the Lakers was stopping Kareem. His teams, strong in their regular-season records, tended to wear down in playoff games. Opponents always based their strategy on stopping him and he rarely got very much help from referees. He was held, fouled and elbowed more than any other player in the league, all with the semitacit approval of the referees; for in truth, if they did not allow his opponents some small advantage there would be no way of stopping him. It was, in a way, the highest compliment that could be paid a professional athlete, the fact that they adapted the rules to limit his dominance, and he raged against it constantly, though his rage was often secret. It was, he knew, something which went with his territory and in this league his territory was too vast.

He was private, distant, black, obviously alienated and obviously privileged. He lived famous and rich and successful in a nation where everyone stopped and stared at him; discourteous as their behavior might be, there was always an implication that the fault was *his*, for being so tall and thus so different; were he more normal, they would not have *needed* to stare. So he had learned to keep his distance; almost nothing good came from casual contact with strangers. He was suspicious even of those who were supposed to be his friends. In high school, his coach had once said to him, "You're playing like a nigger." The taunt had been meant to incite him to a higher level of passion; it was neither the first nor the last wound.

Even teammates approached him cautiously. Only Lucius Allen, a guard, by contrast tiny, a friend and teammate from both college and professional days, was allowed to tease him. Tease Kareem he did, warning his friend that unless he shaped up, he, Allen, was going to get *Awtrey*, Badass Awtrey, to shape him up. Badass Awtrey was Dennis Awtrey, a journeyman white center with the face of an angelic bartender, a player of little distinction beyond the fact that he had once taken Kareem out with one punch, to the latter's enduring shame. That punch and his ability to get under Kareem's skin had, to everyone's surprise, helped keep Awtrey in the league a full decade.

Kareem was rich, he was a Muslim, he was serious about his religion; he had studied Arabic at Harvard, he had an impressive collection of Oriental rugs, he was in the process of writing a book for a serious publisher on the subject of rugs. He was an admirable citizen and yet acceptance, which came so readily to athletes of far less ability and principle, came slowly to him. Part of it was his size, part of it was his decision to become a Muslim, and part of it was his style of play. He played with conservation of energy that befit a man in a league where there could be over a hundred games a season and, worse, he played with conservation of emotion. That for the fans was the hardest thing to accept. He played hard but his style was cool. One could imagine him playing and listening to a Miles Davis cassette at the same time, playing to his own mood and tempo, not the tempo of the crowd, in the process putting distance between himself and the fifteen or twenty thousand who had come to see him. It was as if he held back the part of himself that should have said he *cared*. The crowd cared, its lives in other areas were sufficiently incomplete; this game, this minute, this basket, mattered; the crowd wanted him to care as well. He did not deny them his skills or even, in a curious way, his passion; rather he denied them passion revealed. Walton by contrast showed his exuberance on the court, he was totally boyish without cynicism or restraint, both star and cheerleader; as the crowd cared, so too he, most explicitly, cared. Kareem was different. He was, thought Walton's friend Jack Scott, the perfect product of the NBA machinery: he understood the mechanics of the league, the demands of its schedule, and he understood how to keep his integrity while adjusting to the rhythm of the league.

Now, in the Portland Coliseum, he started walking towards the court for practice. A number of reporters approached him.

"Kareem," one of them began, "how do you like playing alongside Magic?" The words seemed to die as they came out.

He turned them away. He did this silently, without even a scowl, but with so distant and imperious a look that nothing was encouraged, indeed would even be tolerated. He walked onto the court. The one player he seemed to have time for was Abdul Jeelani who, his own practice session an hour away, came running on the court to talk to him. Allah was praised and Allah was proud.

All of this made Kareem less than a great media figure. He frustrated not just the representatives of print, he frustrated CBS, virtual sponsor of the league, both on the court and off the court. In interviews at halftime or after a game he was always intelligent and correct.

Question: "Kareem," would say the announcer, usually Rod Hundley, composing what was by sports announcing standards a question, "you played a great game out there today!"

Answer: "Thank you very much."

So much for the personal touch.

This season, frustrated by Kareem, CBS had fastened on both his young effervescent teammate Magic Johnson, and Larry Bird of the Celtics, the other rookie. Both were asked for exceptional numbers of endorsements, sneakers to wear, colas to drink. Magic, who came from a strong family, was a marvelous media draw, and Bird, his social pathology much more like that of many black players in the league—busted home, disappearing father, rural instincts in a world run by city boys—was by contrast dour. When the camera approached, Magic smiled and Bird turned inside himself. CBS, worried about weak ratings, now hyped the Boston-Los Angeles games. The matchups were, said Brent Musburger, The Magic Man versus The Bird. Magic loved it, it was all hype and fun—Bird hated it. Forwards—and he was a forward—did not play against guards.

In CBS's first game of the year Kareem had hit the last basket in the final seconds and Magic had raced over to embrace him in what was dangerously close to an unnatural act. Along Madison Avenue there was a great sigh of relief. The camera had caught all of it, including the stunned look on Kareem's face.

Now, after the Laker practice, the press waited for Magic. Everybody wanted a piece of him. It had been a long time since a black athlete had come into the league who was so enthusiastic and thus so reassuring. Perhaps not since Willie Mays in another sport and another era had there been a black athlete so ingenuous and so boyish. But no one had ever had to sell the innocence of baseball—baseball was as innocent as the memory of every village green, even to those who had never set foot on one. But basketball was different. Its media franchisers, the people in the commissioner's office, the people who ran CBS Sports, the people who sold the commercials for television, were finding it worrisome. Not only was it less linked to the American myth, not only were its players blacker—and more obviously so, given the skimpiness of their uniforms compared to baseball and football—but they had also become, over the years, more politicized, prouder and more outspoken. Some, like Kareem, had been unwilling to play for the U.S. Olympic team. Madison Avenue already had its doubts about professional as opposed to college basketball. Athletes were increasingly viewed by Madison Avenue as articulate but surly and ungrateful or, just as bad, grateful but inarticulate.

Thus did the network and the league fasten on Magic. Now every time the Lakers visited a new city Magic would hold interviews, not one large mass interview with everyone present, but individual interviews, thirty seconds with each station.

"My impression, *Magic Johnson*," the television reporter was saying as his hand jammed the microphone towards the young player, "is that *you* enjoy playing basketball."

The smile appeared. "Yes, I like it and I like it in front of all these people."

Next interview: "Magic, I can call you Magic, can't I? What's the greatest difference between the professional game and the college game?"

A big smile. "Every player is good. Can't take any naps out here."

Next interview: "What do you think of tonight's game?"

Still the smile. "Well, it's tough. Every game is tough."

Next interview: "Who's the toughest player to guard?"

"Lloyd Free, because he can take it in by himself, doesn't need the pick to score; you lay off him, he's going to hit it."

Final question: "What's the hardest thing about being a professional?"

Pause. Smile disappears. "Doing all these interviews."

Then he was gone. Over in the Portland locker room Jack Ramsay had finished running through the Los Angeles offense for his team. Now they had all gone. He was sitting staring at his own blackboard as if to discover one last secret with which Tom Owens's thin body might neutralize the stronger, more agile one of Kareem.

"Jack," a reporter began, "if you win tonight that's five hundred career wins."

"I don't think about things like that," he said. "I don't know what five hundred victories means. Maybe it means I've stayed around the league a long time. I know what I want tonight. I want to stop the big guy. I know what that means."

The crowd gathered early under the Laker basket to watch Magic. He brought with him not just his own joy but a public display of his excitement. At his best, he was one of the most innovative new players in the game; he appeared to invent a new pass and a new move every time he had the ball. He had the height of a forward, 6'8", but he played guard, where men in the past had only been 6'4", or, at best, 6'5". He had the potential for changing the way the game was played. In basketball there is something called the transition game: a team is on offense, it puts up a shot, the shot misses, the defensive team takes the rebound and starts downcourt. The second or two in which the teams change over, offense to defense, defense to offense, is called the transition period; traditionally, it was the bigger men who had to rebound, and then, because they were not very good ball-handlers, they passed the ball off to smaller guards who were ballhandlers. But because Magic was so tall he was able at once to rebound and then lead the attack up the court without passing off himself. That made it harder for the defensive team to set up and it dramatically altered the flow of the game. Still, the other players were not sure he was a *player* yet. That was their word, a player. All the hype and hoopla worked against him. Hype and hoopla were white, written by whites and sold by whites, and they did not often connect to the core of basketball. Magic's shot was puzzling, he was always a little off-balance when he took it, the ball coming out of a jumble of arms and elbows and legs, all seemingly going in different directions. Perhaps, thought some scouts, he was not a good enough pure shooter. Coaches were a little wary because he did not seem to be a player for a set offense and most coaches liked their teams to run set patterns—Magic was at his best when the patterns had broken down.

The NBA jury had decided within the first week that Bird was a *player*. It was still out on Magic. That night there was no evidence that he had arrived. Portland played exceptional team defense. Owens and Washington denied Kareem the position he wanted, and on occasion when he attained position, the ball. T. R. Dunn, the team's strongest defensive guard, had taken away Magic's game. Abdul Jeelani, a great streak shooter, had come in and hit two quick baskets. There had been a time-out and behind the Laker bench a fan, powerful of lung, had yelled, "Hey, Kareem, how does it feel to be the second-best Abdul on the floor?" Late in the second half some calls went against Kareem. He screamed at the referee and the injustice. No referee on the court seemed taller than 6′2″. Can a mortal of human dimensions mete out justice to an immortal of 7′2″? For a moment, Kareem appeared out of control, the mask stripped away; he became an immense tangle of arms and legs screaming down at some tiny smaller species. The angrier he became, the more his arms and legs seemed to go in different directions—a huge black crane yelling at a small gray object. The crowd loved it, loved seeing someone so tall become so angry. It validated their evening, *they* had done it to him. No wonder he usually conserved his emotion. He could only fire up an opposing crowd.

In the end, Portland won by fifteen points. The locker room was like a Blazer alumni association meeting. All the old players were back: Petrie, Neal, LaRue Martin, Greg Smith. For Petrie, coming to games and visiting the locker room to joke with old friends like Larry Steele who were still active marked something he had been able to do only in the past few months. For his career, one of the most successful in the game, had been abbreviated by serious knee injuries, and this had put him into so deep a depression that for a long time he could not bear any association with basketball. He had been Portland's first great star, for a long time its most popular player, and there were many who believed that his jersey, like that of Lloyd Neal, should have been retired there.

He had come to Portland in 1970, the first year of the franchise's existence, after graduating from Princeton and he had, for a harried Stu Inman, the chief scout given only two months to select players, turned out to be a superb first-round draft choice. He was a guard, a rare pure shooter, his touch some thought was as good as that of the legendary Jerry West. Once during practice Petrie had bet Wayne Thompson, a writer for the Portland *Oregonian,* that he could not only hit eight jump shots in a row, but hit them in such a way that each time the ball would come right back to him. He had proceeded to do exactly that, with his first seven shots, although on the eighth the ball went through the hoop but did not come back. Still it was a feat of skill which stunned Thompson for it meant not just making a basket, but making it at so precise an angle that the ball would touch the back of the rim and bounce right back. That, Thompson thought, was a real shooter. Petrie, in a city starved for sports heroes, had been chosen with David Cowens as co-rookie of the year, a rare honor, made particularly impressive because he had been competing against such formidable rookies as Bob Lanier, Rudy Tomjanovich and Pete Maravich. He was an immensely popular player, young, handsome, white, he looked like a sports hero should, and his skills were evident even to neophyte fans—which, in fact, was what Portland's fans were. But what started as an uncommonly happy experience had quickly dimmed; the next year the team added another superstar, Sidney Wicks, considered by many the outstanding college player of the year, and the talents of Petrie and Wicks never meshed, nor had their personalities. Defeat and a certain malaise followed; later those years were known in Portland and by others in the profession as the Wicks-Petrie years, a time remembered for two players of rare ability who were utterly at cross-purposes, and who, playing in the right circumstances on other teams, might have flourished. Other basketball men counseled the Portland management to trade one if not both players (Wicks particularly) while their market value was still high and before they both took on a loser's mentality.

Geoff Petrie had never thought of himself as having a loser's mentality. Quite the contrary. He thought he was a winner laboring under uncommonly difficult circumstances, playing with weak expansion players against experienced, far stronger teams, and often playing in considerable pain. Very early in his second season he had torn the cartilage in his knee, a very bad tear, and had immediately undergone an operation. The repair of knee cartilage, he was to learn the hard way, constituted the most serious possible business for a professional athlete, particularly a professional basketball player. But he was young, basketball was not yet a business to him, and he was caught up in the mood of Portland, a city which had quickly looked to him as a hero. Sidney Wicks had just arrived and everyone's hopes for the second season were still high. Though other basketball players protected their knees, the most vulnerable part of a basketball player's anatomy, with the care a great surgeon might devote to his hands, and though most players with an injury like that would have taken minimally six months to a year off, Petrie, moved by collegiate sentiment, had returned in scarcely more than six weeks. Much later in his career, knowing far more about the seriousness of the injury, knowing that a repaired knee was never again the same, *never*, and knowing more about the coldness of the world of professional sports, Geoff Petrie realized he had made a terrible mistake. Nevertheless he returned, he played in considerable pain, and other knee injuries, some, friends thought, compensatory ones, soon followed. Because his knees were in constant pain he began taking Butazolidin, "bute," as a painkiller, and for a time it was helpful. But soon he was up to four and six pills a day, and getting less relief. At that point Bob Cook, the team doctor, became alarmed at how much bute Petrie was using and, fearing it would affect his blood balance, warned him off.

At the end of the 1976 season Petrie had hurt his knee again and missed the last five games of the season. That spring Portland changed coaches and Jack Ramsay had become the fifth coach of the Portland Trail Blazers in their seven-year history. Almost the first question that Ramsay had to deal with was what to do about Petrie and Wicks. Ramsay, Petrie thought, indicated that he wanted him to stay and play, but there were now complicating problems. Petrie's contract had run out, and at the same time he needed another knee operation. Petrie wanted the new contract *before* he had the operation. He had already become a good deal less sentimental about professional basketball. Portland, it turned out, wanted him to have the operation first and then would sign him. For a time it appeared that he was close to signing, but the deal fell through. Shortly thereafter, on the eve of the beginning of Portland's championship season, Geoff Petrie was traded to Atlanta in a deal that allowed Portland to pick up Maurice Lucas from the ABA dispersal pool. His knee, it turned out, was more seriously damaged than anyone thought. He could not play that year. He had another operation, his fifth major knee operation, but the knee remained a problem. Still, he was assured by his agent, Larry Fleisher, that other teams were very interested in him, most particularly the New York Knicks. He might, after all, still be the best pure shooter in the league. Willis Reed, coaching New York, put an offer on the table for five years at an average of roughly $325,000 a year. Petrie, somewhat anxious, for the real depression had not yet set in, flew to New York to meet with the Knicks officials and sign a contract.

It was June of 1977. Portland had just won the championship. Everything was in order, but first he had to be examined by Dr. James Nicholas, the New York specialist on athletic medicine. Petrie visited Dr. Nicholas in the company of Fleisher, Willis Reed and several Knicks officials. Years later, Petrie remembered not just Nicholas's words but the cold tone: "I'm sorry but I have to tell you that you have one of the worst knees I've ever seen. I'm afraid, young man, that I am recommending to the Knicks against signing you. I don't think you can ever play basketball again."

Petrie, hearing those words, hearing that his career was over though he was only twenty-nine, felt a terrible anger, most of it aimed at the doctor who was standing right there terminating his basketball life so quickly and seemingly so casually. "Do you know who's upstairs waiting for me right now?" the doctor had added. Petrie, lying there on the table, wondering where his life had just gone, had answered that no, he did not. *"Joe Namath,"* the doctor said, proudly. "I'm going to check his knee right now."

Petrie felt a kind of pain stab him, thinking, *What do I care about Joe Namath? Why is this man telling me this? This man who has just ended my career.*

That year, in the midst of the basketball madness known as Blazermania that had not just come to Portland, but seemed to settle there, Geoff Petrie, Portland's first basketball hero, went into a profound depression. He had tried to rehabilitate his leg, an arduous and excruciatingly painful experience, and in the end he failed. His career, as Dr. Nicholas had said, was over. Basketball had been his entire life since he was twelve years old and he found that he had an instinct for the game. Petrie's father died two years earlier and he had immersed himself even more deeply in the game; he found that it offered, in an otherwise difficult life, security and confidence. It was the one thing he was good at. Even in his student days at Princeton, basketball had been there, comforting for him; he might stay up until 2 a.m. drinking with his buddies, but at 8 a.m. the next morning, every day of the week, he would be up working at the gym, shooting baskets, feeling minute by minute happier and freer. Sometimes in his best college and professional games, there were moments when he felt immortal, sure even before he took them that his shots would go in; it was as if he were simply floating above everyone else. That was what being an athlete meant, he was sure. Now that was gone. He became a different person. He was difficult for his wife to live with. His confidence seemed to evaporate. He avoided seeing old friends. He did not go to basketball games. It was particularly difficult to see teammates like Bill Walton who were still connected to the game, still alive while he was dead. Every athlete, he later realized, has to deal with the end of his career, with its promise of early death, but he felt cheated, they had taken him in the prime of his career. It had taken a long time for him to be able to watch games again, to associate with old friends. But for the past few months he had been able to manage it. Though he worked in real estate, he helped an old teammate coach at a nearby junior college, and he discovered he could again find pleasure instead of pain in the game he had once loved and then hated.

THE JOY WAS palpable in the locker room that night of the win over the Lakers, Ramsay's five hundredth win, the win over Magic Johnson. In a corner the reporter Steve Kelley was talking to T. R. Dunn about his defense, telling him about a conversation he'd just had with Magic in the Lakers' locker room. Magic had made light of Dunn's work. "Just one of those nights," he had said to Kelley. "It wasn't the man, it was me." Dunn, a gentle man with an awesome body, almost never talked. Not to coaches, not to reporters, not to friends. Everyone called him Tee. The longest statements he had ever uttered had come when Stu Inman asked him why he preferred using the initials T.R. "My name is Theodore Roosevelt," he had said. "If that was your name you'd be T.R., too."

Now, with credit for his fine defensive game being snatched away by Magic, he was trying to respond. "Well, of course Magic Johnson is entitled to his opinion, and that's only right but I have my opinion too and I don't want to take away from Magic Johnson's opinion. My opinion is that we played good team defense." Kelley, stunned at that many words, scribbled them down. Later he referred to it as the night that T. R. Dunn made a speech.

In the corner Ramsay was savoring the victory. "I don't see any team beating us the way we played tonight. We played good team defense. We positioned Kareem well. If you don't take position away from him he'll shoot the right-hand hook all night and he'll kill you. Tommy did a good job on position. How many points did Kareem get?" Someone said twenty-four. "How many did Tommy have?" Ramsay asked. "Twenty-four." Across the room Lionel Hollins, who was still not playing but was still captain, was standing on a table, holding a basketball. Everyone had signed it. It was Ramsay's five hundredth victory. Ramsay took the ball. "I don't care about the five hundred. The sixteen [it was the sixteenth victory of the season] is what matters. I thank you for that."

He was fifty-four years old that fall; most of the other coaches were in their late thirties or early forties. He had become an old man in what was, because of the travel and the complexity of pressures, a young man's business. His contract had guarantees but he always felt as if there were no guarantees; a coach was always on the edge. If things did not work out, if the right players did not arrive, if they did not play as they should, it was the coach who would be fired. He thought of himself as a highly disposable piece of merchandise.

Five hundred wins. He remembered his first one as clearly as the last. It was in Philly in 1968. He had taken veteran professional players and made them use a full-court press. He had played against the great Wilt Chamberlain who had traded himself from Philly to the Lakers, with much smaller players, but the press had done it and he had won. The final score had been Sixers 114, Lakers 96. The players that night were a true extension of him and of his passion.

The passion had always been there, even in the beginning, as a high school coach. As a player he had been intense, but as a coach he was even more so, being, in his own mind, far more responsible for the outcome. Now, more than ever, his signature was on a game. A Jack Ramsay team comported itself in a certain way, it fought hard, it was always in better condition, it was smarter than the opposing team, and it knew exactly what it intended to do when it went out to play. It was drilled, prepared and disciplined. Thus it could often beat teams possessing greater talent. Even as a high school coach he hated defeat. When his teams lost he would kick lockers, and if he went out to dinner with his wife and friends he would not talk; he remained lost in a world of missed passes and defensive players who had not defended.

As a high school coach in Wilmington he produced good teams and he wrote letters to all nearby colleges whenever he smelled a vacancy. Very few colleges wrote back. Then in 1955 he was asked to return to his alma mater, St. Joe's, as head coach for $3,000 a year. It was to be an enormously happy and fulfilling time for him. St. Joe's was a small Catholic college in Philadelphia playing basketball in what was called the Big Five. Basketball was the most important sport at the school. In those days the NBA was not yet very big, and New York City college basketball, once the best and most visible game in the country, had been wrecked by betting scandals. But the Philly game was big, there were college doubleheaders before packed houses, the games were on local television, the fans were frenzied in their loyalty, the rivalries ancient and passionate. The college game outdrew the pro game. Over a period of eleven years Jack Ramsay became a figure of immense stature in Philadelphia. He rarely got the best kids, but a Ramsay team bore an identity like a trademark—tough, smart, well-drilled, well-conditioned, eager kids who would knock down walls for St. Joe's and their coach. There were no disciplinary problems. They were all overachievers. The legend grew. Soon, it seemed, every tough ambitious young Catholic kid in the Philly area wanted to play for St. Joe's. Jack Ramsay did not recruit. We like you if you like us, that was his attitude. Thus, not having asked them to come, his authority was absolute. When Matty Guokas, a high school star, son of a former NBA player and a former St. Joe's player, chose to go elsewhere, Ramsay was shocked. Why, he wondered, had Guokas slipped away? The answer was simple. Ramsay had not even visited the Guokas home, so Guokas had assumed the coach did not want him. A year later Guokas transferred to St. Joe's. When Paul Westhead, later to be a Big Five coach and then a professional coach, was one of the most sought-after players in the Philly area, he came out one day to the St. Joe's gym, by bus. No fancy car brought him. He proceeded to locate the gym and finally found the tiny cubicle which served as the coach's office. Inside the office was the legendary Jack Ramsay, whom all the schoolyard players talked about. Ramsay looked at Westhead carefully. Instead of asking him to attend his school, as all the other coaches had done thus far, Ramsay simply asked: "Why do you want to come to St. Joe's?" Westhead, of course, was hooked.

Ramsay loved it there. The rules were an extension of his value system and the players were a true extension of him. He had complete leverage over them. St. Joe's was, in the world of increasingly high pressure athletics, a special place. If the team was invited to play in a postseason tournament, everyone would be consulted, faculty, players. After all, a couple of classes might be missed. Should they go? (They always went.) These were nice blue collar Catholic kids of the fifties, out not to challenge authority but to find it. Once, early in his career, one of his teams had been invited to the National Invitation Tournament in New York. Before the first game he called the team together for a meeting. Very quietly he told them how hurt he was by the fact that even though they were playing and winning, some members of the team *were smoking cigarettes.* It was a big thing at the time. There were no accusations, no punishments. But it was clear, they had let him down. The two smokers had stayed behind and apologized; the nonsmokers, who had let Ramsay down by not pressuring the delinquents themselves, brooded over their failure. It was that kind of sheltered time and place.

He was not simply a coach for them but a complete role model. Many of his players went into coaching. He was rigorous and yet kind. When he scrimmaged with them after a practice in three-on-three pickup games, all his competitiveness showed. His basketball was passionate but it was fun. In those years he perfected a Ramsay trademark, Ramsay as a coach—off the bench, kneeling on the court, towel under one knee. The idea was that he had *entered* in the game, was in there with his players. The sixth man. He was closer to them that way and further from the crowd. The college players loved it; they felt him with them.

He had received his Ph.D., he was Doctor Jack now. Other schools, larger, richer, made overtures, but he had no interest; everything he wanted in the world he had: community, professional fulfillment, faith, all blended into his career. But as his teams got better, the pressure subtly mounted, and even St. Joe's began to recruit better players. In 1961 the real world arrived at St. Joe's. Three of his players admitted shaving points in early season games. Ramsay had broken the news to Jack McKinney, his assistant. "How could it happen here?" he kept asking. "How could they do it? How could I have failed?" For a time he thought of leaving coaching. He wondered whether he had been too obsessed with winning. Had he put too much pressure on these young men? Had he understood clearly enough the complexity and limits of their lives, or had he instead simply tried to make them function for him? Had he disregarded them as individuals in his desire for them to perform as basketball players, to win for him? (That was a question which would bother some of his professional players twenty years later, but Ramsay had little sympathy then; these were professional players and they were highly paid. He was in charge of molding not their character but their game.) The St. Joe's president, Father Joseph Greib, had talked him into staying, telling him that a man like Ramsay was exactly what the players needed, a man of full dimensions. He remained at St. Joe's for four more years. But then, in 1966, all the emotional stress finally showed. He began having serious problems with his vision. His right eye clouded and he could no longer read with it. What was even more frightening was the doctor's warning that his left eye might go too. He talked with several specialists without getting any real assurance. They all seemed to think it was a result of self-imposed stress, something which did not surprise his wife, Jean, already midway in her career as a basketball widow, aware that in spite of his love for her and his children, there was something compulsive about him that drove him and haunted him as few other men were driven and haunted. About that time, Irv Kosloff of the Philadelphia 76ers asked him to become general manager. Compared to the highly competitive world of college basketball, the professional game in those days seemed far more relaxed. He had received professional offers before but had not been very much intrigued by the pro game, which he regarded as largely push and pull, run and shoot; he suddenly had little choice. He could no longer afford the pressure of the college game. He accepted the job with the 76ers.

THE PHILADELPHIA YEARS were not entirely satisfactory. Professional basketball was an entirely different world from college ball, more talented players playing for very different reasons, motivated by money as much as by glory. The world of college basketball he had known, betting scandal or no, was still youthful and innocent, built upon a thousand myths of American rites of passage. For the St. Joe's players believed in the American success story: if they worked hard, they would be rewarded. Diligence paid off. Each game was important, photographed carefully in the memory bank, to be recalled with clarity not just at the end of the season but thirty years later when, much older, they would gather at reunions and remember the pass and the shot that had won the game.

The professional game was nothing like that. There were too many games, and each game became part of a featureless plateau. If a professional player was lucky he might be able to recall several playoff games, but few others. Besides, these players were stars, they had already been heavily recruited in college, and they tended to be a little spoiled, talented but weak in fundamentals. Because of the way they were recruited, college had often *not* been an extension of the home; they were properly cynical about college, and thus about life as well. Many of them now were black and tended to be more talented than comparable whites. They had put in long hours perfecting their moves but now, success assured, they preferred not to show that they were making any effort; with a white crowd then, some part of the effort, in the sadness of our culture, must be concealed. If for the good white children of St. Joe's there was a clear continuing line of progress, home to college to life, work hard, study hard, be rewarded, there was no such line for the children of the ghetto; their parents and grandparents had often worked very hard and the society had been remarkably reluctant to bestow rewards. As Jack Ramsay entered the professional league the players were more and more often black. They were more often quite cynical about the world around them and they were also about to benefit from a dazzling new pattern of high salaries. A certain athletic excellence had worked for them all their lives, a particular shot had been their meal ticket. Now here was a coach trying to change them, trying to make them pass up that shot more often, trying to make them surrender the very thing that had always set them apart.

Nor were the fans the same. They were no longer part of that extended Catholic family which had cheered St. Joe's and revered Jack Ramsay because he was they and they were he. These were tougher, more cynical fans (for it was said that in Philadelphia the baseball fans would boo the Easter bunny, and the basketball fans would boo Santa Claus). A once powerful 76er team was already beginning to break up and Ramsay, making what were generally considered to be injudicious trades, helped expedite the breakup. Thirteen years later, when he returned with Portland, the fans could still boo him, as much as anything for trading Chet Walker, a great local favorite, for Jim Washington, a rebounder who had failed to rebound. Ramsay had moved very quickly from general manager, a job which clearly bored him, to coaching; by the time he took over as coach, Wilt Chamberlain—around whom past glory had been built—had seized the opportunity offered by a new league, the American Basketball Association, to trade himself to the place where he had always wanted to be, California.

In his first year with the Sixers, despite the disappearance of Chamberlain, he had done well, winning fifty-five games. But then in his second year, the team, without any big man, began to slip. His trades were not good nor were his draft choices. The fans were frustrated by him and he in turn was frustrated by the players. There were times at night when he would sit alone in the locker room after the players left, unable to talk to anyone. It was, he once said, as if he could not understand players like these who did not listen, who kept repeating their mistakes. It offended his very being. The second year the record was 42–40 and the next year it was a little better—47–35. Mark Heisler, a Philadelphia reporter who much admired Ramsay, wrote a story saying that fans should not be deceived by the seemingly improved record; it could be explained by the fact that there were now expansion teams in the league, and they had proved easy competition. Ramsay was furious with the story. How could Heisler write that it was not a better record? Ramsay demanded to know.

"Well, I thought that with the expansion teams . . ." Heisler began.

"Who the hell cares what you thought," Ramsay said.

The fourth year, the draft choices still bad, it was 30 and 52 and the fans were mutinous. Some of his players thought he had lost his touch, that he yanked them from a game too quickly, and that he measured them against himself, asking how, with the same talent, he would have played. No one doubted his ability, but the question was whether he could mold his passion and temperament to the more subtle rhythm of the NBA. Some of the men on his team wondered if he really respected NBA players. Still, there were job offers, his reputation was still strong. Seattle, for instance, was interested; it was, ironically enough, about to unload Lenny Wilkens as a player-coach. But Ramsay's wife, a dedicated easterner, placed Seattle on her map as an offshore island of Japan. Not everyone in America, having visited the two cities, would pick Buffalo over Seattle, but Jack Ramsay did.

Buffalo began as poorly as Philadelphia had ended. It was an expansion team in its third season. In each of its first two years it had won twenty-two games. Worse, the players were not Ramsay players, they were big and heavy and lacked the one thing he coveted in the game, speed. Buffalo played a front line of three centers: Elmore Smith, Bob McAdoo and Bob Kauffman. All three liked to set up near the basket, and they got in each other's way and generally made it easy for opposing teams to defend. The first season for Ramsay was difficult. These were again not his players, and he would talk with them, telling them what he wanted, and there was no resonance. There were tense scenes in the locker room when he asked players if they would like to step outside and settle matters there. Gatorade cans and beer cans were thrown against walls regularly in the sixty-one defeats which marked that season.

But he made his professional reputation in Buffalo. There he took lesser players, many of them incomplete, and patched together an exciting, explosive, though flawed team. It was demonstrably a personal triumph; he got rid of players of far greater reputation and brought in players who could play within their limits. Above all, in those years, there was what he did with McAdoo.

Bob McAdoo, when he arrived in Buffalo, was an NBA puzzle, a wonderful, delicate scoring machine. At 6'9" he shot like the tallest guard in the league. But at only 210 pounds he seemed too frail to play center. He seemed destined to become one of those dazzling but basically limited NBA superstars, a man unable to blend his talents into a team, a player who could do one thing better than anyone else, but whose statistics seemed to hide other serious weaknesses. Bob McAdoo was the product of a simple black background in Greensboro, North Carolina; he was quiet, often moody and introspective, and he expressed himself primarily by playing basketball. But Ramsay from the start saw him as an NBA center; if he was not strong enough to play close to the basket, he was deft enough to play away from it, to shoot over the heads of bulkier men, and to lure them away from the basket. So it was that Ramsay, with great patience and caring, began to work with McAdoo, trying to refine his game without losing or altering its genuine natural brilliance. It was not easy. Mac was the best, he had always been the best, the best pure shooter in high school, junior college, college and now the pros. Yet here was Ramsay trying to teach him other aspects of the game, to shoot a little less and to pass a little more, to understand how that would put extra pressure on the defense, help the team and, in the long run, bring Mac even better shots. Mac did not say much, he was quiet and withdrawn, but his teammates saw it there, written on his face, a kind of disbelief, mixed with resentment: *What is this old bald white man trying to teach me about a game that I can play and he can't?* It was not easy, there were gains and then regressions because so much of Mac's self-esteem was built around one thing, scoring. Once, late in the first quarter of a game, Ramsay had pulled Mac and told him he was shooting too much. Back he went into the game. In the second quarter he did not shoot at all. Midway in the third quarter he still would not shoot. Ramsay called time. "Mac," he said, "whatever I told you earlier, forget it." McAdoo enjoyed his best years under Ramsay in Buffalo. There was a curious emotional kinship between the two men and when Mac's name was linked with those of other superstars who appeared to have been ruined by big contracts, Ramsay, his own path now quite different, always defended him vociferously. Mac, he said, was different because he had a passion to win. As for Ramsay himself, he knew that when he finished with McAdoo, he was a better coach, more patient and more subtle, and finally adjusted to the league. He could bend with the rhythm of the NBA.

In his second, third and fourth years in Buffalo, the teams were exciting and always made the playoffs, but he soon had troubles there. Not so much with the players now, but with the owner. Paul Snyder was the epitome of the new professional sports owner, young and self-made and very rich. He had made his money in frozen foods and ancillary businesses, and since he had succeeded so well in a field like that, he saw no limit to his basketball expertise either. Though the team played well, players' salaries had spiraled, and Buffalo turned out—there after all were few tax deductions for blue collar season ticketholders—to be a tough basketball town. Snyder's interventions became more frequent. Ramsay was not averse to meetings but he did not want to be told by a frozen-food magnate who should play and who should not play. Nor did he want to hear, after taking his patchwork team to seven games against Washington in the playoffs, that Milwaukee, which had not even made the playoffs, had a better season because it drew more people.

The last year was not a happy one. The team won three fewer games. Both Snyder and Ramsay became angrier. Snyder's presence became more evident, his suggestions more frequent. Ramsay, he told the coach, was playing too many players. Because they were playing so much, they were coming to see themselves as great players and they were demanding too much money. It was Ramsay's fault. Ramsay, already stretched thin from coaching this team in spite of its weaknesses, did not want to hear very much more. He knew nothing of the frozen-food industry and would not dare to tell Paul Snyder how to run *it*. The least Snyder could do was reciprocate and stay out of basketball. After one loss Snyder stormed into the locker room and started shouting that Ramsay's substitutions had cost them the game. "I don't want to hear it," Ramsay said, his own anger barely controllable. "I don't want to hear it." A Snyder hand had fallen on a Ramsay shoulder and Ramsay had furiously shaken it off. Bob MacKinnon, then the general manager, fearing the genuine violence in the air, separated them. That spelled the end in Buffalo. He was on a one-year contract but there was deferred money coming. It was clear at the end of the season that he would not be coming back. He and Snyder had a meeting. "I think we should change coaches," Snyder said. "I think we should too," Ramsay said. "How do we do it?" Snyder asked. Ramsay sensed immediately that it was a question of the deferred money and that Snyder wanted him to quit in anger so that he could avoid paying it. "Well, I think you should go ahead and announce that there's going to be a coaching change," he said. So it was that Jack Ramsay left Buffalo, neither fired nor rehired. Stu Inman, looking for a coach, had seen the final game of the Washington playoff series, and asked Ramsay about coming to Portland. The first thing Ramsay thought of was not how far west Portland was, it was no longer near Japan; the first thing he thought of was that Bill Walton played there and Walton lived by speed.

Buffalo did not remain a franchise very much longer. Paul Snyder threatened to move the franchise to Miami or Toronto unless Buffalo businessmen and citizens became more grateful and bought more season tickets. More were bought. But the next season he nevertheless started selling off his star players, including Bob McAdoo, who went to New York for some $2.5 million. There were no replacements of comparable talent. The commissioner, often given to talk about protecting the integrity of the game and the fan, was very accommodating and let the deal pass. In time Snyder sold out for a very handsome profit to John Y. Brown, a fried-chicken king. And soon there was no franchise in Buffalo. "Paul Snyder?" Jack Ramsay once reminisced in Portland, "don't feel badly for Paul Snyder. He's a very good businessman. He made a very good dollar out of this game."

FOR A BRIEF moment after the Los Angeles game they were a family. First the nine-game winning streak, which none of them had really believed, then a few close defeats, and then back-to-back victories against Seattle and Los Angeles. Those teams were real; thus the Blazers were real. Maybe they could do it without Walton and Mychal Thompson, and now even without Kunnert. Kermit Washington, who played 33 minutes and got 14 rebounds against the Lakers, was telling a reporter that he felt he should be stronger and contribute more. "He probably means it," Bucky Buckwalter said. "Don't disillusion him." Ramsay, in celebration, had gone out for drinks and dinner not with basketball people but with a few friends that included Larry Smith, the conductor of the Portland Symphony Orchestra. Smith's tour in Portland was finished. He was explaining to Ramsay what his chances for a slightly larger orchestra were, how tough the odds were, how many more qualified conductors to lead there were than orchestras to be led. Watching Ramsay's face it was easy to see him translating the story into his own experience; he was dealing with a man who had even less job security than he did. He was a man of five hundred victories. The five hundred and first, it turned out, was possibly the hardest.

For suddenly the team went into a slump. A few defeats became, as they can in basketball, a psychological state. A slump was particularly dangerous to this team; for it was without a true core of its own, and without either a defined personality or great talent. On its best nights a lineup hastily patched together of overachievers could wear down more gifted athletes. Now, with injuries, there was less and less relief for most of the players, fewer options for the coach; under the pressure of defeat, there was a greater danger every night of the Portland players playing not so much strong as tight.

The losing streak started innocently enough. Three days after beating Los Angeles they had gone to Seattle and lost a very close game by four points. But Bobby Gross broke his thumb during the Seattle game, though he did not realize it at the time, and continued playing. It was one more injury to a key player who had only recently been working himself back into shape after other injuries. With Hollins, Steele, Thompson and Kunnert already out, the injury was crushing. For Hollins and Gross gave this team what little offensive movement it had, and constantly made the other players more aware of each other; with Hollins out Gross functioned almost as eyes and ears for some of the other players. Without him and Hollins it was a noticeably slower, more stilted team.

Two days later they lost again to Phoenix, this time at home, again by one point. After the game Ramsay sat by himself in the locker room. Gradually everyone else dressed and left and still he remained. It was clear he was seeing the game again as it had unfolded in the last seconds, a last minute steal by Gar Heard of a T. R. Dunn pass and worse, Dunn—everyone on the court knew that Dunn would not take a shot—telegraphing the pass, the terrible sensation that the steal was going to come even before Heard moved. After the Phoenix game they went on the road to Atlanta. Tom

Owens, exhausted by playing too many minutes now that Kunnert was out, had been unable to play against Atlanta. His back hurt too much. Until that night he had played in 197 consecutive games as a Blazer, clearly (as he himself noted) a Portland medical record, and then he had given out. That shifted more of the burden onto Lucas and Washington. In the first half against Atlanta, Washington, playing with even greater intensity, had 13 rebounds. But Hubie Brown, the Atlanta coach, aware of how shorthanded the Blazers were, kept running fresh faces at him, and in the second half Washington simply wore down. Luke played both center and forward, and seemed at times distracted. Sometimes he played hard and sometimes his mind was clearly elsewhere. He had made 12 turnovers in the Phoenix game and then 9 against Atlanta, 4 in the last quarter. Portland led by 5 going into that last quarter and then Atlanta with its fresh troops had come on and won by 7. Luke thought part of the reason for his turnovers was that his hand had not properly healed, and part was because he was trying too hard; Ramsay thought that the contract dispute had thrown his concentration off, and that he was not in good condition. On a team that was shaky, he was a central figure. Kermit was new to the team, still to a degree under a psychological cloud because of his fight with Rudy Tomjanovich, wary of assuming leadership in any case and especially wary of seeming to cut into Luke's turf if he assumed leadership. He had been starting while Luke was injured and when Luke was ready to return, he had gone to Ramsay and suggested that Luke start and that he come off the bench. Ramsay liked the sense of team feeling that Kermit's idea suggested. He brought them together. "Luke," he said, "Kermit thinks you ought to start and then he can come off the bench. What do you think?" "I think it's a good idea," Luke had said. The positive attitude was not, Ramsay decided, likely to become contagious; the anger was too deep.

From Atlanta they flew to San Antonio. Ramsay called a team meeting and everyone showed up but Luke. Ramsay sent Buckwalter out to look for him. Buckwalter found him in the hotel lobby giving an interview to Steve Kelley of the *Oregonian* on the subject of salary inequity and the fact that the Blazers would do things for Walton that they would not do for him.

"Hey, Luke," Buckwalter said, "there's a meeting."

"One minute," Luke said, waving him aside, "I'm talking here."

"Luke, they're waiting on you," Bucky said.

Lucas continued the impromptu press conference. Weinberg, he said, did not know how to treat players, did not understand the emotion of it. "I've never talked to the man socially," he said.

"Luke, Jack's getting impatient."

"I'll be there in a minute," he said. To Kelley, becoming more nervous by the second, sure that Ramsay would hold *him* responsible, there was an ominous feeling about the moment. "If I was white," Luke was saying, "I wouldn't have this problem."

A few minutes later he showed up at the meeting. "Luke," Ramsay said, "we can't have this sort of thing."

"What are you going to do," Luke said, "fine me? Then go ahead and fine me."

"It's more than that, Luke," Ramsay said. "It's more than that and you know it." It was a very tense moment and most coaches would have left it there, there had been enough confrontation and there was no need to seek more. But Ramsay was dissatisfied, there was a larger point to be made. He followed Luke to his room and told him the fine was not important. What was important was the obligation of a senior player, a star, to his teammates. Younger players looked up to him. Yes, Luke had finally said, he had been wrong and yes, he owed his teammates more than that.

They shook hands. The fragile truce continued. That night San Antonio, a team which Portland needed to beat, won by 7 points. Luke had 7 turnovers, a total of 28 in three games. Ramsay was more frustrated than ever; Luke, he told friends, was a terribly complicated player, capable of giving you both a good game and a bad game in the same night.

The next day Stu Inman called Ramsay. "How's Luke playing?" he asked.

"Just well enough for us to lose," Ramsay said.

Suddenly it was not just a game or two, suddenly it was what all basketball people, players and coaches alike, feared most, a losing streak. For basketball people believed that their game was far more psychological than football or baseball. Players, if they were going well, believed they could do certain things, shoot and make certain shots, stop certain players on defense. That had been part of the immense intangible value of Walton: he was so superior a player and his talents so directly encouraged other players; because he was so good on defense they were able to play better defense too, for they had less territory to cover; he passed so well that they got better shots. But the reverse was also true. As basketball players lost their confidence, their ability diminished, they no longer believed. They would hesitate and become tentative. Natural shooters began to *push* their shots. Fine passers overreached themselves and passed into the hands of opponents. Rebounders found themselves unable to take the position they wanted. Players began to doubt not just themselves, but their teammates as well. Contemporary professional basketball was a curious amalgam of great skill, great ego and great anxiety. The anxiety, about self, about career, about the relationship with the coach, lay just beneath the surface. A player who got twenty minutes in a game and suddenly was used for only twelve often took that as a major signal: perhaps he was through with this team, perhaps, even worse, it was a sign that his career had crested and he was on his way right out of the league. A confident team glowed with the communal sense of its own ability; a team filled with doubt seemed to signal with its eyes and its body language to opponents, to referees, that it was vulnerable. Some of the veteran players like Larry Steele could remember the great opposing teams which had come into the Portland Coliseum: the old Knicks, the Celtics. There was, even in their pregame drills, a lazy controlled arrogance, as if they were saying it did not matter where they were playing, they might as well be playing at home, it did not matter what the crowd wanted or who the refs were, all they had to be was themselves. They were better, and because they were better and everyone in the league knew they were better, they would get the calls from the refs. They were almost regal. For a brief time Portland had been like that. In the year of destiny, the year after the championship season, when they were 50 and 10 before Walton was hurt, they were sure that nothing could stop them; they had come out on the court, any court, absolutely sure of themselves. Early in that season they had gone into Atlanta, to play a team which had been on a winning streak of its own, and the game was much ballyhooed. They had simply blown Atlanta out, and won by forty points. Afterwards, in the locker room, which had been unusually joyous that night, Lloyd Neal had held up his hand with the championship ring on it and shouted, "I guess we showed them that they didn't give us these rings by no fucking mistake." It was the way everyone on the team felt. They were the best. They could do what they wanted every night and no one was going to stop them. They would get the calls from the refs—they were the best and they deserved to get the calls.

After the Atlanta game Portland re-signed Jim Brewer. He had been let go early in the season when Luke returned, and he had returned to Cleveland where he had a home, waiting for the phone to ring, trying to decide what to do with the rest of his life. He still wanted to play and Denver, a team struggling with its own limited fortunes, seemed briefly interested, but in the end they had signed a player named Glen Gondrezick, a white player, a Colorado boy, much admired by fans for the way he scrambled on the floor. Brewer's agent had thought it a white-black decision. Brewer was glad to be back with Portland. "Terrible time for my wife," he said. "I'm waiting around the house all the time. Every day I've got a long list of things I'm supposed to do, but all I do is hang around the house looking at the phone, taking up her space." The hardest thing for him had been fighting the idea that life was over. "You think basketball is life but it's not. It's a front. You're isolated all those years you're playing ball. Shielded from everything, like living in a glass bubble. Everyone wants to help you, give you discounts on food and clothes, cars, so they can say *Jim Brewer shops here.* Or [his voice mimicking the people he knew] 'we're giving a party and Jim Brewer's coming.' Easy to get the idea that you're someone that you're not. Then one day it's over. The hard part is after the last game. That's when you need the attention the most and then suddenly it's not there. Then you have to deal with the fact that it's still all going on, the players are still there, the coaches are still there and the season ticketholders are still there. You want to say, 'Hey, my career was too short. I can still jump.' Every day I had a list of things for the *new* Jim Brewer to do in his new life. And every day I didn't do any of them. I sat around the house trying to figure out what went wrong, and waiting for someone to phone and give me another piece of my life."

FOR THE TEAM the news was worse and worse. The one thing that Ramsay had hoped for, the late-season return of Mychal Thompson, was now out of the question. Towards the end of November Dr. Bob Cook had taken Mychal to Switzerland to be examined by the Swiss specialists who had pioneered in the operation—more common among skiers than among team athletes—he had undergone. The specialists reported that Thompson was making very good progress, that the operation was almost surely a success and that when he returned to play he would have lost none of his exceptional speed. But they warned against his trying to come back too soon and putting too much strain on a leg that was possibly not yet fully healed. He was now almost surely out for the season. Ramsay had hoped that the team might manage to struggle through the first two-thirds of the season, and then—with Thompson playing center and forward—become a serious challenger at the end. That hope was dead. Meanwhile, the losing streak went on in Houston. Portland, with both Owens and Kunnert out, desperate for a big man now, used Lucas at center. It was not a position he liked playing in the NBA; everyone, instead of being smaller, was suddenly bigger. Playing center against Houston meant he had to go against Moses Malone, 6'10", still, it seemed, almost a boy. Because Malone was so powerful, so quick, like a towering dancer on the court, Kermit Washington had to help Luke out on defense. Both played well. Luke had 20 points and 13 rebounds, Kermit had 25 points and 14 rebounds, and both were exhausted after the game. Kermit was sitting by his locker talking about Moses: "Most basketball fans," he said, "see Moses, and they all think, look how tall he is. What they don't see is the quickness. How can a man that big have feet like that? No one watching that game sees his feet. They're amazing. And the strength. Mo just wears you out, those hands—long quick hands—always working on you. That's a night's work."

THE IRONY OF Portland's need for a big man and Malone's emergence as one of the dominating centers in the league was not lost on either Moses Malone or the Portland fans, or, increasingly, on the Portland coaching staff. For a brief, unhappy time in the fall of 1976, Moses Malone had been the property of the Portland Trail Blazers, and the decision to trade him had become over the years a subject about which the front office remained extremely sensitive. When the ABA merged with the NBA and players from the defunct ABA teams were auctioned off in a special dispersal draft, weak NBA teams picking first, Portland traded the rights for Geoff Petrie in order to choose Lucas; with its own pick, it took Moses Malone. Then two years in the ABA, and all of twenty-two, Malone had been the first player ever to join the professional game directly from high school. Though Bucky Buckwalter, then a Portland scout and the man who had signed Malone to his first professional contract, had warned his Portland colleagues that Malone was the most exceptional young talent in the ABA, it was clear that Portland had picked up Moses not as a player but as bait, either as part of a trade or to be exchanged for a draft choice and cash. Malone in those days bore a considerable stigma in the eyes of most NBA basketball people: his association with the ABA. There was a built-in prejudice against almost any ABA player, a belief that the other league was filled with gunners and hot dogs and that its statistics meant nothing. There was also a degree of doubt about Malone himself, who was very young, black and virtually uncoached in fundamentals, who had not been to college and was said to be monosyllabic (which he often was, by choice, especially in front of older, whiter, people). But the greatest stigma which Moses Malone bore was his salary, and here the front office was more than doubtful, it was adamant. Moses Malone, scheduled to play behind an apparently healthy Bill Walton, was making $300,000 a year, all of it upfront, an exceptional contract, and a sum of money which Portland's owners most assuredly did not want to pay *any* backup center, despite Walton's history of injuries. ("Mo," Maurice Lucas once said, "reminds me of Agnew. If Agnew's so dumb, how come he's not in jail, and if Mo is so dumb, how come he's richer and got a better contract than all those people who think he's dumb?") Thus Moses Malone had been regarded from day one as bait, that and nothing more, and he soon became most painfully aware of his status. When he arrived at the Portland airport he was met by Berlyn Hodges, one of the team officials, to be driven the forty miles to Salem, where the team was at camp. Hodges immediately turned the car radio on and as they drove they listened to the local news. Suddenly a local sportscaster came on and, in a voice rich in authority, announced that Moses Malone was on his way to Portland. In the car Mo leaned forward to hear a little better. The Blazers had picked him up, the sportscaster said confidently, expressly for the purpose of dealing him. Hodges, knowing the story was true, reached desperately for the radio to switch stations. Malone, already fairly noncommunicative, seemed to pull back into himself even more. Hodges, desperate for some conversation, anything to change the mood and break this terrible silence, had thereupon asked Moses Malone what his hobbies were, a question he later realized was very white indeed. Malone had a tendency to mumble his answers, and there were those who knew him well who thought he did this quite deliberately, to keep people at a distance, and to protect his privacy, preferring to live silently and stereotyped rather than noisily and misinterpreted. So it was that Berlyn Hodges, in answer to his question about hobbies, heard Moses Malone mumble something like "swimmin' pools." "Your hobby is building swimming pools?" asked the astonished Hodges. "No," corrected Moses Malone, as tersely as he could, "swimmin' and pool. Man, *playin' pool.*" They had gone the rest of the way in a now welcome silence.

From the beginning the coaching staff did not respect Malone and did not think him smart enough to play in Portland; if there was to be a stereotype, then Malone himself contributed to it, becoming even more monosyllabic than usual. When it was time to be taped before a practice, he would lie on the trainer's bench, point at his feet and say to Ron Culp, the trainer, simply "feet." Once, during a scrimmage, he had held up his hand to stop practice. "Wrist" is what he said to Culp though what Culp heard was "rest." "Jack," Culp yelled to Ramsay, "Moses wants to come out and take a rest." "No," said Malone, pointing to his wrist, "not *rest, wrist.*"

The one person on the Portland staff who was enthusiastic about Moses's possibilities was Buckwalter, who had scouted him, signed him and coached him in the ABA; but Buckwalter was then merely a Portland scout, not a member of the inside team. It was clear, he felt, that the anti-ABA stigma that tainted Malone in some way marked him as well; *he* had been in the ABA, he had coached there and *lost;* thus in some way he was on trial as much as Mo.

That was too bad, he thought, for if there was one player in the ABA who in Buckwalter's estimation bore a guarantee of greatness, it was Moses Malone. In 1974, the year in which Malone graduated from high school in Petersburg, Virginia, Buckwalter was serving as general manager of the Utah Stars, who badly needed a center. Buckwalter, much traveled through the South in the course of an erratic career, by chance scouted Malone in a high school all-star game, and set out to sign him to a professional contract. He believed Malone was a *player,* unbelievably quick for someone so young and tall, and was convinced that Malone could play in the professional game. So it was that he set out to sign Malone to a contract that spring, thus giving Moses the distinction of being the first player to go directly from high school to the pros.

The morality of his mission did not disturb Buckwalter. He had spent more than a decade in the jungles of college recruiting, watching and participating in the process with increasing apprehension; it was college recruiting, with all its promises, few fulfilled, with its disregard of true education, which he thought immoral, not professional recruiting. He was moreover pleased by the fact that by the time he arrived on the scene, Moses, having been sought out by one hundred other schools, had signed a letter of intent with Lefty Driesell of the University of Maryland, he of the honeyed voice and the smooth sell. For Driesell was considered in those days virtually without peer in the art of selling first and foremost himself and then, not coincidentally, his college, to young aspiring players and (often more important) to their mothers. Given the fact that more and more basketball players were black and came from homes where the fathers had made only cameo appearances, Driesell's exceptional skill with mothers was enviable. Lefty was viewed, in the vernacular of the trade, not as one of the better cars-and-girls-and-other-sweet-pleasures-out-there recruiters, but as a supple good-Christian-life-and-high-quality-pro-contract-to-follow-because-of-it recruiter. It was, both Driesell's critics and admirers thought, a brand of salesmanship barely removed from the sale of used autos, the ability to project instantaneously a sense of lasting friendship in which basketball played some part, but the true foundations were love of God and family, of which of course Lefty had just become a member. Buckwalter thought that Driesell was a magnificent recruiter and that he himself was by contrast virtually a failure, not nearly as good at sincerity and piety, and undercut frequently by an unfortunate tendency towards candor. On occasion he had heard his voice tell parents that other schools might in fact be better for their sons than his own. Regretting those moments, he had from time to time made his own stab at sincerity, sitting there with the mother, the boy in another room, talking not about basketball but the kind of Christian life Buckwalter wanted him to lead. Invariably when he did this, he noticed, the mother's eyes seemed to harden and look right through him. Sincerity was not his game.

Lefty Driesell, having just beaten out several of the new outlaw colleges for Moses, was not about to lose his prize recruit to an upstart fly-by-night professional team like the Utah Stars. Soon the competition between college and pro team became heated. There was already a brand new Cadillac outside the Malone home, an obvious symbol of Moses's desirability to some team.

Buckwalter made his initial presentation and Moses Malone looked at him very seriously and just nodded and then uttered what Buckwalter had never heard before, the Malone Mumble, a sound that went like this: *mmmm*, it went, *mmmm*, signifying neither approval nor, Buckwalter suspected, disapproval. Buckwalter was immediately impressed by Malone, by the fact that he was a serious and careful listener and, quite plainly, a very proud young man. When Buckwalter mentioned that he could become the first young man ever to go from high school to the pros, Malone seemed to pick up. A little later one of Mo's friends, one of the countless people who seemed to hang around the house offering themselves to both sides as friends and possible advocates and informants, had taken Buckwalter aside. "That was smart, Coach," he said. "You know Mo's been dreaming since he was a little boy about being the first player to go from high school to the pros. He *wants* that. Not bad, Coach." Soon after, Lefty Driesell arrived in Petersburg to protect his prize, and for the next few days there was an escalation of battle, joint meetings which everyone attended, meetings filled with accusation and counter-charge, everyone talking about *what was good for Moses Malone,* while the object of all this attention sat in the corner, nodding his head, half watching and, on occasion, mumbling just lightly enough to encourage each side to think that he was with them. There was much talk from Driesell and the other Maryland people about what was "right for Moses." The importance of education. Things that last for you your entire life. The prospects for a national championship at Maryland. A national championship, Buckwalter retorted, was for rich kids who went to UCLA. The *Sanctity* of a College Degree, Driesell argued, was something *Important in Life.* A college degree was fine for rich kids who had it made but if Moses went pro now he had four more years to earn big wages, answered Buckwalter. Well, said Driesell a day later, at least try college for two years before turning pro. The sanctity of a college degree, Buckwalter noted, had just been cut in half.

In all of this Morris Buckwalter kept a close eye on Moses Malone. Then he had a sudden epiphany: all the visitors in the room were white and believed that Moses, because he was young, black and silent, was dumb. But Moses, Buckwalter was convinced, was not dumb; he understood more clearly than anyone else what was happening. He had at so precocious an age broken the commercial code of America in general and basketball in particular. The code was simple: the more that all these white strangers said they were going to do for you, the more, in fact, *you* were expected to do for *them.* This meant they could be made to do *even more* for you. Moses understood this, Buckwalter believed, and was enjoying it. That made it easier for him, for Moses clearly knew the rules, and the battle was fairer.

Soon Buckwalter sensed it was going his way. The Malone requests became more sophisticated. There seemed to be a lawyer hiding away somewhere (indeed there was: Donald Dell, a Washington lawyer, alerted by his friend Driesell, was now monitoring the case; and he had told Moses that he could call him anytime he had a question, as a friend, but if he signed anything, it was all over). That meant the price was escalating, and Buckwalter was pleased. In the end Buckwalter and Jim Collier, the Utah owner, had arrived at Mo's house with money, hard cold cash, $100 bills, ten of them, and Collier had taken those bills and spread them on the orange crate which served as a table. "Mo," Buckwalter had said, "when you sign, this is yours. This is for you and your friends. This is not like Maryland where you never really see anything." Then he had reached into his jacket and brought out a photo of a green Mark IV Lincoln. "Mo, this is your car," he said. "We don't want you to drive around in a tacky little Cadillac." Moses Malone had looked at that photo a long time and then he had asked, "Do you think I could have a TV set in it?" Yes, of course he could, Buckwalter had answered, a color TV set to be sure. The next day there was a call from Lee Fentress, Dell's partner, announcing that he represented Moses Malone. There was one last meeting with Driesell, now distraught, who quoted at length from the Bible and told Malone, "The Good Lord won't mind you waiting for a year or two." He talked more about the Bible and Moses's responsibility. "Stop jivin' me, Coach," Malone said, and the battle was over.

Buckwalter coached Malone in the ABA and thought him a marvelous young man and a great talent, and he had been disappointed during the Portland preseason camp when no one seemed to take him seriously. The coaches were clearly unimpressed with his game, Walton was in great shape, a powerful team seemed in the offing, and Malone was clearly an expensive project, indeed so expensive that he was probably cost-ineffective. Malone, of course, sensed their doubt and withdrew even more. The players regarded him differently. They saw him as dazzling, he was so big and so quick, his moves to the basket so instinctive and original for so big a man. Steve Jones, who had played with Malone in the ABA, thought him a 6'10" Earl Monroe. All Mo wanted, Jones believed, was a little respect, and he was having a hard time gaining it. If Walton went up for a right-handed hook shot, that was all right, but if Bill hooked left, no. "You can use your right hand on me, Bill," Moses said, "but don't come in here with that dinky left-handed garbage. Don't you do that to Mo." He and Luke had their own war going, they had played together in St. Louis, they were old friends; Luke would make a move on the basket and Malone would block his shot. "Don't you bring that weak shit in here on Mo," he would say. "Listen, Mo, you better pack your bag and be gone because I'm the one who's going to stay and you are *not* going to get any minutes ahead of me," Luke would say. Mo would answer, "Luke, the only reason you stay and I'm gone is because I make so much more money than you do. Where Moses goes, he will play. And be paid for it."

The players liked him, and that eventually came to include Walton, who lobbied to keep him; Malone could play backup center and backup forward. Walton thought the skill was beginning to impress Ramsay. Still, it was a business decision. The early exhibition games were not good, no other team seemed interested. Suddenly Portland was not only trying to move him, but panicking, that huge salary now facing them. Portland called New York and Eddie Donovan had asked, "Is he better than Gianelli?" mentioning the name of a relatively weak New York journeyman center. Finally Buffalo made a conditional offer in exchange for a first-round draft choice. Two nights later Portland played in Oakland in an exhibition and Moses Malone was awesome; he pulled down 12 rebounds and scored 24 points in only 26 minutes. Everyone knew now that he was a player. Ramsay, who had been wavering, decided that they had to keep him. On the following Monday they held a meeting, voting unanimously to do so. But even as they were talking, Harry Glickman, the general manager, came in the room and told them it was too late, that Buffalo had just picked up the option.

Later that day Ramsay appeared at a practice session. The players were subdued; Moses had already packed and gone. "We just traded Moses to Buffalo," Ramsay said.

"What did you get for him?" Walton asked.

"We got a first," Ramsay answered.

"You didn't trade him away," Walton said, "you gave him away."

Moses Malone did not stay long in Buffalo, moving six days later to Houston for *two* first-round picks, and with his departure from Portland, any chance of a dynasty was gone, for then the team's hopes depended far too much on Walton and his fragile lower body, in particular his feet. Two years later, while Bill Walton, injured and his career once more in jeopardy, was sitting out the entire season at Portland, Moses Malone, then twenty-five and playing for Houston, was voted the most valuable player in the league. Portland fans still got to see Moses, whenever Houston came to town.

FROM HOUSTON THEY flew to Salt Lake City, where they lost in overtime against the pathetic Utah Jazz. Ramsay had seen the game as the perfect place to end the losing streak. Portland lost because it had three technical fouls called against it. When you were losing you simply did not get the calls. Referees, like everyone else, were human; they did not like losers. One technical was called on Ramsay late in the game when, upset by the lack of calls, he had said to Bob Rakel, the ref, "Call the foul, Bob." That had done it. Lucas had drawn a technical earlier in the game and then with twenty-five seconds left, frustrated by the lack of calls, he had said, it was mild stuff by the norm of NBA protest, "When is this bullshit going to end?" That was his second technical, and it caused his banishment from the game. It also put a game Portland might have won into overtime. Number seven was against Chicago at home. The next night again at home, this time against San Diego, a team they had inhaled earlier in the season, they were beaten when Lloyd Free hit a three-point shot in the final seconds. Lloyd Free was someone whom Portland, preparing the compensation case, had made very clear it did not want. A film replay of the shot seemed to indicate that Free's feet were not outside the three-point line and Harry Glickman, the most emotional of the team's fans, had gone charging down after the game to confront the referees. He was restrained by security men. When Steve Kelley mentioned this in the next morning's *Oregonian*, Glickman denounced the report to other Oregon sportswriters. Tempers were wearing thin. In all of this Ramsay tried to remain controlled. Underneath he seethed, and his players were aware of the conflict inside the man, the rage and the attempt to control it. After a home loss he sometimes now headed for an all-night health club and worked out on the Nautilus. He was wary of showing how much these defeats meant. He knew they were playing tight and he was afraid they would play even tighter. He had decided after several years in the league that he had to make certain adjustments and part of that, for the sake of his players' sanity, was to conceal how much defeat meant. Now, during the losing streak, his postgame interviews were models of comportment. "I saw a lot of things out there tonight that I liked." "We're closer than ever to winning. Just a shade away." "We could just as easily have won eight in a row as lost eight in a row." But in fact nothing was going right. In the Utah game, David Twardzik hurt his leg again and had to leave in the first half. One more injury. Ramsay was aware that Twardzik, from whom he had wanted twenty minutes a game, was beginning to wear out.

David Twardzik had been a member of the championship team, a very distinctive member with what appeared at the time to be the sole surviving crew cut in American sports. Only H. R. Haldeman's similar haircut had rivaled it for national media exposure in the mid-seventies. The implication was clear: Twardzik, both man and basketball player, was, in spirit if not in age, a relic of the fifties, a short scrappy white guard who takes the charge from opponents, dives after loose balls and drives in among far taller men, disappearing for a moment, as bodies bang, only to reappear at the other side of the crowd, to shoot a layup and usually to draw a foul as well. For millions of fans who had bounced their last basketball in high school and who wondered why a college scholarship had never come, Twardzik in those days had represented a second youth. No other player, in style, in dress, in look, so easily blended into the faces in the Portland crowd. What few in the crowd saw was the rare basketball intelligence which had set him apart from hundreds of other comparable college seniors and made him special; he saw the floor, he saw the small slivers of daylight among the big players which allowed him to drive, or get the ball to one of his own big men with just enough of an angle to score. Nor did many see the exceptional dedication which had driven him, knowing that his size was against him, to practice and practice his drives, using not the normal angle and arc of shooting, for bigger men would destroy those shots, but far more difficult angles with rare spin shots which they could not block. There was nothing happenstance in his game. Knowing the limits of his body he had deliberately set out to compensate and it had worked. He had also realized that to stay in the league he would have to sacrifice his body, that his game, if successful, would require him to be knocked down again and again on hard wooden floors.

Going on the wood, the players called it. No small man had ever planted his body so skillfully in the path of so many bigger and yet unsuspecting players, thus forcing them into the foul, as Twardzik. Once, after he had sneaked up and set himself on the blind side of Artis Gilmore, so that when the giant 240-pound Chicago center would, as he went for his shot, turn into him, Stu Inman had taken Twardzik aside. "David," he had said, "there is a fine line between courage and absolute foolhardiness, and you just crossed it." Now, in his eighth professional season, his body was simply wearing out. His back had been used as a shock absorber all those years and it hurt constantly. His thighs were always sore, his neck gave him systematic pain, and every night Ron Culp had to attend to a series of severe skin burns on his legs. Often he wore neck braces after games. His body was slower to respond. His speed seemed to be diminishing. Once he had been able to take the ball upcourt, size up the floor, give a quick fake, plant his first foot and drive to the middle, somehow, almost miraculously gaining both the basket and the foul. Now more and more frequently he planted the same foot, drove and found a defensive player already come over to cut off the access. Younger guards were giving him problems on defense; his court intelligence was still exceptional and on defense he could compensate for the wear in his body by anticipating what an opposing player would do, but it was harder and harder for him to deal with the quick explosive guards of the league. With his shots all coming close in near the basket, he had once been one of the highest percentage shooters in the league; in the championship season, where most guards might shoot .460, he had shot a remarkable .612 and the following year .592. This year he was wearing down, shooting jump shots of twelve feet, and his percentage was closer to .450.

"Did you see what David did last night?" Bobby Gross asked Kermit Washington. They were having lunch after a loss during the losing streak.

"Yeah, three jumpers. Must have been thirteen feet each," Kermit said.

"It's an allergy," Gross said. "The body is beginning to reject the wood after all those years. Bound to happen."

Twardzik was a tough kid; he lived absolutely within his own ethical framework. He often seemed apart from the other players. If he was close to anyone on the team it was perhaps Ramsay and Culp. He roomed for several years with Steele but they did not talk much or seem very close. The crew cut had gone now, replaced by longer reddish-brown hair which some teammates claimed was styled, and a beard. Other players doubted his height, officially listed as 6'1". His own explanation was that he was on occasion 6'1", most notably when he was in Denver where the altitude was such that his body expanded. His parents were both the children of Polish immigrants; his father had worked in the coal mines before taking night courses and working on computers for the Air Force. Because of that the Twardziks often lived in government housing. Others might not have considered that a blessing, but he did because it meant that there were always plenty of kids to play with. His father was his first coach and he had been forced constantly to compete against two older brothers; his father's first lesson had been simple—be afraid of no one. Twardzik considered his entire professional career to be something of a fluke. He had been a good high school player on a team which had won a Class B title. He was sure he was too small for college ball, for he saw the size of the guards emerging, not just in the professional game but in college as well. He had nevertheless made one Pennsylvania all-star team and some college coaches had seen him there. Not the biggest colleges, but still colleges. A man named Sonny Allen, who coached at a school called Old Dominion in Virginia, had come up to him after the game and said that he liked the way Twardzik played, and that he was interested in having him come to Old Dominion. Could he fly there that weekend? Twardzik had never heard of Old Dominion, then in the process of making a reputation as a basketball power, nor did he know that Virginia was the Old Dominion State. "Coach Allen," he had immediately answered, "I've heard a lot of good things about Old Dominion." The first thing he had thought about when the coach had invited him to come down was that he could get out of school for two days. The second thing was that it was to be his first airplane flight.

His luck had held. At Old Dominion he played in the perfect system for himself—highly disciplined; moreover there was an ABA franchise in Norfolk, and that made it a professional basketball center. Professional basketball coaches, assistant coaches, scouts were always moving through, and if they had a day off they went out to scout the nearest college game, which was often Old Dominion. Because of that he received exposure that he might have missed at almost any other college. He was drafted by Virginia in the ABA in the top three rounds (they were secret that year), and by Portland which chose him in the second. Virginia offered a three-year contract with two years no-cut; the money, like the money offered by Portland, was not very good by pro basketball standards, $30,000 a year and then $35,000 with a $10,000 bonus for signing. The no-cut clause was crucial; it guaranteed him a chance to prove his worth, which was the only thing that mattered. He never doubted that he could, given a chance, make the grade. The ABA was better about playing smaller guards than the NBA anyway. He had just gotten married and he could not believe his luck; he was able to buy a house within a year of graduation. (There had been a house they liked for $65,000, and one for $30,000. Nervous about his future, unsure of the world of basketball or the world of mortgages, he had settled for the smaller house. In that sense he was rare among professional basketball players, who seldom bought small. It was an indication of the conservative mind at work.)

The years in Virginia were not bad. It was a shaky franchise in a shaky league, but only once in his last year there did the management fail to pay players on time. It was nevertheless always hard going, a team constantly shadowed by financial desperation which, in order to survive, methodically sold off its best players—Julius Erving, George Gervin—to richer teams in richer cities. In that sense, Twardzik later decided it was an early lesson in both the economics and loyalty of professional sports. If Julius Erving is for sale, then everything is for sale. At the beginning of his fourth year in Virginia he had signed a handsome new contract for $75,000, $80,000 and $100,000 a year; shortly after, the team folded. When the league collapsed, Portland had the rights to him. Logically, that new contract should have been honored in the merged league, but because the Virginia Squires had folded during the season, the contract evaporated on a technicality, and with it the leverage gained in four years of building a career. He was immensely vulnerable in dealing with Portland. It was in a monopoly position. He seemed at best a type, and the colleges graduated a thousand plucky little white types a year. Portland, as it was wont to do with vulnerable players, turned the screw and signed him to a long contract at minimal rates. Instead of what Virginia would have paid him, he got $50,000, $60,000 and $70,000 in his first three years in Portland. In 1979, his fourth year in Portland and his eighth in the league, he was making $75,000. Ramsay intervened for him after the championship season and asked Weinberg to renegotiate his contract, but the owner had refused. A contract was a contract, even an inequitable one.

When he first arrived in Portland he had to prove himself. In the beginning Ramsay had been dubious. He had no need for some old-fashioned St. Joe's heroism on this team. He wanted certain skills, speed above all else. Only Inman sensed Twardzik's potential. "You're going to love him," he told Ramsay. Is he fast? Ramsay asked. "Not particularly," Inman said. Can he shoot? Ramsay asked. "So-so," Inman said. "I don't know about him . . ." Ramsay began. "Jack," Inman said, "you're going to love him." In a short time that became true. Ramsay liked Twardzik's sense of the floor, his finely honed feel for where all the other players were, for which way the defense was leaning, for how to tilt the defense off-balance and then exploit it. In time they became close friends, a closer friendship than Ramsay had with most contemporary athletes; they were after all cut from similar molds and shared a similar value system. Nothing asked for free, and nothing given. Twardzik seemed, in the fluid, often rootless world of professional basketball, with big contracts and all the attendant flash, curiously old-fashioned. Even with the crew cut gone the crew cut spirit lived. He was clearly suspicious of much around him—owners, players, media people. Yet basketball was something which had been very good to him and had given him a place in the sun. After Portland had won the championship a reporter had asked Twardzik what it all meant and he had answered that without professional basketball he might still be carrying a lunch box and working in a factory. The Portland management loved that. He was the political and social opposite of his former teammate Bill Walton.

In the championship season Walton had at the beginning been disrespectful of Twardzik's game; highly aware of racism in sports, he had decided very quickly that Twardzik was simply some plucky little boy kept on to appease white fans. Ramsay, sensitive to that kind of tension and wanting Twardzik for the team, had asked Hollins and Lucas to talk to Walton and to let him know it was not a racial quota thing; he genuinely wanted Twardzik's floor leadership because it was hard to think of a player who made as few mistakes on the floor as Twardzik did. Walton gradually came around to an acceptance of Twardzik's game, but the personal tension was always there. Other players, some of the holdovers from the past who did not like Walton, kept their opinions of the big man to themselves; it was not, they thought, worth hassling a star who was also a management favorite. But not Twardzik, he backed down from no one. He believed that Walton had a tendency to hassle others, often the lesser players, about little things, so he hassled Walton right back. It was as if he had failed some kind of UCLA elegance-of-your-game test and was thus supposed to pay for it. Walton sometimes teased other players about their clothes, but he himself wore a shirt with an eagle on it that Twardzik considered the ugliest shirt in American history. "There's the world's ugliest eagle," he would say. In Twardzik's opinion, Walton was constantly testing Ramsay, always with great subtlety (Walton, he thought, was a master of subtlety), never on big things, just pushing for a little advantage not so much to use it as to have it and create a little air space, a little extra territory. Ramsay might be talking to the team about that night's game plan and Walton would take one last shot after the talk had started. Or perhaps two. Nothing big, but something that was always there. Once when Walton was shooting while Ramsay was talking, Ron Culp, the trainer, a friend of both men, looked up and saw on Twardzik's face a look imploring Ramsay not to accept it, to react, to draw a line. The line was never drawn. Twardzik was close to Ramsay, closer every year; he was Ramsay's choice to run the team as assistant coach if Buckwalter was off scouting and Ramsay was ejected from the game. He considered

Ramsay a man of high principle. But like Larry Steele and Culp, who later blamed himself for being part of it, Twardzik thought management and Ramsay had yielded too much to Bill Walton, and that they were paying for it this year with Maurice Lucas and his anger. He believed, like everyone else on the team, that Portland would have been delighted to renegotiate Walton's contract when he asked out, under what pretext he did not know, and that Luke, whose contract was not being rewritten, was aware of that. In the end no love was lost between the two of them. When Walton made his criticism of the Blazer medical practices, Twardzik defended Cook, who was his friend. "Yes," he said, "I've been back there when Bill Walton was getting shots, and yes, I saw the needle, but no, I never saw the straps that held him down." Walton, furious, thereupon announced that Twardzik was a homer—that is, a player who played better and put out more for the home fans than on the road.

In this season, perhaps his last, he seemed removed from the team. He played hard. He gave physically of himself as before. Yet he seemed to hold back something, perhaps a sense of passion or of genuine involvement that was mandatory for a fine professional athlete. His attitude seemed to say: this is what your management policies have wrought; I'll do my share, but don't expect me to do what you yourself don't do. A defeat somehow did not seem to matter that much to him. His friend Ron Culp thought Twardzik was playing out of personal loyalty to Ramsay more than for any other reason. Culp sensed a major change over the years in Twardzik's attitude and he believed it a melancholy one. One of the things that Culp came to hate about the harsh world of professional basketball was watching the attitude of players change. They arrived enthusiastic and optimistic but the nature of the game and the season and the money and the pressures changed them and made them progressively more cynical. To most Portland fans Twardzik exemplified the surviving company man in professional sports. Yet privately he was very bitter over the way he had been treated. Sometimes it was more than he could bear to think about. He and his wife would talk about it and become so angry that they would have to put it aside and talk more positively about life. Then, when he was on the road, he would think of his salary in comparison with that of young and untested players and he would become bitter again.

IN DECEMBER, THE CBS television network and the league received a blow to their pride and their finances. General Motors, one of the great weather-vane advertisers for all sports, and a central buyer for this year's NBA package, decided to withdraw its advertising for the season. Chevy had earlier agreed with CBS to buy some three minutes a game of the regular NBA package—roughly $100,000 a shot—and the time had been put on hold. For CBS, GM was a vital ingredient in a larger advertising package (in sports advertising there was always a package): a beer, a shaving cream, a life insurance company and, above all, an automobile. The car was crucial. Advertising people believed that most of the selling done on prime time was to women. But sports was a different world, a lonely surviving male bastion, and a place where things could be sold to *men*. Men still made the decisions about what kind of life insurance the family would buy, what beer it would drink and most importantly, what kind of car it would drive.

Thus every network sports package liked to have a car. It was known in advertising circles that General Motors really wanted to buy into *college* basketball, a sport played with greater intensity for higher ratings, to a younger, more affluent, whiter audience, but Ford had locked up the college games on NBC. Thus GM had tentatively agreed to the NBA, but with some degree of resignation. It was not a hot vehicle, clearly not really worth the money, but there were not many good male vehicles around. It was a case—not uncommon in advertising—where a buying decision was made partly to keep someone else out, a sort of defensive action. On Madison Avenue, the decision of Chevy to pull out was viewed as a true reflection of the weakness of the draw: a major advertiser was not only pulling out of the NBA but it was doing so in full awareness that a competitor might freely come in.

With Chevy out, a good deal of nervousness ran through CBS Sports. At last, after much hard selling and at much lower prices, Subaru came in, delighted to sell Japanese products by means of American sports. But it had not been an easy sell, and the deal was well below, it was said, the $18,000 for a thirty-second spot that CBS wanted (a figure roughly a third or a fourth, depending on the time of the season, of what professional football got for a comparable spot). Still, the package now had a base. The car was in and the beer was in too.

The beer was Miller Lite. The Miller Lite people, and their agents in the advertising world, had considerable reservations about professional basketball, but they were at least for the moment ready to stay the course. They thought there were a lot of things wrong with the league, and with the way

CBS presented it, and they were not especially eager to use basketball players in their commercials featuring former athletes. Perhaps in another time they might have dropped the entire NBA package. But they did not have that luxury now. For Miller, challenged by Anheuser Busch Natural, was engaged in a great war of its own for the low-cal beer championship of America. Millions of dollars were at stake. Natural had even stolen some of the ex-jocks who played such a large part in propagandizing Lite. Advertising was particularly important for low-cal beer; it was a product without a history and a tradition. No American father, after all, had ever taken his son to a local pub and ordered up a Lite for him in observance of his eighteenth birthday. So Miller was using advertising to create its own history. It ran charming whimsical commercials rich in nostalgia, displaying prominent ex-jocks; their history and nostalgia became, by implication, Miller Lite's history and nostalgia. As they were burly and hairy, Miller established that its product was not sissified, but one favored by good old boys in neighborhood pubs largely devoid of women. The Miller commercials were done with rare skill and the same athletes often reappeared in different commercials, becoming gradually a kind of great ongoing national jock family. They had roots; so too, clearly, did Miller Lite.

Though some of the CBS basketball advertisers were shaken by the defection of Chevy, the people at Miller took it in stride. In spite of its failings, the NBA remained an available way to reach young Americans. If Miller pulled out, Natural and its renegade jocks, some of them former members of the Lite family, might soon appear as NBA sponsors. There was, for example, the case of Mickey Mantle, a former baseball player who was the advertising man's ex-jock dream, a shy country boy who had had the good fortune to play in the nation's richest market for his entire career. Mantle had played constantly in great pain, and had drawn big money only near the end of his career, a surviving white power-hitter among more and more black stars. In an age where the best players switched teams readily, Mantle had played for only one team and that seemed to symbolize the best of old-fashioned loyalty. Mantle had however not seen fit to extend his loyalty in baseball to loyalty in beer drinking. First speaking for Lite, he had soon switched to Natural. The money in the low-cal beer war was very big. Most Americans after all had white collar jobs and had to watch their waistlines. If Miller pulled out of the NBA, Natural would surely move in.

CBS, the network which was in effect cosponsor of the league, was now

paying a great deal of money for a property whose ratings had declined seriously. Along Madison Avenue there were persistent rumors to the effect
that in 1982, when the current contract expired, CBS would try either to get
out of the game completely or to curtail its coverage markedly and pay considerably less for the honor of achieving those soft ratings. The television
money was of course central to the league's solvency and legitimacy; roughly
40 percent of the NBA teams, it was said, were in the black only because of
the television money—some $800,000 per team—and there were fran-
chises so shaky that if the television check was as much as a day late, they
anxiously called league headquarters to inquire about its whereabouts.

Even with Miller in, CBS was still struggling. All the commercial slots
for NBA games were not filled. Sometimes with Sunday games coming up,
there were desperate deals known as fire sales on Friday afternoon; then,
anxious to unload the time, the network virtually gave it away. Shrewd advertisers could hold back and then come in for as little as $5,000 for a
thirty-second spot. The network's wariness and lack of enthusiasm was reflected in the way it now nibbled at the NBA schedule. Much to the annoyance of the owners, there were two NBA schedules, one for the league which
began in October, and one for CBS which began only in mid-January after
the football season was virtually completed. When CBS finally deigned, a
few weeks later, to cover its first regular Sunday afternoon game, it was,
predictably enough, Los Angeles versus Boston ("Can the Magic Man pull a
Bird out of his hat?"), a hype, not of teams but of rookie superstars. The
game, much to everyone's relief, drew well, an 8.5 rating (meaning that 8.5
percent of television-owning families had tuned in), well above the disastrous 5.6 average of the previous season, but not every game could be
Boston-L.A. There were twenty other teams in the league, a handful of
them good and interesting and relentlessly competitive, but many of them
weak, and most of them without a marked public identity. The CBS executives, looking at their schedule, had a sense that they might get a season
rating in the low 6's. To make the league coverage palatable to average television fans, CBS now needed to ignore some two-thirds of the teams.

At the same time as CBS was struggling to save its shaky product, Roone
Arledge's mind was as far as it could be from the problems of the game. He
was the man who had done so much to make professional basketball a via-
ble television property, and who had subsequently done just as much to deprive it of viability. He had in fact established himself as the most talented

huckster-dramatist in all of television sports, to the point where ABC had given him, as a reward, the real world of real people: he was now in charge of ABC News as well. Roone Arledge was onto bigger game now. He was determined to overtake CBS where it counted the most—every weeknight, on the evening news where CBS had been traditionally preeminent. Walter Cronkite, the symbol of that preeminence, was due to retire in a year; without Cronkite, Arledge was sure, CBS would be extremely vulnerable. Arledge loved the attention CBS now paid to ABC News, the top people there were, he told friends, really uptight. Besides he now had the perfect story with which to drive up ABC's ratings. Iranian students had in early November taken sixty-five American citizens hostage at the Tehran embassy. It was, he knew immediately, a great television story, intensely human with grave international implications, and best of all, with great pictures. As a man whose roots were in sports, where the instinct was to do things *live* and exploit them, rather than in the soberer and more restrained world of news, he sensed the potential and was determined to make ABC the station to which hostage buffs would automatically turn. He had immediately added an extra show to the late-evening schedule. The hostage story had the emotional impact of little children lost in a cave, except on a far greater scale. An entire nation was soon hooked. When, four or five days into the story, subordinate executives suggested that because nothing had happened that day they might drop the second section, Arledge knew better. He had by chance been at Lake Placid dealing with his other world, that of sports and the Winter Olympics, and everyone he had met had asked him about the hostages. The late-evening hostage special would stay. Non-news, he believed, if the country cared, was as important as news. So it was a good time for him and for ABC News, which was on the rise; in January 1980 the main ABC evening news show, once the absolute joke of the industry, would pass NBC in the ratings. Arledge loved that. He was wearing two hats, shuttling between his News office on West Sixty-seventh Street and his Sports office on Sixth Avenue and Fifty-fourth by means of his chauffeur-driven Jaguar (the better to give the right mod signal to Madison Avenue). Always difficult to reach even in the best of times, Arledge was now more difficult than ever to find; there were, said his employees, now *two* places not to find him.

Arledge's stamp was most indisputably upon professional basketball, as it was on almost all major sports. A key element of modern professional sports was its symbiotic relationship with television, and for twenty years Arledge had been by far the most important figure in that relationship: pioneer, entrepreneur, writer of the rule book, violator of his own rule book. Television had helped convey basketball, like so many other sports, out of its own arenas into the mainstream of national entertainment, making it a principal means for American companies to sell American products; it was thus responsible for much of professional basketball's sudden health and, equally, much of its more recent illness. Television had helped basketball find a mass audience and had amplified for Americans the artistry of the game. It had also made the game more potent commercially; the audience was larger, and there was more money to be made than before. People had once paid a relatively small amount of money simply to see a game; now large companies were willing to pay millions of dollars to sell products and that meant that sports at every level, professional and college alike, had become more of a business and less of a game. All of this happened within a decade. It was a perfect example of what television newscaster Daniel Schorr had once called the "greenhouse effect" of television—things observed by the cameras tended to grow abnormally fast and large, often unhealthily so. Certainly that was true of professional basketball. Its norms and economics were no longer the norms and economics of a simple sport played in small arenas in a few cities, but the norms of television and Madison Avenue. Moreover, as basketball people were eventually to learn, as quick as television was to seduce an institution, it was equally quick to turn against one with which it was disenchanted.

Football had of course become an immense popular and commercial success almost overnight, and the basketball owners watched that explosion enviously. Professional basketball had entered the sixties a small sport played in eight cities before dedicated fans. It was largely without glamour. In some cities there was always doubt, right up until payday, whether the payroll could be met. The first television contract, desperately agreed to, had been with NBC. The ratings in the early sixties were so poor that in the world of Nielsen they were reported as the ultimate ignominy, IFR. *Insufficient for Reporting.* To no one's surprise NBC got out of the game as quickly as it could. Then in 1965 ABC, the weakest of the three networks, a company with nowhere to go but up, took basketball over. Weak in both prime-time programming and news, ABC had been forced to make its move in sports and to put its best young people there. The contract was for five years, starting at $600,000 a year for the entire league, and going up in increments of $100,000 a year until it reached $1 million in the final year. In that first year there were only nine teams and several were on the edge of bankruptcy; the ABC contract prudently contained a clause letting the network out if more than one team failed. In retrospect, the network officials realized later, the clause should have allowed them to limit the number of teams *coming in.* But it was a good league, filled with fierce and genuine rivalries, teams which had competed for years and loved to beat up on each other. Making the NBA attractive on television became the responsibility of the most talented man in the network, Roone Arledge.

Arledge was at the very center of the sports revolution in television. He was young, he was not tied to the past (for there was no past to be tied to) and he understood what the camera could do as few producers did. Other producers sent four or five cameras to a game; Arledge might send eleven. He was a man of impulse in a profession built around impulse; he understood that television was action, that it was live, and that the camera could convey it as words could not. Where others in sports sought rules to guide them, Arledge gloried in the fact that it was so new a business that it *had* no rules. He was new and he had nothing to unlearn. His cameras would catch the *scene,* the cheerleaders, the band, the personal responses of the players and coaches and create an intimacy that the average sports fans had always sought and never gained; he wanted, Arledge once wrote in a memo, to bring the fan to the game, not to bring the game to the fan.

He was the executive producer of ABC Sports in his late twenties; when he began televising the NBA games he was all of thirty-three. Later, as his string of successes mounted—*Wide World of Sports,* college football, the Olympic Games, *Monday Night Football*—people wrote of him as a television genius. His longtime colleague Barry Frank saw him differently. Arledge's great talent, Frank thought, was not that he was brilliant, but that he was *everyman.* Arledge knew what he wanted to see and what excited him, and in a world filled with cautious men, who no longer knew what they wanted to do or, more important, why they wanted to do it, he held faithfully to his own instincts. He never lost touch with himself. He trusted himself because his taste was so elemental. Roone Arledge had learned to program what Roone Arledge wanted to see. Introduced in the early seventies to soccer and told that it too would be like basketball, the coming game, Arledge held back. "I don't like it," he said. Why not, Roone? a colleague asked. "Too slow," he answered. "Too many people. Too much running. Too little happening. I don't understand the rules. If I don't, the rest of the country won't. I'm not ready for it, and the country's not ready for it." At the same time he was brilliant at televising the Winter Olympics, taking seemingly arcane sports which Americans knew nothing about and by means of deft camera work and quick biographical sketches of the competitors, depicted at home in Austria or Liechtenstein, making both the sport and the athlete come alive in places where snow had never fallen. What Arledge understood about his medium was its immediacy, that sports did not necessarily need a history or roots, that he could, if necessary, and if the sport translated itself into pictures, create a constituency for it. Nor did he mind, if an event seemed potentially boring, focusing attention on the broadcast booth, and making the action there as important as the action on the field. He thus gave the nation Howard Cosell. ("Howard," Arledge said to him after his debut as a football commentator, "we are not paying you by the syllable.") In those twenty years in sports, no one did it better than Arledge and ABC.

Arledge had not been a basketball fan but he was quickly impressed by the beauty of the game, the power and the grace of the athletes. What ABC had to prove to a disbelieving national public, he believed, was that this was not simply a bunch of tall awkward goons throwing a ball through a hoop, but a game of grace and power played at a fever of intensity. He was artist enough to understand and catch the artistry of the game. He used replays endlessly to show the ballet, and to catch the intensity of the matchups, Dave DeBusschere against Gus Johnson, Wilt Chamberlain against Bill Russell, Bill Bradley against John Havlicek, Jerry West against Earl Monroe. He was aware of basketball's limitations: baseball was part of the American past, the World Series never had to be sold, it created its own myth; pro football, more recent as a national sport, had a primal force that the entire country responded to. Professional basketball was different: it was not rooted nationally, it had flowered only in a few select urban areas, and a few rural places. As a national sport it was young and uncertain and its growth, he believed, would take time. Even when ABC had the ideal media match-ups, the New York Knicks against the Los Angeles Lakers, the ratings by football standards were small. But the game was intense and artistic and had one advantage over football and baseball—it was played indoors, and its intensity was thus bottled up in an arena, and tangible even for the fan seated in his home. In the meantime he intended to exploit as best he could the traditional rivalries, for that was one of the best things the league had going for it, genuine rivalries in which the players themselves participated. Those rivalries, Boston-Philly, New York-Baltimore, needed no ballyhoo; the athletes themselves were self-evidently proud and they liked nothing better than to beat their opponents, particularly on national television. They were, in those days, obviously motivated more by pride than by money, and the camera readily caught that pride.

Where once under NBC there had been no ratings at all, Roone Arledge carefully stroked the sport upwards. It was never easy. The owners, he soon decided, were the most selfish and egocentric he had ever dealt with. Nevertheless the ratings began to climb: first a 6, then a 7.4, then a 7.6, then an 8.1 and in 1968–69, the final year of that contract, with the entire league dividing up only $1 million, an 8.9.

But Arledge, like others, was concerned about the increase in the number of teams. He mentioned his concern to Walter Kennedy, then the commissioner, who seemed to agree. But whether Kennedy ever mentioned it to the owners, Arledge never knew. He had a strong sense of the owners' growing contempt for Kennedy and Kennedy's consciousness of it. Kennedy, he believed, was a nice man fighting hard to hold on to a job, wary of stepping on the toes of his owners who more and more treated him with open contempt. Arledge had no sure sense of the ideal size of the league, perhaps twelve teams by 1970 going to sixteen teams twenty years later. But there was no stopping these owners. Arledge felt that they were different from other sports owners; they wanted television, but they treated it with contempt and would make no concessions to it. He had to fight with them constantly to schedule the matchups he wanted for Sunday. Worse, he recalled Jack Kent Cooke, the Los Angeles owner and a particular nemesis, steadfastly, even at playoff time, refusing to clear a few seats in front of the main television cameras, so there were always heads popping up to block the action at crucial moments. "Bush," Arledge would scream to his associates in the control room when it happened. "It's *goddamn bush.* Can't you get these bush people to do anything? I mean it's their goddamn game." Several times he warned Walter Kennedy about expansion, that it was all going too fast, that the league was plunging ahead too quickly from one era to another. "Take your time," he said. No one listened.

ABC followed its first five-year contract, which had ended in 1969, with another one for four years. Again the money was still relatively small by pro football standards, some $6 million for the last year. During the course of the second contract the ratings continued to be good, all 9's until the final year when it reached 10. But the sport had grown too quickly for its own good. Where there had been nine teams at the start of the first ABC contract, there were now seventeen. What was more, instead of being delighted with the good fortune their contract with ABC had produced, the owners were restive. Many of them were new. Few remembered the days just ten years earlier when no other network wanted the sport at all. They seemed to be aware of nothing but the greater price being paid for football. It was all ABC's fault, they were sure. In 1973 the time came for a new contract. ABC had an option for renewal and a handshake deal with Walter Kennedy. Everything seemed settled. But suddenly it was clear that several powerful owners, led by Jack Kent Cooke, wanted to switch to CBS. In meeting after meeting new owner demands were met by ABC, leaving the owners with no legal basis for reneging. At this point, the key owners on the television committee went out for drinks with Barry Frank, once an Arledge associate, now an agent for the league. "Let's think of all the ways we can to fuck ABC," suggested Alan Rothenberg, then Cooke's attorney, according to Frank's later testimony in court. (When Rothenberg himself testified, he denied saying it.) Frank, knowing ABC, knowing Arledge, had the ideal proposal: demand that *both* CBS and ABC program the games in October and November between 1 and 2 p.m. on Saturdays. That was a revolver to Arledge's head; Saturday afternoon in autumn, with college football, was the jewel of his sports programming. There was no way ABC would replace Ohio State–Michigan with a professional basketball game. The NBA switched to CBS. Arledge charged conspiracy and contested the case in court and lost. One voice in the NBA warned against the switch—Celtics coach Red Auerbach, who could spot a fellow pirate when he saw one. He also thought ABC was doing quite well with the game and he was worried about what would happen if Arledge turned against them. "You don't really think a man like Roone Arledge is going to take this lying down, do you?" he asked. No one listened and the NBA switched.

ARLEDGE, OF COURSE, was furious. He had lost a valuable property which he had personally nurtured to success and he felt betrayed, not by CBS, that was part of the network game, but by the NBA. The first thing he did was destroy pro basketball on Saturday afternoons. Never had ABC promoted its college games as it did that fall, as Arledge set out to show Madison Avenue what was a real part of the American sporting scene and what was a vulnerable one. It was like a mugging; by the next year CBS and the NBA had gratefully retreated to Sunday afternoon. But that was not enough. He wanted, friends thought, vengeance, and he also had a lot of open time on Sunday afternoons. In the past Arledge had been successful because he knew how to focus on the special beauty and rhythm of a given sport and, through the magic of his cameras, virtually invent a national constituency for it. Now, going against CBS, he set out to test television's true power, to show that television was so rich and powerful that it did not need reality. It could create its own reality. He became the founding father of a new genre in television sports, known forever after in the immortal phrase of Bill Leggett of *Sports Illustrated* as TrashSports. It was a program called *Superstars*. The idea had been around the network world for a long time—superb athletes from different sports competing in various events against each other. Others had turned it down. Now Arledge wanted it. Everyone around him told him it was a terrible idea, that it was hokey and would not work. Arledge thought otherwise. "If I were a fan I'd like to see these guys compete against each other," he said.

So it was born, Roone's own decathlon. He could select superb athletes who were also attractive and verbal; he could, if he chose, control the racial mix, and if there were long dull parts, he could leave them on the cutting-room floor. So what if it was hokey? People, he told friends, *liked* it, and wanted to watch it. That was good enough. So what if it was sports without the ecstasy of victory and the agony of defeat? It worked. He also took *Wide World of Sports,* his Saturday show, and added a Sunday version. This new Sunday afternoon was a staggering success. The ratings hovered around 12. From the start it virtually killed network hockey and left Madison Avenue with a sour feeling about professional basketball. Soon NBC had the college basketball game and the college game was increasingly exciting. In part as an obeisance to television, colleges now allowed freshmen to play, and though the college game had rarely been played before on Sunday, when NBC asked for Sunday games and offered huge sums of money, even suggesting which teams should play, and where and at what time, the colleges agreed. The college game began to draw better than the pro game. In the first year of the CBS contract the ratings plummeted from a 10 to an

8.1; soon the decline became steady and very serious. Along Madison Avenue it was known as Roone's Revenge.

The emergence of TrashSports coincided with the NBA's own new malaise. With so many new teams the old rivalries simply evaporated. In addition it became harder for the old teams, which happened to be teams in the great media markets, to replenish themselves as their players grew older, for now more teams were drawing on the talent bank. There was even more travel, and the players, already locked into an endless schedule, now had far greater travel burdens; they appeared constantly exhausted on television during the regular season. And where once it had been only the owners who were greedy, now the players were greedy as well. The existence of the new league, the ABA, meant that salaries were skyrocketing. Most damaging of all to the intensity of the game was the arrival of no-cut contracts. Given a no-cut contract, too many games and a deadening travel schedule, many players responded by playing on automatic pilot, coming alive only at playoff time. Just as the camera had caught the vital intensity of the earlier days, now it with equal fidelity captured the increasing indifference of the players. By contrast, college basketball reeked of authentic intensity and competition, kids hurling themselves on the floor for loose balls.

At CBS nothing seemed to go right. The network which had always been number one in everything, and which had a certain elitist smugness about its position in broadcasting, was being challenged by ABC on other fronts. High executives came and went in CBS Sports. In 1978 the NBA and CBS began negotiating a new four-year contract. The NBA was now a troubled, declining product. No one else seemed very much interested in picking it up. Whereas in 1978, the last year of the previous contract, CBS paid the league some $13 million now—to CBS's surprise—the owners wanted much more: $80 million for four years. A man named Bob Wussler began the negotiations; midway through, CBS let him go. At that moment Larry O'Brien, the NBA commissioner, rushed into the CBS executive offices to say that he had a handshake deal for four years at $74 million. Along Madison Avenue there was a sense that this was almost comic, so much money for so marginal a sport. No one else after all very much wanted the product. At best, experts thought, a figure of $50 or $52 million was closer to reality. For a time the CBS executives thought of challenging O'Brien in court, though that would be a messy business, fighting the very partner you needed. In the end, CBS accepted its lawyers' advice and agreed, reluctantly and very unhappily, to the $74 million figure. The partners in the marriage had decided not to get a divorce, but it would be hard for them to dislike each other more. By the middle of the 1979–80 season, the owners were angrier than ever with CBS and at the same time terrified that CBS might not renew the contract next time. Some of them wished they had Roone Arledge back.

None of this bothered Roone Arledge very much. Professional basketball was distant from him now. He rarely watched. That which had mattered so passionately just seven years earlier was virtually forgotten. He was a man of two kingdoms and the smaller one, sports, had already been conquered. He was much more interested in beating CBS in its news ratings. Guessing that Dan Rather was likely to be Walter Cronkite's successor, Arledge made an incredible offer for him, which CBS was forced to match. At the same time, as the NBA season moved forward Arledge was preoccupied with the Iran story. Early on, one of his news producers had added a slug over the late-night half hour, "The Iran Crisis: America Held Hostage." It was blatantly editorial and blatantly a hype, and precisely what those who had once admired Arledge in sports feared from him now in news. Would there, they worried, now be TrashNews? At first Arledge did not like the slug; he feared that it locked ABC in. But soon he saw that it *worked,* that it tied into the rage and frustrations many Americans felt about their status in the world. In those days the pressure of both jobs mounted and Roone Arledge, most decidedly not held hostage, was having the best time of his life.

THE PLAYERS THEMSELVES seemed numb. Game after game was on the road. Each day there was less confidence, and each day the locker room was quieter and the bus more subdued. Game by game there was less camaraderie. Each player seemed to shrink inside himself. Because they were playing poorly there was an awareness that Inman the Shadow was working the phone, and while the Shadow was primarily interested in dealing Luke and Lionel, who knew what moves lay in the hands of the Shadow, building up his awesome phone bill? He might in talking with some flesh peddler from a distant city say at the last minute, "Oh, all right, we'll throw in T. R. Dunn too." Or Tom Owens. Or Ron Brewer. Anything to change the lineup. No one raged at anyone else. They were all very polite. But they all seemed isolated. There was, thought Buckwalter, an *acceptance* of defeat; it might be better, he thought, if they raged at one another. If someone would only blame someone else. Everyone knew that Luke was probably going to go, and that he wanted to go, but no one said anything to him, not about wanting to leave and not about the turnovers. He was an intimidating presence and among those he intimidated were his own teammates. Besides, they were professionals and he was a professional and their attitude was that he was entitled to make the best deal for himself that he could. But they were uneasy. Some of them blamed him, some of them blamed management, for not getting the whole thing over with.

Chicago, the night before, had been loss number nine, a dismal defeat by a dismal team. A tiny guard named Del Beshore had gotten 8 assists in 25 minutes against them. Mark Landsberger, a white forward, dominated the boards, getting 14 rebounds in 28 minutes. That night Buckwalter walked the streets of Chicago, trying to burn off the misery. "Landsberger," he said, *"Mark Landsberger!* If he plays on a Washington playground and hits three buckets, the people there would break into polite applause. *Landsberger!"* Now they were flying to Kansas City. The announcer Steve Jones said Kansas City was good because the hotel where they stayed served excellent gumbo.

So they filed in, the players for a few hours of rest before Ramsay held a practice; Jones to change quickly into a warmup so he could get his daily tennis game. To the players the NBA was a constant series of arenas, coffee shops and small college gyms where they practiced; to Jones it was a series of tennis matches—he had someone lined up in every city. Later, consuming some of the famed hotel gumbo, Jones discoursed on the season he had spent as a player in St. Louis some years before. "The St. Louis Spirits," he said, "right nickname. Greatest collection of head cases in basketball history." There had been a story in the paper the previous day about Marvin Barnes, known as "Bad News" or, more intimately, "News," perhaps the greatest head case of all in recent basketball history, a man of talent equaled only by his capacity to self-destruct. "Marvin comes, Marvin goes," Jones said. "Marvin signs, Marvin unsigns." The report had been that Marvin was going to sign with San Diego. "I'm here to help my man, *Bill,*" Jones said, doing an imitation of Barnes. "So the next morning Walton is up looking for his man, and his man is probably gone. Saddest story in basketball. Most talented player I ever saw come into the game. He's blown it all, and it's *all* gone, but I never saw a better player than Marvin Barnes when he came in the league. As quick as Walter Davis. The rebounding instincts, timing and strength of Moses Malone. Could shoot like Marques Johnson. Marvin broke every rule there was, sometimes I think he studied the rules just so he could break them. He was his own worst enemy. Anything he had, and he had a lot in those days, he gave away. Stayed up all night to five o'clock, six o'clock. Always late to practice. *Always* being fined. One year they fined him five thousand for breaking all those rules. Then they beat New York in the playoffs and News just tore New York apart, and they gave him back the money. He thought they would always give it back. He was so talented but no one had ever disciplined him. Just too talented to discipline. Marvin loved the street people, they were his people, he said. 'These are my people, these people love *News*,' he'd say. He'd be out with them until five o'clock every morning. All he knew were night people. He'd come to a game and make the trainer rub him in baby oil so that his body would gleam. '*News* likes to look good for his people.' Meanwhile the ballboy isn't taking care of the other players like he's supposed to because he's out behind the arena shining up Marvin's Rolls. 'People want *News*'s car to look good.' Marvin thought it would never end and that those people gave a damn about him."

There in the restaurant Jones moved back and forth between love of Marvin Barnes, the pleasure in telling the stories and anger over what had happened. "One time we're supposed to fly to Virginia and Marvin misses the plane. We're at the airport and it's four o'clock in the afternoon and he's not there, so the coach calls him at home. Wakes him up. 'You're not going to make the plane,' says the coach. '*News* will catch a later one,' Marvin says. He goes back to sleep. The coach calls again. 'There is no later one,' the coach says. So Marvin goes back to sleep another time, wakes up about five o'clock, charters a plane to Virginia. Costs him fifteen hundred. We're in the locker room, the game is about to begin, and who comes in with the biggest pimp's hat you ever saw, a mink coat that must have cost $10,000 and underneath that, his basketball uniform? *Marvin!* He's eating a Big Mac and stuffing fries down his throat. 'Have no fear,' he said, '*News* is here.' That night he goes out and scores maybe forty-nine points and gets maybe twenty-five rebounds. He was so good, his body was so strong, he thought it would last forever, that he could do anything he wanted with his body, keep whatever hours he wanted, put anything inside him he wanted and there would be no price. Too damn much natural talent, maybe it all came so easily to him he never took it seriously." Last year, after a pathetic performance in Boston, Marvin had been waived out of the league. Boston had been one great party from the time he arrived to the time, thirty-eight games later, when he was let go. Every time paychecks were to be issued the Celtics office was deluged with phone calls from the friends of Marvin Barnes, all wanting a slice of his paycheck—the restaurants, clothing salesmen, car dealers, landlords, the IRS. San Diego would be his last chance. "The nicest kid you ever saw," Jones was saying. "Marvin's only problem was being too kind and generous. I don't think he'll make it through the season." He was eating gumbo and talking about a man who was only twenty-seven years old. "You try and tell these kids how rare it all is to get this far," he said, his voice different now, colder, angrier. "The Man gives you one chance at it in this game. You can't waste it. You can't be black and waste *anything.* Not a damn thing."

With Marvin a large part of the problem had been drugs. He was young and rich and generous, and there had always been, after every game in every arena, a coterie anxious to be his friends. Inevitably there was among these people someone with a connection, a very good *instant* friend. In the NBA drugs were a constant shadow; in other sports the shadows were slightly different. In baseball, white and rural in its roots, less rigorous in its daily physical demands, players in season having too much time to kill in alien cities, there was a surprising number of serious alcohol problems. Football—with its physical violence, its constant pain from injuries, and its single game a week—produced many players addicted to pills, uppers and downers. Basketball players had little time for boozing, and tended, if a stimulant was required, towards drugs. With heavy schedules, the days were gone when everyone except a few religiously inclined souls went out and caroused at night, when by legend a coach might assign a benchwarmer the job of taking out a first-string buddy from an opposing team on the eve of the game to drink into the early hours. The new vice was drugs, not surprising considering the salaries, the mod rootless lifestyle of many players, and the easy availability in city after city of good dope. Smoking pot was fairly normal. Light use of cocaine on many teams was simply a part of the season; on some teams, and with some stars who could afford it, the use was heavier. The athletes themselves were now less like old-fashioned jocks and more like musicians past and entertainers present; cocaine, being part of the entertainment world, was bound to be part of the sports-entertainment world. Coke, said one thoughtful league official, went with the territory; it was the Cadillac of modern drugs, great highs at (so its users believed) a limited physical cost. The exact incidence of cocaine use in professional basketball was impossible to determine unless, as one coach said, you were "a good eye, ear, nose and throat specialist and you checked every player out." Possibly, thought the same coach, 20 percent of the players used coke to some degree. A few teams—usually the weakest ones, where discipline was breaking down and players were on the margin—had serious coke problems. How many players in the league had coke habits was anybody's guess. There was general nervousness among coaches as they watched for what they believed to be the telltale signs of heavy coke usage—arrogance, it was said, mixed with paranoia. Whenever a player's game began to decline there was a lot of quick gossiping in the NBA backchannel among coaches, general managers, and other players, comments that coke might be the reason. Suspicions were constantly in the air. In all of this Portland remained one of the straighter teams; Kermit Washington seemed the symbol of that. While in Los Angeles with the Lakers he had, in accord with that local custom whereby film stars and athletic stars are gathered and mixed, been invited to the home of one of the great movie actors of our time. Everyone there, it seemed, was sniffing coke and offering some to Kermit. He was terrified, had waited some ten minutes and then had grabbed his wife. "Come on, Pat," he had said, "we're in the wrong party in the wrong house."

IN THE LOSING streak their strengths became shakier, their weaknesses more noticeable. Other teams now scouted them more accurately. With Hollins out and Twardzik able to play only in limited spurts, Ron Brewer and T. R. Dunn, neither of them good ballhandlers, had the job of bringing the ball up. Opposing teams were clearly homing in on this—attack the Blazer guards, the scouting reports said—and doing it with considerable success. The scouting reports also showed that if Kermit Washington was playing at power forward instead of Maurice Lucas, then though that perhaps meant better rebounding and defense, it also threw the Ramsay offense off. For Ramsay's offense called for the power forward to come out high, away from the basket, and help set the offense, either by passing inside or moving towards the basket and taking a quick twelve-foot jumper. But Luke was a better passer than Washington and a better and more willing shooter. Washington hated to take a jump shot. He thought it was the mark of a selfish ballplayer and he was not confident about his own shooting. When he got the ball in the offense he tended not to respond by instinct but to hold the ball. In the split second before he was ready to pass, the defense had closed again. This all meant that opposing teams could ignore Washington as a shooter as they could not ignore Lucas, and that they could, in turn, double up on Tom Owens as they could not when Luke was playing. That in turn meant that Owens did not get as many nor as good shots as in the past. Washington was, the coaches were now realizing, a player with some limitations, he did not set a pick particularly well and he did not drive to the basket as well as he should. But he was a player of such desire and passion to win that his overall game tended under normal circumstances to obscure his weaknesses.

Washington himself took the losing streak harder than anyone on the team with the possible exception of Ramsay. Kermit became harder to talk to, more aloof. In postgame locker-room interviews his words became more elliptical. He would say things like "I have to rebound better and work harder on defense" and the translation was, for someone alert to nuance, "the other people on the team better work harder on defense." He was trying not to let the losing streak destroy him. There was a time, when he was in college, he said, when losing seemed like death. It had destroyed him. He had become so tight that he had come down with a severe ulcer and his health had stood in the balance. In the professional game, he was trying to reduce that tension, reduce how much defeat meant. During the losing streak he had gone to the library and taken out a biography of Gandhi, hoping to find solace and comfort from the great man's life. Because he wanted approval so badly, defeat seemed personal with him. It transported him back in time from what he had become to what he had been.

Sometimes when he talked about Swen Nater, his friend in San Diego, he would say that he understood Swen because he was passed around a lot as a little boy. I can understand that, Kermit would say, I was passed around too. That was a sad phrase from a difficult childhood. Passed around. His mother was a graduate of Howard University, where she had received good marks. She was very smart, he thought, but not so good at dealing with the pressures of life around her. She was always telling people to be truthful and honest and they were always letting her down. Probably she had been too idealistic, he thought. His parents split up when he was about three.

There had been a terrible fight, one that he was not supposed to see. Years later he thought that his father had wanted some credit cards back from his mother. His mother's brother had come over and there had been a family fight, and someone hit his uncle with an iron, and there had been blood. Everyone had been shouting and yelling. He witnessed everything, the accusations, the fighting, the blood. He had been absolutely terrified by the sight of the people he loved fighting with each other. That was the last time he saw his parents together. His father took custody of the children. Then his mother had come by one day and taken him and his older brother and run off with them. It had been an aimless, ill-planned flight and they had been poor all the time. He remembered vaguely the bleakness of the trip; they stayed once with the Salvation Army and there had been days with virtually nothing to eat. He had a memory, he was not entirely sure it was true, of not eating for three days and then being given a ham and cheese sandwich and devouring it so quickly that he never even chewed it. Finally they had to wire for help and his father showed up to take them home. For a time he and his brother lived with various members of the family— grandparents, aunts, uncles, father's family, mother's family, changing homes. There was a feeling, he remembered, of never really belonging, of perhaps not being wanted. He was convinced that the fault must somehow be his, and became terribly shy, quiet to the point of being mute. He said as little as he could because he was afraid that anything he said might be wrong. Finally they ended up with his great-grandmother on his father's side. She was a stern, strict old lady, but she also had time to love both boys. The rules were strict but he knew she cared. When he and his brother Eric brought their report cards home from school and their grades were predictably bad, they would tell the old lady that they had done well. She, after all, could not read or write. Pleased that these two little boys had done so well, she would mark her X on the card in the appropriate place. That was as good a time as he remembered. His father remarried and the boys moved back with him; his stepmother was clearly less than overjoyed to find that the Washington ménage contained two little boys. The home did not become warmer. He had no memory, as a little boy, of anyone hugging him. He was closest to his older brother, Eric; it was as if the two of them were connected to each other, against the rest of the world.

The neighborhood that he grew up in was just shy of being a ghetto. Perhaps it would be a ghetto to white eyes, but by comparison with far worse black neighborhoods, it was not that bad. Still, his area was not without danger; by all rights he should have been a street person, but he was afraid of the streets. There were always gangs and he was never a member of any gang. He was often afraid when he went out on the streets; there were certain sections you simply did not enter. When the chance came to join a gang he was too frightened to take it. It was, he decided later after he had gotten out, a neighborhood of great hopelessness. For the kids the streets were the real world, not the schools, nor, all too often, the homes. Some survived the streets, but many did not. Many of those he knew had burned out young—drugs, gangs, prison. The worst thing about growing up there, he thought years later, was that no one knew any better. You simply went through life accepting what you had because it was the only thing you knew. The only real role model was failure. Oh, perhaps there were a few black sports stars on television. But there was no connection, no sense that those people on television had anything to do with this sad beaten neighborhood he lived in. He had as a boy loved to go to movies. Whenever he did and there was a black man in the movie, playing the role of a soldier, he was always sure that the black man was going to be among the first to die. He was rarely wrong. There were two worlds out there, one that successful people came from and one that black people came from. He grew up in that neighborhood afraid, afraid of offending his family, afraid to be in a gang, afraid not to be in a gang. He had no self-esteem at all. If anyone he was with said anything, Kermit Washington was always quick to agree.

The schools were a reflection of the community. The teachers were, almost to a person, unable to help. It wasn't that they were bad people, simply that all too often they were caught up in the same cycle of expected failure. They did not, Washington later decided, really believe that a black child could achieve anything. Living differently, getting out of that area, was beyond their own vision. What had happened to them would happen to their students. Kermit Washington remembered himself in those days as a skinny awkward boy without friends, except for his brother and perhaps one or two other buddies. He considered himself a poor student, unsure of his ability at anything. He was relieved at the end of every class when the bell would ring and he had gotten through without being called on. He was not a good athlete. He was so skinny that even in the summer he wore long sleeves and a long jacket so that no one would see how thin his arms were and make fun of him. In his senior year at Calvin Coolidge High he was about 6'4" and perhaps 150 pounds. Other kids called him The Blade. He played some school football largely because he had a friend on the team and he did not like to walk home at night alone; by going out for football he found some companionship.

He felt he could not do well at anything. He received uniformly poor grades in all classes. Then one day in biology class the students were dissecting frogs and the teacher, Mrs. Joan Thomas, watched him and said, "Kermit, you're doing an excellent job." He was terribly embarrassed and he was sure that she was making fun of him. All the other kids began to laugh too, sure that she was mocking him. After all, Kermit was the boy who had never been praised before and who was often the butt of a teacher's frustrated criticism. "No," she corrected them, "I mean it. Kermit is doing an excellent job." That was the first time that anyone had ever told him that he was good at anything in his entire life. With that he began to feel confident in biology and he began to study and get good marks. Soon he had good marks in biology and poor marks in everything else. Then Mrs. Thomas became his homeroom teacher and she looked at his report card and told him that he ought to try to do better in other courses too. "You know, Kermit," she said, "you're intelligent and you could get good marks if you wanted to." He was stunned by that, by the idea that she thought he was intelligent. In his last year at Calvin Coolidge he made the honor roll. He was very proud of that.

Yet it seemed unlikely that he would be able to go to college. Not many poor black graduates of Washington's school system went to college unless they were either superb athletes or superb students. He was neither. He was a terrible athlete. In his senior year he had played on the basketball team but had not even started, and he had averaged perhaps four points a game. District of Columbia high school basketball in those days was a center for college recruiters from all over the country, the East, the Big Ten, the Far West, but among those whose names were never heard was Kermit Washington. Then, in his senior year, his stepmother made it very clear that when he graduated he was supposed to give back his key to the house and move out. Suddenly, almost desperately, he had to think of the future, and he wanted to go to college. But he had no money. His brother Eric had won a football scholarship (he later played for the St. Louis Cardinals), so he decided he better win one too. He was too skinny for football. But he was tall and so he decided that basketball would have to be his sport.

Almost overnight, in his senior year, with the season virtually gone, he began to practice three hours a day. Then he heard of an all-star game for Washington players. Those chosen would compete against another all-star team from Pennsylvania. Everyone in playground basketball, which was big in Washington, knew about it, and only the best players were even invited to try out. Half terrified by the audacity of what he was doing, Kermit Washington, not even a starter at Coolidge, had shown up for the tryouts. At first the officials were not even going to let him compete because he had not been invited. But he talked his way into the competition and as soon as he did he regretted it. He had made a fool of himself, he was sure, coming here to play against the best players in the city; they were all much better than he was. He could not shoot, he knew, because he did not have a shot. The gym was almost empty except for lots of quite snappily dressed white men, recruiters. Among them was a young man named Tom Young who had been an assistant at Maryland, where the teams were always bigtime, and who had just taken a job as head coach at American University, a weak school in basketball. Young was there looking for prospects. The kids he could have recruited in the past for Maryland, the superstars, were now beyond his reach, and he would have to take what he could get. Young was, in his own words, working the scrap heap. But he noticed one young player, not very good, almost bad in fact, skinny and in some ways terribly unsure of himself, with no instinct for the game. But very quick, and tall and eager. So desperately eager that he dove after every loose ball. This was not a kid he would have gone after in his plusher Maryland days, but American was not Maryland, he could no longer be choosy, and this young man had a look of such eagerness. What was intriguing was that Tom Young had spent a lot of time around Washington playgrounds and high schools and he was acquainted with all the people who were supposed to be experts; none of them even knew who this boy was. Young continued to watch him and he noticed another quality: the people who ran this tryout were treating the boy very badly and yet the boy never complained. So Young, who could not be choosy, and who saw something in the boy that he could not even de-scribe, decided to offer him a scholarship to American. Forty kids try out, he thought, and I get the worst one.

So Kermit Washington thought he was lucky in the fall and Tom Young thought *he* was lucky, because over the summer Kermit Washington grew four more inches. He arrived as a freshman, skinny as ever, still very quick, determined to build himself up. He had spent the entire summer playing basketball and now he decided to build himself into a basketball machine. He lifted weights every day, right up until basketball practice; each night, before he went to bed, he put on a weight vest and ran up the seven flights of steps in his dorm several dozen times, building up his wind. No one, he decided, would be stronger or in better condition. Tom Young told him to lift weights only three days a week but he refused. "Coach, I'm not good enough to play unless I'm in better shape. Otherwise we can both forget it." In his freshman year, playing against the varsity, the older, heavier players beat on him in what was almost a personal manner. Joe Boylan, the freshman coach, wanted to stop it, there was clear personal animosity there, but Young said no, Washington would have to learn to take it, things would get rougher in real games.

At the beginning of his college years he was shy and retiring. College changed him. Later he decided his life could be divided into two parts—the part before college, and the rest. He met his wife to be, Pat, when he was a freshman; she seemed smarter and more confident than any young woman he had ever known. She had watched him in a freshman basketball game and he had caught her attention by scoring four straight points for the wrong team, two when he had tipped the ball into the wrong basket and then, after the referee had lined them up the wrong way, two more. She thought he was very cute and tried to talk to him afterwards, but he was the shyest boy she had ever met. When she finally met him she tried to compliment him: "Boy, you're awfully skinny." She thought that was very flattering, all girls liked to be told how skinny they were. Instead it was absolutely the wrong thing to say and he seemed to freeze and become even shyer. Finally she started going out with another member of the basketball team in order to be near him, but that didn't work. Next she forced her roommate to go out with *his* roommate, and thus she could go to his room. But even then he wouldn't talk to her, he simply sat there, reading a book. So she picked up a book at random and started reading too. This made him even more nervous, so he put down the book and picked up a basketball and started playing with it. "I can play with a basketball too," she said, and grabbed the ball. But he still refused to talk. She realized that somewhere someone had beaten him down, and had convinced him that he had nothing to say, nothing worth listening to. When they finally started to go out together, sometimes when she would call him on the telephone there would

226 | David Halberstam

be long pauses at his end, as if there were something frozen there. "Why won't you talk?" she asked. "I don't know, I wish I could. It's the way I am, and the way I guess I have to be," he answered. She wondered how the two of them could be so different; they were both black, her parents were hardly wealthy or even middle-class, her father had a simple job in the New York welfare department, but hers was a strong family with an absolute determination that she and her sister, who later went to Harvard Medical School, would go to college. She had been brought up absolutely sure of her place at school, her right to be there. He by contrast was terribly unsure, as if terrified that someday they would find out about him, a whistle would be blown and he would have to leave this haven and return whence he came. But there was something touching about him, his curiosity about everything, his desire to study. At night she would go with him to the playground and he would shoot and she would retrieve the ball until the lights were out and it was too dark and then they would go back to study. They would walk through the pleasant white middle-class section of Washington in which American University was located, and he would talk about how one day, if they worked hard, they might own a house like one of these. Hearing him say it, she had a sense that it was a dream that he was trying to conjure into reality.

Gradually he was becoming a good player, and building himself up. He played through the school year in the gym, played on the Washington playgrounds in the summer, and on various Urban League teams. The playground games were often great ones for, unlike most bigtime basketball, the fans and the players were as one, the players black and the fans were black, and the fans wanted what the players wanted, not so much the score, but the moves, the artistry of it. They wanted, Kermit Washington came to realize, three things. The first was a dunk, but even better a superdunk, someone near the basket spinning and reversing and then slamming the ball home. That was black property. No white boy could do that. Second, they loved a blocked shot, two men going up in the air at the same time, *mano a mano,* the intention so parallel, all of it taking place in the air. And third, they loved a *mean, mean* rebound. That was why all those rims on baskets on the outdoor playgrounds were always bent, he thought, and why too many players off the playgrounds knew only one phase of the game, jumping and moving to the basket. They did what they loved, what came to them by instinct, and what their fans appreciated, their fans who were their friends. No wonder then that in America's ghetto schools some white coaches were always puzzled: their players might on occasion lose a game, but if the level of artistry was high enough they would be elated; or if they won, and the game was slow and boring, without *moves,* they would be mildly depressed.

He began to be more confident. He did better in school. Pat helped him there; she was a good student and she could write essays. In the beginning he was almost unable to write reports. He did not know what a paragraph was. He could barely write a simple sentence. But gradually he became better and his marks improved. When he went home to his old neighborhood during the summer his friends teased him. "Kermit, what's happened to you? You beginning to talk like a white person now, man." He knew he was changing, he did not think it was a bad thing to change, to want to be better. It was also important for Pat to like him. He was sure she would not like someone who could not write a sentence or make a paragraph. He began to become a better basketball player too. His body filled out and he continued to build himself up. But in his first two years he remained something of a soft player. He was not aggressive enough. Then, working in the weight room at American, he met a graduate student named Tray Coleman, a former football star at the University of Nebraska, who was just a little too small to play in the pros, but who looked like a walking body-building advertisement. They had, by pumping iron together in the weight room, shared sweat, shared grunts, become good friends. Coleman began to push Kermit Washington: he was a good player but not good enough, he was not aggressive enough and because of that he was not going to make the pros. "Kermit, you are not a stylish player," he said, "and you are not that big. So you'd better be more aggressive." "But Tray," Washington had answered, "I'm not an aggressive person. It's just not my nature to *be* aggressive. I can't be what I'm not." "Kermit," Coleman had answered, "you are black. Very black. Look at yourself if you don't believe me. That's handicap enough. You don't have to worry about adding any more handicaps. You've got the biggest one there is. So you'd better *be* aggressive." Washington had protested that it wasn't him. "You do it and after a while it becomes you," Coleman said. "Listen, boy," he added, "you better not be afraid to act hungry because you *are* hungry. Don't be cool. You aren't good enough to be cool. There's a lot of blacks that feel they have to act cool. That's because they're afraid they might fail. Don't let that be you. You can't afford it. It's all right in this world to act hungry. White people do it all the time." So he had become gradually more aggressive, and as Coleman had predicted, it became part of his game. He became, in a somewhat better than average college circuit, a great college player, intense, quick, an excellent rebounder. At the end of his junior year he was drafted by the New York Nets of the ABA. They offered him a five-year contract at roughly $100,000 a year to leave school and play for them. Half a million dollars! It was, given the poverty of his life, a limitless sum of money. But American had saved him, had let him play and had let him study, and he owed it something. He turned the offer down. Later that day Tom Young, the coach, simply hugged him. Kermit Washington had never felt better about himself.

By his senior year he was one of the best players in the country. He would read almost with disbelief stories in the *Washington Post* about coaches of opposing teams and how they were planning to stop Kermit Washington. *Kermit Washington,* that was him. For the last two years he had led the nation in rebounding. In the last game of his senior year he was on the edge of becoming only the seventh player in the country to average 20 points and 20 rebounds for his entire college career. He had to make 39 points to do it and he had never been a great scorer. He was so nervous the night before that he could not sleep at all. On the day of the game he could not eat, and when the crowd, the largest in history at American, started cheering as he was introduced, he could barely walk. That night he scored 40 points. He was also a scholastic all-American. In his senior year he taught courses in the social sciences. It was a life which just a few years earlier he could never have envisioned. A few weeks later he was made the first-round draft choice of the Los Angeles Lakers, chosen number five in the whole country.

The year before that, in Wilt Chamberlain's last season, Los Angeles had come close to winning the championship, and the Lakers were now sure that they had a strong team, particularly in the front court. There was no place for Washington to break in. In college he had played center, and he had been big enough and strong enough and above all quick enough to play against other centers. Bigger men were almost always slower. But he had been drafted to play forward, and he was in addition unprepared for the difficult transition from college star to pro. College star after college star had been destroyed by failure to make the adjustment. Most had after all almost always been the strongest players on the court, first in high school, then in college, always a little bigger and a little stronger than their opponents, and had never bothered to develop more subtle skills, because those skills had not been needed. Few coaches, moreover, had much interest in broadening a player's game. Strength was enough. Then overnight the player arrived in the professional game where everyone else was strong and everyone was big and everyone was quick. He might well have a no-cut contract, but he almost certainly found himself playing out of position. College centers play with their backs to the basket and their offensive moves are simple, one quick fake and a spin; professional forwards *face* the basket from a greater distance and they have to move without the ball and to put the ball on the floor in order to play their position correctly. They must have an acute sense of place. For someone 6'9" and 6'10" moving with the basketball is extremely difficult; it is an altogether different procedure, and not surprisingly, a completely different game. Power was no longer enough, agility was now necessary too. Similarly, those deft and graceful in college, successful because they were so good at the ballet of basketball, now needed to add power and strength to their game. What made it even more difficult was the fact that there is virtually no individual coaching and teaching in the NBA; the schedule is too difficult, the pressure to win consistently too great. There is an assumption that a player arrives in the league in full possession of all the basic skills. Either that or he sinks.

For a long time Kermit Washington sank. He had arrived with a good team, as a high draft choice, well paid, desperate to prove his worth, sure he could succeed here as he had succeeded in college. He had been told in advance that he would play very little in his rookie year, but like all rookies he had not believed this and it had come as a hard lesson when it turned out to be true. He had played in only half the games, averaging only ten minutes a game at that. What was worse, in the second year things did not improve very much, not many more games, not many more minutes. For the first time since before college, he began to doubt himself. He was playing some backup center and some power forward, and it was clear that if he had any future in the league it was at power forward. But he was awkward there. He had no sense of the game. On offense he froze or took shots that were wrong, angry at himself, even as he was releasing the ball. Now, for the first time in three years, he became frightened of failing. Bill Sharman was the coach and Washington went up to Sharman and asked him to teach him the game. But Sharman, harassed by pressures beyond his control, worried about his own position in the organization, had little time for instruction. The third season was even more disappointing. He knew now that the Laker front office thought he was a writeoff, a failure; worse, they had concluded that there was nothing wrong with his body, and therefore he was dumb. Nice kid, couldn't learn the game, was what they said about him in private. That was particularly painful; it wiped out all the hard-won achievements in the years at American, the success both athletic and academic, the personal triumph over his own negative image. He had by painfully hard work become someone in his life and now they were taking it away again. There had been one game against Golden State when he bounced off Rick Barry, fouling Barry clumsily, and Barry—who had little tolerance for fools—had turned to him angrily and said, "Listen, you better learn how to play this game." That had stung. He stayed up late that night seeing the play, hearing Barry's words, seeing not the anger on his face but the contempt, all of it made much worse because he knew that Barry was absolutely right, he had better learn to play the game.

By the end of the third year he was desperate. It was not the money that was at stake, his contract was good; it was his sense of self, so laboriously put together and, he realized, so precarious. He waited until the season ended and then, in desperation, he had gone to Pete Newell, a former college and professional coach, then with the Lakers in a peripheral capacity, and asked if Newell would teach him to play forward. He was terrified about asking, he barely knew Newell, but he had always heard what a great coach he was. He was afraid that Newell would mistake his request, think that he was trying to gain points in the organization or get a better contract, or simply that he was too pushy. But the alternative was too grim—it was failure and a return to what he had been. Newell in turn was astonished. In recent experience, no player in the league seemed willing to admit that he still had something to learn. Washington had picked the right time to approach Newell. He had left college coaching (where his teams, with less material, had regularly beaten John Wooden's UCLA teams) because he did not like the direction the game was taking—too much emphasis on recruiting, too little on coaching, too much on selling the school to the young men, and too little on the young men selling themselves to the school. He did not like his job at the Lakers; when he talked basketball to Jack Kent Cooke, the owner, he was always being challenged by one of Cooke's cronies who knew nothing about basketball. Bill Sharman had just been fired and so Newell felt less inhibited about working with a player. "Why do you want to take lessons?" he had asked Washington. "Because I want to play like Paul Silas," Washington had answered, which was good enough; Paul Silas was an example of the best of the NBA players, a triumph of character and intelligence over pure athletic skill.

So Newell was intrigued by the request, and he had said, Yes, they would meet, at 7 a.m. He was sure the hour would put Washington off. It did not. The first few weeks were terrible. Pete Newell was, in most human situations, an absolute gentleman, intelligent, soft-spoken, his clothes and manner more that of an Ivy League professor than of a basketball coach; but in the privacy of the gym, he was radically different, tough, demanding, the coach as drill sergeant. He was even tougher than usual with Kermit Washington; if he was going to take on a charity project he wanted to be absolutely sure that the project was worth accepting, and he was going to find out whether there was a real person inside there or not. He did not much care about Washington's time. They went at it for a terrible first two weeks, relentless, demanding drills, three hours of them, repeated, and repeated until Washington did not know which was more ready to collapse, his brain or his body. Each day when he came home he was unable to walk for two or three hours. At the end of those two weeks Pete Newell decided that Kermit Washington had a chance to be an even better player than Paul Silas. He was a slightly better jumper, and he was quicker. So they began special tutorials for a professional player making $100,000 a year. These were the kind of drills Newell usually gave to seventeen-year-old college freshmen, on footwork, on balance, on moving the feet, keeping the hands in the air. Sensing when Washington was tired, and no longer wanted to bend his body, Newell would yell at him, "Low! Low! Get down low! Bend! Bend!"

They were an odd couple, just the two of them in the Loyola gym, the old gray-haired man pushing the young black player. Newell told Washington to study the book on Paul Silas, take film clips of his games home and memorize them. All that summer they worked long sessions together two and three times a week, and in the end Pete Newell thought he had a player. He began to tell Washington to take jump shots, not because he was a particularly good shooter, but because he needed to be able to score and, even more important, he had to believe that he could. Forwards have to have small jump shots. Not great ones. But acceptable ones. In the beginning Kermit Washington was terrible. Gradually he became a competent shot.

He still hated to shoot from more than six feet away, as if he regarded shooting as uncharitable and thus something he shouldn't do very often.

The lessons changed him. For the first time he understood his position and what was expected of him. At the start of the 1976 season he was a different player. Jerry West was now the Los Angeles coach, and Washington knew that West, one of the league's greatest stars, did not like his game and wanted to trade him. It was wounding that so great a player thought so little of him. But then the game had come so easily to West, each move was so natural, he thought, that it was difficult for him to appreciate a player for whom it was so much harder. By now Kareem had become the Los Angeles center and Washington was the ideal forward to play alongside him; Kareem was a great shooter and a good rebounder, but not that physical; Washington was not a good shooter, but he was a fine rebounder, and he was a physical player. For the first time in his professional career he was playing with confidence, averaging nearly ten rebounds a game. That was the year in which Portland went on to win the championship, but during the regular season Los Angeles played Portland three times, with Kermit Washington in the lineup, and won three times. Suddenly basketball was fun again. Then in the fifty-ninth game of the season Kermit Washington's leg went out. There had of course been plenty of warning—athletes' bodies usually give repeated signals—but in professional sports there is a tendency to ignore the warnings. Washington had been feeling pain in his knee for weeks; he would put heating pads on his knees before a game, and ice on them after, and took a lot of bute, the anti-inflammatory drug, that dealt with the pain but not with the problem. He knew he was taking a risk in using the bute, that he was in effect killing not the cause but simply the body's warning to him. He now had trouble walking after games and could not drive his car for more than five minutes at a time without getting out, in terrible pain, and stretching his legs. If he was walking down a decline he had to angle his leg because he could not properly bend it. Moreover the pain was not just in his knee, but went through his entire body and into his head, and he was gobbling aspirin before every game because the headaches were so bad. He knew that because of the pain he was changing as a person, becoming more irritable and edgy, less secure. He also knew what was wrong with him: he had tendinitis, jumper's knee. This was particularly unsettling, since his game was premised upon one thing, his jumping ability. As the pain increased he stopped working out at Laker practices. If he played back-to-back games he could barely walk the next day.

Pat Washington was appalled by what was happening to him. "I can't understand why you're doing this, you're taking too much risk," she would say. "You don't understand," he would answer. "I have to do it. If I rest I might not get back in. They might make a trade." She tried to argue, *it's our risk too,* she said, and the more she did the more he simply withdrew into himself. She had become, she knew, the outsider. He was the basketball player; he knew what was at stake, and she did not. Reason said he should rest and let the inflammation subside. But he refused to take himself out of a game, or to miss a game. One night the Lakers were playing Denver and he drove the baseline past Paul Silas. Silas never touched him, but then Kermit Washington heard a terrible pop and he instantly knew what had happened. He went down as if shot. He had known pain all his life but he had never felt pain like this. He was absolutely out of control, rolling up and down the floor like a little kid. He finally looked down where his kneecap was supposed to be. It was no longer there. It had slipped over to one side and where it was supposed to be, there was simply a big dent. In medical terms he had severed a patella tendon, which was in front of the knee and served as a brake. It was as if someone had taken a pair of scissors and cut the strings which held his knee in alignment. The trainer rushed over and told him to try to raise his knee. He could not.

The season was over for him and, it turned out, for the Lakers as well. They iced his knee and operated on him at six o'clock the next morning. He was terrified that his career might be over; not many athletes make it back from so serious an injury. During the surgery and then in the days and weeks after it the pain was beyond anything he could remember. It was as if his whole body was wired to this single point which sent out nothing but pain. It was pain that was total, pervasive and unrelenting, and he lay in his hospital bed wondering how anything, any human endeavor, could make pain like this worthwhile. When Pat Washington brought his daughter Dana to visit him, she had frolicked on the bed. Afterwards he had been forced to tell Pat that much as he loved his daughter, Dana should not come next time, the pain was too great. Finally he ended up in a cast that stretched from hip to foot. The doctors told him he probably would not be able to play basketball again. He fell into a deep depression; when the Lakers made the playoffs he could not bring himself to attend the games. He had been injured in February and it was not until June that he could start running.

This time it was Pete Newell who pushed Washington, insisting that he not quit, that he try to play again. The leg was almost atrophied from the injury. Washington was not even sure he could bend it and run, but Newell was so single-minded that he dared not slack off. It was as if Newell were offering him a personal challenge. Every day he forced Washington to do more drills, to accept more stress on the leg. It was the worst summer Washington could ever remember, harder in many ways than the brutal training summer of the year before. Each day he was sure he had to quit; he would come home and tell Pat that he did not think he could go back the next day, and the following day he returned. The worst thing about Newell was that he was acting as if Washington had never even hurt his leg. One day Newell introduced him to a sliding drill. Washington tried it and the pain took him right back to the moment of the original injury. "No way I'm going to do that," he told Pete Newell, "*no way* I'm going to do it, even for forty-five seconds." "You're going to do it, and you're going to do it for twenty minutes, or your career is over," Newell had said. So he had stayed with it and gradually his leg came back and he had been able to play again.

He had played surprisingly well. He was, the doctors decided, a quick healer. Then on December 19, 1977, in the twenty-fourth game of the season, playing against Houston, he went up for a rebound against Kevin Kunnert of the Rockets. Kunnert had gotten the ball and Washington, as big men often do under the boards, used his arm to push off on Kunnert's jersey, in order to get some leverage and propel himself faster down the court. Kunnert, a very tough, physical player, threw two quick elbows. That surprised Washington, who thought they were friends, and he retaliated with a swing, and then Kareem had grabbed Kunnert and Washington had hit Kunnert and he went down. The intensity and physical toughness of the game had suddenly ignited into violence. Then out of the corner of his eye, Kermit Washington saw a figure in a Rocket uniform rushing towards him and he had swung as hard as he could, and the uniform had belonged to Rudy Tomjanovich.

The big basketball players, the power forwards, are among the strongest and most agile athletes in the world, men of great quickness and speed and powerful frames rendered stronger by the miracles of modern weight rooms. They have the outlines of great heavyweight boxers except that they are bigger. (The boxers stand 6'2" and 6'3", and the basketball players, just as agile, stand 6'9" and 6'10"). Looking at men like George McGinnis and David Cowens on the court it is possible to believe that in another time, when sport was more primitive, where colleges did not compete for football and basketball players, and where class distinctions were more crucial and economic opportunity more limited, they might have been competing for the heavyweight boxing title of the world. The game is physical, there is always contact, holding, pushing, elbowing. And there have of course been fights. But never with results like this.

Kermit Washington hit Rudy Tomjanovich as hard as he could right on the face, a punch doubled in impact by the fact that Tomjanovich was running towards Washington at the time. It was a terrifying moment. The impact of fist upon face sounded, Kareem Abdul-Jabbar said later, like a watermelon being dropped on concrete. Washington, two hundred thirty pounds, all muscle from many long hours in gyms, had smashed Tomjanovich's entire face, and come within millimeters of killing him. It was, the chief surgeon in charge of putting him together remarked, like piecing together a badly shattered eggshell with Scotch tape. "I have seen many people with far less serious injuries not make it," the doctor said. He had seen that kind of damage before from fights, but only as the result of someone being hit by a baseball bat or a two-by-four. It was the worst damage he had ever seen from a human fist. For a time the question was not whether Tomjanovich would play again but whether he would live.

Washington ran through all of that moment over and over again, both in his mind and later in court. He had held Kunnert and tried to push off, coming off the boards. That was a foul, something you did every game, and tried to get away with. Kunnert had pushed back, a quick elbow and a punch—something confirmed by the film, by other Laker players, and even by Tomjanovich's teammate Robert Reid. (Years later, when they had by chance found themselves playing together in San Diego and then Portland, there was always a distance between Washington and his teammate Kunnert; Washington resented the fact that Kunnert in court had never acknowledged his own culpability in the origins of the fight.) Then he had swung and everything had gotten out of control. He remembered Tomjanovich simply as a blur in a uniform. It was a terrible thing, but it was not deliberate, it was a part of the frenzy of the game. The commissioner, Larry O'Brien, had already been worried about the growing number of fights and the potential for serious injury—football players fought but rarely hurt each other because they wore so much equipment; baseball players fought but rarely hurt each other because they were not that strong, the game was less physical, and because usually so many people intervened that the fight never got serious. He immediately suspended Washington and fined him $10,000. This meant a loss of about $60,000. He bore the burden of what he had done to Tomjanovich, and even worse, what he had almost done. He tried briefly to get in touch with the man he had maimed, with no success. Tomjanovich was in the hospital, first fighting for his life and then gradually undergoing a prolonged, difficult, delicate series of operations to rebuild his face. He wanted no part of Kermit Washington, his sympathy or his friendship.

Washington found that he had been judged and convicted, not just by the commissioner and by the media, but by the fans as well. All the years of effort he had devoted to gaining approval had been stripped away. The management of his team, the Lakers, made no move to defend him, nor did anyone from the Lakers get in touch with him. Meanwhile the mail was the ugliest he had ever seen, hundreds of letters, all filled with racial epithets. He was shattered by the fact that people who did not know him could hate him so much. "Have you heard from the Lakers?" Pete Newell had asked him. "No," he had answered, "but I've sure heard from the rednecks." He could not remember a time like it. Pat was in the last month of pregnancy with their second child. They felt completely alone. There was a question of whether Kermit would ever be able to play again. Larry Fleisher, the head of the Players' Association, called him to suggest that the association be allowed to protest O'Brien's decisions, the fine and the suspension. It was a clear violation of due process, Washington had been judged and convicted without any hearing. It would never stand up in the courts, Fleisher said, and they would surely win. But Washington wanted none of it, he kept putting Fleisher off, and Fleisher realized finally that Washington had been through too much already and that whether or not he believed he should be exonerated, he simply could not bear an additional replay in court. In the years that followed Washington nevertheless became the center of a complicated legal action in which Tomjanovich sued the Lakers (and won some $3 million in a Houston court); and he came to hate the law and all its works, the courts, the lawyers, the questions, even when they were directed against the Lakers; he hated what was implied, that he was some kind of animal, a monster the Lakers had failed properly to control. He never said so—he had become too wary and he knew his position was too vulnerable—but he believed that the entire legal action was in part racially motivated, that if it had been a white player hitting a white, or a black player hitting a black, that there would have been less media fuss, a less energetic intervention by the commissioner, and less passion in the courtroom. He believed this but he said nothing.

He felt a public enemy, a marked man. When his wife shopped, people in the stores who had once been so friendly now were cold. "How could your husband have done that?" asked a woman Pat had thought was a friend. He and Pat lived as quiet a life as they could; each day they took their daughter Dana to the seashore and then to a small park with a swing where they could play with her. In that time he wondered whether he would ever return to the basketball court again. It was clear to him that the Lakers were finished with him. There had been one fight earlier in the year between Kareem and Kent Benson, a white center for Milwaukee. The Lakers had stood by Kareem but Washington was sure they were not about to do the same for a second black player involved in a fight with a white. As he waited the only person he had any contact with was Pete Newell. One day Washington showed up at Newell's door with a huge color television set. With it was a small plaque that said, FOR COACH NEWELL. THANK YOU FOR MAKING ME A BETTER BASKETBALL PLAYER. KERMIT WASHINGTON. Pete Newell tried to turn down the gift but Washington insisted he keep it. He eventually relented and accepted it, partially because Washington seemed the loneliest young man he had seen in a long time.

A few weeks after that the Lakers traded him to Boston. Red Auerbach had always coveted him. Washington loved playing in Boston. He felt at home there. He had never seen an athlete like Dave Cowens before. In turn Cowens loved playing alongside Washington. "It's great fun," Cowens said, "you can always hear him grunt when he's rebounding." At the end of the season Lakers owner Irv Levin switched teams with San Diego owner John Brown, and Washington came to San Diego.

Even now, rehabilitated, accepted by teammates and fans in two different cities, he was aware that he had been part of something terrible and frightening, that he was on the edge of having committed, however involuntarily, a dark deed. He was also in a more pragmatic way aware that he was a target now, not just for fans, but for other physical players. Unlike

238 | David Halberstam

anyone else in the league, he dared not get in a fight, so there were sharp limits to how much contact he initiated. That was something he could deal with; the shame of what he had almost done was more serious. He had a dream, more than once: he was at a restaurant and went to the men's room. There a man pulled a gun on him and, terrified, he had hit the man. Then Kermit ran from the men's room to the parking lot, where he was picked up by two cops, one white, one black. They accused him of killing a man. The black cop shackled him and the white cop put a black hood over his head, and they took him to a courtroom. There a judge looked down and announced that he was guilty of murder. Washington understood that nightmare perfectly.

THAT NIGHT IN Kansas City they were blown out: it was a rout. The score at the end of the first quarter was 37–17, at the half 64–39. It was an absolute collapse. Kansas City ran a clinic for them. Phil Ford, the quick, fearless guard, penetrated at will and then handed the ball off to other players. Near the end of the game the only excitement was the noise from the crowd trying to tell K.C. Coach Cotton Fitzsimmons to keep Otis Birdsong in so he could score forty points. Fitzsimmons did not listen and Birdsong scored only thirty-eight. "That did not," Birdsong said later, "seem like a Jack Ramsay team out there." The Portland locker room was absolutely silent. The players could not talk to reporters nor among themselves. They waited for the explosion from Ramsay. There was none. Ramsay stepped outside the locker room to talk to reporters. "Kansas City was exceptional tonight. They played very fine basketball. These things happen in the NBA. This is the first time it's happened to us. It's not the end of the world." At least they were flying back to Portland.

IN AN INELEGANT game which marked Lionel Hollins's return after thirty games, they finally won one, beating Denver 106–98. Hollins seemed to change the entire nature of Portland's play. Opposing guards could no longer prey on the Portland ballhandlers, and he seemed in addition to bring badly needed confidence and equally badly needed ball movement. As he played, Bobby Gross moved better, and so did some of the other players. It was not a very pretty game to watch, but Ramsay was pleased, the losing streak was over.

Denver was one of the shakiest teams in the league and its economics reflected the importance television played in the sport. In the old ABA, Denver had been one of the stronger franchises, and the Nuggets had been an intelligent, well-balanced team which did well during the regular season but faded in the playoffs. Like many ABA teams it was located in a limited television market. When the ABA folded (in part because of the lack of television money), Denver had been one of the four semiviable teams admitted into the NBA. It arrived, saddled with debts from the past, liable for an NBA entrance fee, and with no prospect of NBA television income for two years (no one after all could stick it to a new NBA owner like an old NBA owner). To survive, Denver management was forced to push season tickets and that inevitably meant hype, and the exploitation of superstars, name players who might not in the long run bring Denver a winning team. So they were caught in a cycle. The ownership was weak and Denver had in recent years made a series of disastrous trades, breaking up the embryo of a strong team. A year earlier they had made the archetypical bad trade, sending Bobby Jones, one of the best defensive forwards in the league, a fine team player, and a man coveted by almost every coach in the league, to Philadelphia for George McGinnis, an incomplete superstar of dazzling but limited abilities. But, it was reasoned, a George McGinnis sold more tickets than a Bobby Jones. The trade had immediately made Philadelphia a far more coherent team and weakened Denver. Worse, the Denver management had panicked. Hearing that the New York Knicks, they of the big Gulf & Western megabucks, were thinking of signing David Thompson, the team's other superstar, Denver had re-signed Thompson for *$800,000* a year, then the highest salary in the league. David Thompson was surely an exciting player though no one was sure yet how well he would fit into a complicated team offense. That meant Denver, which had allotted something like $10,000 annually for scouting, started the season with a player payroll of $1.7 million, of which approximately $1.3 million was allocated to two players, neither of whom had shown the ability to play a complete professional game, or, for that matter, to play with each other.

In the Denver game Hollins's play made a crucial difference. He moved the ball, and Gross responded to his movement, and suddenly the other players had been transformed; those who had been playing listlessly in the past three weeks began to move, those who had played with limited vision began now to see. It was an exceptional demonstration of how one player, even a small man, can transform his teammates. On defense Hollins had helped double up on the Denver guards at precisely the right moment to force turnovers or to take away good shots. After the game Ramsay had finished his normal Quotations from Chairman Jack, we-played-good-team-ball, we-doubled-well-on-defense and lingered, talking about Hollins. It was a very deliberate act on his part, especially for a coach who was always extremely guarded and careful in his praise of players. "Lionel means so much to us," he said. "He is an exceptional athlete." The word *athlete* was one Ramsay did not quickly employ easily, and to him it meant not physical skill but more, completeness of person, physical, spiritual, intellectual ability and finally, the passion to prevail. "Lionel," he was saying, "is a very special young man. He always wants to win and he knows a great deal about how to do that. If he has any fault it may be that he wants to win too much and he tries too hard and takes too much upon himself. Then we have to slow him down." It was rare praise of a player from Ramsay and it was quite deliberate, a quick stroke of a troubled player whose injuries Ramsay partially suspected and who moved back and forth from instinctive team loyalty to growing alienation because of his contract troubles. Ramsay was clearly trying to tell Hollins how much he needed him, and he was also, because Hollins and Lucas were close friends, or at least seeming close friends, trying to separate Hollins from Lucas's greater bitterness. Ramsay believed Lionel was potentially the one player on the team who might stand up to Luke. Unfortunately, Hollins was caught up in contract problems as deeply as Lucas. Ramsay's belief—that if Hollins had been signed and his contract problems were out of the way, he would probably have played in most of the thirty-one consecutive missed games—was therefore purely academic.

The player in question, Lionel Hollins, was pleased with the game, though beating Denver didn't amount to much. Still, he was skeptical about the whole business of professional sports, and about the Portland management. Just a day or two before there had been a story in the paper about the problems Earl Monroe, wanting to play his thirteenth and final season, was having with the management of the New York Knicks. Monroe was a special hero to Hollins and other black players because of his style. He had been an ornament to the Knicks in good seasons and bad, he was fiery, original and creative; disciplined when the teams were good and required discipline, undisciplined when the teams were bad and the crowd demanded, if nothing else, a show. Now management, the fun-loving folks from Gulf & Western, were quibbling with him about money. They were trying, Hollins thought, to take the man's dignity away from him in the final moments of a rare career. Lionel Hollins had been in high school when Walt Frazier and Earl Monroe comprised the New York backcourt and the Knicks were the most exciting team in basketball. Television had loved the Knicks then, a great team in a major media market, three blacks, two *whites* in the starting lineup, and it had beamed their images into the tiny home in Las Vegas where Lionel lived. He soon came to idolize both guards. Walt Frazier's poster—huge and in color, showing the great New York backcourt man, eyes sly as could be, almost hooded as if to conceal their devious intent, the *steal*—had adorned Lionel's room. Hour after hour, Lionel had practiced on the court, not what some local coach told him to, but in the new modern manner, what he had *seen,* not Monroe's spinning whirling dervish moves (for they were not natural to him) but the graceful moves and steals of Walt Frazier. In November 1975, he had gone, as a rookie, into Madison Square Garden with Portland and had played first against Frazier and then Monroe. In those days a great deal of hand-checking was still allowed—that is, defensive players were allowed to rest their hands on the bodies of the men they guarded and if their hands were strong enough, to hold them and delay them. Sometimes the hand-checking became quite rough, but that night Lionel Hollins had been afraid to hand-check with any strength, afraid that if he did, Walt Frazier, still his idol, still a god, might be injured. Frazier was even then beginning to slow down, but he could still surprise Hollins with his quick bursts of speed. Later in the game Hollins had been assigned to guard Earl Monroe, and it was even worse, like guarding a black ghost, for there would be a jerk of the Monroe body as if some unnatural spirit from another planet had entered it, and then a Monroe hitch and a spin in the opposite direction and Hollins, like many before him, would be guarding not Earl Monroe but a recently vacated piece of Manhattan real estate. Yet after the game Earl Monroe had asked reporters the name of the young Portland guard and they had told him, Lionel Hollins, and Monroe had said he's going to be a fine, fine player. Now the Knicks were trying to unload Monroe, deprive him of his rightful chance to finish his career in New York City where he had faked out so many players, rookies and veterans. There was no loyalty at all in the business, Hollins thought, if something like that could happen. He would take care of himself while he could.

* * *

IT WAS BECOMING harder and harder to unload Maurice Lucas. San Diego was interested, but Portland had no intention of sending Lucas down to a rival team in its own division where he might be able to team with Walton. Besides, San Diego had nothing to give back in return. Whatever talent it owned had already come over to Portland as compensation for Walton. Detroit was interested, but Detroit had little to offer; it was a team beset by more problems than Portland, devoid of high draft choices. With Portland playing poorly, rival managers pulled back from Lucas, sensing that he might be the problem. Just as he had feared, Inman found himself dealing with a stock whose market value was dropping. Ramsay had told Lucas that if he wanted out of Portland the way would be to play the best ball of his career. But that was happening only in brief flurries. Inman was still in touch with New Jersey about a deal for Calvin Natt, but the word from New Jersey was that Kevin Loughery, the coach, was uneasy about dealing with Lucas.

All of this made Inman more tense than ever before. It was his job to get Ramsay the players he needed for his system, within the pay scale acceptable to the owner. He was already worried about the stress that Ramsay was subjecting himself to. Ramsay kept saying that he was all right, that he was only going to work out for a few hours at the Nautilus machine and that if any spare pieces of its machinery came flying through the window, not to worry. Inman himself was a chain-smoker and a multicup coffee drinker in the best of times. "Keep that nicotine man away from young basketball players," his friend Bobby Knight would say when Inman lit up anywhere near a locker room. During a game he did not like to talk; his fingers drummed nervously on the press table in front of him. At halftime he would dash out to smoke a cigarette, forbidden now in the arena itself. He could not go out for drinks and dinner after a game; he was too tense. Instead he would go home and scramble a few eggs for himself and watch television for an hour.

His position was not enviable. Lucas had always been a difficult player for Inman to accept, and he no longer could discuss the problem rationally. At the other end of the spectrum his relations with the owner, though they had worked together for four years, remained somewhat tentative. He knew a vast network of basketball people, had dined with them, teased them, done them favors and had in turn received favors from them. Watching him scout was like watching an old-fashioned pretelevision politician work his turf. Telephone calls placed to him at the Blazer office went through directly; no secretary screened the caller. He was good at the professional con, he could charm almost anyone. But he was not particularly skillful with Larry Weinberg. Weinberg, stiff and somewhat formal, was not the kind of man who encouraged the laughter and friendship born of the locker room. Inman respected Weinberg and it appeared that Weinberg—as much as any owner in so whimsical and uncharted a profession, who like the others gave large sums of his money to untested egocentric twenty-one-year-olds—trusted Inman. Or, to use a more accurate word, Weinberg *accepted* him and his professionalism. With everyone else around him Inman could check up on their college team, know its record, sing, if necessary, the words to the fight song. But he dared not with Larry Weinberg sing the words to any college song. None of his moves worked with Weinberg and because he dared not be too angry with the man he worked for, he was very angry indeed with Maurice Lucas.

Unlike Ramsay, who dealt in the present, Inman dealt in the future. Already this team was in the past for him and he was thinking, not as Ramsay was, of the next game, but of the next season, and the season after that. That was the main difference in their attitudes. Ramsay's job was always on the line. Sometimes Inman wished Ramsay would go with his lesser players and give them more of a chance to develop, even at the risk of losing a game or two. The future, he was sure, would reward such foresight. But Ramsay could not afford the luxury of loss. As Inman traveled the country, from Avis car rental at the airport to Holiday Inn to whatever Burger King or Pizza Hut was open late at night, he was watching not just seniors, the prime meat, but also freshmen and sophomores, looking always for growth, for potential. His business was in looking at poverty-stricken nineteen- and twenty-year-old boys, and trying to decide what they would be like in ability and character as twenty-six-year-old millionaires. He judged their faces and their eyes. Sometimes he would say of a talented college senior that he had not liked his face, that there was not enough animation in it. There was a certain amount of teasing about this, but gradually an acceptance of its validity. The talent level in the NBA, he believed, was surprisingly even; what made the difference was character, and the ability to adjust and sacrifice and assume a smaller role in the pros than a player had enjoyed in college. Some of his colleagues believed that Inman's preoccupation with character was potentially excessive, that the Portland organization might be overdoing it, going always for the same type of player, becoming too homogeneous. Character was important, but talent was important too, and there was, some suspected, too great a reluctance on the part of management to take chances on players who bore the reputation of being difficult.

Inman did not want to coach in the league. There had been offers. But the league was too harsh for him, and there was too little time for teaching, as he knew it. Near the end of Portland's second season, when Rolland Todd had been fired, he had filled in for the last twenty-six games. His halftime pep talks, much given over to Larger Objectives in the Game of Life, were considered classics. *"Who* is John Johnson," he would say to a player, "where is he coming from? What does he want out of life?" Another time he had addressed an assembly of black college players at a postseason all-star game in the South. "What is a winner?" he had begun. "What's the description of a winner in our sport? What does he look like?" "Well," shouted someone in the first row, "he's six-eleven, weighs two hundred and thirty pounds, has red hair and went to UCLA." A player named Charlie Yelverton had taped some of Inman's pep talks and played them after the game to visiting teams. Yelverton was gone the next year.

He was in the process now of creating a team without Walton. The Walton team was dead. Its demise was hard to accept because it had been so brilliant. It had been the kind of team professional basketball men spent their entire lives dreaming about, wanting only to have a small share of it. Yet it had actually come together in Portland, in no small part through his handiwork; he had seen the different pieces before they were even pieces, and it was difficult to realize that a team as fine and young as that could be gone just as quickly as it had come together. Many of the people connected to it, including the fans, were still living in the past, waiting for the magic to strike again. Ramsay was a little that way. He still looked at Lucas and Hollins and Gross and thought of the past and the good days. Sometimes, a few of his players thought he coached as if Walton were still there. Some of the younger players wondered why he had not come down harder on Lucas and why he seemed so tolerant of Hollins. Some of them thought he was physically afraid of Luke. The truth was different. Ramsay was tolerant of Lucas and Hollins because they had been part of that championship team, and part of that moment. He was not alone; some of the players themselves, Lucas, Hollins and Gross especially, were still in a way rooted in the past, waiting for things to happen that would never happen again. Inman was less sentimental. Walton was gone, and Lucas was almost certainly gone. He was not sure about Hollins. He liked him as a player and as a person, but he was not sure they would be able to meet his salary demands. The new team was bound to be different. It would never be as elegant or as graceful as the Walton team. Perhaps no team in basketball ever again would be. It would have less finesse and more muscle. The guards would have to be much quicker. He did not see Twardzik or Dunn being back. The jury was out on Ron Brewer. The first step in the new team, though they were unaware of it, had been the acquisition of Mychal Thompson, quick and strong. Kermit Washington was a valuable piece, low on natural talent, a manufactured player in Inman's phrase, but valuable and strong and generous to others. Generosity was rare in this league and he wanted to hold on to that. Perhaps they could get something for Luke. The Washington Bullets were interested in dealing Mitch Kupchak. So the team was in the middle of a transition. Perhaps in two years, if they were lucky, it might jell. Portland had a lot of draft choices in the next few years. Unfortunately a team like Portland, almost always a winner, drafted around number fourteen or fifteen. Players at that level rarely changed a team very dramatically. But they were in the position now of trading two medium-level first-round choices for one very high one, and getting a key player from the top four or five players. What Portland needed above all else was a guard. Inman liked Kelvin Ransey of Ohio State. He went into scout-talk about Ransey. Good tough kid. Sturdy body. Probably won't get hurt. Played well under pressure in a good program. Excellent statistics in a top league. A Phil Ford type, but maybe a better shooter than Phil Ford. Then there was Darnell Valentine of Kansas: a kid you had to love. Very bright. Was thinking of going to law school. He had had an outstanding freshman year and a good sophomore year, but had tailed off in his junior year. Inman did not know why. Perhaps personal problems. Well, Inman had a lot of friends out in Wichita, Kansas, where Valentine came from, he would make a few phone calls. You had to love a kid like Darnell Valentine.

Inman was a true basketball junkie. He liked to sit down a year ahead of time and pick the top fifteen players and the order they would go in the college draft. He did this with stunning accuracy. Kelvin Ransey, he said, we need a guard like Ransey badly, but he'll go number three or four or five in the country and we won't draft that high, we'll draft somewhere between twelve and perhaps fifteen. So unless we can make a swap, two draft choices for one, we won't get him. Often when he was scouting Inman traveled with other scouts who were his buddies. There was loneliness on the road, but this way they could hit a particular three-game tournament, sit there, talk through their judgments with each other, and then go out to dinner. On occasions like these they often spoke of the direction that professional basketball was taking. It was the sport that all of them loved, and it was their lives; but they were worried about what it was doing to their colleagues and to the young men themselves. Among the men Inman met this way were Pete Newell, who had once coached at California, and now was a scout for the Golden State Warriors, Wayne Embry, an immense black man, a former player as wide as he was tall who had been general manager of the Milwaukee Bucks, and who now ran several McDonald's hamburger shops and was slowly being phased out of the Milwaukee operation; and Jerry Colangelo of the Phoenix Suns, a smart scout and general manager for an unusually well-run franchise. Newell was special to Inman, like a father figure; Inman had played against Newell-coached teams and had in fact coached one of Newell's sons. Newell was the epitome of the gentleman in sports. When Inman talked about Newell there was a special reverence in his voice. Newell, he said, had been a great coach who remained true to himself; he had always been willing to walk out of good jobs, whether at Cal-Berkeley or with the Los Angeles Lakers.

They all thought the problem began not in the professional ranks, but in the colleges. Where once, Pete Newell said, a school was content to play before 3,500 people, now the television money was so big that every school was forced to build a new 19,000-seat arena designed to showcase its blue-chip players and lure the national television cameras. "When I was young, college basketball was an extension of the college itself," Newell said. "Now it is a piece of some television network." If you could recruit well and get star high school players, the network—in this case NBC—would schedule you. Where, given the number of players required, it took years to develop a major athletic program in football, basketball with so small a number of players was particularly seductive to a college looking for an instant reputation. Pete Newell hated the change in emphasis in college programs from coaching, which at its best could be a form of teaching, to recruiting. "Some school calls now and they're looking for a coach. But they don't ask, is so-and-so a decent man? Is he a moral man? Would you want him to handle your own kids?" Newell said. "They ask whether he can recruit. 'Can he sell?'" Now schools were receiving $40,000 and $50,000 a game for a special appearance on the NCAA game of the week, a game no longer scheduled by the two respective college athletic directors, but by the NBC Sports programmer, in competition with CBS, which had the professional game. Because freshmen were eligible now (a change made which enhanced the game's attractiveness to television) college teams had the continuity that they had lacked in the past. A particular star might play for a full four years without a break; there was as much or more continuity in the colleges now as in the pros. It was not, Newell said, that the kids today were so much different from kids twenty years ago; it was that they were subject to much greater temptations much earlier.

Embry agreed passionately with this. He was very bitter about what was happening because he was black and most of the victims were black. The new materialism in society reached right down to these eighteen- and nineteen-year-old kids and hurt them. "They think they know everything, and they think they're street-smart. Street-smart maybe, but they've been on a very small street compared to what they're getting into," he said.

What Embry considered to be the real tragedy was the way the colleges, which were supposed to be centers of learning, were giving kids a value system entirely different from the old values instilled in the home. "They're so smooth, so friendly when they recruit, there's not a question that these men don't know the answer to." The only hope the young blacks had was education, some kind of education, and these recruiters were teaching them how to bypass education, how to take pointless courses that would permit them to spend their lives in gyms. "These recruiters, if a kid has a question for them," Embry said, "then the answer is always *Yes, Yes,* we can take care of that. *Yes,* we can fix that." He himself had been lucky. He had been a poor farm boy from Ohio and was recruited by many schools, two in particular, Ohio State and Miami of Ohio. He had loved the idea of Ohio State. The Buckeyes were big stuff in Ohio and he had been brought to Columbus feeling the shadow of a great university upon him, feeling that he was small and that there was something magic there right at his touch, books with so many secrets, wise professors who knew so much and who would make him into a bigger man. He had almost felt giddy. The giddiness ended that night when he had dined with a high state official who said that Ohio State needed Wayne Embry and that Embry could study three times a week in this official's office and make $90 a week. That was in 1955 and $90 a week seemed like a lot of money. He had known the moment he heard the official's words that something was terribly wrong with Ohio State, that those books and professors were not what they should be, there was a terrible lie out there somewhere. Miami of Ohio by contrast had offered him tuition and room but demanded that he work in the dining hall to help pay for it. His parents, poor as they were, had been outraged by what had happened in Columbus and told him he better expect to work for anything he got. That had been true before college and it was damn well going to be true after it, his father had said. He chose Miami and it had been a happy choice. But now, for the other poor black kids, the inducements were worse than ever. What they seemed to be saying was that you can cheat on life, so long as your jump shot goes in. "And that, my friends, is not always as long as we think," said Embry.

It was their fear of the growing corruption and commercialization of college sport, and the willing participation of too many coaches in it, that made Newell, Inman and Embry allies of Bobby Knight of Indiana. Knight was anathema to many of his colleagues, and sometimes it seemed the entire world of college coaching could be divided up according to how people stood on the question of Bobby Knight. Knight was sensitive, volatile, deliberately and often shamelessly provocative and a brilliant coach, who was absolutely devoted to the integrity of his players. At first, given the nature of Inman, Newell and Embry, it seemed unlikely that they would be buddies of Knight, with his barely submerged ferocity and his instinct to blaspheme, his desire to challenge almost anyone he met, whether there was a need for a challenge or not, and his tendency to ride not just refs, but his own players. But the three men cared about him, understood his special passion and respected him though they often worried privately about his tendency towards self-destruction. But in a profession and a society less and less hospitable to the disciplinarian, Knight remained a strict disciplinarian. Things were done only one way. Where other coaches were often privately contemptuous of alumni groups, a corrupting influence all their own, Knight was less private in his lack of respect, and there was even a clause in his contract which said that he did not have to speak to any alumni groups if he chose not to. When he did speak, the occasion was not always successful. ("What do you think of Ohio State?" someone in an alumni audience had asked. "Are you from Ohio State?" Knight had asked in turn. "No," the man had said. "Then why do you ask a stupid goddamn question like that," Knight said.) For players, there were special drills designed above all else to instill respect for the coach. Geoff Petrie, the former Portland player, remembered attending a Bobby Knight basketball camp. A young player had been dispatched to find a four leaf clover. Finally after much travail he had actually found one and, proud of his accomplishment, he had held it up to the coach. Now he would surely be rewarded for his endeavor. Knight took it, examined it closely, then crumpled it up and threw it away. "You brought me the wrong one," he said. Asked once, after his team had won a national championship, whether he would be interested in coaching in the pros, Knight had answered, "I'll never coach where a player makes more than the coach."

At Indiana, Knight's behavior was troubling to many faculty members. Some saw him as a kind of reincarnation of Woody Hayes and Richard Nixon. Others saw him as a man too powerful for the university, coaching a sport too powerful for the state. Others, distinguished professors of great achievement, argued that it was possible that he might be one of the two or three best teachers on the entire campus. The reason that Newell, Embry and Inman were committed to Knight was that in their view he remained special and old-fashioned and absolutely true in the one most basic and now most perverted principle, his commitment to his individual players as human beings, however, upon occasion, roughly expressed. He was honest in his recruiting, seeking only players he genuinely intended to use and who he felt could graduate from Indiana. Long before they signed their letter of intent he told them what he expected of them—that he would not create stars, they would have to listen to him and they would play within a system. He told them he would insist, above all, that they graduate from Indiana. Knight was proud of the fact that during his years at Indiana, of the thirty-two players who had remained eligible and had reached their junior year there, thirty-one had graduated. That contrasted extremely favorably with the national ratio; it was estimated that four out of five pro basketball players and two out of three pro football players had not received their college degrees. "I think what some coaches dislike the most about Bobby," Inman once said, "is that in a world where all the rules are constantly being broken or bent, Bobby is absolutely straight and absolutely clean." He once suggested that each school in the NCAA be allowed in effect to give out only as many basketball scholarships as the number of seniors who had graduated from its program and received their degrees the previous year. Since the suggestion cut to the very heart of contemporary athletic immorality—which was to take a young kid, allow him to play as long as he was eligible, and accept no responsibility at all for his receiving either an education or a degree—Knight's colleagues were not greatly amused and there was no rush to act on his recommendation.

In the previous year, Embry, admiring of what Knight stood for in his relationship to his players, had helped him recruit a young black player from the Chicago area named Isiah Thomas. Thomas, a player of speed, skill, courage and the rare ability to change the tempo of the game, was one of the most sought-after players in the country. Embry had come to know the Thomas family, which was dreadfully poor, and he worried that other members of the family might pull Isiah down if he stayed too close to home. Embry thought Thomas a truly remarkable young man of great human promise as well as athletic ability and he thought the worst thing that could happen to him was to go to a school where he would be catered to. Bobby Knight, whatever else, catered to no one. Embry not only helped in the recruiting himself, but he brought in Quinn Buckner, now a Milwaukee guard and a former Indiana star who had fashioned a rare ongoing four-year love-hate relationship with Knight while at Bloomington. With all that heavy weaponry brought in, Indiana seemed to be ahead in the bidding. Then in a dramatic last-minute confrontation, Gregory Thomas, one of Isiah's older and more volatile brothers, had appeared, and there had been a series of charges and countercharges, threats and counterthreats about Isiah's future with Bobby Knight. Gregory included Embry and Buckner among the potential exploiters of his brother. Knight, enraged, had finally blown up. "You're an asshole and you're a failure, and the worst thing about you is that you want Isiah to fail the way you did." He turned to Isiah and got up. "If you stay near him you're going to be ruined. I'm getting out of here. I'm sorry we lost you." Then he walked out. The next day Isiah Thomas, in tears, had come to see Knight and had pleaded for a chance to go to Indiana. There he had gone and soon he too was fashioning a love-hate relationship with Knight worthy of that between Buckner and Knight.

IT WAS A frustrating time for Maurice Lucas. He was with this team and he was not with it. He wanted to be traded, and they had said they would trade him, but nothing happened. They told him that they could not get what they wanted, and that they were not going to give him away. He doubted their word, he knew of the preseason trade with Chicago that Weinberg had vetoed and it had convinced him once again that they paid him at one level and spoke of him with the media and with other teams at another level. Ramsay, whom he trusted more than anyone else in the operation—they had their own convoluted relationship of admiration, tension, resentment and pride in what each had done for the other—kept telling him that the quickest way to ensure a good trade was to play well. But it was hard to do on a team like this which was floundering, and when his own status was so uncertain. He did not care that much where he went, though he liked the idea of New York, because it was a great stage, filled with purveyors of what he called the pub, media wretches both electronic and print.

Portland as a city did not mean a lot to him. He had created a genuine niche there and he was immensely popular, a formidable figure on the court with that powerful body. Many Portland fans had remembered, as Luke did, that the winning seasons began not when Bill Walton arrived, but when Maurice Lucas arrived. When he came on the court at the beginning of a game, or when he had collected a particularly important rebound, they even had a special sound for him, a long low cheer, using his name, turning it into a veritable train whistle: *"Luuuuuuuke."* He loved it. They did nothing like that for any other player. He ran camps for underprivileged youngsters in Portland and he was a popular and identifiable figure. But Portland was, he thought, also a very white city. *Very* white. Not much in the way of streets there. He liked to think of himself as a person of the streets. He had been a street kid in Pittsburgh, a city with dark and dangerous streets that he at once loved and wanted to escape. When he was a boy he had been a swimmer on a championship local relay team and he had fancied himself a great swimmer, and he had dreamed of medals still to be awarded. But swimming was not a black sport, pools were not readily available for blacks and no college eagerly passed out scholarships to black swimmers, nor was the television screen filled with the exploits and financial triumphs of swimmers black or white. So he had turned to basketball.

It was a passport in Pittsburgh from one neighborhood to another, past invisible barriers set by different local gangs. He was proud of his street-smarts, his sense of the mood and the tone of the streets, how to blend with it. He knew the various tricks, shooting craps, making a little money playing cards, scalping some ill-gotten tickets to Forbes Field. He liked the feel of the streets, the rhythm and the action, the fact that these streets came alive just when other streets in other places were closing down. He knew how to evade trouble when he wanted to, and how to find it when he wanted. Both his parents were tall, his father 6'4", his mother a handsome and imposing 6 feet. His father, a butcher, was gone by the time he was two, his mother supported the family by working as a secretary in the tuberculosis foundation. When he was in high school he began to grow. Once he was of middling size and then suddenly he was 6'2"; and then even more remarkably, in one three-month period he grew 6 more inches. For a time that was difficult, he was skinny and he had outgrown all his clothes, and the girls did not like someone who was that tall and skinny and whose pants did not reach his ankles. But then he began to grow into his body and regain his coordination. He also worked on weights. Because he was so tall, he sensed now that basketball could mean something to him.

Pittsburgh was not a particularly good basketball town, certainly not by the standards of the modern underground basketball railway. Washington, Philly, New York, Chicago were the great cities, so one summer he went to Philadelphia. There the summer league, called the Baker League, was nationally famous, and high school, college and even professional players competed in it. During that summer he practiced six and seven hours a day, playing against men already in college, studying their moves and the way they used their bodies. One time he played against Ken Durrett, then a big college star at LaSalle, and he felt after that game that he was different, that he had been a boy before and now somehow he was a man. Then one day Earl Monroe, then at the peak of his fame as a star of the Baltimore Bullets (and, before Julius Erving had replaced him, a special kind of hero to black fans and players since he could do what *no one else* could do), showed up. The word had been out for several days that Monroe would play and the crowd was much bigger than usual. When Monroe missed the start of play the disappointment among the other players and the crowd was tangible. Then, ten minutes into the game, a huge beautiful car, half the length of the street, had shown up—it was a Rolls, Luke had known instinctively—and out had come Earl Monroe. He was wearing the most ragged shorts imaginable, terrible ratty sneakers and an absolutely beautiful Panama hat. That, Luke knew immediately, was true style, the hat and the shorts and the Rolls. The crowd had begun to shout *Magic, Magic, Magic* (his playground nickname, different from his white media nickname which, given the nature of sportswriters who like things to rhyme, was the Pearl). Monroe had put on a show that day, dancing, whirling, faking, spinning, orchestrating his moves as he wished, never any move repeated twice, as if to repeat were somehow a betrayal of his people. He had scored some forty or fifty points. Luke had watched him, taking his eyes off Monroe only long enough to watch the crowd watching him. The Black Jesus, he had thought, that's what he is—the Black Jesus.

Luke had gone back to Schenley High with the feeling that he was grown up. He watched the big men in the Baker League and saw how they handled themselves. Off-court was as important as on-court, they took up space, the best ones seemed to warn others away, and he had understood immediately that this was part of the role. It was not a good idea to smile too much, either on the court or off it. By his senior year he was a high school all-American, and recruiters started appearing from the fancy schools and some of the new outlaw basketball schools, those schools which had gone bigtime overnight in basketball, and were always willing to bend the rules in their recruiting, and in their treatment of players. Everyone in America, he thought, wanted to buy him a steak and lend him a car. He chose Marquette in the end because he loved the spiel of Al McGuire, an almost lyrical con man, for Luke was already a good enough con man himself to recognize a master when he met him. McGuire's first words had virtually sold him: "Everyone else is going to promise you a lot of shit and give you a lot of shit and I'm not going to promise you anything." Luke had loved that, and he settled back to wait for the next McGuire flurry which, he was sure, would contain certain promises. McGuire did not disappoint him. "I'll get you on national television five times a year and I'll make sure you graduate." He checked with other blacks and the word came back that McGuire was good with blacks, he played them five at a time, which some coaches were still reluctant to do, and he did not try to change them and the way they loved to play. "He's as crazy as we are," one friend said. "You'll feel at home here."

So he had gone to Marquette, his bridge into a white world. Later he would learn to deal with whites with great skill, understanding that he had something they wanted, his celebrity, his position and his size, and he doled out his favors accordingly. But in the beginning he was a scared young black kid who had never been around that many middle-class white kids before, middle-class perhaps to themselves and their parents, for Marquette was hardly a rich man's school, but rich indeed to him. It was the whitest atmosphere he had ever known, everyone always sitting around drinking beer, a white thing to do (and even worse, talking about how much they were going to drink, which was *very* white, he decided), instead of drinking wine, which was the black thing to do. The environment was very Catholic and it seemed as though there were priests everywhere. Luke was Baptist, a soft one, but Sunday, in his own words, "was a day I'd always go out and make me a hustle." He became somewhat obstreperous in theology class, asking one day if Jesus was white. The professor had hemmed and mumbled and Luke knew he had hit the right question and he immediately followed up. "Well then, how come he always looks so *white* in your pictures? Why does your Jesus always look like he comes from London or Paris when if he was from Egypt or Israel or one of those places he wouldn't look like that? Everyone down there," he added, "is *dark*." In general, though, he liked Marquette; they let you alone and they did not try to make you into something you were not.

The fatal mistake, the one which haunted him for the next seven years, came at the end of his junior year. Marquette had gone to the finals of the NCAA, but McGuire's bizarre behavior had cost them two technical fouls and possibly the game. But Luke was sure that he had made a national impression. He scored twenty-one points in the final, and there were people telling him how big a star he was and how many pro teams wanted him. Chicago seemed particularly interested in him and he thought he heard the magic figure of $100,000 a year mentioned. So he had declared himself a hardship case, making himself eligible for the draft after his junior year. His expectations were high, and Chicago, as promised, drafted him in the first round. But the money was not there. In Luke's view, Chicago clearly felt that he was out on a limb, he had nowhere to go, for he could not, having once been drafted, return to school, and it offered him roughly $40,000 a year, sawing the limb out from under him. He thought of trying to go back to Marquette, but authorities there did not seem eager to have him. Just at that moment, there was new ownership of an ABA franchise in St. Louis, and it was throwing money around. His agent called and said there was a good offer for him, roughly five years at $75,000 a year, with some additional money deferred. It sounded marvelous at the time. He did not realize that it was not very big money for the league, and that more important he was locking himself into far too long a contract, in effect betting against his own abilities.

All that he came to learn later the hard way. The first disillusionment came when he arrived at the St. Louis camp and found that Marvin Barnes was already there, playing his position and being paid roughly six times as much a year. That was a sting. But in those days he was a young black kid, advised—he later came to believe—poorly (he, like a number of players, eventually sued his agent), and the money had sounded like a guarantee of permanent happiness. By the end of the second year St. Louis had folded, the league had folded and in the third year he went to Portland. The contract of course followed him. There he found himself an all-star forward on a championship team making $75,000 with two full years on his contract still to run, unable to convince the owner, despite the coach's intervention, to raise his salary without extending the contract even further. He did extend, and the extension simply created its own problems, for he had dealt with Weinberg with limited negotiating power. Now he was locked into an even longer contract, which he soon saw was unsatisfactory. He had been caught, he later realized, and there was no easy way out. He was very fond of Bill Walton; they were as close as players could be in that league both on-court and off-court. But never for a moment did Maurice Lucas forget that Bill Walton was white and when they played together he made six times as much as Lucas did.

NEAR CHRISTMAS, THE New York Knicks—only ten years earlier the absolute symbol of team play and then, as if overnight, a group of overpaid and self-indulgent players—arrived in Portland. Now, slowly, having put aside the attempt to buy key players from other teams (and having learned the very hard way that other teams usually only trade or sell key players when there is something drastically wrong), the Knicks were trying to build themselves back through the draft. They seemed on the verge, for the first time in a decade, of a genuine beginning. They had several promising rookies in the backcourt, including a player named Michael Ray Richardson whom Inman had coveted, and a young center named Bill Cartwright who in a normal year—that is, a Magic-less, Bird-less year—might have been Rookie of the Year. What New York most evidently needed was a power forward. This need had, among others, occurred to Maurice Lucas. The day before the Knick game, Steve Kelley asked Luke about whether he would like to go to New York. New York, he answered, was the perfect team for him.

"I could really help them," he said. Besides he would love to play in New York, there or Los Angeles, New York the city of the big pub, and Los Angeles a city of endless glamour and excitement, and the chance to play alongside Kareem. In New York he could play with a young rookie center like Cartwright and help break him in. The veteran and the rookie, plenty of turf for both—he liked the idea. Kelley printed the interview and the next day Ramsay was furious. He had chased another writer, John Strawn (to whom Luke was giving an impassioned critique of the racism of the previous night's referees), out of the locker room before taking Luke aside.

"You play for the Portland Trail Blazers," he said, "you are under contract. The other players here are your teammates. It is not your job or part of your contract to give interviews in midseason about who you would like to play for." He was very angry. He felt that Luke had crossed over a line of loyalty in the interview. Off-season, talk like that was one thing, it was theoretical; but during the season it was another thing. Now the New York Knicks were opponents. "I don't want to read any more interviews about who you want to play for," Ramsay said. Ramsay was a First Amendment man; he was, to the surprise of many of his old friends, even an admirer of Jane Fonda. He admired her courage and independence. But he was furious at Maurice Lucas. In season there were limits to freedom of speech. Luke was frustrated by the entire episode. "Hey," he told Strawn, "I didn't do anything. The man came and asked me a question and so I answered it. *They*'re the people talking about trading me."

For Portland at that moment was working very hard to trade Lucas to these very same Knicks. But the people in charge of the franchise were nervous about Luke; if Portland and an ultimate team coach like Jack Ramsay wanted to unload him, perhaps there was something wrong. New York had suffered too much in recent years, first with Spencer Haywood, then with Bob McAdoo, to risk adding a player who might value statistics above team play. New York was warier still of the price. An easy mark in the decade just past for other teams anxious to unload superstars, it had paid huge sums for saviors who had not saved. At one time New York and Portland were talking seriously about a deal in which Luke would go to New York for Toby Knight, a forward who was considered a tweener, that is, he fell between being small forward and power forward. Knight was an able but not overpowering NBA player. What had soured the deal was that Portland had wanted in addition, according to New York sources, as much as one million dollars.

The negotiations in the Lucas deal were now being handled by Larry Weinberg, the owner, and Weinberg was a very demanding negotiator. "That is," one of the New York officials said later, "simply the toughest man to do business with in the entire league. Maybe the smartest, at least in the narrow sense. But certainly the toughest. It's as if he's so afraid that you're going to screw him in a deal, so the only way he can do business success-fully is by screwing you first." That New York found Larry Weinberg tough to deal with did not surprise other owners and general managers around the league, nor the radio and television stations that broadcast Blazer games, nor in fact his own players. Weinberg had a reputation for knowing all the angles to every deal, for delegating very little that mattered to him and for being particularly difficult as a deal neared completion. Difficulty at this stage was almost a trademark of a Weinberg deal; a general agreement was near, everyone seemed happy, and then Weinberg, taking stock, might de-cide that he had not been sufficiently tough and would up the ante just a notch, some additional cash, or a marginal draft choice.

In the past Weinberg himself had managed to stay in the background during almost all Blazer transactions. But the growing controversy about Lucas, which Steve Kelley was reporting regularly in the *Oregonian*, had drawn Weinberg in. He hated the inevitable public attention; he was that most unusual kind of sports-team owner, a man who craved anonymity. In the past the attitude of the Portland media and the Portland public to the Blazer management had been largely one of gratitude, simply for having brought a team to so distant an outpost. But the championship season had made fans more sophisticated and raised their expectations, and the con-troversy over Walton's medical treatment had for the first time brought management practices into serious question. The *Oregonian*'s criticism was something new too. Largely because of Steve Kelley's reporting, Larry Weinberg was becoming what he least wanted to be, a figure of controversy in Portland. He had become principal owner by chance. There had been a local campaign in the sixties to get a professional franchise, and to build a handsome new arena worthy of a professional team. Many in the city re-garded the acquisition of a professional sports team as a decisive factor in the city's future. SAD SACK CITY OR MAJOR LEAGUE TOWN, wrote the *Oregon Journal*. In the early fifties the world of professional sports was eastern, cities like Philadelphia had two professional baseball teams, New York had three, and St. Louis was considered the western outpost of American sports. Then television arrived, helping to connect California to the rest of the nation, and soon after that, the 727 jet, which made intermediate travel easier. Teams began to move west: in 1960 the Lakers went from Minneapolis to Los Angeles, that most lakeless of cities, without even changing their nickname. From then on other western franchises made economic sense. Portland had always been known as a good sports town, and the NBA was interested in coming, but Oregon money was hard to find. Harry Glickman, a local boy and a sports promoter, became aware of the problem when he tried and failed to get funding. The money was indisputably there, no one doubted that certain Portland families had been rich, were still rich and were certain to become richer. Glickman, puzzled by this lack of local enthusiasm, talked it over with a friend named Gerry Pratt, then a local business writer. "Harry," Pratt explained, "the first thing you have to understand about people in Oregon is that they hate notoriety. They are not high-rollers. They have a very conservative attitude about their money. They do not like to be upfront with their money and they do not like to spend it publicly."

So it was that when the franchise was finally secured, the money came from three out-of-town Jewish businessmen. That of itself was not surprising; the league already had a high percentage of Jewish owners. The sport had been a city game in the thirties and forties and fifties when there were still Jewish backcourt stars with quick two-handed set shots. Besides, if old WASP money avoided notoriety, then new Jewish money often sought it out by involvement in sports, show business and politics. "Anyone who invests in sports," Herman Sarkowsky, the first principal owner of the Trail Blazers, once said, "has an ego problem to start with."

The team entered the league in the fall of 1970. Sarkowsky was the principal owner, Bob Schmertz and Weinberg were the other two, somewhat smaller shares. The entrance fee was $3.7 million, but the Blazers would, in their first year, get a share of the television money. They were all young, they had all made fortunes, primarily in real estate and housing, and they had talked often of doing something like this together. The real estate connection was not irrelevant. One of the attractions to owning a major sports team for a modern American millionaire was the ability to depreciate the athletes for tax purposes, a procedure which could make even a bad team valuable. No group of businessmen better understood depreciation than real estate operators who knew how to buy buildings and set off other income by depreciating them and then, when the depreciation ran out, to sell out for a profit. The practice helped explain the revolving-door ownership of the Boston Celtics, one of the league's prize jewels, as owners came and owners went, always with a tip of the hat to the IRS. During Senate hearings over whether or not professional basketball should lose its special antitrust exemption, one of the things which had genuinely angered Senator Sam Ervin was a look at the books of some of the teams. Athletes who were making $30,000 a year were, on the owner's income tax returns, being written off and depreciated at an annual rate of $200,000. It helped in professional sports, as in real estate, to be able to depreciate.

The triumvirate did not last long. Soon Schmertz wanted more satisfaction and became a principal owner of the Celtics. Then Sarkowsky, who had always coveted a professional football team, was offered a chance to own the Seattle professional team, the Seahawks. Because there was a rule prohibiting a principal owner in football from being the major owner in any other sport, Sarkowsky in 1976 sold much of his stock to Weinberg, who that year became the principal owner of the Blazers, firing Lenny Wilkens and hiring Jack Ramsay as his first move.

"I want," Larry Weinberg once told a friend in the building industry, "to be able to make very tough decisions and still be able to feel good about myself as a human being." That was vintage Weinberg. He was an imaginative, shrewd, relentless businessman who left nothing unturned and unscrutinized, but he also had a passionate desire to be a good citizen, a good family man, a good citizen of Los Angeles, a dedicated and influential friend of Israel, a major contributor to liberal causes and liberal politicians. One of his greatest disappointments as a builder was that he had been unable to convince federal authorities of the wisdom of having government sell housing units to the very poor with very low mortgage rates. The very poor, much more than the middle-class or the rich, he had always believed, needed to *own* their homes, and thus to have a stake in the society. He had helped convince his friend Hubert Humphrey of the logic of this; unfortunately Humphrey was narrowly defeated in the 1968 Presidential election and the idea had died in the subsequent turmoil of American politics.

In the world of sports, an area much given over to glamour or at least the illusion of glamour, Weinberg was old-fashioned. Where some other owners showed up with the young lady of the week, Weinberg seemed to go nowhere without his wife. "I like the fact," a woman in the Blazer office once said of him, "that he is unafraid to show how much he loves his wife— that's very unusual in this country right now." There was nothing facile about him. He seemed almost inept at small talk, and there was a certain stiffness in his manner and his dress, as if he had never quite become accustomed to his power, his position or his money. He did not pal around with athletes, as many owners did. The only player he had gotten to know socially was Walton who, as a white superstar and former UCLA hero, was a figure large in Weinberg's Los Angeles circles. Jack Scott, Walton's then close friend, was mildly amused by the friendship, by the fact that Weinberg would come out to the Walton-Scott house dressed down for the occasion, eat whatever nonmeat dinner they were serving that night, seaweed or whatever, and protest, in an odd muffled way, its excellence. "Why don't you get to know Maurice Lucas?" Scott had asked one night when Weinberg had mentioned how much he liked the fact Walton was involved in politics as a man and citizen. "He's every bit as bright and verbal as Bill, and every bit as involved in politics. Maybe more involved than Bill. I'm sure you'd like him just as much as you like Bill." "I just don't seem to know Maurice," Weinberg had answered. "He's very easy to know," Scott had said (thinking to himself, "I know why"). "You ought to try."

Weinberg had very strong convictions about doing the right thing, about behaving in an honorable way, but he did not articulate them very well, and in the basketball world at least they often seemed in conflict with his desire to be the toughest businessman around. When Jack McKinney, Ramsay's former assistant, had gone to the Lakers, he was involved in a serious bicycle accident early in the season. The accident had nearly taken his life and left in question whether McKinney would ever be able to function, let alone coach again. Jerry Buss, the Lakers' owner, who was better at moving through the locker room than almost any other owner, stroking his players, had acted in what McKinney felt was a most insensitive way. When at the end of the season McKinney was let go by the Lakers, he heard of it from reporters; Weinberg, awkward and clumsy at precisely the things Buss was skillful at, had been generous, helpful and caring in making sure that McKinney, a former employee, received the best possible medical care and attention. Weinberg wanted to do the right thing in the right way, and he brought to basketball all of his experience from almost thirty years of stunning success in the building business. There he had been honorable and successful and he had never renegotiated a contract. So be it, he would never renegotiate one in basketball either. A contract was a contract. That the basketball business was far more emotional, and that what worked in housing would not necessarily work in sports, did not matter. That the housing market reflected a true open market and NBA basketball was a monopoly league with a draft system which limited personal choice for the player did not matter. He seemed afraid, above all, that his players might take advantage of him. If there was a weakness in his makeup, it was his powerful rectitude, bordering on righteousness.

Larry Weinberg had been born in Brooklyn, had loved basketball as a boy, had wanted to play it, but then one day in high school he learned that the math team and the basketball team practiced at the same time. So much for his basketball career. "You did not," he once said, "choose which way you wanted to go in those days." He had gone to Cornell, then to the Army in World War II, where he had been seriously wounded; he had come out of the Army with a 100 percent disability. After the war, trying to repair his health, he had moved around the country to various colleges, ending up at UCLA in 1947. There he found that none of his friends could afford housing. They were largely young veterans with young families; they had, like himself, a few thousand dollars in their pockets; they had come to California, discovered the sun and wanted to stay there. But the houses available, even small ones, cost $9,000 and $10,000, often just out of their reach. Weinberg felt the houses should cost no more than $7,500 and, being good at math, felt he could build a modest home, particularly in large quantities, for that price. He mentioned his idea to a cousin. "It's too late, Larry," the cousin told him, "the boom in California is already over." The Federal Housing Authority was not very much help. It told him his houses were too small. Finally he convinced them to stake him. He used his own money, Army discharge money, disability money, stored-up bar mitzvah money. The prototype house was a success and he went into a project, selling thirty houses at $7,225 and $7,500. With that he became a full-time builder and one of those postwar success stories. Larry Weinberg turned out to be a superb businessman, original, careful, inventive, shrewd, a tough and unsparing reader of bottom lines, and, more than anything else, imaginative in sensing the total possibility of what housing represented to young people. He caught the demography of California exactly on the rise, at precisely the moment when the American dream was to own a single-unit dwelling, and when government loan programs favored precisely that kind of ownership. He was the right man in the right place at the right time doing the right thing. He understood that to most middle-class Americans with no inherited wealth, true net worth was the equity they had in their house. He was unusually imaginative in creating interrelated businesses that built the house, mortgaged the house, sold the carpets, did the drapes and bought the dishwasher—the drapes, the carpet and the dishwasher could all go on the same mortgage. Did this new development need a shopping center? Larry Weinberg would build one. Even when small-unit housing began to slow down, his company, called Larwin, remained on the rise: in 1967, when the national housing market was up only 11 percent, Larwin revenues were up 50 percent. He was, in the true sense, inventing communities. By 1969 he faced a dilemma. The company, still family owned, had become so big that he constantly needed more money. The choice was either to go public or to sell to someone else. So he sold to a huge conglomerate from Chicago, CNA. The eventual total for the deal was $200 million. Half of that went to Larry Weinberg. In Portland, estimates of his wealth ran around $100 to $150 million. He was one of the wealthiest owners in the league. Soon after he sold his company he bought into the NBA.

There too, in the strictest sense, he was a superb businessman. No organization in the league was as well run in the narrow business sense. Devoid of competition for the sports dollar, he was in an enviable position, and he knew how to maximize it. The radio revenues were exceptional. The television contracts were getting better. Soon, with the arrival of cable, he would be packaging his own game broadcasts, a Blazer network. There was a Blazer candy bar (of dubious distinction). The team was said to turn an annual $4 million profit, one of the highest, if not the highest, in the league.

Yet there was always the doubt whether his own business skills could be translated into professional sports, whether he was too rigid in his outlook for so volatile an enterprise, whether—as his coaches had always felt—his attitude about renegotiations was in the long run shortsighted. Certainly he was not enjoying this year and the increasing notoriety it was bringing him. He hated reading the articles which questioned his stewardship and he hated seeing his name in the paper. In his own mind it was absolutely clear that his stewardship had strengthened the team and that his own role had helped bring Portland its first championship. Yet the athletes and all these agents were becoming hard to deal with all the time. Walton had been his favorite, boyish, impressionable, almost innocent, filled with enthusiasm. But Walton had been immature, he had later decided, an attractive young man who would not take responsibility for his own decisions. He was very upset now with Lucas and all the things he was saying. That was all very unnecessary. Luke wanted to be traded. Fine, Larry Weinberg could accept that, but he wanted fair value. Thus it was clear that the better Luke played, the easier it was to trade him. He had explained this to Luke, and had pointed out that because of this they were both on the same side of the fence and they both wanted the same thing. But then Luke had played poorly. Larry Weinberg found Luke's performance puzzling.

THE KNICKS WERE shying off Lucas anyway. The idea of paying big money to Portland made them nervous, for they had just gone that route, attempting to purchase a championship by going after highly paid superstars. A team once lovely to watch had become a vague assortment of overpaid egotists. The contrast to its predecessor was unusually painful for basketball fans. The Knicks of the late sixties and early seventies had been a sheer pleasure to watch. It was not a big team or even particularly physical; in fact it was like watching four guards and a forward play. But every Knick player could shoot, every player could and did pass, and the intricacy of the team's movement, to say nothing of the unselfish nature of its play, had brought a special pleasure to a city which loved basketball and was exceptionally sophisticated about the rhythms of the game. In New York, basketball was as much part of the culture as football or baseball, and thus the team was celebrated as few professional basketball teams were. Because New York was the great media center of the nation, the first Knick championship spawned almost a dozen books, much to the chagrin of the true basketball traditionalists, the Boston Celtic fans, one of whom pointed out that the Celtics by contrast produced roughly one book for every four championships.

The old Knicks had marked the end of one era in basketball and the beginning of another. Most of the players, apart from Bill Bradley, had come into the league in the mid-sixties when salaries were still small. Bradley, son of a banker, returning from a tour at Oxford as a Rhodes scholar, had options in his life other than basketball. Besides, he was a white superstar of middle-class origins who had captured the imagination of basketball fans even while in college. A book hailing his achievements had been written by a major writer before he even left Princeton. In addition a new league was about to start. Given that much leverage, he was able to sign as a rookie for more than $100,000 a year. Soon, in order to preserve harmony on the team, his teammates were equally well paid. When Bradley entered the league the average salary was $12,000; a decade later, when he left, it was well over $100,000. The coming of big new money was never a factor on the Knicks; most of the players were already tough and disciplined, their value systems well developed.

For all their closeness on the court, the Knicks were not particularly close off-court. In those days professional teams had a twelve-man roster and the joke about the Knicks was that when they arrived at an airport, twelve players got into twelve cabs. They lived in very different worlds, but they allowed each other the requisite air space. Their roles, off-court and on-court, were clear. If there were any tensions on the team it might have been between Bradley and Cazzie Russell, since they had both been great college stars and were competing for the same position. The other Knicks often teased Cazzie, who was legendary for using words he did not entirely understand and, it was said, for cheating while working aloud the word games from newspapers on the team bus. Cazzie, teammates claimed, carried a small dictionary so that he could look up words. *"Ergo,"* he would say aloud, as if struggling for the answer, "that means . . . *hence.*" "Come on, Cazzie," a teammate would say, "we saw you look it up." Bradley, worried about creating additional tension, always held back from the teasing. He also kept his mouth shut about money. Though he had gotten the first big salary on the team, it was soon assumed that most of the other players, especially Frazier and Reed, were now paid more. That was not necessarily true. Instead, very quietly each year, liberated by his lack of dependence upon the game, given his ability to quit whenever he wanted to, Bradley had negotiated a one-year contract for the next season. That gave him maximum leverage. Without anyone knowing it, he was one of the two or three highest-paid forwards in the league. But he remained as disciplined socially as he was on the court and in order to diminish friction he was absolutely taciturn about his salary.

Gradually, as the Knicks team developed and assumed its character, the roles seemed to fit the players. Willis Reed, who might not have sought the part, became the big man, the player who took care of his teammates on the court when there was a fight. Dave DeBusschere was the blue collar player who earned his money and always gave a full night's work no matter how tired his body. Walt Frazier was the media star, the player who always gave the New York reporters the good postgame quotes. Earl Monroe, the ultimate one-on-one player ("Could you go one-on-one with Monroe?" a reporter once asked Frazier. "God couldn't go one-on-one with him," Frazier, quotable as ever, had answered.), came over from Baltimore. Knick purists were at first appalled by the trade, but they misunderstood Monroe's greatness, and his generosity of spirit. He changed his game, disciplined it, and fitted into the existing machinery as if he had been born to it. Only Bill Bradley held back from assuming his assigned role. Princeton graduate, Rhodes scholar, he was supposed to be the resident jock-intellectual, and the media sought to crown him as such. But Bradley feared this might cause more problems with his teammates and he refused the coronation rites. One of the unwritten rules of that team was that no one challenged any other player's image. There were two reasons for that. First, a player might destroy something important to a teammate, and thus diminish his sense of self; and second, if you *did* correct a player's self-assessment, you were automatically more involved with him. Thus both of you might be losing air space and freedom. Out of that was fashioned a very strong, very smart team. It won two championships in four seasons and if Dave DeBusschere's back had not given out during a championship playoff series against Los Angeles, it might have been three. Excluding the Celtics, that was as close to a dynasty as anyone had come.

Even that minidynasty was over quickly. The second New York championship was in 1973. A year later all three of the team's big men—Reed, DeBusschere and Jerry Lucas—retired. It had always been a small team physically, and now it had lost all three of its big men. Management, competing in a city filled with first-class entertainment and tough critics, panicked and decided that rather than rebuilding slowly through the draft, it would use that big New York money to accelerate the process. The 1974 team was a disappointment. At the end of it, hearing that Wilt Chamberlain might come out of retirement, Mike Burke and Eddie Donovan of the Knicks front office flew out to Los Angeles to meet with Chamberlain and his lawyer. At the Los Angeles airport, they found neither Wilt nor his lawyer, but instead Sam Schulman and Bill Russell of the Seattle Sonics, who had a car and a driver and who most courteously drove them to their hotel. Burke learned a lesson: beware of Schulmans bearing limos at airports.

What Seattle was offering, it turned out, was Spencer Haywood, once a young athlete of superb promise, an Olympic hero at nineteen. Yes, said Schulman, he was still a great player, very young, only twenty-six years old. But there was a certain tension, rivalry was a better word, between him and Russell. Spence wanted to *be* Russ. That was the problem. Better for him to play elsewhere. Schulman, who had pioneered in the signing and overpaying of superstars, was now pioneering in another area, the unloading of them. He was getting out of that business just as New York, desperate, was getting in. So the Knicks got Haywood, for some $1.5 million plus his own rather considerable salary.

Haywood's New York years were not happy ones. Powerful and physical as a young man, his game had never developed. In the pros he was not strong enough to play center, nor supple enough to play forward. He seemed an island apart from the rest of the team, a painfully shy, often anguished young man, unable to deal with such great expectations. He seemed happiest when he was off by himself working for a small radio station as a disc jockey. There, in his enclosed booth, the outside world cut off, he seemed absolutely relaxed and content. Willis Reed by then was the coach, and Reed was of a tougher generation; people around the team sensed Reed's diminishing respect for Haywood. Buffeted more and more by the expectations of the fans and teammates and his coach's evident disrespect, Haywood's game began to deteriorate.

When that fix had not worked out the Knicks tried another. They bought Bob McAdoo from Buffalo for $2.5 million. McAdoo was a truly brilliant athlete, and under Jack Ramsay his game had been reasonably controlled. New York hungered for him, but the McAdoo who arrived in Madison Square Garden seemed a different athlete. It had all begun with the negotiations after New York had purchased him from Buffalo. His agent, Bill Madden, told the New York management that he wanted a contract that would guarantee Mac's finances for the rest of his life. That was roughly five years at $500,000 a year. Mike Burke, representing the Knicks, was not so sure it was a good idea. The problem was not, he said, the money—the Knicks certainly wanted Mac to be happy, and they did not, having paid that much to Paul Snyder for him, want to be cheap now. The real question was Mac's future. With that much guaranteed money, would he lose incentive? And would this affect his game? It would not take a large loss in incentive to make a difference, Burke said, perhaps just 10 percent. That, in the case of a professional athlete, could be quite a lot. If I, Burke added, had a comparable lifetime guarantee, I'm not at all sure I would work as hard as I do. Madden answered that incentive was not a problem. Bob McAdoo, he said, was a professional athlete of the first order, and a rare competitor. It was not in him to give anything less than his best. Still Burke wanted one more meeting. This time Willis Reed, now coach, also participated. Reed felt even more strongly the way Burke did. He had been a witness to the two different generations of NBA players—his own, which got big money only very late in their careers, and the new breed, less tested, which had big guaranteed contracts from the start. There was no doubt in Reed's mind that a guaranteed contract diminished incentive and made an athlete less coachable.

In the end the Knicks capitulated. They had come so far, paid so much already and fan expectations were so high, that they were not about to back out of a deal. They paid McAdoo roughly what he wanted. The result was unfortunate for everyone involved. McAdoo, playing on a young uncertain team, reverted to the worst of his former game; once again, it seemed, his self-image came from points and statistics, as if the very size of the contract itself forced him to be the big man and score points. He seemed diffident and moody at practices. He and Haywood were never able to integrate their games. He soon became something of a movable commodity, going in one year from New York (for three first-round draft choices, the beginning of a new team) to Boston to Detroit, which in turn within a year let other teams know that Bob McAdoo was very available, finally, to New Jersey.

In New York Willis Reed was fired. He had been hired largely because management, frustrated with the failure of its black superstars, believed that a forceful black coach, in particular a former center, might be able to do what a white coach could not do. Reed, a very proud man, whose career in New York was a uniquely dignified one, became very bitter. He felt he had been treated unfairly and judged unfairly. Red Holzman, who only a few years earlier had been let go because it was believed that he could not handle the new modern black athlete, was brought back from oblivion. Bill Bradley, symbol of the great teams, finally retired to run for the Senate, stopping long enough to write an article for *Sports Illustrated*, "You Can't Buy Heart." Under these circumstances the Knicks, now slowly building back by means of the draft and not multimillion-dollar purchases, were hesitant about moving on a deal for Lucas, particularly a deal where the outlay of cash was an important factor. They had been burned twice before.

That night in Portland they played well and beat Portland 111–103. Luke, aware that Knicks management was watching, played brilliantly and scored twenty-nine points, one of his two best games of the year.

IN SAN DIEGO, Bill Walton, still weak of foot, worked very hard in the month of December to keep his body in shape. He was an eternal optimist about his professional future; in the past that optimism had been one of his great strengths but never had it been more needed than now. Because he believed he would play again, he kept himself physically strong and somehow, because he was physically strong, he remained mentally strong. He even, with some reservations, took regularly a special drink intended to give him additional minerals to strengthen and hasten the healing in his foot. By late December there was some evidence that the healing process was accelerating. He could sense around him now the doubts of other Clipper players with whom he had less and less contact, of the Clipper management— in any case increasingly interested in the terms of its insurance policies on him with Lloyd's of London—of writers and even of close friends. They believed, he knew, that his body was not strong enough to withstand the hardship of an NBA schedule. His problem as the fall turned into the winter (if there is a fall and it can turn into winter in San Diego) was keeping himself in shape. He loved to run, as he loved to hike and climb mountains, but running placed unacceptable stress on his foot, and even his walking had to be limited. So it was that he resorted to the Nautilus equipment. That was a relatively late addition to his training program; at UCLA John Wooden had disliked all bodybuilding equipment, fearing that it would make his players musclebound and slow. It was only when he had joined the NBA that Walton, whose game was always premised on speed, discovered the need for more strength. In the NBA there were plenty of players who were both quick and muscular. After reading a book in which Wilt Chamberlain recommended it, he turned to the Nautilus machine, built his body up in very selected areas, and decided that he was, if anything, quicker than ever. Now, waiting for his foot to liberate him and filled with surplus energy, he liked to get up very early in the morning and go to a health club. The club was virtually empty and he was virtually alone when he did this, which pleased him; there were no fans asking, *Bill, how about the foot? Big Guy, when are you going to play?*

He knew he was not a sympathetic figure to most sports fans. He had said too many things in the past that were controversial. Moreover, like any athlete he was wary of fan idolization, he had seen it swing for and against other athletes and he had seen it swing for and against himself. He was aware that fan loyalty, always a question in some cities, became far shakier with the coming of big superstar salaries, and that athletes were now judged not by what they had done in the past but only by what they produced that very day. There were no allowances made for a slump or for an injury. In the past the athlete's special skill had stood between him and the fan who envied him his job, and that situation was volatile enough; now, in addition, millions of dollars stood between them. Thus he was bound to be judged harshly, drawing big money whether he played or not. (That, he believed, was part of the business, just as was the fact that Portland paid him $400,000 a year, but listed his value, in the compensation hearings with San Diego, at $9 million. Just a part of the business.) His injuries, which did not show up on X-ray machines, had always been suspect. Worse, he had been both a critic and a beneficiary of the commercialism of American sport. He had not liked the NBA as it existed—too many games, too much money, too much materialism. But he had signed on and taken his share of the profits. For that he would not be forgiven.

In his senior year at Helix High School, John Wooden, in person, had actually come and scouted Walton. There had been rumors that Wooden might visit, but no one believed them because it was well known that Wooden *never* personally scouted players, it was beneath his station and his dignity. Yet there he was, seated in the stands with Ted and Gloria Walton. The other Helix players, normally so controlled and disciplined, had immediately started putting the ball up from all over the court. Gordon Nash, the coach, had called time, given them a full thirty seconds of silence and then told them to forget who was in the stands and play their game. That night at dinner at the Waltons' house, Wooden told Walton, "You're the player we want. We won't give you anything. We're not going to promise you that you'll start but we think you can. But you're going to have to earn it." That of course had impressed all the assembled Waltons, particularly their seventeen-year-old son, since the other coaches had been telling him how they were going to make him the *star* and how when he came to their school he would average forty points a night. Wooden of course was selling the game Walton had always been playing, for every high school coach in California seemed to coach in the shadow of John Wooden—quick, fast-breaking offense, tough man-to-man defense, speed above all else. To Walton, Wooden was selling nothing less than a basketball player's Eden.

For UCLA was a beautiful school, one of the loveliest in the country; its faculty and intellectual climate, as America's power and affluence steadily moved westward, had been continually on the rise. It was also one of the first major American colleges to go after black athletes. Long before Jackie Robinson had starred in major league baseball, he and Kenny Washington had starred in football at UCLA. Thus in the sixties, as basketball became more and more a black-dominated sport, UCLA already had an enviable reputation. It was, moreover, situated in an ideal place, gentler of climate, and less rigid of lifestyle, than many areas blacks now wanted to forsake. The pull of California upon blacks was not to be underestimated. "I have always been captivated by California," the then Lew Alcindor had said in announcing that he would, of the hundreds of schools seeking his presence, enter UCLA. Added to that was the style of Wooden's game with its emphasis on speed, which most black stars felt showcased their game far more than the old-fashioned game.

At the center of this Eden was John Wooden who, in an age when recruiting was becoming the dominant factor in college ball, did almost no personal recruiting (there were other highly skilled people on his staff who did it for him) but rather attracted talented players with the reputation of the college, its physical setting, its record as a draw. When UCLA sought out Lew Alcindor of New York, it had done so in the most subtle but high-powered way imaginable. Wooden, holding to his vow that he did not recruit out-of-state players, made no visits to Alcindor (although Ralph Bunche and Jackie Robinson and several UCLA graduates already in the NBA helped lobby for the old school). He did, however, make one request of Alcindor's high school coach: "I just want him to see our campus last."

Wooden was a very good coach who emphasized absolute fundamentals and he had his players work for hours on the most elemental parts of the game, shooting without the ball and rebounding without the ball. He was a somewhat prissy man of quite rigid personal habits, an old-fashioned religious midwesterner, spare of emotion, who had finally surfaced to full acclaim not in his native Indiana, but in this new America of the counterculture. "James Whitcomb Riley in the land of Ken Kesey," Herbert Warren Wind once wrote of him. Wooden emphasized in his coaching what he called The Pyramid of Life, diagrams of which, autographed, he handed out by the

thousands. This depicted a pyramid built of such blocks as Industrious-
ness, Friendship, Loyalty, Cooperation. Using the proper mortar (Resource-
fulness, Reliability, Integrity), it was ultimately capped by Competitiveness,
Greatness and Success. Well, why not? The proper players always seemed to
arrive, a Walton to succeed an Alcindor, a Keith Wilkes to succeed a Wicks,
and a Marques Johnson to succeed Wilkes, and always, it seemed, on Wood-
en's terms.

But Eden had not always been Eden, and there were those who coached
against Wooden earlier in his career who thought his moral principles fell a
little short of the Pyramid's specifications. In those days he was something
of a holy terror. He disciplined his own players harshly, he was known to
overheat his gym so that opposing teams would wilt in the fourth quarter,
and he ragged unmercifully not just refs but opposing players. Other coaches
naturally disliked this and he did not always have an enviable reputation
among his peers. The ragging of opposing players, other coaches felt, was
simply ugly; ragging referees seemed to pass on a dangerous subliminal
message to college students, that if life did not go the way you wanted it to,
it was because someone like a referee was whimsically screwing you, and
the way to beat it was to try and trick the referee first. But gradually there
was a feeling, starting in the mid-fifties, that Wooden was coaching better
and attracting better players, and as his teams improved, so finally did his
manners.

What other coaches resented about UCLA was the surface purity of
Wooden and the more complicated morality of its athletic program. For the
articles about Wooden that dealt at length with his virtues rarely mentioned the presence of a man named Sam Gilbert, a wealthy Los Angeles
builder and fan of UCLA basketball, who helped with some of the more
mundane aspects of bigtime basketball, such as keeping egocentric superstars happy. Gilbert liked to boast that he, not Wooden, really took care of
the boys, helped them with their personal problems, helped them find jobs,
and helped them with their pro contracts. Gilbert was the self-proclaimed
Godfather of UCLA basketball. When it became possible in the seventies
for underclassmen to claim hardship and enter the pro league before their
class graduated, UCLA was virtually unique in how few major players it lost
that way. The reason, students in the UCLA program thought, was as much
Sam Gilbert as it was John Wooden. It was, said one Wooden watcher, "as if
Gilbert's there but he's not there."

In the glory days before freshmen were eligible and before there was a tendency of high school graduates to go where they could play immediately, Wooden liked to recruit two high school superstars where one might do the job. UCLA teams were always deep, with players sitting on the Bruin bench who could have started and starred for virtually any other team in the country. The year that Bill Walton graduated, Swen Nater, his backup center, who had played remarkably little over three years, was a first-round draft choice in both leagues and ended up rookie of the year in the ABA. Other coaches resented Wooden's practice; it struck them as greedy. Wooden preferred it, for the depth of the bench gave him added leverage over some of his more egocentric athletes. If he had a strong bench he did not need to start a particular player and if he did not start a player, the player's pro prospects began to look dimmer. Sidney Wicks was fond of telling how, as a sophomore, he was a better player than some of the starters. He had gone to Wooden and pointed this out. "I couldn't agree with you more," Wicks liked to quote Wooden as saying, "and as soon as you do it my way you'll start." Some professional coaches believed that Wooden was the last coach who had been able to discipline Wicks.

UCLA was an ideal place for Walton to play. Walton loved speed; Wooden's style also emphasized the team concept of basketball, built around a center who could pass; and Walton loved above all else the special pleasure of the rare and original pass, of a teammate making an exceptional cut in order to get free and his being able to get the ball to him. Wooden was aware of the problems posed by the celebrity of his players. He worried privately whether Alcindor, great player that he was, was healthy for his program, because as a superlative player that the entire nation wanted to see on television, he received too much publicity. It inevitably detracted from the attention paid other players. Wooden did not like the dunk in basketball because he thought it too showy, too much the embodiment of individual basketball. If he encouraged it he would be encouraging his players to highlight their personal skills at the expense of team. Those who dunked soon found themselves on the bench. To some of these modern young men, black children of the California ghettos in the rising consciousness of the fifties and sixties, Wooden occasionally seemed to be a little bit of an old lady, a little conservative. Indeed, some of the blacks resented him just a little, thinking him reluctant to deal with them as whole men. When he told one black player that he thought that it was a bad idea for blacks to date white coeds, some of the more politically and socially conscious players expressed considerable resentment. It was Martinsville, Indiana, of the twenties talking to Watts of the seventies. Sometimes, among themselves, the players would make fun of him. But if you were a player, Walton remembered later, and you doubted him and thought him too old-fashioned, you simply looked at his record and doubted yourself for doubting him, because everything he did had always worked. His practices were meticulous, broken down minute by minute, every minute written down on little three by five cards. Practice began at 3 p.m. and ended at 5:30, and everyone went by Wooden's watch. No minutes were ever wasted. If you ran to build up your wind, you ran with the basketball. The practices were considered great fun—the UCLA second team in many of those years was better than almost any starting team in America—and part of Wooden's leverage against his players was his threat, if they malingered, of keeping them away from practice.

Bill Walton loved the basketball program at UCLA because it was so tightly disciplined and so meticulously well run, so little left in the hands of chance. By contrast he loved the rest of his college years because they represented the height in personal freedom. He was lionized, but in a very light sophisticated way, and on his terms, not so lionized that he lost his privacy. He loved the informality of the school, the quality of its education, the political excitement that UCLA in the early seventies seemed to be at the center of. Where he wanted discipline in his life there was discipline, and where he wanted freedom there was freedom. He switched early in his career from engineering to history and his grades were excellent. Professors there were impressed by the fact that though this shy young man had already been on the cover of national magazines he was trying to be not just a genuine student but a genuine citizen as well. He participated in political protests: at UCLA in those days that was done at no exorbitant price. Perhaps an angry editorial in some paper in some distant city, perhaps a gentle warning from a somewhat embarrassed and apologetic athletic director. But he spoke from the security of a safe environment, and a personal position as the best college basketball player in the country. Thus emerged the Walton of the twin cultures, first the finely disciplined, totally sacrificing and dedicated basketball player, immensely respectful of immediate authority, singularly purposeful about what mattered to him, quite willing to obey all the rules and procedures of his craft; and second, the Southern Californian who embraced the counterculture, let his hair grow as long as his coach would permit, smoked dope, moved openly among peace protesters, the tallest demonstrator on campus, a friend and fan of the Grateful Dead, the Walton who was public in his criticism of American racism and who answered his phone by saying, "Impeach the President." For a time the two worlds did not clash. In his first three years at UCLA Walton observed Wooden's rules faithfully; following his junior year they had flown to Atlanta together for an award ceremony. On the plane they were seated next to each other when the stewardess came by and asked what they wanted to drink. Walton asked for a glass of wine; the stewardess returned a few minutes later with a glass of ginger ale. Why this? Walton asked. "That gentleman there," she said pointing at Wooden, "says you're not having the wine." Wooden had nodded. "As long as you're traveling with me, you'll not drink wine," he said. So be it, so it was. Score one for Martinsville.

But lives are not so easily categorized and separated. Finally freedom and attitudes in one category inevitably seep over to the other. The Social Walton as opposed to the Basketball Walton was a man experimenting with life, and enjoying the experimentation daily; life was now an extension of his political views. By his senior year his UCLA team had won two championships in two years; and some of the players were clearly restless with Wooden's rules and pieties. Some of the seniors, including Walton and his close friend Greg Lee, were challenging the dress code and hair length. Practices were a little different from the past, perhaps not as intense. After all, two championships down, one to go, this was clearly the best team in the country. After all, Wooden told friends, these were modern players, different from the players of the past, less automatically accepting of regimentation. Perhaps it was important to be more flexible, and though he did not like it, Wooden bent somewhat. In his senior year Walton talked with Wooden about his need to smoke marijuana after a game. He asked for permission to go back to his motel room or his apartment after a big game and smoke. He needed this, he said, to relax. It took him hours to come down from the excitement of competition. Wooden said he was absolutely against it. Walton insisted; he was so tense after a game it was costing him sleep and affecting his readiness for succeeding games. Finally, reluctantly, Wooden had given his permission. All right, he had said, but don't tell your teammates about it.

It was an important moment: Walton was so good that the rules did not apply. For much of the season Wooden benched Greg Lee; other players on the team believed that Lee was benched for Walton's sins. Wooden also began later that year to tell people Bill Walton was a leader on the court but a follower off it. It was a line later picked up in Portland. Not everyone who knew Bill Walton agreed with that judgment; many of them, including close friends, thought Walton a very strong young man with an exceptional knack for doing exactly what he wanted to while being forgiven by those who opposed his actions because his athletic skills were so exceptional. Nor was John Wooden finally very fond of that team. Later he publicly blamed himself for becoming lax in dress and practice regimen; it had led, he told associates, to lack of discipline on court. That year, in the NCAA playoffs against North Carolina State, a good but hardly great team, UCLA had blown a considerable lead near the end and State had come charging back. The UCLA players, including Walton, had seemed confused and disorganized and had looked to the sidelines for Wooden to call time. Wooden normally had a perfect sense of the tempo of a game, when to stop and when not to, but this time, though the flow was going against UCLA, he did not call a time-out. It was, thought one of his friends, as if this was quite deliberate, he was in the process teaching them their final lesson—that they had done things their way all season long, and they could do things their way now.

Walton had entered the professional game not just as the best college player in the country but more, potentially the most dominating player to come into the league since Kareem five years earlier. His stature was so great that the very flip of the coin between Philadelphia and Portland for his NBA draft rights occasioned a full media celebration, including embraces on the part of the victorious Portland owners. The ABA had in desperation offered him a franchise of his own in Southern California, San Diego or Los Angeles, whichever he chose, stocked, if he so chose, with nothing but his former UCLA teammates. His signing with Portland was a major occasion. When a reporter asked Herman Sarkowsky about reports that Walton's legs, particularly his knees, were vulnerable, Sarkowsky, in words he would live to regret, said that was something which had been blown up by the media.

Perhaps part of the problem was UCLA; UCLA was Eden but the rest of the world was no Eden. In his three years at UCLA his teams went 86 and 4, the good guys always won. But life, let alone basketball, was not an 86–4 proposition. The good guys did not always win. UCLA always had the best players available; by the nature of the NBA draft, it was Walton's fate to go to the team with the worst players in the league. Life had always been a high; and Jack Scott—for three years Walton's closest friend and roommate in Portland—regarded Walton as a classic example of the exceptional modern athlete who had been unconsciously spoiled, not because he wanted to be spoiled, but because those around him had competed to spoil him. When Walton was injured, Scott thus believed, he was less able to deal with the depression and conflict than someone who grew up with lower expectations and greater exposure to reality. That was how Scott felt after Walton broke with him in 1978, at least. That break was particularly bitter for Scott because he lost not just a close friendship but also a connection through this influential and talented athlete to the ruling sports elite, to the inner circles of the sports establishment.

Scott was a classic radical of the sixties, intense, passionate, sincere and absolutely single-minded, so pure in his convictions and so devoted to them that he always had difficulty believing others could not see what he saw, and seeing it, would not come to the same conclusions that he had come to. Like so many other radicals he opposed the main political currents of American life, but where other radicals in those days concentrated on such issues as Vietnam, Scott concentrated on what he regarded as abuses in the world of sports, tracing into this smaller, closed inner society the injustices he found in society at large. He was an important influential figure in the sixties in his criticism of covert racism in college and professional athletic programs and abuses of sports medical practices. In a field where in the past few people had been politicized at all, he was a completely politicized person. Everything with Scott was potentially political. In his own book about Portland's championship season, Scott tells how during the playoff games, when there was a brief referees' strike and scab refs had worked the games, he had questioned the integrity of the calls of Earl Strom, one of the strikebreaking refs. Strom was being escorted to the referees' locker room by cops after a game, and Scott asked him whether some comments by Portland players about scabs might have made a difference. Strom, one of the most emotional referees in the business, had immediately screamed, "I don't know who the hell you are," and charged Scott, his arms flailing, punches flying. As cops pulled Strom away and ushered him into his room, Scott himself tells how he had shouted, "I plan to file charges, Strom! You blew your cool and you know you're in trouble!"

Scott was at once curiously mild, almost gentle, in manner, and yet constantly at the ready for some form of protest. Within the professional game he was especially critical of the free use of painkillers, both pills and shots. He saw this as a central theme, an example of rich owners abusing vulnerable individual athletes; he believed the system of professional athletics placed far too much pressure on the athlete to make himself available to play, whether his body was ready or not. Scott wanted badly for the players on a team to choose their own doctor; thus the doctor's loyalty would be to the players, rather than to management. He was highly critical of Larry Fleisher, the head of the players' union, for not pushing harder in this area; it was hard for him to accept the fact that for most contemporary athletes, the opportunity to earn huge salaries, however briefly, was far more important than control of the medical room, that there had been a quid pro quo, bigger salaries worthy of entertainers for higher risk. Walton's own salary, $400,000, made him an accepting if not an eager supporter of the structure as it existed.

Scott and Walton had corresponded when Walton was in college; when Walton joined the NBA, Scott—recently released with pay by Oberlin College, where he had been athletic director—decided along with his wife, Micki, to live with Walton and his lady friend, Susan Guth. They moved into an opulent new home that had been built to Walton's exceptional physical specifications for some $100,000. There were two shower heads, the higher one for Walton, the lower one, in his own immortal words, "to wash the soap off my balls." There was a commode of such elevation that a log was kept nearby so the mortals who used it could rest their feet on something. The kitchen counters were styled not for the person who did most of the cooking, the relatively small Ms. Guth, but for a seven-footer who might one day surprise everyone by becoming active over a hot stove. Soon, in part because some of his radical friends complained about the house's grandeur, Walton sold it for about $90,000 (thus becoming, it was said, the first person in modern Oregon history to lose money on a real estate transaction); two years later Walton's buyer sold it again, this time for $300,000. That house, watched off and on by the FBI because of a strong suspicion of a Scott–Symbionese Liberation Army–Patty Hearst connection, was a center for local radicals. At a party there Wayne Thompson of the *Oregonian* once spotted Dennis Banks, the Indian leader, several other less famous Indian leaders, Daniel Berrigan, the radical Jesuit, and John Froines of the Chicago Seven. It was a center of both basketball and politics, the two main forces in Walton's life, though in his early days in Portland his political existence seemed more consuming than his basketball one.

Later, after both Ramsay and Lucas arrived, basketball became relatively more important to Walton and he gradually saw less of many of his radical friends. How deep his politicization and his radicalism went was always hard to tell. How deep could it go in a superstar athlete from Southern California who went to college at a time when political dissidence was fashionable? Later, after Walton and Scott broke over complicated personal disagreements, a mixture of politics, friendship and ego, Scott became critical of the depth of Walton's politicization, particularly after he announced himself a born-again capitalist. Clearly basketball was always far more important to him than politics; clearly too, his political structure was, however much was written about it, and primarily because of his basketball achievements, only partially formed. He was in those early Portland years a very young man, subjected by others and by himself to far too much conflicting political, social and athletic stress. "I feel," he once told Scott, "like someone out of the movie *Shampoo*." By that he meant a semi-innocent bystander to a hustling, disoriented society in which other people always wanted more out of him than he could give. Yet he was by nature so passionate in his various avocations that whatever he did, politics or sports, he did so enthusiastically that there was not even any minimal restraint. Later, when he and others looked back on the time, there was always the question: was he the most naive person around or was he, as some claimed, deftly in charge, skillfully manipulative. It was a question that few of his close friends, and possibly even himself, ever answered or could.

He in fact entered the NBA with serious injury problems which the lighter college schedule, two games a week against less physical players, had not revealed. His knees had been a problem in college but in later years as everyone became more sophisticated about Walton's body, Bob Cook, the Portland doctor and then friend, believed that his medical problems originated not with his knees but with his feet. The knee injuries, he felt, were compensatory injuries suffered as Walton tried to protect his poorly constructed feet. Even his jump, Cook came to decide, the unusually deep crouch, Walton squatting before the jump much lower than other players, more like a frog, using an unusually deep knee bend, was an indication that he was using his entire body to relieve the strain on his feet. He was, in short, dependent on the most fragile underpinnings. Bad wheels, as they said in the league. Dr. James Nicholas, the New York doctor who had nursed Joe Namath and his knees through a career that defied medical logic, had once looked at Walton's feet and legs and said simply: "You don't belong in this league, young man."

That was something he, but regrettably few others, knew. He had constant foot problems in his early NBA years, terrible pain, surely the stress from the breaks yet to come, but no one could locate its source. Seventeen games into his first season he felt the pain in his foot. That pain and others like it would hang over his entire career. The Blazer management, anxious to hype tickets and sustain the high fan enthusiasm that had begun with his arrival (the number of season ticketholders had jumped from 2,971 to 6,218 when he was drafted and signed), kept saying that his status was a day-to-day thing. Walton hated that, and he never forgave the top front office for saying it. He believed that it placed the entire burden for not playing on the athlete and, at least unconsciously, minimized the seriousness of an injury, implying that it was at least as much in the head of the athlete as in his body. What made this even more of an issue was that Walton at the time was unalterably opposed to any kind of painkillers or shots, which were generally standard fare in professional athletics. Walton, well educated, wary of commercialism in sport anyway, extremely knowledgeable and genuinely respectful of his body, represented a new attitude on the part of the athlete as to what his obligations were. By refusing shots and pills, he was unwilling to play hurt. That was the term, playing hurt, and professional athletes in the past had always been willing to play hurt. Thus he was defying a good old American sports ethic of guts, toughness and loyalty to team. Worse, he was denying it while being remarkably well paid. And, worse than that, he was continuing as before to vent his political opinions, thus defying the first law of public relations for the concerned athlete: thou shalt be political and sound off in America against accepted ideas and institutions only when thou art playing at thy highest level of performance. All of this angered fans, and the Portland papers reflected it; reading them, he was convinced that he was really reading the attitudes—and goads—of the Blazers management.

In that period he accepted only the two coaches, Meschery and Wilkens, and Cook the doctor, as people who he felt were sympathetic and understanding to him. He was trying to stay true to himself and he was seen as a malingerer. He was willing to play with some pain, but pain in his feet made him exceptionally vulnerable. His first year was absolute misery. He was a pure vegetarian, ate no poultry or fish, carried his own food and water on the road and talked of becoming a breathetarian—someone who breathed but did not eat. He told Lenny Wilkens the Portland cold was robbing the life from his body. He told Scott he was thinking of giving up his unselfish style of play and concentrating, as he believed his teammates did, on personal statistics. He even tried to leave the team and the league, but found himself bound in his contract. He played in thirty-five of the scheduled eighty-two games that year.

In the second year he changed. He had built himself up on the Nautilus. His proper weight was 230 and he had come in the year before at 200; this time he came in bulked-up at 260. Desperate to play, he had adjusted his diet and now he was no longer a pure vegetarian; he ate seafood and poultry. Far more important, in his eagerness to play he began to compromise on his own personal medical policies. In that second year when his feet hurt he started to take Butazolidin. His younger brother, Andy, whom Scott thought the most radical of the Walton sons, found the bottle of bute in the medicine cabinet. The two brothers had stood there and screamed at each other: Bill Walton enraged by his violation of his privacy, Andy Walton equally enraged by this violation of personal ethic, by the cooptation of his brother by a system his brother rejected. "It's a mistake," Andy kept yelling at him. "It's a mistake and you're going to regret it. Not me, but *you*." Bill Walton took his first injection later that season. The team had, after a slow start, finally begun to play well, there was a modest winning streak, Walton himself was beginning to think of playoffs. In February 1976, warming up for a game against Golden State, Walton felt an unusual pain in his right leg. At first he thought he had simply been taped poorly and he went back to the locker room and was retaped. But the pain kept nagging. He played the first quarter and part of the second and the pain got worse. He began to limp. Culp and Cook cut the tape, looked at the leg and decided it was tendinitis. Cook suggested he take a shot, which would relax the leg and ease the pain. Walton thought about it for a very long time, thought of all his opposition to shots and the reasons for them, and then he thought of how much he wanted to play, and how much misery he had undergone. He and Cook and Culp were all friends, bound by a mutual concern for his body. The room, he remembered later, was very silent, an extended silence. It was to be his decision. Finally he had said yes. They had given him a shot and he played the second half, barely able to run, and afterwards Cook had taken him to a nearby hospital—where they X-rayed him and found a severe fracture of the fibula—a badly broken leg. He was out for seven weeks. He was furious with himself for what had happened, and the blame could be placed only on himself.

The controversy over Bill Walton's foot, which was to lead to his departure from Portland, and much acrimony, some of it legal, began on January 31, 1978, in a game against Milwaukee. At the time the Blazers were playing the best basketball in their history and, some thought, the best basketball in the history of the NBA. Their record at the time was 39–8. There was talk of their winning more games than any other team during the regular season (the previous record was 69) and a belief that they were a team of destiny. This was not just the illusion of fans and sportswriters, but of professional basketball people, and in fact the Blazer players themselves. Later Walton compared that excessive desire to be the best and to enter the record books with the excessiveness that marked the activities of CREEP, the Committee to Re-Elect the President, which led to Watergate.

That may well be a legitimate comparison but there was also no doubt that Walton, with his unique competitiveness, played a large role in Portland's obsession to win. During the Milwaukee game he felt a soreness in his right foot and when the game was over he peeled off his sweat sock, expecting to find a raw blister. Far more disquieting, he found no blister, but the pain continued. Still the team was winning, he was playing well, the pain seemed for a time acceptable. He played through the month of February until, with the pain steadily increasing, he finally had to take himself out during a game against Philadelphia on February 28. As he came out of the game he told Culp, "I'm tired, my left leg is tired—just very tired." At the time Portland's record was 50 and 10. No one seemed to know exactly what was wrong with Walton, though he did have a major neuroma in his right foot (plus a nagging fatigue in his left one), and on March 3 there was an operation to remove the neuroma. Without him a brilliant team became a less than ordinary team; it won 8 and lost 14. Destiny was becoming a good deal more elusive.

In his early days as a professional Walton had been suspicious of sports doctors; he believed them an extension of management. But over the past two years he had become extremely close to the Portland team physician, Dr. Robert Cook. Cook was not just the team doctor, he was, along with Jack Scott, one of Walton's two best friends; the bonds between Cook and Walton were a shared love of outdoor sports, backpacking, white-water canoeing and a mutual concern for so vulnerable a body in so exceptional an athlete. Cook was thirty-six at the time, already tested in far harsher terrain than basketball locker rooms—he had been with the first wave of combat troops arriving in Vietnam in 1965 and there he had seen enough gore and brutality and leg amputations to last several lifetimes. He was young, modern and hip. Before moving to Oregon (because he coveted the outdoor life for his young family) he had served as the team doctor to the Baltimore Bullets, and he soon found he liked sports medicine. The reason was not so much the derivative fame and glamour of the role, though no one was immune to that, but that the patients were so remarkable in medical terms. Unlike many ordinary patients, the professional athlete was a truly exemplary patient, his work was his body and any injury to his body threatened his livelihood and, in the most primal way, his sense of self. Moreover, a sports doctor had a rare opportunity to explore the outer reaches of what the human body could do. Cook liked athletes personally, he was aware of how high a price many of them had paid to become what they were, and he was proud to have fashioned several close friendships with them. Cook believed that at the time when he first met Walton, the young center did not know how fragile his lower body was. The general perception, when he entered the league, was that it was his knees, not his feet, which were the problem, and indeed, Lloyd's of London had, in his rookie year, excluded his knees from its insurance on him. But the more time Cook spent with Walton the more he became convinced that it was the foot and ankle area, the lack of cushion it offered so strong a man in so physical a profession, which was at the source of his ills. His foot was, for any star athlete, simply a monstrosity. Bob Cook had read a book once by an English doctor which said that the superior athlete is greater than the sum of his parts; in no case, Cook believed, was this ever more true than of Bill Walton. Everything about his foot was wrong. To start with, the arch of his foot was incredibly high, more like that of a woman in high heel shoes than that of a normal person. That was already dangerous, for it put added pressure on the tiny bones in his foot as he came down for a rebound, increasing rather than relieving the stress. Worse, Walton had a tight heel cord, which kept the entire foot and ankle area bound tightly and allowed it less flex and cushion, making him even more vulnerable. If that were not bad enough, he had hammertoes. It was as if rigid, inflexible feet had been attached to his otherwise magnificent body as a cruel joke. In 1980 Telford Taylor, one of the most distinguished jurists in America, a man who had served at Nuremberg, was sitting as a court-appointed special master approving the amount of compensation that San Diego had paid Portland in the Walton case; as such he became involuntarily an expert on Walton's left foot. The expression Taylor used to refer to the problem was "an ominous malfunction."

So in those days Cook had tried to educate Walton about his body and its limits. Their job, he believed, was one of conservation; they were, given the pressures of the schedule and Walton's fierce competitiveness, drawing heavily on a very limited bank. Practices and workouts in training camp should be cut back, because every jump and every landing in some way threatened the body and the career. Cook was conscious of the fact that there was a pit-stop quality to sports medicine. The pressures, after all, were so much greater. There was the brevity of the career, the immediacy of need. In the world of sports, everyone and everything, coaches, fans, media, teammates, schedules, the ritual of championship games, created a psychology of need that was absent in many other fields. In addition, Cook believed, the higher the level of achievement, the greater the pressure on the athlete. A great athlete developed a constituency, be it fans, media, teammates, which came to expect him to play and to play at a level beyond anyone else; these were pressures not faced by average athletes on average teams. In the championship season of 1976–77 Cook thought he had, under the pressure of winning, exceeded the bounds of pure sports medicine which Walton himself believed in.

There had been some gambling involved and the gambling worked. Near the end of the championship season Walton had had a severely infected ingrown toenail. It had been exceptionally painful and Cook had taken off a considerable amount of toenail and a certain amount of tissue. It was then so sore that Walton was not even sure he could get into a basketball shoe. So Cook had injected his big toe before every game in the Philadelphia championship series. Pit-stop medicine, Cook thought, though of relatively limited risk. A far more serious risk had come earlier in February of that year. Walton had tendinitis of the Achilles tendon, probably from the pressure of carrying a weak foot to high levels of athletic achievement. It was sore and it was inflamed. There was a considerable danger of rupture, one of the most serious athletic injuries imaginable, often a career-ending injury. The conservative thing to do was to place the foot in a cast for three to six weeks and then rehabilitate it slowly over another two months. But if his foot was in a cast, Walton's own season would have been over and, just as surely, Portland's season as well. Given the history of injuries which had haunted Walton's professional career, it would have been another immense disappointment, and would have added even more to the doubts that existed about his psyche, among those from whom he most wanted respect, his fellow players. So, with Walton's approval, Cook had fashioned a knee-length elastic dressing, providing in effect a man-made extra tendon. Walton knew the risks and wanted the dressing badly. It was a reasonably imaginative procedure and it had worked remarkably well.

Cook's ability to keep Walton healthy during the championship season had helped solidify their friendship. He now was certain that the general assumption about Walton in professional basketball—that he was a malingerer and that he would not, in the jock phrase, play hurt—was absolutely wrong. On the contrary, considering the vulnerability of Walton's body, he had played with pain as a constant, going back to his high school days; his career represented in fact the kind of rare triumph of spiritual will over physical limitation that only a truly great athlete could have managed.

The operation for the neuroma in March 1978 on his right foot was a success. But almost as soon as Walton started testing his left one, he again felt pain in it. Cook tried a series of injections so they could at least pinpoint the problem, but the pain seemed to move around. Specialists were consulted, among them Robert Kerlan, a well-known Los Angeles sports medicine expert; according to trainer Ron Culp, who accompanied Walton, Kerlan made no mention of a stress fracture during his examination. (The point was later of some importance. According to Cook, Kerlan's written report said nothing of a stress fracture either; however, a copy of the report with a small notation at the bottom mentioning the possibility of a stress fracture did show up in Harry Glickman's office. According to the Blazer people, and they are adamant on this point, this copy showed up only *after* Walton had been hurt and had gone public with his charges against the Blazer medical practices.) Other doctors, specialists in the foot, were consulted. Walton was even sent to a hypnotist. Later, this rankled; the implication was clear that the pain was not real but in his head.

When Walton's foot trouble began, everyone had been confident he would be ready for the playoffs. Now the playoffs were approaching and the still-unidentified pain continued to nag him. The team, which had been so brilliant for the first three-quarters of the season, was floundering without him. Walton felt suspicion of him growing—from the fans, even from the media and—the most difficult to take—from teammates and coaches. He felt that Ramsay was questioning him; nothing said, but a look, filled with need and urgency. Bob Cook, he felt, had his doubts. At one point, according to Walton, Cook told him: "You're looking at it [the foot] too closely." (Cook, though he often uses that phrase in dealing with patients, does not believe he used it with Walton, he was only too aware of how much pain it would take to keep Walton out of a playoff game.) But above all there were his feelings towards his teammates. They were his closest friends, but now there was some distance between them. Was he really one of them, they seemed to be wondering, was he just a little spoiled, unwilling to bear what they bore? The situation was rife with pressure, much of it self-generated; he was the supremely competitive athlete, this was the highest level of competition imaginable, he had been a part of what might be the greatest team ever to play, and now everything was about to go down the tube. Just before the playoffs he began to work out with his teammates, without jumping or running. The first playoff game was April 18. The day before the game Culp had asked Walton about the foot and Walton had answered, "It's no fucking better." Culp had asked if Walton wanted to go out and visit with Bob Cook. That meant shots. Walton said no, he did not.

In the first game, Walton played thirty-four minutes. Though he had sixteen rebounds he could neither run nor jump. He was largely ineffective and Seattle won. Cook kept trying to locate the pain and finally succeeded, just before the crucial game with Seattle three days later, on April 21. It was, he believed, in a soft indented point near the ankle, called the tarsal sinus area. That he had located it at all was encouraging; what was more encouraging was the fact that it might be diagnosed as the tarsal sinus syndrome, a condition known to afflict people who had suffered ankle problems in the past. Shots might well relieve it. Ron Culp asked Walton if he would like to go talk to Cook about shots, but he refused, he didn't like the idea of shots. No one on the team pressured him directly; the situation was pressure-filled enough. Later that afternoon he called Cook and asked to come out, and the two men sat in Cook's office for more than two hours, talking about the foot, the particular area involved, the medication and its possible dangers. Walton had involuntarily become something of a lay expert about his feet. His questions, Cook thought, were very professional. Cook remembers telling Walton not to go ahead unless he was completely comfortable with the idea. Sitting there, Walton weighed all the odds, all his own misgivings, feeling the pressure on him, and finally decided to go ahead. Cook gave him three shots of Xylocaine, two in the ankle and one higher up. The relief was immediate. It was like being let out of jail, Walton remembered. He went out into the parking lot, jogged a little and did some light jumping. The pain was not totally gone, but it was reduced to a level he could deal with. "If my foot feels like this tomorrow," Cook remembers him saying, "Mister Marvin Webster is in for a big surprise."

That night the painkiller wore off and he began to feel pain again. When he woke up the pain was considerable. He did not practice at the light shoot-around, which both teams had near midday. By the early evening the pain was worse. An hour before the game he asked Cook to shoot his ankle again. This time Cook gave him two shots but the effect was more limited, it reduced the pain but not as much as it had the previous day. Cook recalls Walton saying there was some discomfort, but it was not profound. He also recalls Walton asking about the possibility of an injection on the inner side of the foot and Cook says he answered that this was not anatomically safe, that this was the center of the foot mechanism; many tiny bones were there and a shot was too dangerous. So Walton went out and played. At first he was all right. During one break in the first quarter he walked towards the Portland bench. "Is Bob [Cook] coming with us to Seattle?" Culp remembers him asking. Culp replied yes, he was. "Great," said Walton.

Then the pain began again. His foot was killing him and he was sure he was limping badly. He remembered looking at the bench hoping someone would come in for him, but no one seemed willing to catch his eye. Finally it dawned on him that no one would take him out but himself. So he called time and hobbled to the locker room.

That was it. He did not know at that moment which was worse, the physical pain or the emotional pain, the sure sense that his foot had been seriously injured again. He refused to talk to reporters. After the game Cook took him to Good Samaritan Hospital for X-rays; the radiologist there studied the photos and could find no break. The next morning another radiologist looked at the same photos and called Cook saying there was one small area which bothered him. He wanted to shoot some more. Walton and Cook went back, and the doctor shot nine times and on the tenth shot picked up a small fracture. Walton had a broken left foot and they put it in a cast immediately.

That began a terrible time. The worst had happened, he had played and been hurt; he had gone against his own precepts on injections; at the crucial moment, when the pressure was greatest, he, like everyone else, had given in, violating his principles. He felt very isolated, no longer a part of the team, which was struggling badly against Seattle. He did not show up on the bench for the remaining games, as injured players usually do. Cook covered for him, saying that Walton was staying away on his instructions. Walton was angered when Rick Barry, broadcasting the game for CBS, called attention to his absence. Soon there were various articles discussing the seriousness of his injury; one columnist for the *Oregonian* said that he was one of a handful of people in the world who had a rare bone disease. All Walton really wanted was to take his family and get away from Portland. He felt cut off from basketball, though not, as yet, from Cook and Culp, and about three weeks after that final game he was one of a handful of people invited to Bob Cook's birthday party. He and Culp went together and spent some $1,500 for a Yamaha trail bike. They were still, it seemed, friends.

The friendship did not last very much longer. He went into a depression, the injury was serious, the pain from the foot was considerable, his future was jeopardized, and he felt desperately alone. At both a physical and spiritual level he was unhappy with what he had done. Now the season was over, players had departed, the fans had gone on to other things. That immense pressure which had crystallized around him in those few passionate days just before the playoffs had dissipated, as if a summer storm had suddenly come and gone. He became increasingly embittered, and his bitterness focused more and more on the Blazer management, on its medical practices, and on Cook and Culp personally. They had been, he decided, responsible for the shots. He saw them now as pushing him to have them; what was worse, he had thought of them as his friends, men who were devoted to him and his good health. But the shots, he was now sure, had endangered his whole career; the pain had been a warning signal, and by playing in spite of it he had deadened the foot's capacity to protest what he was doing, and almost certainly, he was convinced, led to far graver injury. Now, frustrated and lonely, he began to see Culp and Cook in a different light; they were his friends, but the risk had all been his, the pain was all his and the damaged career was all his. They were able to go about their normal careers, and he was not. It had not, he decided, been a balanced friendship. He began to wonder, as all athletes do, whether they had been friends merely with the human being, or with the athlete. Friends were supposed to protect him from things like this. Instead, he felt, they had helped lead him into it. He became very bitter. Other friends thought he was angry at them because he was in fact angry at himself.

In those days he was spending most of his time with two friends—Scott, who hated the idea of shots, and a young Portland writer-lawyer named John Bassett, who wrote for the counterculture *Willamette Week*, and who virtually alone among Portland sportswriters had been critical of Blazer management policies in the past. In June 1978 Cook took the cast off Walton's foot; Cook seemed more optimistic about the progress he was making than Walton did. He spent a summer during which the pain did not go away and became increasingly worried about his future. He did not think the Portland management, including Ramsay, sufficiently sympathetic to his problems. Soon criticism of Cook and the Blazer medical policies began to appear in the Portland papers, with Scott and Bassett as the sources. Ramsay had once asked how the pain was and Walton replied that it was considerable. Well, Ramsay had said, sometimes you just have to run through the pain. That struck Walton as being insensitive. On August 1, 1978, at Walton's request, Walton along with Scott and Bassett met with Weinberg, Glickman and their lawyer. Walton read out a statement attacking Blazer medical practices and demanded that he be traded. After a long difficult meeting Weinberg agreed to do so. Though from time to time Walton wavered in the future (in large part because Portland had the perfect players to complement him, and he knew that if he was traded the price would strip his new team of its better players) in the end he would leave.

The entire episode had left almost every participant bitter. Walton remained angry at Cook and Culp, and they in turn resented his attack on their professional ethics. Part of the friendship between Cook and Walton had been based on Walton's faith in Cook's concern for his health, far beyond that of the ordinary team doctor for the star player. Cook, angry, now referred to Walton as a "sociopathic personality" and complained that he was refusing to take responsibility for his own actions, that his position as a great athlete had too long protected him from personal accountability. Scott, acting as Walton's agent, arranged what he considered to be a remarkable contract with Golden State, which would permit the players to choose their own doctor, a key part of Scott's vision of the new athletic structure. But Walton turned down Golden State and signed with San Diego, a team in his hometown. He also split Scott off from his inner group; no one knew exactly why, but he told friends that Scott's ego and desire to get publicity were a problem.

Scott, deeply wounded both personally and professionally, gradually became critical of Walton. He remained for a time a pariah in Portland, regarded by most fans there as the man who had masterminded Walton's departure. While Walton was still indecisive about his future, Scott gave an interview saying that Walton would go to San Diego because it was his home, and the medical practice had little to do with his decision. Little noticed at the time, and treated cautiously because Scott was regarded as an outcast, it was rediscovered and bannered in local papers after Walton made a decision to sign with San Diego. In September 1979 after Walton had gone, Jack Scott called Bob Cook. The two had been antagonists in the past, but now Scott's tone was different. He seemed, Cook thought, to be very nervous. "You and I," he told Cook, "haven't always agreed in the past, but we were Bill's best friends and he used us both for his own purposes and then he cut us out." Cook, sensing a lawsuit in the air, kept notes on the phone call.

ON JANUARY 7 the Trail Blazers held a practice at the Jewish Community Center in Portland. They were to play Indiana the next night, and then go on a prolonged eastern road trip, so Ramsay made the practice relatively light.

That day Larry Steele watched his teammates scrimmaging. He sat on the side of the court, wearing sweat clothes. Everybody else would be going on the road, but Steele would not. His knee was not coming around very quickly. He was putting weights on his feet and then lifting them in order to strengthen the knee. He did eighty repetitions of this exercise, and when the eightieth repetition felt as good as the first, he added 2½ pounds more to the weight. He had started at 2½ pounds and now was up to 7½. On this day he locked his bad knee and raised it 240 times in drills. It was, he said, a grinding monotonous business, made more grim by his own doubt that the knee would ever come back enough for him to play again. Nevertheless he hoped to reach ten pounds within two weeks. When he finished lifting, he worked by himself shooting baskets for two hours. He was pleased by the amount of time he now had with his family, but he missed being part of the team. There was a vacuum in one part of his life; for sixteen years he had always been part of something, and now that was gone.

Off in the weight room, LaRue Martin was working pumping iron on the heavier weight apparatus. LaRue liked to work out at the JCC because he wanted to keep in shape and at the same time let the coaches know that he was available in case they needed him. He knew that with Kunnert injured, they needed help at center; he had mentioned to Ramsay recently that he was ready to come back and help anytime the coach wanted. He was *sure* he could do it. Just the other night LaRue had dreamed that he was back playing. He was still with Portland, and Larry Steele was there playing forward. Larry was open in the corner and LaRue playing center tried to get the ball but the ball was heavy and seemed frozen in his hands. Coach Ramsay was on the sidelines, kneeling as he always did, his face absolutely red. Was Ramsay angry at LaRue? LaRue couldn't tell. In his dreams, which were frequent in basketball season, LaRue never shot at all, he just rebounded and tried to play good defense, playing unselfishly, the way the coaches wanted. After this practice he talked to Ramsay again, mentioning his availability, but Ramsay had again not seemed very interested. Well, there was a new franchise being started in Dallas. He had talked with his wife about living there. Would she mind living in Texas? Dallas would certainly need an experienced big man. He knew he could still play and he knew he was better than Kim Hughes, a white center playing for Denver. He could eat Kim Hughes *alive*. Still, he was glad that Kim Hughes was able to play ball, that was important for him and his family.

The Blazers were still struggling to get above .500, and this was the worst time of year for all but the good teams. By now most players were caught in the numbing cycle of the schedule, too many games, too many defeats, one game turning into another, bodies steadily wearing down. Only on teams that were consistently winning was this time of year any fun, and even then, the bodies often were exhausted. The five-game road trip had started badly; the last game of the home stand had been a getaway game against Indiana, one of the weaker teams in the league. Like Denver, Indiana was perennially shaky in its financial base, and so other teams had been able to exploit it in recent years with ripoff trades. But against Indiana, Portland had played a stupid listless game as if asking to lose, which it had finally done. That night there had been a fierce ice storm which had virtually shut down the city, and the next morning, half asleep, the players had struggled to the airport through a frozen, deserted city. At the airport Ramsay, angry about losing to *Indiana,* at *home,* positioned himself as far away from his players as he could, while still remaining within the general confines of the waiting room. Most of the flights were canceled, but Portland's flight to New York through Seattle was open. Steve Jones, the announcer, was trying to negotiate with some United Airlines people in order to get the two referees from the previous night's game on board. "Never know when you might need a favor," he was saying. He was talking with one of them, Dick Bavetta, about George Gervin, the San Antonio guard, slim, graceful, known as The Iceman. Ice had scored fifty points the night before. "A few weeks ago I refereed a game with San Antonio," Bavetta said. "We were ready to start the game but the ball didn't feel quite right. A little soft, you know. So I threw it to Gervin. 'How's it feel, Ice?' I asked. Ice bounces it once or twice, throws it back and shrugs. 'A ball's a ball,' he said. Scored forty-five points that night. It doesn't look like he's doing it, and you think to yourself, Ice isn't doing it tonight, and then you check at the end of the game, forty-five points." Finally they announced the plane. Ramsay walked down to the ramp ahead of the players. A man dressed in western clothes stopped him. "Hey, Coach Ramsay, I'd like you to meet my father." Ramsay stopped. "He's from way back east," the man said. Ramsay, good easterner, smiled. "From Philadelphia?" he said encouragingly. "No, no," the man said impatiently, "from back east. In Oklahoma." Where am I now and where have I gone, Ramsay thought, we lose to Indiana at home and Oklahoma is way back east.

The first day they stayed in New York City and practiced at the New York Athletic Club. Afterwards Ramsay had called the team together and issued an ultimatum. Players would get playing time from now on, he said, based only on how they played. In this season, he emphasized, not on how they played in the past. He was sick of the whole business, he said. It was a speech aimed as much as anyone else at Lucas and Hollins. Hollins was not even with the team at the moment, he was back in Portland with some vaguely defined flu, but Ramsay was annoyed because Dr. Cook was having trouble keeping in touch with him. None of the team members took the warning very seriously; they felt that Ramsay was softer on Luke and Lionel than others, in part because of the championship season loyalty and in part because the team lacked talent and therefore he could not discipline those who held back. The other players felt some resentment over the way Ramsay was treating T. R. Dunn. Dunn, a reserve guard, had played well at the beginning of the season and had been a major force in the team's early wins. Even now during the losing streak he worked harder at practice than most of the other players. But he was not a good scorer or a good ballhandler and because of that his court minutes were going steadily down. He more than anyone else seemed a victim of the team's malaise. As his minutes dropped, so too did his confidence, and this quickly showed in his play, which became more stilted. Sometimes now late in the first half, wanting to cool off an opposing guard, Ramsay might send him in, and tell him, "Now play with confidence, Tee!" But suggestions like that did not quickly restore Dunn's confidence. He did not complain, he accepted the judgment, and his play suffered accordingly.

But it was a reflection of the tension and divisions that haunted a losing team. As the team played with less success, the players' anxiety levels mounted; as their anxieties grew they inevitably saw Ramsay differently than they had when the team was winning. Then he was the omniscient coach who paid attention to all details, who knew his opponents' every move even before they appeared on the court. His confidence had become his players' confidence. Now, in the depth of their malaise, they saw him as someone who did not commit himself to them emotionally, who was interested in them not so much as human beings but as basketball players, and then only to the degree that they could perform for him. They believed that he had little time for those who were not contributing, and warmth only for those who were playing well. By his standards Ramsay was sure that he was being exceptionally patient with both Dunn and Ron Brewer (who was also playing in a funk), but the other players were not so sure; they thought defeat increased the distance between player and coach.

For the New Jersey game they moved to a motel in the New Brunswick area, a tiny island in a sea of seemingly disconnected new suburban towns built outside the inhospitable tax structures of New York State and Manhattan. For the moment the New Jersey Nets would play in the Rutgers gym, but soon, because all of this was part of a new America and the tax benefits in the new America were considerable, there would be, for games to come, a brand new multimillion-dollar sports complex awaiting them. It was a rich populous new area, absolutely without a city or a center, designed for the automobile and the overtaxed. The players were restless, because they could not, as they did in New York or Chicago, walk around town. It meant that many more hours watching daytime television in their motel rooms.

Lucas had lunch with Larry Fleisher on the day of the game. Over the last decade Fleisher had become one of the two or three most powerful men in the league. Perhaps, thought some observers, *the* most powerful man, excepting always whoever happened to run CBS Sports at the moment. The commissioner was theoretically the most powerful man, but there was a feeling among many owners that Larry O'Brien, a former Kennedy-Johnson pol, had turned out to be a weak and disappointing commissioner. O'Brien's political connections, which were what the owners had sought when they hired him, had proved valuable in arranging the merger with the ABA, and there had been a brief sense of gratitude to him. That gratitude had diminished as the owners compared him (almost always unfavorably) with the far shrewder and more dynamic football commissioner, Pete Rozelle. Rozelle was the symbol of the marriage of modern bigtime sports to modern media and modern corporate power. Having him as commissioner of the league was like having the head of NBC and CBS as commissioner of the league, so complete was the marriage he orchestrated. By contrast many basketball owners now regarded O'Brien as slow and ineffective, and virtually incompetent in dealing with the media. Thus there was a vacuum at the top; owners or general managers could no longer dominate the league as Coach Red Auerbach had once done. In that vacuum, given the changing legal and financial structure of basketball in the last decade, Fleisher had come to be of central importance. He was the head of the NBA Players' Association which, unlike the football players' union, was strong, well organized, and highly sensitized to a large variety of social as well as political issues. In addition, Fleisher personally represented many of the top players in the league, a fact which some of the owners resented, believing it a conflict of interest. Given Fleisher's new status, they were wary of voicing such opinions. Just a few years ago being a player representative meant virtually nothing. The owners and the owners alone determined in which city a player would work, and what the essential salary level would be. But then, largely because of the rise of Fleisher's union, the legal structure had changed and the players could now decide their own futures. Fleisher's personal influence was now taken very seriously by many owners (particularly inasmuch as the players were often black and the owners found it hard to believe that blacks would make these vital decisions by themselves). Owners believed Fleisher could guide players in paths that he alone chose. Perhaps he could. In any event, where once he had been shunned, now his goodwill was coveted.

Fleisher had the good sense to be amused by the dramatic change in his social status. The holds when he called an owner on the telephone had become briefer, there were now invitations to dinner, and Christmas cards. Twenty years earlier, when he had first been drawn into the game, he had done it because it was all fun. He was newly escaped from Harvard Law School, which was not fun, and he had come to know a few of the Boston Celtics and done their tax returns for them. He had liked the players immediately. They were not just stars and heroes, the best players in a game he loved, but they were also, to his mind, honorable men, educated and sensitive as well. Tommy Heinsohn, his first contact, was wonderful company, earthy, educated and funny. When they had asked him to represent a union which was not yet a union he had been delighted; he liked them. Like any basketball fan, the little boy in him was delighted with this association with his heroes; the lawyer in him was distressed by how few legal rights they had in a society where the other labor laws were far more equitable. Fleisher enjoyed, as a basic right upon graduation from law school, the opportunity to take a job with anyone who wanted him. So did all his classmates at law school. So too did all the journalists he now began to deal with, many of whom questioned the right of players to be free of the restraints of the reserve clause, but who were themselves free to look for a better job in another city anytime they wanted. What was hard for him to believe was that these athletes, men looked up to by most of American society, did not enjoy such basic freedom, and were thus denied their true market value in American society.

For the first eight years he represented the union without taking any money because there was no money and because he was appalled by the way the owners treated players—they were denied, in addition to the right to choose their place of work, medical plans and pensions. The athletes themselves saw the union in the early days as a means of getting the most primitive of protections, a simple pension plan. These were men immensely vulnerable to a special set of anxieties, of careers ending overnight because of injuries, and fears that after the brief days of glory they might end up driving cabs. But Fleisher from the start saw the future in larger terms. He recognized in the legal structure of basketball a rare surviving monopoly, a structure in fact worthy of an antebellum plantation. More, he was aware that given the place of sport in American life, particularly with the coming of television, these men were not just athletes, they were entertainers as well, yet at an enormous disadvantage compared to other kinds of entertainers.

From the beginning Fleisher was only marginally interested in an improved pension plan. What he really wanted to do was something historic. Everyone, he thought, wants in his career to do something large, something special. A quick dance in the history books. In his case it would be to form a union in basketball and gain recognition for it, not for some small benefits, but because with a union he could muster the financial resources to challenge the existing legal structure and thus free his players from the reserve clause. From the beginning he was touched by the quality of the players he was dealing with. The hard core of the union came from the Celtics. That was not surprising; Red Auerbach went after players of the highest intelligence and character, and then of course paid them horribly. That made the Celtics a mass of contradictions. They had great coherence as a team, great personal loyalties to each other, great respect and love for Auerbach, who had created this unique institution and honored each of them by making him a part of it, and then of course great anger at him for paying them so little.

The essential irony of the world he was entering, Fleisher thought, was the contrast between owner and player. He considered many of the owners to be fly-by-night operatives in for a fast tax deduction, or primitives who had made some quick money in another field and who, on the basis of that success, considered themselves universal experts. Many of them managed to see themselves quite differently, as benefactors of the athletes, indeed as civil rights leaders because their players were black, and they were immensely critical of anyone who tried to represent (and thus in their eyes, mislead) their players. The owner often quite unconsciously looked down on his players. In part it was a reflection of the fact that the owners thought the athletes were stupid, but it was also a feeling that they should be eternally grateful for the chance to play a little boy's game and be paid for it. With blacks, Fleisher thought, the attitude was far more blatant and nakedly expressed, the racism barely concealed; there are not thousands, but *millions* out on the playground who want your job, so you should be even more grateful. What intrigued him was his belief that many of the players were in fact men of rare character and intelligence and dignity, Silas, Russell, Wilkens, Robertson, Attles, men who had fashioned remarkable careers out of desperately little advantage. Young men of comparable strength and character and different color often ended up in the U.S. Senate.

In the decade of the sixties, Fleisher could feel the players change as the society around them changed, especially the black players who were being touched by the great social revolution in civil rights. The players each year were becoming more sensitized and more politicized; the changes he believed were quite dramatic, but the owners, isolated from the players, did not see them as changing, they saw them as the same dumb jocks. Perhaps, he sometimes thought, the problem was with the very word *owner.* Most people in America who were owners, owned property—land, factories or machinery. Maybe even airplanes. But these were owners whose possessions were simply the human beings on their teams. Since the human beings were becoming constantly more aware of their limited circumstances, and since the owners were not changing, Fleisher was sure that a genuine collision lay ahead. The first decision, when the union was very weak, had been a crucial one. They would go after only the best players on each team to be their representatives. They wanted first and foremost the peer respect worthy of a Russell or a Pettit or a Wilkens, and secondly they wanted players skilled enough to be immune from front office pressure. Better to build slowly but build a strong core than to move too quickly and become vulnerable to owner pressure. The second decision was to choose a successor to Tommy Heinsohn as head of the union. It was clear that the new leader should be young and of exceptional talent, so that he would not be vulnerable to pressure from owners. Also, considering the new racial balance of the league, he must be black. They decided on Oscar Robertson. Robertson was young, strong, smart, an exceptional shooter and passer and a quarterback of rare ability, the best player, Kareem Abdul-Jabbar once said, ever to play the game. Whites could see his talent; but what whites did not know was the special niche Oscar had in the hearts of black athletes everywhere. For it was Oscar, as a player at an all-black school in Indianapolis called

Crispus Attucks, who had led his team to the state championship in 1955 and 1956. The state tourney in Indiana was something of a national event, and until then it had been a white-dominated event. In 1956 Robertson's all-black team had beaten an all-white team, and at that moment one of the great myths in American sports had died. There were thousands and thousands of blacks who had never set foot inside Indiana who knew what had happened. Heinsohn and Fleisher and Russell had gone to Oscar and asked him to head the union and he had been delighted. The future was thus ensured.

The first great victory had come because of the quality of the union membership. It was in January 1964 at the time of the All-Star game. For some four years they had been trying to build the union, with only mixed success. The owners were unbending. They boasted that they did not have unions in their other businesses and they damn well were not going to have them in basketball. Besides, they would say, they had talked to their players and everyone knew athletes, they weren't interested in things like unions, that was political, what they were interested in was playing ball, chasing girls on the side and making a little money for themselves. But if the union at the time of the 1964 game was relatively weak throughout the league, it was strong among the best players. On that occasion there was limited NBA television coverage (NBC was already bailing out), but ABC was planning to telecast the All-Star game. Implicit was the idea that if the ratings were good, ABC might televise the entire coming season. Since football was just entering its televised golden age, with expanding revenues for all clubs, the owners needed little imagination to be tantalized. Knowing they had leverage, the players decided to strike. The issue was a pension plan—the most minimal kind of pension plan imaginable. The owners refused to grant it. The leaders of the players were Heinsohn, Russell and Wilkens. The strike was a shaky business; a few minutes before game time it was still uncertain whether they would go through with it. The breakdown was about eleven to nine in favor and some influential players like Wilt Chamberlain wanted to play now and negotiate later. At that moment Bob Short, one of the owners of the Los Angeles Lakers, furious over the dissent on the part of his players, sent word down to the locker room that the two Laker All-Stars, Jerry West and Elgin Baylor, better get dressed and get out on the floor immediately or they were gone. It was a grotesque moment and it had a sobering effect on everyone in the locker room: West and Baylor were two of the most respected people in the history of the game. Yet here was an owner treating them as though they were untested rookies, *do this, do that, go here, do what I say.* The mood in the room swung completely, and solidified behind a strike. ABC meanwhile was squeezing the owners. If the players were not dressed and on the court in twenty minutes, ABC said, there would be no coverage this year *or* next year. With that the owners folded and promised a pension plan, thus giving the union a foot in the door, and greater legitimacy with all the league's players. It was a major breakthrough, and it taught a significant lesson to Fleisher. Television, he decided, was an instrument for modernizing the structure of the game. The owners so badly wanted television as a source of revenue that they were willing to accept it as an additional source of power, even though they could not control it. Television in addition allowed the modern, articulate athlete to speak directly to his fans. On television, Fleisher thought, players always won and owners always lost. It was a major ally and the owners now had placed themselves in a position where they needed it badly.

Still the union's struggle went slowly. The pension plan was piddling at first. In the mid-sixties, the players found themselves fighting for a comprehensive collective bargaining agreement which would greatly expand their bargaining rights and give the union the legal status it needed. The owners fought all the way, but by now the union had gained strength. The owners still pretended it wasn't there. When Fleisher went before the owners' meeting to ask for the bargaining plan, Fred Zollner of the Detroit Pistons got up and walked out. "I don't have a union in my other business and I'm not going to have one here," he said. Walter Kennedy, the commissioner of the league, went out and brought him back. "I think it's different now, Fred," he said. Fleisher began his presentation. The moment he started, Jack Kent Cooke, owner of the Lakers, began to talk as loudly as he could to an owner next to him. But again the players were armed. They warned that they would sit out the 1967 playoffs, a crucial part of the network package. The network's reaction was predictable. Again the owners crumbled. Now the union had the legal recognition it had always sought. Now too there was a rival league. Television strikes again, Fleisher thought. He felt free for the first time to go after what he had always wanted, the reserve clause. A legal challenge in a case like this demanded a class action suit, that is, one group representing many allegedly injured parties; it was far too broad and costly a struggle for a single player with a short career and limited funds to wage.

But the union was something else; it had the status and the resources to pursue the battle. In 1970, when the two leagues wanted to merge, the courts—at the request of the union—held against the merger. When the owners, sensing trouble in the courts, tried to get Congress to give them an exemption from the antitrust laws, the union fought back. In the past the political path had always been easy for owners, they were always well connected, they had given generously to congressmen and senators, and made good seats available for them as well. The athletes themselves had by contrast been either invisible or mute. But now this was a new generation of athletes, they were articulate, well informed and attractive (and they were still in good repute, they had not yet gained the huge salaries which tainted them somewhat in the public mind). Havlicek, Robertson, Russell, Bradley, Wilkens, Silas were all lobbying for the players. Many congressmen were fans. The old power of the owners no longer worked. Teddy Kennedy found that he was listed as a cosponsor of the owners' legislation. He was besieged by complaints from players. One of the Senate's leading liberals, he did not want to appear on so public an issue to be antiunion and antiblack. He asked his staff aide, Eddie Martin, how they had gotten lined up on this. "Oh, I called up Red [Auerbach] and he assured me that all the players were against this union," Martin said. "He assured you wrong," Kennedy said. The owners' attempt to get a congressional exemption failed.

Now, freedom for the players seemed right around the corner. At the same time the owners wanted desperately to merge with the vulnerable shaky ABA, and to secure Julius Erving and David Thompson to help their television draw. But the union opposed the merger. What held the two sides apart was the issue of compensation, that is, what one team would receive if a veteran player at the completion of his existing contract signed with another team. Would there be a payback in other players? So the union and the owners struggled over the issue. The owners complained that if there was no compensation, all the best players would end up in Los Angeles and New York.

The union was sure that it could win a fight going through the courts, but that it would be a long and expensive battle. The negotiations between the two sides dragged on. Finally in June 1976, Jeff Mullins, a veteran player in his last year who was on the settlement committee, had turned to Fleisher. "How long does it take a case to reach the Supreme Court?" he asked. "Three or four years," Fleisher answered. "Well, then, why don't we let them have compensation for three or four years?" Mullins said. How simple, Fleisher thought, how smart these players are. He made the suggestion and it became the basis for the settlement that permitted the merger and in the long run brought ultimate freedom and market value to the players. Compensation ended in 1980. In fifteen years, the union had not just arrived but revolutionized the sport. Power had passed to the players and to Larry Fleisher, who had set out in life to do one thing which he considered important, and had done it.

In Somerset, New Jersey, after Ramsay finished his lunch with his assistant coach and Fleisher finished his lunch with Lucas, the two of them met for ten minutes. There was a time, just twelve years earlier, when agents coveted the goodwill of coaches and were often supplicants. A favorably disposed coach could take a longer look at a rookie in opening camp, or could give a bench player a few more minutes, minutes which turned into added negotiating muscle. Now that was past. Already Fleisher held in his hands the contracts of twenty-five of the best players in the league. Now, if Ramsay sought a certain player, and Larry Fleisher said a good word about him or about Portland as a city, it might make a difference. They treated each other now gingerly and respectfully. Ramsay wanted to know what was bothering Luke. "Jack," Fleisher said, "he hates what's happening. He hates the way he's being paid."

"We're going to deal him," Ramsay said. "It isn't as easy as he thinks."

"Deal him, Jack. Try a little harder," Fleisher said.

Fleisher felt some sympathy for Ramsay. Ramsay and Lucas were caught in the same dilemma. Fleisher had seen it coming in Portland for several years. Because Weinberg was so much smarter than the other owners he was probably the first owner to understand as far back as the mid-seventies that immense legal and financial changes were going to take place in basketball, and that the power of the owners was going to be drastically reduced. That meant senior talented players would have great freedom of movement and would become, as a result, very expensive. Thus Portland, starting around 1975, had initiated a deliberate policy of signing its young players, just out of college, to very long contracts, four years, five years, at relatively small salaries. Often only one or two years were guaranteed. It was an almost perfect no-risk deal for the club: if the player panned out, he was safely in the fold for a long time. If he failed in the league, there was no price tag at all. Fleisher, who as head of the union saw all the contracts, immediately understood what Weinberg was doing. Brilliant, he had thought, brilliant but perhaps shortsighted. What Weinberg was doing made great sense in business terms but not in human and emotional terms, and these were at the heart of basketball. It would, if a player turned out to be good, mean that two or three years into his career he would become deeply embittered. Fleisher had seen too many players turn sour for reasons like that and he knew that bitter players were rarely good ones. Worse, that which burdened one player often became contagious. He had thought at the time that there would be trouble in the future, and now the future was here.

Fleisher did not represent Lucas officially, though he was unofficially representing him. He was not negotiating with Portland because Portland simply refused to renegotiate Lucas's contract. Some three years earlier, when Luke extended his already long contract in order to get a salary increase, Fleisher had been afraid something like this would happen and he had warned Lucas against it. At the time, during the championship season, there had been a questionable clause in Luke's contract giving the club two option years. That was plainly illegal and there was a chance that it might invalidate the entire contract. Because Weinberg did not renegotiate on principle, and because Lucas's then agent, Donald Dell, did not believe in renegotiation either, Lucas had felt himself locked in and unwilling to wait until his current contract expired. "You're going to regret signing this," Fleisher had told Luke, "I've seen it happen before." "Maybe," Luke had answered, "but what else can I do—look at what they pay me now." Fleisher had a strong sense of Luke's doubts, but could see that he was also a man cornered. It would turn out badly, he thought at the time, and it had turned out badly. Now, back to back at this lunchtime in New Jersey, he had dealt with Lucas who was angry and frustrated and Ramsay who was angry and frustrated. Weinberg, he thought, might be a very smart businessman, maybe smarter than anyone else in the league. How wise he was, was another question.

PORTLAND WON THE first game on the road, against a weak New Jersey team. Calvin Natt, object of Stu Inman's affections, looked like a strong player with a good sense of the baseline. From there the Blazers traveled to Washington. Weinberg had arrived and given a huge party for his wife the night before the game. (The players knew something was up that evening when they spotted Ramsay in the hotel lobby, dressed in surprisingly conservative clothes. He had finally blushed and admitted why the florid pants and jackets had been put aside.) The next afternoon, replete with important friends, Weinberg had driven out to see his team play the Washington Bullets. The signs were not good. Tom Owens was talking beforehand about how physical the Bullets' Wes Unseld was, and how Unseld always wore him down. Kermit Washington was saying that he never played well in Washington because it was his hometown. Lionel Hollins was not even there, but was still allegedly fighting the flu in Portland. The Bullets led by 21 at the half and blew out Portland. The final score was 127–95, and the game was worse than the score. Later Weinberg complained to some friends that Ramsay did not seem intense enough.

They had gone from there to play Philadelphia, an awesomely powerful, arrogant team. Philly seemed to drift though a game, tease its opponents and then, near the end of the game, turn on just enough power to win. When Philadelphia walked out on the court, there was a tangible sense of its physical power; the bodies alone were enough to intimidate other teams. There was Darryl Dawkins, the man-child, his fifth year in the league, only twenty-three years old, 6'11", 265 pounds, all, it seemed, muscle. His game had not caught up to his body but the potential was always there. "He put an arm on me and I felt like a flea pinned by an elephant," Kermit Washington said after the game. "He could be the next Wilt. He doesn't know how strong he is." Dawkins's coaches partially agreed. They thought Dawkins limited by a fatal tendency towards kindness and happiness. He had invented an imaginary planet and called it, of all things, Lovetron. He still loved to dunk, and earlier that year had done so with such force that he shattered a glass backboard in a game against Kansas City. That had sent a rival player, Bill Robinzine, running, his hands over his face as the glass fell. Dawkins, who liked to give names to his dunks, had named that one his "Chocolate Thunder Flyin' Robinzine Cryin' Teeth Shakin' Glass Breakin' Rump Roastin' Bun Toastin' Wham Bam Glass Breaker Am Jam." But it was not just Dawkins, there was Caldwell Jones, seven feet tall, a center anywhere else, a forward on this team, then Steve Mix and Bobby Jones. To say nothing of Julius Erving. The idea of what Philadelphia players could do was a good deal more frightening than what they actually did; it was symbolized by Dawkins, who seemed to coast through most games, moving in and out of focus, coming alive just long enough to terrorize opponents, then departing long enough to keep the game interesting.

In addition there was always Julius. Erving was probably the most exciting player ever to play the game; opposing coaches still warned their players
not to watch him, otherwise the game would simply slip away. Yet for all of
that Philadelphia was not drawing very well. It was averaging around 11,000
fans at home and drawing about 2,000 more on the road. The night before
the game some of the Portland coaches had gone to see a six-man indoor
soccer game in Philly, a new instant sport. It drew an impressive 6,500.

PHILLY WAS HOME for Ramsay. That afternoon Jimmy Lynam, the coach of
St. Joe's, Ramsay's old school, and another in the line of Ramsay protégés
who had gone into coaching, had dropped by, along with Matty Guokas, a
former Ramsay player in both the college and the professional game. They
were sitting talking about referees. Ramsay was telling how in the previous
game Wes Unseld had pushed Tom Owens out of the way, like a bulldozer
clearing a few small rocks. The next time there was a break in the action,
Ramsay said, "I yell at the refs, 'Hey, *watch* Unseld, *watch* Unseld.' So the ref
does, and Unseld doesn't do a thing and they're looking at me laughing."
    "When I was playing in Houston Jack Marin was on the team," said
Guokas, "and one time Mike Newlin starts for us and it's the first play and
Newlin drives to the basket and he gets hammered, and so Mike looks up at
the ref, it's Richie Powers, and Richie gives him a look, which says, 'Hey, it's
only the first play of the game.' But Marin is sitting with me on the bench
and he yells out, 'If it was Walt Frazier you'd called it.' About ten minutes
later Marin goes in the game and he takes one little step on a move to the
basket, no contact at all, and Richie calls it—offensive foul. So Jack begins
to protest, barely gets his mouth open, and Richie hits him with two techni-
cals, and he's out of the game. Refs," he said, "you figure them."
    At one time the Philly-Portland games had been brilliant, a test of sys-
tematized team basketball against basketball of natural talent and far less
discipline. In particular during the championship season, basketball aficio-
nados had been drawn to the matchup between Julius Erving of Philadelphia and Bobby Gross of Portland. That matchup had captivated professional
basketball men; yes, Walton had been dominant and yes, Lucas had been
impressive but it was Gross, maximizing his skills and his intelligence
against the single greatest athlete in the game, who had stirred the imagination of fans. As for Erving, well, basketball fans talked about him as ballet
lovers talked about Nureyev and Baryshnikov, and, indeed, saw genuinely

comparable skills in his use of his body. For Gross, only twenty-three at the time, the idea of playing against Julius Erving in a championship series was a professional athlete's dream come true. Gross regarded Julius Erving as the most remarkable individual athlete in the game, and quite possibly the greatest athlete in the world. He doubted there was any sport that Erving, with his combination of size, speed, power and delicacy, could not succeed in. Gross, like many other basketball players, was proud that Julius had chosen basketball.

The one position in the matchups where Portland might be weaker than Philadelphia that year was at small forward, where Gross was pitted against Erving. Before the series the Portland team had talked at great length about the best way of handling Erving. Lucas and Twardzik, who had both played against him in the ABA, warned that there was no real way of stopping him but that it was important not to let him dunk. Erving did this with such power, force, grace and originality—each move seemed invented at the very moment he made it—that it was not simply a matter of scoring two points. His moves electrified, not just his teammates, but the crowd as well, and they often changed the tempo of a game. Thus it was important to concede him some points, but to try to prevent him from dunking. Otherwise a game could quickly get out of hand. Ramsay, in these pregame sessions, had emphasized that while Erving was a great player, there were limits to his game, he was not an exceptional passer and he did not play strong defense. Because Erving, both as an athlete and as a man, intelligent, proud, respected, was so important to black players, he was to them an almost mythic figure, the epitome of the *black* game, there were some blacks on the Portland team who somewhat resented Ramsay's briefings. It was as though he were denigrating one of their gods.

In the championship series Ramsay had not been exactly sure how to play Erving. At first they had tried to force him to the left. But that had not worked, he was too quick and too strong and even when he was forced left and the angle to the basket was tiny, he could still manage to slice through and make some rare, instantly invented spin shot. Besides it also meant that Walton, trying to help double up on defense, was coming over from too great an angle. This not only neutralized some of Walton's defensive ability, it meant that Walton was in danger of arriving too late, fouling, and getting in foul trouble. By the third game they had changed their strategy. They would drive Erving right, give him a wider angle towards the basket, almost it seemed encouraging him to drive there, but also creating a situation in which Walton had a much better angle on him, had to move a shorter distance and was less likely to get in foul trouble. That was part of the strategy. The other part was for Bobby Gross to run and run on offense, in an attempt either to get free, or to wear down Julius. That was a key part of Gross's game, moving without the ball, and now at Ramsay's urging he ran more than ever. They had decided to make Julius work so hard on defense that he would have to give up something on offense. In the third game Gross kept running, even at times when he was sure he could go no further, because for the first time he could look at Erving's face and see the fatigue. Erving's face was drained and Gross, delighted by the sight, found he could run a little more. He knew he was not stopping The Doctor, but he was taking away part of his game and making him work harder for his points. It was an exceptional performance.

Erving, Gross thought, was simply a wonderful player. It was an honor to be on the same court with him. Julius dribbling the ball upcourt could move faster than Gross sprinting up the court without the ball. If he was not the greatest jumper in the world, then Gross wondered who was. Few fans, he thought, understood what Julius's leaping ability really meant. A teammate could hit Julius with a bad, low pass, a pass which most players would bobble, and Julius would reach down, gather it in, flex his body and still manage to dunk. But it was not just the leaping ability. It was The Doctor's hands. They were huge and yet surprisingly delicate, with extremely long fingers. It was odd, Gross suspected, for a player to be so fascinated with another player's hands, but Julius Erving had beautiful hands. They allowed him to hold the ball lightly and yet still control it, to do tricks with the ball, to drive past the basket and then at the last minute to score by putting all sorts of different spins and reverse spins on the ball in ways denied mere mortals with mortal hands. Gross, in comparison with most American males, had huge hands, but even they forced certain limits on his game. He could not dunk without holding the ball tightly; otherwise he might lose control of it. That alone denied him many of the angles available to Erving. There was only one thing a generous God had denied Julius Erving, Gross thought, and that was a great jump shot. He had a good one but not a great one. Everyone who played against him was thankful for that.

By contrast, Gross's own game was very much a product of his particular assets, the principal of which was his extraordinary eyesight, almost as good, some members of that team thought, as Walton's. Gross had never realized that his eyesight was unusual until he noted that others, even professional players, lacked it. He would ask teammates after a game why they had not made a particular pass and they would answer that they had not seen the opportunity. As a boy he had been better with visual puzzles than anyone he knew. In high school he would notice a teammate holding the ball while a man came open and then a second too late he would watch the reflection of the play come into his teammate's eyes. What surprised him was that the same things happened in the pros. When he showed up in Portland for his physical exam, the optometrist had been amazed. "You can see sideways," he told Gross. He had asked Gross to put his hands almost completely behind his head and Gross could still see them. He had clear 180-degree vision. Thus passing was at the center of his game. It was what set him apart, and because passing was the mark of an unselfish player, his game was uniquely unselfish.

Because Gross had been so dependent upon a team feeling for his own game to flourish, he more than almost any other player had suffered as the Blazers had slowly come apart. Philadelphia by contrast in the intervening three years had become stronger; Philly players who had less sense of teamwork had been traded and this was a much better 76er team than the one in the past. On this night Portland played hard against Philadelphia but the 76ers, with a much stronger bench, had simply worn them out. Portland was down by only two points at the half. Then Erving seemed to take over. He always had the ability to ignite a game by himself. The game would have its own pace, perhaps a little slow, the players were tired, and then suddenly The Doctor would explode, moving faster and higher than anyone else, and there would be six quick points on the scoreboard. Once in the third quarter he had taken off on a fast break and he had gone into the air just before the foul line and soaring higher and higher he had with an almost 270-degree sweep of the arm slammed the ball home, much like a flying carpenter driving home a nail, all synchronized into one perfect move. A moment later Bobby Gross, who was guarding him, responded by taking the ball, driving, spinning as he neared the basket, and then at the last minute reversing his body and dunking the ball into the basket, which was by then behind him. Erving, lost in that particular shuffle, had stopped and watched approvingly. A smile had come on his lips, a small one. Not bad. Perhaps not the real thing, but not bad either. A quick reminder of the confrontation past. A few minutes later Julius leaped in the air, appeared to be going towards the basket at an impossible angle, changed directions in midair and dunked. *That* was the real thing. Philly won by eleven. The road trip was becoming depressing and Portland was heading for Boston.

IN PHILADELPHIA TOM Owens had received a call right before the game telling him that his father had died of a heart attack. He left the team immediately and went back to Bronxville to make arrangements. It was a melancholy trip for him. His father had been seventy-four and the two of them had planned a long-delayed trip to Ireland that summer. Bill Owens had been a maintenance man at the Lotos Club, a fancy Manhattan private club. The family had always been very poor, white but poor, Tom Owens was acutely aware of that as a boy sharing a bed with his brothers as they grew up; but now, when he went home for the first time, sitting in his father's apartment, going through his personal effects, including his old tax returns, he realized just how poor they had been, and what an immense effort it had been for his parents to raise three sons. The largest amount of money his father had ever made, he learned to his shock, was $8,200 a year. He had no idea it was that little. It was like discovering, upon your father's death, a kind of secret poverty. Looking at the receipts, all he could think of was how much courage his parents had had. As a professional basketball player he made more than $8,200 just for a sneaker endorsement; some of his teammates who had the plusher sneaker contracts made four times as much for endorsing sneakers they did not necessarily choose to wear. He looked at these tiny pieces of paper which represented part of his father's story, and he tried not to feel bitterness towards the bleakness and powerlessness of his father's position in life. Even at that moment his lawyer was enmeshed in endless seemingly fruitless negotiations with Portland over his next contract, a contract, since he was already thirty years old, likely to be his last. One of the questions was whether the contract would start at about $250,000 a year as Portland wished, or $325,000 as Owens and his lawyer, John Lizzo, were demanding. One year, he thought, was the equal of what his father made in an entire lifetime.

When he went back to his father's house for the funeral it had made him still more determined to sign a proper contract with Portland or go free agent. The negotiations had been dragging on for almost a year. It was his last shot at big, at least by his terms, money. But Portland to him always seemed to be offering too little too late. Before the season had started he had wanted three years starting at $250,000 a year and going up very slightly. That was by NBA standards relatively modest for a starting center. Portland had instead offered him $175,000, which was what he was already making, though Houston was still paying part of that salary. Now Portland was steadily coming up in the offer, but he would soon become a free agent and now he figured he might as well sample the free-agent waters. There was little incentive for him to sign now. Also he felt a certain anger over the way Portland had acted. At one point, when his agent, John Lizzo, had asked for $250,000 a year, Weinberg had responded, "Are you really serious?" Lizzo had answered, "Who's got the problem of being serious? You're the people who offered $800,000 a year to a man who can barely walk." Now, with Portland willing to pay what Owens had originally wanted, but with free agency just around the corner, Owens and his agent were asking $325,000 a year. Owens, looking at his father's income tax returns, so tiny, so private, thought it all odd; he was not at all sure he was worth that much money, but if Marvin Webster, barely playing for New York, was worth $600,000 or so, then he was worth $325,000. It was all relative, he decided.

PORTLAND CAME INTO Boston to play the Celtics, tired, shorthanded, with a losing record, 24–25. Ramsay was sensitive about Boston, and he did not, above all else, want a bad performance there. A game in Boston was a part of history and in some way more important because it was against Auerbach. In a relatively new and uncertain league, Boston was the only team with any real tradition and past. Even the sheer ugliness and crumminess of the Boston Garden seemed to reflect that. It was wonderfully human and old-fashioned in contrast to the sterile new arenas around the league, each modeled on the other, products of quick deals between owners eager for tax and rental breaks and municipalities eager for bigtime national status, all located inevitably in new white suburban areas. The Garden was located in a fading center of town, over a railroad station; it was an area much richer in pimps and hustlers than in wholesome suburban families, a Ramsay postdefeat walk here was always high adventure. As a building, the Garden was old and tired, and it smelled of beer drunk and beer spilled, and cigarettes and cigars smoked. Even in the afternoon when the place was deserted, one seemed to still hear the fans, for the Boston sports fans were among the nation's most impassioned, cheering not just a Russell block of a

Chamberlain shot, a Havlicek steal of an inbound pass, but even more, still venting their anger at Mendy Rudolph, a referee now departed this life, but large still in the hearts and rage of Boston fans (who believed he favored the Knicks), his calls against the Celtics neither forgotten nor forgiven. The Garden boasted the most championship flags and the worst locker rooms, and showers worthy of a poor junior high school. Both the championships and the foul lockers were regarded as the work of Auerbach, the championships a reminder of Celtic power and strength, the locker rooms, a mild humiliation to the visiting team. The home team had foul lockers too, but it was believed that while the Celtic players gradually became acclimated to them, visitors did not. Even as the Blazers practiced, there was a sense of Auerbach in the building, deciding which player's number would retire next, Jo Jo White or Don Chaney (would Chaney be forgiven for jumping to the ABA?), and readying his victory cigar for one more victory. Auerbach was the best, he had coached to 1,037 pro victories and though he was no longer actively coaching, the record was there; since Ramsay too wanted to be the best, he always wanted to beat not just Boston, but Auerbach.

Auerbach was the architect of it all, the man responsible for so many of the Celtics' past victories. Now, beginning this season with the Celtics staging a major comeback, he was the man with the golden touch who had rejuvenated the franchise. For twenty-five years he had been smarter, and shrewder, and more innovative and finally more *concerned* than anyone else in the league. He was brash, and crafty, and bullying, a man of equal parts character and con, high integrity and low craftiness. His ego was immense, but he used it as a force; he at once stepped on it and stumbled over it, but was never impaled by it. In the Celtics' pecking order he was the first among nonequals, only then came the players. When other teams won championships the players were almost always in the center of the team photo, the coach and the owner standing on the side; in the Celtics' photos, it was always Auerbach and the owner of the moment in the center, the players to the sides. He had always been that way, brash, arrogant, absolutely sure of himself, from the moment in 1950 he had arrived in Boston. There, met at the railroad station by local reporters, he found himself questioned about the future of one Robert Cousy, a favored player from nearby Holy Cross who had dazzled college crowds with his passing and thus become a local darling. "Cousy? *Cousy?*" he had said. "Listen, I'm here to win basketball games, not to play some local yokel." His talent and feel for what the game should be were without challenger; he helped change the game, encouraged speed and created the model for the modern team. Indeed his talents were even worthy of his ego. During the early seventies, much national media attention was focused on the Knicks and their coach, Red Holzman. "That's nice about all the media attention Holzman is getting," Stu Inman of the Trail Blazers once said to Auerbach. "He's such a terrific coach." "Yeah," answered Auerbach, "but he ain't got no charisma like me."

He was a man far ahead of his time, smarter than other general managers and coaches, adept at understanding the draft rules when they were not, shrewd if necessary at getting crucial players like Jo Jo White placed, if need be, in military reserve units back in friendly Washington. Intolerant and opinionated in many areas, on the most important question in sport in the fifties and sixties—the use of black players—he was the most tolerant and farsighted man imaginable. He immediately adapted his game to them and the quicker, more exciting game they created. He played them in numbers not yet deemed acceptable elsewhere—two, three, *four*, even *five* at a time. More, his team was in the purest sense family, and if blacks were Celtics, then they were family. Any mistreatment of them was mistreatment of him. If the blacks were refused service at some southern restaurant during an exhibition swing, not just the blacks flew out of town immediately, but he and the other Celtics went as well. He was capable of bullying the blacks in practice and he did things in the fifties and sixties with them that one might not so readily do in the seventies, but in those days the codes were different and the blacks, who were then Negroes, accepted it. He used to call them *schvartzes,* the Yiddish word for black, though actually, in American-Jewish colloquial practice, closer to "nigger." He insulted them by doing that, but then he insulted everyone else in the same way, so it was all right. Or almost all right. They were black, but they were also *Celtics,* part of that special family, and they all had their special character and pride.

The Celtics were different; average players, joining Boston, blossomed and became better. Celtics were, above all else, winners. There was a dress code because winners should dress like winners. At first the dress code had been instituted by Auerbach, but soon its guardians were the senior players, the tradition was self-perpetuating. As in any good family, Celtics took care of each other, both on the court and off the court. They practiced harder, remained in better shape, and they won the important games, usually in the third and fourth quarters, by putting out more effort precisely when they were most tired. Then they would always run hardest, and then too they took that special pleasure in seeing fatigue and defeat in the eyes of their opponents. The integrity of their game, and integrity was the precise word, was based on superior conditioning. No one was allowed to let his teammates down, they were family, and besides they needed the playoff money. That was part of Auerbach's plan, keeping his players physically lean and well conditioned, and financially hungry. Outsiders like Paul Silas coming to the Celtics midway in their careers were skeptical of the idea of the Celtics as a family until they experienced it. There was a team ethic which helped guarantee a player's integrity, and it was supported by the fact that the playoff money was at stake; they all badly needed it. So in many of those years through the late sixties the Celtics had defied trends, not just in the way they played but in the way they perceived themselves and their teammates. After the final championship victory over the Lakers in 1969, his last professional game, Bill Russell had closed the Celtics' dressing room to reporters so that the players could savor that special moment of victory with each other. "We are each other's friends," Russell had said, and those words rang, not foolishly innocent, but immediately true to the ear.

It was also very consciously a male world. Auerbach himself had never moved to Boston; his home was in Washington and he kept his wife and family there. Players were thus expected to keep their wives and families somewhere else as well. He did not, they believed, want them buying houses in Boston; in Boston they could rent. That, of course, emphasized the impermanence of their position and the need to play hard in order to retain it. He wanted a strong masculine world. He was the head of the family, and by dint of his great will and shrewdness and force, the players were, no matter how much bigger physically, the sons. There were no daughters in *that* family. In that he was not unlike Vince Lombardi; his role in their lives went far beyond basketball, and he intended it to. Wives distracted, they wanted more money, they were an alternate source of authority, they got in conflicts with other wives. The postseason triumphant tours of foreign lands by the championship Celtics, the long season finally over, did not include wives.

Tradition was also important; things were done a certain way because they had always been done a certain way. Paul Silas, newly arrived as a Celtic, took one look at the cheap benches in the locker room, and asked for chairs instead. "These benches have been good enough for thirteen years and they're good enough for you," Auerbach said. Celtics did things because they had always done things. They did not buy houses because they had never bought houses. Silas, a serious family man and a shrewd investor, had bought houses wherever he lived in the NBA and he broke the Celtic tradition by buying in Boston. Soon all his teammates bought houses.

There was also a part of the Celtic tradition that said the veteran star made the most money. First Cousy, then Russell, then Havlicek, then Cowens. It was a shrewd ploy by Auerbach since it meant that he had to negotiate seriously with only one player. That's the top money we've ever paid, he could say, and everyone else would fall into line. Thus he could use the entire idea of Celtic tradition and its inherent loyalties to enforce a tight pay scale. To challenge the salary scale meant a player was challenging the Celtic idea of team. Every star got his turn, every star-to-be awaited his turn. Auerbach paid his players less than other teams were paying in the fifties and early sixties; the players accordingly were always on the edge of financial rebellion, their anger at him tempered only by their love, and their belief that since they were Celtics, they were thus something special. Auerbach did this not just because the Celtics were poor, though in those days there was a series of owners who passed through stopping only long enough for tax breaks; he did it for reasons of power and principle. Auerbach did not think big salaries and indulgence conducive to the Celtic team style. He believed, friends suspected, that if salaries were too big, the players would become soft. The playoff money would not mean as much to them, and they would therefore not enforce their disciplines upon each other. With playoff money an important factor in their lives, the players would not allow any member of the team to slip out of condition or pursue personal statistics to the detriment of the group as a whole. Besides, salary was connected to the issue of authority. If Auerbach set the terms for the team in something as basic as salary, and kept the structure coherent, then it added to his authority. But if he lost control to agents and players, then the interior structure of the team might unravel as well. It was a matter of will. Control was important; he cared about power and authority as much as Dick Daley of Chicago ever did.

Thus in the era of the fifties and sixties Red Auerbach was a dominating figure, and he found it relatively easy to maintain control. The legal structure of the league had not yet changed. No part of the legal-financial revolution had yet touched his players. They were still anxious to be Celtics. The gap in salary was always compensated for by the spiritual pride in being a member of those teams. Then it all changed, and his power began to crumble. The age of sports dictators was clearly over, men like Larry Fleisher and Howard Slusher were on the rise, and Auerbach reacted badly. For a time he would not deal with certain players if they had agents. Salary considerations began to dominate his decisions, and he was in a far more competitive market. For the first time he began to make mistakes; the Celtics, once the proudest and most stable team in basketball (other than, as someone noted, UCLA), had clearly begun to unwind. Players came and went. In the previous season the Celtics had won only 29 games and lost 53, and had had three coaches within a period of ten months. Clearly an era was over.

Above all Red Auerbach disliked Larry Fleisher, the lawyer who represented so many of his players and headed the union. It was a natural collision of two strong-willed men. Fleisher was a growing force in basketball, the kind of man that Auerbach had rarely had to deal with in the past. He was smart, he was connected, he had other options besides dealing with Boston—there was another league—he was as tough as Auerbach and he could not be, as so many men had been in the past, intimidated by the fury of Auerbach's tongue. To a degree, one mutual friend thought, Red was particularly infuriated because Fleisher was so much *like* him. A Fleisher player simply would not be drafted by the Celtics. But then in 1969 John Havlicek, by then the great star of the Celtics, and a truly unique athlete in his daily relentless contribution to the team, received an offer from an ABA franchise to jump leagues. The ABA offer of approximately $300,000 was four times what Havlicek was making as a Celtic. Worse, Havlicek was represented by Bob Woolf, a tough local sports attorney, and was also consulting on the side with Fleisher. It was a rare example of a senior player having a true shot at the marketplace. Auerbach could not lightly attack Havlicek; he was white, he was a great local favorite, his personal integrity and lack of selfishness and commitment to his team were beyond question. Auerbach could not allow Havlicek to get away, nor could he bring himself to deal with the attorneys. Finally, playing as hard as he could on Havlicek's very considerable loyalty, he summoned the last bit of Auerbachian skill and worked out a compromise. He would deal with Havlicek directly, but Havlicek would keep his attorney informed step by step. Havlicek eventually signed for $140,000 with the Celtics, a huge increase; Fleisher, who later represented Havlicek, believed that his loyalty cost him several million dollars. The trouble with John, Fleisher thought, was that he loved basketball far too much. It was almost impossible to negotiate for him. By the late summer with training camp about to open he would always be desperate to play, and Auerbach knew it.

But it was hard now for Auerbach to deal with the new forces. Paul Westphal, regarded by most of the Celtics as a great player of the future, was traded to Phoenix in part because he was represented by Howard Slusher. Don Chaney, a classic role-model player, slipped away to the ABA because Auerbach did not take him and his desire to be paid more quite seriously enough. Then in 1976 Paul Silas, four years with the Celtics after a long and honorable career elsewhere, was ready for a new contract. He, as much as anybody on the team, had become the embodiment of what being a Celtic meant, playing with intelligence, sacrificing his personal game for the benefit of his teammates; he was not only an exceptional player himself but an important positive influence on younger players. He admired many of the things Auerbach stood for in trying to create the idea of the Celtics, the principles of honor and character and integrity. He too opposed the idea of paying huge salaries to young untested players who had yet to show either professional skills or depth of character adequate to deal with riches. At the time Silas was thirty-three years old, he had been in the league twelve years and he was, finally, making roughly $175,000 a year. He believed this to be his last chance for the big money. He wanted $1 million over three years. He knew that many untried rookies were now making $300,000 a year. He was represented, naturally, by his close friend Larry Fleisher. The Celtics offered him $285,000. He wanted a three-year contract (in fact he was to play four more years), the Celtics offered only two. Silas remained insistent about the money, he had waited his turn, he had never tried to renegotiate up to fairer value in the past. Auerbach refused to budge. "That would be more than I'm paying John [Havlicek] and David [Cowens] and I'll never do that." He would not break the Celtics pecking order. He would not undo his salary schedule. Cowens, who loved playing alongside Silas—it physically liberated him as a player to play the way he wanted—begged Auerbach to sign him. "You're making a terrible mistake," Cowens said, "pay him whatever he wants." Cowens was a rare modern athlete, he did not let his salary define him, and he thought in fact that most modern athletes, himself included, were vastly overpaid. "You say that now," Auerbach answered him, "but a year from now if he's making more money than you and if his talent slips, you won't feel that way." With that he traded Silas, giving up the classic Celtic player, picking up in return Sidney Wicks and Curtis Rowe, who turned out to be as different in their attitude towards the team as players could be. The dissolution of the Celtics, already begun, was now accelerating. In Silas's last year the team won 54 games. The next year it won 44, and Cowens, unhappy with his new teammates and the change in team style, temporarily retired. The next year it won only 32 games, and then in 1978–79 only 29.

So Auerbach was forced to adapt. The Celtics were near collapse. It was either change or get out of basketball. He began to build again, making smart trades, paying players bigger salaries, dealing, however reluctantly, with agents like Fleisher. There had been a delay when John Y. Brown became the Celtics' owner, and worked with great dedication to undo Auerbach's work, trading players of quality for those with statistics, before departing to marry a television sportscaster and run for governor of Kentucky. "Watch out for that guy," Auerbach said when he heard that Brown was running for the governorship, "he'll trade the Kentucky Derby for the Indianapolis 500."

THE KEY TO the Celtic resurgence, however, was the decision to draft Larry Bird. Bird was a player of exceptional potential and many pro scouts lusted after him; he had huge hands and even more remarkable court vision. By a fluke he was eligible for the draft after his junior year even though he made it clear that he planned to return and play one more year of college basketball. That scared off most other general managers. Five other teams eager for immediate help passed on him, but Auerbach, believing that a big forward who could pass as Bird did was the rarest thing in basketball, drafted him. Then he waited a year to negotiate. That meant Bird, far more than the average player, had leverage. He was white, he was an exciting player, and he could sign with the Celtics. Or he could wait a few weeks and be included in the 1979 draft. He would not miss a single game if he did. That put extra pressure on Auerbach. There he was with a floundering franchise, and a shot at a player of rare ability, the kind who comes into the league every four or five years. Because Bird was a country boy, a group of businessmen in Terre Haute helped him pick an agent, and finally decided on Bob Woolf. Woolf was well equipped to do battle with Auerbach; he was as quick to go to the media with moral outrage as Auerbach was. Besides, a precious commodity was at stake. Not surprisingly, in the Bird negotiations Auerbach seemed muted. The bellows and screams of the past became light squeals. There was talk about the fact that the Celtics would not pay any new player, let alone a rookie, more than existing stars. In the end Auerbach gracefully accommodated to the modern era. Bird signed for about $650,000 a year, more than any veteran on the team, more than any Celtic had ever gotten. In 1979 the Boston Celtics, once the tightest of teams, began the season with a payroll of $2,651,071, the highest in the league. The world had indeed changed.

Bird was the rarest kind of media player, someone even better than advertised. Every player on the Celtics improved when he was on the court. "I would never have retired," the thirty-nine-year-old Havlicek told Bob Ryan of the *Boston Globe*, "if I had known there was a chance to play with someone like him." His sense of the court was absolute. He seemed to know where every player was at every moment. Bill Fitch, the new Celtic coach, called him Kodak because of his ability to photograph the court mentally. He was, with that eyesight and those huge hands, perhaps the best passer ever to play forward. If a teammate got free, the ball came to him. Though he was a seemingly limited player physically, with a body that was weak by NBA standards, and had limited flex in his feet (which made him run up and down the court like an elderly woman) he was nevertheless one of the league's top rebounders. He simply compensated for his lack of physical gifts by rare anticipation of where the ball was going.

HE WAS A shy, awkward, introverted young man at heart. A cutter just like the Indiana kids in the movie *Breaking Away*, said Bob Ryan. Ryan, one of the keepers of the Celtic flame, had immediately welcomed him as the purest of Celtics and began to promote him, not just for Rookie of the Year, but for Most Valuable Player as well. Though his salary and his skills meant that he was celebrated in the media, he was uncomfortable with his fame. He was clumsy socially, a country boy suddenly let loose in a slick high-powered world. A stranger spotted him riding an elevator to his room in Phoenix and very politely congratulated him on having so successful a rookie season. Bird immediately turned his back, as if to get as far from the man as he could. He hated in particular the pressure of the media, whose representatives were quick and verbal and sure of their words, all the things which he was not. The more he showed up on television the more he was sure it strained his relations with his teammates. That was where his true covenant lay. He was good with them and comfortable with them, because they were linked by the one thing in life he was sure of and comfortable with, basketball. He had, as a good Hoosier boy, tried Indiana University but it was too large for so simple a boy and he had quickly withdrawn. He had for a time worked as a garbage collector. Somewhere in his past there was a brief marriage and a child, and then a separation. Then he had returned to college and played at Indiana State, a more rural college than Indiana. His entrance into the pro league had surprised most professionals. They thought the skills were there but that the body might undo him. Instead his sense of the game and love of the game had served him well. The better the level of the play, the better he was. The Celtics, a dreary team the year before, were a championship contender overnight. All it took was dealing with the right agents and paying $650,000 a year.

That night, with Portland in town, the Celtic glory seemed as ever. Both Russell and Auerbach were back, Russell drafted as a broadcaster by CBS, anxious to boost the ratings of a slumping commodity. Russell was to broadcast a Boston-Seattle game two days later. Auerbach seemed in charge of Russell, shepherding him through the crowds. The fans pressed forward as if to touch the living basketball history in front of them. Russell had been the key to the Celtic dynasty; in the thirteen seasons he had played for the Celtics they had won eleven championships. It was Auerbach's first stroke of genius to perceive Russell's potential for the professional game when others did not; it was his other stroke of genius to be able to deal with Russell over that period. Russell was, if not the proudest man ever to walk the face of the earth, certainly one of the four finalists. The Boston fans and media had, of course, loved Cousy in those years and Auerbach in the most subtle way had manipulated that local prejudice to extract from Russell ever more effort, a rare performance by a player not so much to please the local crowd as to defy it. When Cousy finally retired, Jeff Cohen, then a young sportswriter, and later Auerbach's assistant, had published a piece in a Boston paper suggesting that the Boston dynasty might now end. A few days later he saw Russell in the locker room. "Son," Russell asked, "do you really believe that stuff you wrote about us coming apart?" Cohen, like everyone else intimidated by Russell, nervously allowed as how he did. "Son," Russell said, "you're going to watch an interesting season." That year, without

Cousy, the Celtics won even more games. Auerbach had also shepherded Russell through the latter part of his career when his knees began to hurt, and when he practiced less and less, often sitting there watching practice, drinking coffee, eating a doughnut, reading a newspaper, inciting his teammates to violence against each other. Once Sam Jones, one of the guards, complained about Russell's failure to practice. "This ain't a democracy," Auerbach had answered. Russell sat there half hidden by his paper, and a little later when Jones hit an off-balance jump shot, Russell smiled very slightly. "Nice shot, Sam," he said and went back to reading his newspaper.

Now, as they moved through the crowd, it was clear that Auerbach loved the moment, father and son, and was delighted to be as much of a celebrity as his player. Russell—who had hated playing in Boston and who believed the city racist long before its public school battles surfaced (the Celtics began to draw better after Russell left and the two dominant players were Havlicek and Cowens, both white)—seemed as distant as ever. As the crowd pushed towards him, he pulled back.

Auerbach guided Russell into the Celtics' dressing room, otherwise closed to the media at that moment. Steve Kelley from the *Oregonian* was waiting outside when they entered. "Hey," he told Auerbach, "you can't take him in there. He's from the media. He's CBS. The media can't go in." Auerbach looked at Kelley for a long moment, absolutely stunned that anyone thought that the greatest center of all time, all those championships to prove it, could be thought of as a representative of the media. First, scorn filled his face. Then disbelief. Other reporters, knowing Auerbach, awaited a blasphemous answer. Instead he winked, and closed the door behind Russell and himself.

That night the Celtics put their stamp on the Blazers. The Celtic game in fact was very simple; they always sought players who were fast and strong and they based their game on intimidation. They came at another team and they pounded away, as physically and relentlessly as they could. It was a style perfected over twenty-five years. They intimidated visiting teams and referees alike. Players like Cowens and Silas and Havlicek got the calls from the referees that no one else got because they were the Celtics. As Auerbach intimidated basketball people off-court, his teams intimidated them on-court.

Cowens symbolized it. He was in the twilight of his career, but he still played with a special fury. Off the court he was an absolute gentleman, a serious, reflective man, self-questioning and self-doubting, pledged to an eminently honorable code of behavior. His own athletic commitment was total but he was always surprised that basketball meant so much to others, to crowds who would come and scream, to owners who would pay such large salaries. Basketball was a private and almost personal matter for him, something he simply enjoyed. Earlier that season there had been an ugly scene in San Antonio, home of a notoriously rough crowd. The Boston players were on their way from the dressing room to their bus after a tough game, and a boozed-up crowd began riding them, spitting, shouting obscenities. Cowens stopped, puzzled. He went over to a semicrazed, heavyset lady who was chanting out, "Cowens is a sissy! Cowens is a sissy!" He did not want to shout back at her or argue with her, but he wanted to find out why she hated him so much and why something like this meant so much to her, so much more to her than it did to him or to the other players. He was genuinely perplexed. But on the court he was barely recognizable as a thoughtful civilized human being. He was probably the most totally physical player in the game, he used his body as a missile. As a smaller man playing against bigger men, he was constantly jockeying for position, trying always for that slight extra bit of territory. He was rarely called for fouls most players would have been called for. The one thing he hated in the game and which offended his own sense of purity was the player who faked a foul, who exaggerated the impact of a collision by his own theatrics. At the basketball camp where he taught tough physical basketball, he obstinately refused to teach how to fake fouls. It was, he thought, phony and it was on the increase in the league. Once in a game with Houston he had turned towards the basket and driven on Mike Newlin. There had been light contact and Newlin faked the foul, falling to the floor. The referee gave Newlin the call. Cowens was enraged, he screamed at the ref in disbelief, and then raced down to the other end of the court, where Newlin now stood in the corner. Cowens locked his arms at the elbows and in a moment of almost unparalleled violence, running as hard as he could, he absolutely belted Newlin with all his might, driving him off the court, almost, one feared, out of his career. He then, still raging, turned to the referee and screamed, "Now that's a fucking foul—that other thing you called, that was a fake. Now you better goddamn well call this one."

That night it went well in the Garden. Portland played well in the first quarter, it shot well, and it worked the ball well. It was up eleven points at the quarter. Lucas and Washington were working hard. Then slowly the game turned and evened out in the second quarter. In the third quarter Boston came at them, driving, running, pushing the ball, looking for the crack, looking for what Paul Silas once described as the signs of fear and fatigue in the faces of their opponents. Lionel Hollins had just rejoined the team, and he made some quick turnovers. Rather than playing in a natural flow he was trying to do too much, pushing the ball upcourt faster than his ability permitted, taking longer shots than he should, not getting back quickly enough on defense. Suddenly the Celtics spurted and their margin was eighteen points. The Portland players were exhausted. On the Portland bench Ramsay seethed. He knew what had happened, that they had lost in no small part because the Celtics were in better condition. For two months during this prolonged losing spell he had been remarkably restrained, stroking his players, protecting them from the media and from himself. But now, the game over, he was enraged. He cleared the locker room of everyone but the players and he started yelling at them. "I won't have it! You were outhustled and you were outplayed. I won't have it! Anyone who does not want to play my way is gone! I won't stand for this, and I will not be embarrassed like this in this building." That night, his colleagues thought, he decided to cut himself off from the past, not just from Lucas, but Hollins as well.

LIONEL HOLLINS AND Maurice Lucas were having breakfast. They were in Milwaukee for the last game of the road trip. Both of them were somewhat depressed about the season. There was a story in the paper about recruiting violations at New Mexico, a school, it turned out, that had tried to recruit both of them. Hollins began reminiscing about his days as a junior-college star when many colleges were after him. Stanford wanted him to sign a letter of intent. Arkansas, just beginning to go bigtime in basketball, made a big play. "My grandmother, she had raised me, did not want me going to school down there. 'Lionel,' she kept saying, 'that is like going backwards. I *know* what they do to colored folks down there. You just keep headed in the *other* direction.'" So Arkansas was out. Brigham Young was next. "The man comes from Brigham Young like he's going to do me this great honor! 'Lionel Hollins, you can become the *first member of your race to play at Brigham Young.*' Well, that was not exactly the honor I wanted most, I mean I had been to this Mormon junior college in Utah and I knew a good deal about it, when they cheered for you, and even more about *when they didn't cheer for you,* if you get what I mean. But I went up there anyway. Had one great moment at BYU. They took me to lunch, a university dean and an assistant coach, and the dean asks me if I want any milk with lunch. I said no, I'd rather have a Coke. So the dean, it's like he hasn't heard a word I've said, asks me again if I want milk. No, I tell him again, but I'd sure like a Coke. But the milk is very good, he says. I look over and the assistant coach is breaking up. That's how I learned that the Brigham Young cafeteria does not serve Coke or tea. Or coffee."

They began to talk then about coaches, and categories, soft sell, hard sell. Good Christian sell. Out-and-out crazies. "Did The Mussel recruit you?" Luke asked. The Mussel was Bill Musselman, a coach whose tour at the University of Minnesota had been marked by bitter controversy and charges that he had played a part in inciting his players into an ugly fight against Ohio State. "He didn't just recruit me, he told me I was the best basketball player in America and he needed me," said Hollins.

"Told me the same thing, maybe that I was better than that," said Luke. "The Mussel called me every day, saying, 'I need you, I need you, you got to come up here.' Made it sound like if I went up there, he had a pro contract right in his hand. Hey, man, I wasn't so dumb. I owned a television set, and I had seen the Minnesota Vikings play, all those people in the stands with woolen masks over their faces. So I told The Mussel far as I was concerned he coached at the University of Alaska."

"Called me too," said Hollins, "all hours of the day, telling me how much he *needed* me. I think to myself this man is a little odd. Isn't it cold up there, I asked him. 'No, no, no,' he says, 'that stuff about the cold is all made up by TV announcers and people in the media.' So I go up there and The Mussel does a number on me: Big Ten basketball is the best in the country. All their games are on TV. I'll be on TV more than O.J. and Kareem. If I come to Minnesota I can get to play against Quinn Buckner. Hey, I'm thinking, Quinn Buckner is forty pounds heavier than I am, and maybe I don't want to play against him. All The Mussel keeps saying is '*Sign now. Sign now.*' I tell him I want to think about it. 'You can always change your mind,' he says. 'We'll let you out of it.' I notice that I don't meet any basketball players when I'm there. That's a little odd. Besides it's very cold there. Turns out it isn't just TV lies. So I decide it's not for me and I'm about to go home and I'm at the Minneapolis airport and I hear my name paged. '*Mister Lionel Hollins, Mister Lionel Hollins.* Please report to the desk.' I'm scared, afraid someone in my family is dead. So I go there and there's *The Mussel*, all dressed up, no coach dresses better than The Mussel, and he pulls a letter of intent out of his pocket and tells me it's my last chance. I tell him no and I start walking back to the plane and the one thing I hear behind me is this voice crying, 'I need you.'"

"Tark the Shark had better moves than The Mussel," said Luke. Tark the Shark was Jerry Tarkanian, a coach at various schools whose recruiting was always closely watched by the NCAA ethics committee.

"I agree with that," said Hollins. "Tark was smarter than the other recruiters. All the other recruiters tell you how good you are before you sign and how good you are *after* you sign, which is the big mistake, because they can never discipline you. But Tark, he's got great moves, I mean fast. Tark tells you how good you are, how much he needs you, and then even when you're signing, the ink is still wet, Tark starts telling you what's wrong with your game and how he's going to fix it up. I liked Tark. He was the best of the recruiters who wasn't absolutely crazy. Take The Mussel, he's too slick. Clothes too fancy. But Tark wasn't slick, he comes in and he's carrying a little too much weight, and his clothes are a little rumpled. Tark kind of *waddles* in. See, you're expecting this very slick guy and then he waddles in and he gets your sympathy right away, you feel sorry for him."

"Did he tell you that you *had* to sign with him?" Luke asked, laughing.

"Yes, he told me he had near given his life for me. He had flown into this little town in Utah and it was a bad day, and he's telling me that it was the smallest plane he had ever been in and how the plane had bounced around. 'I risked my life for you, Hollins,' he kept saying, 'I could have died coming in here. Quick, sign!'"

"Well, Tark never risked his life for me," Luke said. "Tark was always talking about Long Beach and how beautiful the girls were and how many of his players went into the pros and how Maurice Lucas was going to be his main man. One time I get a call, 'Maurice, this is Tark. Do you know what I did last night? I didn't go to sleep. I spent the entire evening diagraming new plays for our team. And do you know who they're built around, Maurice? *You.*' Well, I liked that, everything built around Luke, and I went out there and I loved the place, nothing but beaches and pretty girls and everyone in T-shirts. Lovely place, Long Beach." He turned to Hollins. "Did you meet The Chicken Man?"

"No," said Hollins, "who is The Chicken Man?"

"Well, The Chicken Man, we made that name up for him, he is *the connection*. I mean Tark is there giving you that careful Tark speech about how he can't do anything illegal and he can't give me any extra financial assistance but then one night The Chicken Man appears, he's in some part of the chicken business, and The Chicken Man is a great friend of Long Beach basketball. Nothing in the world he likes better than Long Beach basketball, never misses a game, and he has all the moves, fast and quick. Pretty soon The Chicken Man is telling me how much he likes me and how much he likes my family and how he was sure he could find work in the chicken business for one of my parents. Maybe nine hundred or a thousand a month. That's not bad in 1971. I'm thinking the chicken business must be pretty good. I'm ready to go, but then I hear that Long Beach may go on probation. So I mention it to Tark and he says, 'No way, that's a rumor that all these other coaches make up.' But I'm getting nervous because that means no TV exposure. So I begin to pull back. Just then Al McGuire shows up. Clean Al. Talks faster than any man I ever met. Never heard so many different words in so short a time. Half of them I'd never heard before, and probably half of them *he* never heard before. But right off I know that no man who isn't smart could know so many words. So finally I make him slow down and what he says sounds something like this—'everyone else is going to promise you a lot of shit, money and cars. But I'm not going to give you a lot of bullshit and give you a car and buy you steaks.' Well, that's all right with me, because I know the whole car bit, that's the most basic one in the book, the recruiter comes by and he talks to the kid and then he leaves his car behind so the kid can use it, tells the kid he's got other appointments and he'll pick it up in a few months. Only what happens is he leaves the car, and the kid has the car and the kid feels obligated and he signs. I knew that one, and I wanted no part of it. So we go down the street to a pizza parlor for lunch. He buys me nothing but a cheap pizza, Clean Al."

LATER IN THE day a reporter runs into Al McGuire and the reporter mentions Maurice Lucas. "I got him," says McGuire proudly, "for a fifteen-cent slice of pizza."

THAT DAY RAMSAY held another team meeting; he was still angry from the Boston game. It would *never* happen again, he said, one of his teams not putting out enough. Buckwalter thought he was overreacting, that the

Boston game had not been that bad an effort, that if anything the team had tried harder in that game than in most of its games all year. It was simply a weak team, and it was wearing out. After the meeting Ramsay took Hollins aside and told him he wanted Hollins, who had rejoined the team, not Ron Brewer or T. R. Dunn, to bring the ball upcourt, because Dunn and Brewer were poor ball-handlers.

"Are you sure you want that, Coach?" Hollins asked.

"Yes," Ramsay had said. "Why do you ask?"

"Because I'm not doing such a good job of ballhandling either," Lionel said.

That afternoon Milwaukee beat them by one point. Afterwards Ramsay sat in the locker room talking about the things which might have changed it. A foul against Luke which could have gone either way. A foul against Kermit which was not called. A last-minute defensive lapse against David Meyers in which the defensive player had not come out to challenge him, giving Meyers an uncontested shot which he had made. That meant the Blazers were 1–4 on the road and 24–27 on the season. Before the season Ramsay had wanted 45 wins. That had been his goal, get into the playoffs with 45 wins, become a stronger team in the second half of the season. It had seemed within his grasp after the early winning streak.

Ramsay himself was exhausted. He was frustrated by the players, frustrated by the owners. It was all just less fun than it should be. For the first time since he arrived in Portland four years earlier he talked with close friends about leaving. It was, he confided, like being back in Philadelphia when that team was slipping out of his grasp. He just did not know if he could deal with players like this anymore. The championship season, far from starting a dynasty, seemed to have spoiled them. They had come to think they were great players. Well, they were *not* great players, they were good players who could on a given night as easily win or lose. Winning one championship, he said, did not make you a great player.

A week later he went to Washington for the All-Star break. The All-Star game was sandwiched in between several league meetings. It was an ideal time for trades. Normally Inman was the key figure at trade time, but Inman was so sick of dealing with the Lucas soap opera that he had managed to be in Alaska scouting minor league players. So Ramsay took over. He was, friends thought, almost frenzied, a man so desperate for a deal. He located his old friend Kevin Loughery, now coach of New Jersey, and when

Loughery said that Calvin Natt might still be available if Portland made a strong enough offer, Ramsay launched into it. There were other players available, but Stu Inman had been pushing Natt so hard for almost a year that Ramsay was convinced. Inman had spotted Natt early, when he was still a sleeper, a player for a small black southern school as yet unnoticed by other bigtime scouts. It was the body which had first attracted Inman, a very physical 6'6" and 220 pounds, exceptionally powerful for a small forward. And Natt's attitude. "You have to love him," Inman had told Ramsay. "Very strong kid, keeps coming at you, never wears down, plays unselfishly. Very strong body, not much flex in it though." Besides, the talks between Inman and Natt had gone well; Natt was the son of a minister and Inman had immediately liked that. It was a good sign. Even better, when Inman had suggested that being a son of a minister might have helped Calvin's character, Natt had said no, his father had become a preacher only recently, but he himself had been together a long time. Inman had loved *that*. From then on Ramsay was in constant pursuit of either the New Jersey owners or of Larry Fleisher, who represented Hollins and consulted with, if not actually represented, Lucas. Fleisher thought Ramsay seemed almost feverish.

At one point a deal seemed struck: Lucas, Hollins *and* a first-round draft choice for Natt, the New Jersey rookie. Natt was a good player, Fleisher thought, a strong rookie, but the trade seemed terribly unbalanced. He had particular trouble in understanding why Portland seemed to want to give away Hollins. He regarded Hollins as the kind of guard every team in the league sought, a crucial player if you wanted a championship, quick, intelligent, totally unselfish. But Hollins, who had a right of refusal on cold weather cities, turned the deal down. Lucky for Portland, Fleisher thought. Ramsay had been imploring Fleisher to try and make the deal work. So now Portland began to restructure it. Now perhaps it would be Lucas and two firsts for the elusive Natt. There had been a time early in the year when they might have gotten Natt *and* a first for Lucas and certainly Natt for Luke even up, but no longer. In addition there was talk about Hollins going to Philadelphia for a draft choice. Fleisher found that hard to believe, that a player of Hollins's rare ability and team attitude could go for some untested college senior. Suddenly other teams like Washington, which was desperate to change its chemistry, were entering the bidding. Washington wanted to unload Mitch Kupchak, a strong forward, for Lucas. Ramsay clearly wanted to finish the deal before leaving Washington but time ran out. When he rejoined the team in Kansas he called a meeting, intending to tell the players that Luke would be gone and that there was a good chance Lionel would go too.

The players before the meeting had been sitting around talking about the All-Star game, which they had all watched. They had loved the moments of individual brilliance, a blind pass behind his back to a player trailing by Larry Bird, a supreme dunk over Julius Erving by Walter Davis. ("Would you call that a Doctor J. move?" one of the reporters had asked Julius after the game. "No," said Erving, ever polite and courteous. "I would call that a Walter Davis move. A very fine Walter Davis move.") Kermit Washington had been chosen to play in the game, which had pleased his teammates immensely; it was not just the recognition of the fine season he was having, it was further evidence that the Tomjanovich incident was behind him. Rejoining his teammates, he had been like a little boy telling his neighborhood buddies about what had gone on in the big city. "Did you see the commissioner?" one of the players had asked. "*Yes*," said Kermit, laughing, "I saw him and he was nice, *so nice*." They had been introduced and the commissioner had said, "Yes, Kermit is an old friend," and Kermit had thought for a moment, if you're so nice and I'm so nice, where's my $60,000? Magic Johnson, said Kermit, was like a kid at Disneyland. "All he does is hang on to Kareem. Afraid he's going to lose The Big Guy. Everywhere Kareem goes, Magic goes. Everything Kareem says, Magic says. Kareem eats something, Magic eats it too. Afraid he's going to lose The Big Guy."

"Hey," said Lionel Hollins, "if I was Magic I'd hang around him too, wouldn't ever lose him, or let him get hurt. Don't ever lose a big guy. You know after the championship season Lenny Wilkens said that everywhere he went all he heard was Jack Ramsay this, and Jack Ramsay that, and about the Jack Ramsay system, and finally Lenny said, 'Hey, I could have won the championship too if I'd had The Big Guy healthy for a full year.'"

Hollins told his teammates he was probably gone. Kermit said he doubted it. "No," Lionel said, "they've already tried a package deal with New Jersey. I turned it down. But it won't be long."

"New Jersey," Washington said, "that's not the worst."

"Piscataway?" Hollins said. "*Piscataway*, Kermit?"

"Well," said Kermit, "it could be *Detroit*."

"I like Detroit," said Abdul Jeelani, "I'd like to play there."

"Abdul," said Kermit, "you're a nice man, but you're crazy. You do not want to play in Detroit." Detroit was legendary with the players for its poor management, its self-destructive trades, its endless losing seasons, its small but rough crowds. No one wanted to go there. The trade talk was unsettling. They were not a particularly close team, but a trade was always threatening. Every player's role would change. Even for an established player like Kermit Washington it was bothersome. "Now they say that Natt is a small forward," he told Jim Brewer, "but I'm not so sure. He plays pretty big. Maybe he'll play at big forward." Besides, Washington liked playing with Bobby Gross, who was in many ways Kermit's eyes and ears on the court. That might change with Natt, who was said to be a strong player but not a very good passer. Nothing was certain anymore.

Later Abdul sat alone in the dining room. The others had gone. He did not really want to go to Detroit, though he had heard some trade rumors involving him there, he wanted to stay in Portland. But above all he wanted to stay in the league. It had taken him four years to become a rookie, four years to have this one chance. He did not intend to blow it. He knew that a lot of other players were critical of Ramsay now in this long difficult season, but he was not; Jack Ramsay had given him his chance and allowed him to *play*. It might be a bad season for almost everyone else, but it was not a bad season for him; he had made it into the NBA. Besides Ramsay had been surprisingly gentle with him. Abdul was scared when he came to Portland because he knew that Ramsay had a reputation as a tough coach; whenever Abdul had seen him on television he always seemed to be angry. But Jack Ramsay in person dealing with players was very different. His criticism was never personal, he never raised his voice, and he never—as a lot of NBA coaches did—built himself up at the players' expense. Instead he worked to build up the players. When he told them what he wanted it was very specific. When Abdul did something wrong he made it seem as though the mistake was not Abdul's, but the fault of one of those other coaches who had preceded Ramsay. That was fortunate, Abdul thought; ordinary-sized white people, he realized, looked at a huge 6'8" black man with a name like Abdul and could never believe that he might well be shy and sensitive and that words could sting. Abdul Jeelani *hated* coaches who made fun of their players; it had always made him feel poor and stupid, an outsider who had wandered into the wrong gym. Jack Ramsay worked hard to make Abdul feel better about himself, and Abdul knew enough about the NBA to recognize the rarity of such treatment; he was grateful for it.

That night, the deals still said to be near completion but not final, they played Kansas City. Luke had flown in from Portland, part of the team, but not part of it. He dressed for the game. Ramsay, fearing a deal might fall through if he was injured, barely used him in the first half.

At halftime Luke took Ramsay aside. "Coach, why don't I go back to Portland? You're not going to play me. I know that, you know that and this stuff, me hanging around, is bad for the team, bad for me." Ramsay agreed and Luke did not dress for the second half. Jack McMahon of Philadelphia was there at courtside, scouting Lionel Hollins for the 76ers. The last time Portland had come through here, Kansas City had blown them out; this time Portland played a smarter game and won. In the locker room later the players were pleased. A victory here was important. Kermit Washington had fifteen rebounds and he was teasing Tom Owens. They had had a bet on who would get more rebounds. Lucas, already fully dressed, popped quietly into the locker room to get his bag, then slipped away. Ramsay followed him into the hallway of the ratty old Kansas City arena. There they stood for a few minutes with their hands on each other's shoulders. Luke was saying that he was sorry that it had all turned out this way.

"Luke," Ramsay said, "forget all this contract stuff. Just bust your ass. Just play. Let them see. You can still be the best power forward in the league."

"I'll be back," Luke said. "I'll be back." That was it, he walked out of the arena. For four years he had been the most popular player in Portland; all those years the Portland fans had screamed when he came in the game, *Luuuuke.* That was all done with. He wondered where he would go. New Jersey, Washington. Maybe Detroit. The rest of the team was going to San Diego.

THE NEXT DAY they flew to San Diego still unsure of what was happening. Culp had gone so far as to get three new uniforms made up, one for Natt, one for Kupchak, one for Leon Douglas of Detroit, in the unlikely event that everything fell apart. The players were becoming nervous, there was a sense of everything turning sour, too many trades had been discussed in the newspapers. The Portland papers were filled with trade stories. They could have Kupchak for Luke, even-up. The price for Natt was Luke and two draft choices. Secure at power forward with Washington and Mychal

Thompson, they decided to go for Natt. It was a heavy price. Natt it would be. Philly was after Hollins. He would be next.

The following afternoon Lionel Hollins sat in his San Diego room. He was in his jogging clothes. The room smacked of the transitory life of the professional athlete. Warmup clothes were scattered around. The television was tuned to a midday soap opera. Hollins himself was playing solitaire. "Look at that," he said pointing to the television. "With our hours you can't get any program that requires a brain. That's the only thing you have time to watch. If they have anything on that requires a brain, then for sure you're out playing. They got something that's brainless, for sure you're in your room." Hollins had just been traded to Philadelphia for a first-round draft choice and $100,000. Hollins himself was bothered by the trade. He liked living in Portland, it had taken him a long time to make friends, but after five years he finally felt comfortable. His grandmother and three young cousins lived with him in a house he owned. He had been thinking about building a new home. It was hard to explain to people how much owning a home meant to him, a place where all his relatives could live. He was worried about Philadelphia, and how long it would take to make friends there. He understood the trade. He felt he had put Ramsay in an impossible situation, because under its salary scales, there was no way Portland was going to sign him for next year. So Ramsay had pushed for the trade because he wanted something in return for a quality player. What bothered him, he said (he had been quoted to this effect a few days earlier in the Portland papers and it had surely sealed his departure), was that this was his life, his being, and yet decisions about him and where he played were being made by a man who was an absentee owner, and who had barely bothered to watch him play. You like to think, he said, that the man who makes decisions about you cares as much as you do. Hollins had in a few minutes over the phone already settled his contract with Philadelphia for three years: $325,000, $350,000 and $375,000. All guaranteed.

It took Philadelphia, Steve Kelley said laconically later that day, thirty minutes to do what Portland had failed to do for fifteen months. Bill Walton had called a few minutes after the deal had been struck, and had commiserated. Bound to happen as long as Weinberg was the owner, Walton had said. You're lucky to be getting out. "We were pretty good once, weren't we, Bill?" Hollins said. "Yeah," Walton said. "We were pretty good." He told

Walton if he was around after the game they'd get together. Then he hung up the phone. It was funny, Hollins said, we were so young and so cocky. Not just the championship year, but even more the year after. We didn't think there was anyone who could beat us, and we didn't think it would ever end. We walked out on the court before every game and we couldn't wait for it to start. In the year after the championship game there had been one game in particular he remembered. Against Milwaukee. Portland had played brilliantly but Milwaukee was good too, and at the half the score was 78–74, with Portland ahead. I mean, Hollins said, it was a game above our levels. Like we were playing in our dreams. In the locker room at halftime Jack had been angry, talking about how we had to tighten up our defense. "Hey, Coach," Walton had said, "we *are* playing defense. It's just that this is a great basketball game. It's almost perfect. We're not doing anything wrong, and *they're* not doing anything wrong. Enjoy this one, Coach." Ramsay had nodded and accepted their word. In the second half, Milwaukee finally started missing. "We blew them up. Scored maybe a hundred and forty points that game." Hollins paused for a moment. "Perhaps we were all too young to have so much happen to us."

Then he went downstairs to the pool. A Portland television station had set up its cameras by the pool to interview him. As he walked over to the pool, tall, elegant, wearing his Portland warmup jacket, an elderly woman looked up at him. "I've seen you somewhere," she said. Hollins nodded. She could not place him, but she knew something was different, there had to be some reason why this young black man was here at this fancy motel being asked questions by a television reporter.

"Are you a basketball player?" she asked.

He paused for a second and smiled. "I used to be," he said.

At almost the same time, Jack Ramsay sat in his motel room, splitting his time between watching a broadcast of a San Diego Clippers–Golden State game, and going back and forth to the phone as the trades were being completed. The television set in Ramsay's room was very small, so small that it made Walton seem small too. A reporter sitting with Ramsay mentioned mildly that Walton seemed a little slow and did not seem to cover a very large defensive arc. Ramsay immediately challenged the comment. For a coach who was always sparing in his praise of players, whose positive comments were uniquely understated ("I like Kareem," he once said when asked about probably the finest active player, "he's a good player"), it came as a stunning angry response. "No one plays better defense than Walton does," Ramsay said, "*no one*." Well, he seems a little slow, the reporter continued, not realizing he had trespassed into the most private, almost *intimate*, area imaginable. "No one playing understands the game like he does," Ramsay said flatly. When he had finished the silence in the room was complete. The lesson was clear: criticize Walton's game and in a primal way you were criticizing Ramsay. The championship season lived.

THE NIGHT BEFORE the game Tom Owens had taken Kevin Kunnert down to Tijuana to a seafood restaurant which Kunnert claimed to know well. Owens was pleased with how the evening had turned out. "A big evening on the town for Bub," he said. Owens did not so much talk to Kunnert as he broadcast to him—Owens the announcer, Kunnert the announcee. "Bub goes to a foreign country. Bub's in *Mexico*. Right, Bub? Bub even knew a restaurant where you could get a lobster for four dollars. That's a lot less than lobster costs back in Iowa, right, Bub? Those Iowa lobsters are expensive." Kunnert nodded his head in approval. "Bub paid four dollars for that lobster. That was six years ago when he was a *rookie* in the league. So last night Bub goes to this foreign Mexican country where they speak a strange Mexican language and he found the same restaurant, but the guy tries to charge Bub *twelve* dollars for a lobster. No more four dollar lobsters. This Mexican pretended he spoke English and tried to tell Bub that the price of lobster had gone up in six years. He thought Bub was a hick, right, Bub?" Another nod of assent from Kunnert. The big hank of hair on his head shifted directions, guaranteeing that he was a country boy. "Some kind of hick, this big guy. Our Bub wasn't having any. He stood right up to that Mexican, even though it was the Mexican's country. That Mexican was at least 5'5" but Bub wasn't a bit afraid of him. Right, Bub?" Another nod of assent. The hair shifted direction again. "Right, T.O.," said Kunnert. That allowed Owens to continue broadcasting. "Anyway Bub let that Mexican know he was dealing with a bigtime sophisticate and he couldn't pull that kind of shit on him. We just want you to know that out there in Mexico today there's a Mexican who knows that not everyone from Iowa is a hick."

"Well, Bub," said Owens as they got into the bus for practice, "how do you feel about playing against Walton tonight?"

Kunnert, out twenty-four games in a row, simply smiled and pointed at his lame knee.

* * *

WALTON WAS DRESSING when Marvin Barnes walked in. Marvin was on a ten-day contract trying to catch on with San Diego. He was in terrible condition now and his knees were almost gone. Walton had been trying to get Marvin to work out with him on the Nautilis equipment, but Walton's enthusiasm had not proven contagious. Marvin sat down next to him. Walton started telling the story of Marvin in the ABA missing the team plane and chartering his own plane, arriving in Virginia just in time for the game.

"How many points did you get that night, Marvin?" Walton asked.

"Fifty-seven," Barnes answered. He was a slim elegant man in a beautifully tapered suit. He had signed for over two million dollars and all of that was gone but at least some of the clothes were still left.

"How much did it cost to charter the plane?" Walton asked, determined to prove that this was not an apocryphal story.

"Fifteen hundred dollars," Barnes said, "all cash." He paused for a moment. "Those were the days, weren't they, Bill? We were wild then. But we've both grown up now, all that wild stuff behind us now."

"Sure we have, Marvin," Walton said.

It was his third game back. He was exuberant about playing again. The best thing about him in his profession was his love of what he did, a love which was rare even for professional athletes in that it was absolute. He was almost childlike in his pleasure, a big joyous kid who believed he could do anything on a basketball court, and whose enthusiasm was infectious, for his teammates, for the fans, even for those he was playing against. Games against him were more fun for opponents as well as teammates. For others it was one more game in a season too long. For him it was coming alive again.

The teams had entered the game struggling, with almost identical records. The Clippers were 28–30, the Blazers 27–29. It was an even game for most of the first quarter and then Walton came in. The balance seemed to change immediately. His presence was immense and dominating, he was not as he had been two nights earlier, a tiny presence on Ramsay's tiny television screen, but instead a huge dominating figure who seemed to gather himself up for every Blazer shot, ready to deflect its trajectory and the flow of the game. What little confidence the Blazers had left evaporated. Walton played only seventeen minutes that night, scoring thirteen points. He was almost joyous as he ran down the court, and the contrast with the others was marked. On the bench Kermit Washington turned to Bucky Buckwalter. "He really likes to play, doesn't he? It's still fun for him."

THE CLIPPER LOCKER room after the game was celebratory. Twenty reporters, all of them with tape recorders at the ready, surrounded Walton. In came Irv Levin, happy that his expensive property had finally played. "Great game, Bill baby," he said. It was the way the new-breed owners talked. The spotlight was on Walton alone. Did it feel good out there, Bill? How's the foot? "Seventeen minutes, Bill," someone said. "That's a lot of minutes." He was pleased. Yes, he said, seventeen minutes was a lot of minutes. Gene Shue was playing him every other game now, but he hoped soon to play in every game. He was optimistic, his doctors were optimistic.

But the anxieties remained. A few days later he dreamed that the Clippers were playing in Boston. He was sure it was the San Diego team because Swen Nater and Lloyd Free were there. He was sure it was Boston because the arena was so old, a foul, malodorous place. He dressed carefully for the game, annoyed that the facilities were not better for professional athletes. Then right before the game Gene Shue had come to him and told him he was traded. What was worse, he had been traded to Detroit, the worst team for him in the league, far from the California sunshine. At first he had been terribly upset because the last thing he wanted to do was leave San Diego, which was his home, for Detroit. Then right in the middle of the dream, in that terrible old Boston Garden, he remembered that he had a no-trade clause in his contract. He had rushed after Shue to explain that he had a clause prohibiting trades without his approval. But Shue, both in real life and in the dream, was not a man who liked to argue. He had pushed Walton aside, very brusquely. "I don't have time to argue," he had said. "You've been traded. I'm sure it's for the better. Pack your bags and get going." Detroit, he had thought, how could it all end up in Detroit? He woke up shortly after that, thinking how fragile his station was in professional sports, even now.

JACK RAMSAY WAS worried that all the excitement created by the trades and the high expectations would put too much pressure on Calvin Natt. Some fans, angered over the trade of two popular players, might take out their anger on Natt. Before Natt's first game as a Blazer, Ramsay had held him back after the other players had left the practice. Natt had been a little slow dressing anyway—he had played in a college gym for most of the season, where the floor was bad, and he had arrived in Portland with the basic disease of the NBA, chronically sore knees. Ramsay talked to him at the whirlpool bath.

"Calvin," he said, "you're going to play in this league ten years. That's about a thousand games, with playoffs." Natt nodded, pleased at the idea of so full a career. "Calvin," Ramsay was surprisingly gentle for a man who rarely wanted true human connection to his players, "a thousand games. That's a lot of minutes. Take your time, Calvin. You don't have to do it all tonight or tomorrow."

THE WEEK OF the trades was a terrible time for Larry Weinberg, owner of the Trail Blazers. For several days the Portland papers had been full of trade talk and the rising public anger in the city had been reflected by the sportswriters. For the first time both papers seemed to have focused on the long-range financial policies of Weinberg, which had helped cause such conflict and chaos. Even Kenny Wheeler in the *Oregon Journal*, who was rarely critical of management policies, had listed the salaries of all the players, implying clearly that in trading Lucas, whose salary was $300,000, for Natt, whose salary was around $130,000, the Blazers were once again saving money. Weinberg, enraged, had seen Wheeler a few days later and had turned on him and said, "Well, I guess I can fire my bookkeeper now that you're doing the job." Kelley had stung him even more. A few days after the trades, Kelley had written a long tough article, labeled "commentary" by his paper, in which he had summed up all the complaints and resentments, the more public ones of the players, and the more (and long-muted but still intense) private ones of the coaches who worked for him. In it, he had coined a phrase, "Weinbergism," and he had written that Weinbergism was burying the Blazers. "If Funk and Wagnalls was asked to define 'Weinbergism' it might describe it as: 'Inflexibility of management to the point of alienation of team officials, players and part of the population of a city. Dedicated to the pursuit of making money and not satisfying legitimate player requests.'" He ended the piece: "Weinberg lives in Beverly Hills, California. When the Blazers won the NBA championship the trophy remained in Southern California. Weinberg has seen only one game in the last two and a half months. Weinbergism is tearing down the Blazers."

The day he read the phrase *Weinbergism* was, said a close friend, one of the worst days of Larry Weinberg's life. He had always prided himself on his ethics, his rectitude. Honor was important to him. Now, to see his name bandied about like this: *Weinbergism*. For the first time in the ten years of his ownership, *he* had become the issue. That was particularly difficult to take; he was a deeply shy and private man. That he would even enter so public a field as professional sports seemed in retrospect unlikely, but he had been able to remain mostly invisible, in part because he seldom came to Portland. He deliberately tried to avoid attention. The Blazer press guide—$3.25, copies sold, not to writers, but fans, filled with advertisements—told in great detail of the accomplishments of Ramsay, Inman and Harry Glickman, the general manager, but disclosed not a word about Larry Weinberg. *Who's Who in America* listed Glickman, Weinberg's subordinate, but it did not list Weinberg, because he did not choose to be listed. Though he was intensely involved in Democratic politics and American-Israeli affairs, he again remained as private about them as he could. Once Steve Kelley of the *Oregonian* had mentioned to him quite casually that he understood that Weinberg was going east to be among the select group invited to witness the signing of the Camp David accords. Kelley had expected him to be pleased by this recognition, but Weinberg was appalled by Kelley's mention of it. "Please," he said, "please don't write that!" He was not listed in any phone book, and when the phone rang in his home, a voice answered, not saying whose home it was, but repeating back to the caller the number he had just dialed.

Now suddenly he was the center of a storm in Portland. His sin was *Weinbergism*. He decided to do the unimaginable thing, hold a press conference. On the morning of the conference, everyone in the Blazer office was tense. Weinberg had always carefully and skillfully avoided the press in the past. He was contemptuous of those owners like Jerry Buss of the Lakers and George Steinbrenner of New York who used their sports affiliation to hunt for publicity and attention. Long ago in business he had learned that privacy was good for business and suited his shy personality. He could use words well and precisely but he was never graceful, never comfortable. Up until the last minute he had wanted to keep television reporters, cameras and still photographers out. Only his public relations people had convinced him to let them in, pointing out that it would not be a real press conference if they were barred.

Weinberg, it turned out, was very good at the press conference. He was formal and stiff and yet at the same time in a curious way skilled and deft. The skill and the deftness came in associating Ramsay's and Inman's names with all of the Blazer policies and decisions, ones they had agreed with and ones they had opposed. In the back of the room, watching the proceedings, Ramsay shifted uncomfortably from time to time and said nothing. Weinberg was not The Owner for nothing. The reporters never laid a glove on him.

The next day Weinberg was sitting in his office in Portland when Ron Culp called in to say that Kermit Washington had pulled a hamstring and might miss the forthcoming trip to New York. The possible loss of Washington on top of all the other injuries was too much. Suddenly Larry Weinberg started to cry. No one seated in the room with him knew whether he was crying for the injured Kermit Washington, or for himself.

Pat Washington was scared when she heard about the hamstring. She remembered all the pain and the anxiety the two of them had lived with when Kermit had been injured before. She was, she knew, different, less accommodating and accepting of injuries and pressures than other basketball wives. Now, with his hamstring pulled, she was nervous about his making the trip. He insisted on going, in order to be with the other players. The team, he said, was playing poorly and it was important for him to be there for reasons of morale. She reminded him of what had happened before when he was hurt, and how great a risk he had taken with his own body, but as she argued he simply withdrew inside himself. She had become in that instant an outsider. He promised that he would not play, then he had gone on the trip. Two nights later *The Wizard of Oz* was on television. She turned it on for the children and went into another room to listen to the game on the radio. "Calvin Natt's knees are bothering him and we're not sure how much he can play tonight," she heard Bill Schonely, the announcer, say as the teams came on the floor. One more injury, she thought, they really were in trouble. "But *Kermit Washington* has apparently recovered sufficiently from his hamstring and *will* be able to play tonight." Kermit, she thought, how could you, how could you do this to *us*. For the moment she hated basketball and basketball fans and everything about it.

Portland came back from its mini-road trip to play Philadelphia at home. The game marked Lionel Hollins's return as a Philadelphia 76er. The crowd, remembering the good days, gave him an enormous ovation before the game. The past was not forgotten. Hollins, who had missed thirty-six of his first fifty-six games with the Blazers, did not miss a single game after he was traded to Philly. That night in Portland, encouraged by the crowd, he played brilliantly, the Hollins of old, shooting 9 of 15 in 33 minutes, but more important handing out 6 assists and causing several turnovers; he was the crucial factor in a 2-point Philadelphia win. After the game reporters asked Ramsay what he thought of Hollins's game. "Lionel played very, very well," he said. "If he had played that well for us, he'd still be here."

It was Morris Buckwalter who first suggested that they sign Billy Ray Bates and bring him up for the remainder of the season. Stu Inman had already scouted Bates in the minor league and liked him, but it was Buckwalter who thought they might use a space on the roster for him now. This would give Bates a better shot at the team. Buckwalter was a ubiquitous figure in professional basketball. He had been everywhere and done everything, scouted, served as agent, coached in the colleges, coached in the pros; he seemed to have held every conceivable job in basketball, save that of commissioner. But if he had held virtually every kind of job, so too had he left virtually every kind of job, sometimes voluntarily, sometimes, given the nature of the profession, not so voluntarily. He had once coached a Brazilian all-star game in the Pan Am games where he had divided his time between coaching Brazilians, scouting Americans and trying to sign the great Russian player Aleksander Belov, a player much coveted by all American professional teams, to a representational contract. Belov presumably would sign with Buckwalter and Buckwalter would in turn deal him to the New York Knicks. Buckwalter had always been convinced that Belov was anxious to jump and that he had come quite close, with only the intervention of the KGB, which hustled Belov out of Brazil, depriving him of his great opportunity. Still the trip had not been entirely wasted. Buckwalter had noted great skills in an underclassman named Johnny Davis, from Dayton, and had convinced Stu Inman to draft him; it was an exceptional pick for Portland.

If there were journeymen players in the NBA, then Buckwalter was a journeyman coach, a man of surprisingly little personal ambition in a profession peopled, it often seemed, by single-minded workaholics. Buckwalter drifted in and out of jobs, he had a skilled eye for appraising raw talent, he was an exceptional scout, but he seemed to have one major flaw as a coach: victory did not really seem full of meaning for him, and even more important, defeat was clearly not shattering. In the previous season he had coached a team in the Continental league. When the job as assistant to Ramsay came open, Buckwalter was about to fly to West Germany to coach there.

("The Continental league," one of his friends said, "wasn't seedy enough for him.") Where Ramsay was in every sense driven, disciplined and organized, Buckwalter was relaxed, given to missing planes while on scouting missions, sometimes staying at the wrong motel. The difference seemed to show most dramatically in their bodies. Ramsay, Nautilus-honed, was lean and muscled; Buckwalter was by contrast constantly overweight, a source of irritation not to him, not to his wife, but of course to Ramsay. ("Buck's a good man . . . I like Buck . . . but he's thirty pounds overweight and he ought to lose it. . . . It's not really good for him to carry that extra weight. . . .") This season was not an easy one for him. He admired Ramsay greatly as a coach; he believed that when Ramsay had left the college ranks to begin coaching in the pros it had immediately helped legitimize the professional game. But in a losing season, with Ramsay becoming tighter and tighter with each defeat, Buckwalter often found himself walking in a kind of grim and silent DMZ lying between players and coach. Besides, Ramsay was so dominating a personality that he left little for his assistant to do. During the one minute allotted for a time-out, Ramsay would talk for fifty seconds, a complete and concise description of what the Blazers were doing wrong and how they should remedy it. Nothing would be left out. Then, with ten seconds left, Ramsay would turn to Buckwalter. "Anything you want to add, Buck?"

Buckwalter was then forty-five years old. He had been a college star back in the mid-fifties, playing for excellent University of Utah teams. Sometimes now he wished he had cared more about basketball as a boy and had concentrated more on it. But he had lived in another America, when sport was not yet commercialized, when games were still likely to be games, when the average American kid played baseball in the summer, football in the fall, basketball in the winter, and then on the first good day of spring, put away his basketball for a baseball. Now it was different. Talented kids chose one sport and played it year round, nine- and ten-year-olds paid to attend clinics and camps run by professionals. Buckwalter had been drafted in a middle round by the St. Louis Hawks in 1956, upon graduation from college, and offered $7,000 a year for his services. He never thought seriously about accepting it. He had an ROTC commitment to fulfill, and besides, the life of a professional athlete sounded alien. This was in the pretelevision days, and professional sports were generally devoid both of money and of glamour. By the time Buckwalter came to realize how much he loved basketball, he also realized that the game had gone beyond his more limited physical skills. The coming of the black athletes had changed the game and made players like himself obsolete. He was 6'4" but now, with the blacks coming in, he was a small 6'4". Like the old-fashioned players, he had been gifted with exceptional hand-to-eye coordination, but that was now meaningless. *Bodies* were what counted now.

By the early sixties, the game had, in his words, "gone in the air." He remembered when he had first realized it, watching a predominately black team from Cincinnati beaten by a team from Loyola of Chicago with an all-black starting lineup. Watching the game he had felt an immense excitement. This was a sport in which he had excelled—in fact in his time he had been one of the best, there had been All-American mentions—and now he was watching a generation of young black men so superior in their gifts that he could not even imagine playing against them. It was an epiphany. He knew that he was watching only the beginning, that this was not going to be some isolated phenomenon at a Cincinnati-Loyola game. Given the number of superb black athletes in the country, how much greater their educational opportunities were becoming, it was undoubtedly the first wave of something large. The sport, he sensed, was about to change color. Watching that game he realized that all the coaching rules of the past, so carefully drilled into players like him—where to set your body, where to position your feet—were meaningless. Those rules were for a slow game played on the floor by slow players and this was a new acrobatic game where players floated above the floor.

He decided that he wanted to be a link between the old world of basketball and the new world of basketball. The coming of the black athlete had always moved him. As a young Mormon boy in LaGrande, Oregon, he had played with a young black boy. Some of his friends, fellow Mormons, had been appalled—blacks by Mormon doctrine were unequals, and by Mormon practice something worse. Torn between friendship and his church he had simply moved away from his church. Later as a college coach he had worked hard to open up the colleges of the West, many of them Mormon, to black athletes. If these colleges accepted black athletes, he believed, painful though the process might often be for the young men involved, in the end they would gradually open up to all kinds of black students. Subsequently he met a black wheeler-dealer in Washington, D.C., who seemed to know every talented black playground star and for a time they set up an unofficial partnership. When his friend came up with a black player otherwise unable to go to college, Buckwalter made a connection to a series of junior colleges throughout the Far West and, eventually, to four-year colleges. It was a cause for him—perhaps, he thought later, considering the size of the civil rights revolution, a very small cause, and perhaps his participation in it was more selfish than he realized at the time. But it was something he felt he could do in a world he understood and cared about. In all those years he specialized in working the backcountry of the South, watching all-black colleges go at each other in high scoring games, often the only white in attendance.

In the spring of 1978 during one of his swings through the South he had stopped off at an all-star game in Portsmouth, Virginia. It was a game designed for the semicastoffs of the sport, black players not quite good enough for the big, postseason tournaments, like the Aloha Classic in Hawaii, which was a far fancier meat market. The Portsmouth game was funkier, it was blacker, it was held in a local high school gym, the crowd was black and it wanted above all flash and dunk. Looking around, Buckwalter recognized in the men watching the game the second tier of scouts and coaches, men still hoping for a better connection. It was a world not without its own hustle, its quick shilling and conning, its soured hopes and its failure. A lot of the men struck him as sad, shaky and unsure of themselves but their voices were quick and certain as they talked with kids who were even more shaky and unsure of *themselves*. Buckwalter looked at those men from time to time and saw just enough of Morris Buckwalter to make himself nervous. He liked to think he had beaten the system, that he had other options if he chose to get out, that he had been able to live within a moral code, but then he would wonder how different he really was. He had been in the business for twenty years and the morality of it still bothered him, the recruiting of kids, the buying and selling, really. He felt more relaxed about it now that he was in the pros, but he had always been uneasy in his college days. Even as he was selling some kid, he would hear a voice asking whether he was really doing the kid any good. Once when he was at Utah, he had tried to recruit a shy tall young man from Dalton, Georgia, named Artis Gilmore. "I need," Gilmore had written him, "a pair of 15½ shose." Buckwalter almost cried when he read the letter, and in the years since he had watched Gilmore's career with admiration, admiration for how so poor a young man had found the integrity and character to remain so pure and honorable despite the odds. Sometimes he wondered why he put so much time and energy into what was only a sport, boys jumping up and down. Wasn't there, he occasionally wondered, something more important he should be doing? Then he would pick up on a talented young kid and he would understand why he did what he did. It was because he loved it.

There was, on that day in Portsmouth, a young black kid from Kentucky State named Billy Ray Bates, and he had been dazzling, a player of awesome, almost completely undisciplined talent. The crowd had immediately adopted him as its favorite. He seemed to go up for dunks and hang in the air, and then hang some more, and then dunk over much taller players. He touched something deep in Buckwalter, who could look at him and instantly see all the natural ability and then, with his practiced eye, see all the things the young man had never been taught, all the things other kids with better luck would have learned by their second year at Indiana or UCLA or North Carolina. Bates was to Buckwalter terribly poignant, a stepchild on the court. He felt first a sadness that so much talent was being wasted, and then, secondly, a coach's fascination; for Billy Bates was everything a coach could want in a player, at once so terribly untutored and so talented. If I were a player today, that's who I would want to be, Buckwalter thought. The next year Buckwalter was coaching in the Continental league and he saw very soon that Billy Ray Bates was the best player in the league. When in January 1980 it became clear that Kevin Kunnert was out for the season Buckwalter had started pushing Inman and Ramsay to sign Bates, who was again starring in the Continental league. With Kunnert out, Buckwalter argued, there was a place on the roster. Bates, he said, was a great raw talent, well worth a try. If Portland signed him in the normal way and he came to a rookie camp, it was likely he would be shunted aside, quickly lose confidence and fail. But if he could sign on now, in a no-fail way, the pressure would be far less, he would have a chance to learn the plays more slowly, he could practice with the team every day, and he might be able to make it. If he made it, he might become a truly great basketball player. It was almost impossible, Buckwalter said, to exaggerate how much natural talent he had, and also impossible to exaggerate how little coaching he had been given. Inman was interested but somewhat dubious. He had seen Billy Bates, agreed that he had talent but was unsure that so undisciplined a player could fit into so disciplined a system as Jack Ramsay's. Like most basketball people he doubted that Bates's head was equal to his talent. Ramsay himself

seemed unconvinced. He had heard about Bates and he was not very enthusiastic about what he had heard.

Billy Ray Bates was a child of the feudal South, the son of sharecroppers,
an American whose roots ran a short way back into slavery itself. He had
chopped cotton, he always remembered what it did to his back and how
much he disliked doing it, and he had grown up in a sharecropper's shack
owned by a distant rich man of another color. Many of his teammates had
grown up hearing stories similar to his but at a generation or two removed.
It would be hard to imagine an American of Bates's own generation against
whom the odds were so hopelessly stacked. Most of the young men and
women of his time in Mississippi had little choice about life: they could remain in those small rural Mississippi towns until they died, subservient
and obedient, embittered but somehow willing to swallow their resentment, and get by, or they could pack their belongings into the inevitable
cardboard suitcases, take the bus to Memphis, and from there the next bus
to Detroit or Cleveland, in frail hope of finding some industrial job. But
even in the North, as agrarian uneducated black children in a highly indus-
trialized and technological new world, they were, more often than not,
doomed to end up lost on the cold winter streets. Billy Ray Bates was different. He had had a chance to get away because he was a surpassing athlete, so
talented that colleges in his native state, once all-white, competed for his
presence on their campuses. He was born in Goodman, Mississippi, a tiny
village near Kosciusko, the town which had produced James Meredith, the
young man who at great personal risk had integrated the University of Mississippi in the early sixties. Billy Bates did not know for whom Kosciusko
was named; since there were so many Choctaw Indians in the area, he had
always assumed that it was named for a Choctaw chief, not a Polish-
American patriot. The farm on which the Bates family toiled was huge, a
man could work all his life on that one piece of land and never see the end
of it, he thought. The owner was a man named Pat Smithson. He was okay,
Billy thought, in that unlike some of the other big white men he never did
anything cruel to black people. Five or six families lived on Smithson's
farm. Ellen Bates, Billy's mother, helped clean house for the Smithsons. His
mother, he was quite sure, was part Choctaw. There was something in her
face that told him. Also, she kept pet snakes, and told him that the snakes
were her friends. To black people in Mississippi talking about snakes like
that was a sure sign of Indian blood. There were four brothers and four

sisters, and everyone worked in some way or another. Billy Bates as a boy had many jobs: he picked cotton, sometimes he broke clods of fertilizer up as he followed behind a tractor, and sometimes he hooked logs for the lumbermen. The cotton money was the best; there had been times when he worked hard and had made as much as $50 a week picking cotton. But he was not a good picker. His heart was never in it. He tended to pick a little, and sleep a little, and pick a little, and sleep a little, just like the cartoon figure of the shiftless southern black. The white people who saw him thought him shiftless. His father was Frank Bates, known as Shack. Shack was not a good worker, nor finally, Billy came to realize, a very happy man. Billy's early memories were of him laughing and playing, but then when Billy was about five, he seemed to change. He was hot-tempered and began to work less and to get in fights more. Increasingly he would spend the day drinking, returning to his family late in the day when he was drunk. Soon Ellen Bates had to protect her children from their own father. Later Billy Bates came to understand why his father had come apart, and why he had begun to drink. For a black man in Mississippi life was nothing but farming and not even farming for yourself, but farming for the owner. Too much like slavery, he thought. His father died when he was seven. From then on everyone in the family had to contribute even more. When he was a sophomore in high school the family stopped sharecropping and started paying rent. The thing he remembered most clearly about that life was the poverty of it, the fact that they had no electricity, and no indoor plumbing, and very little food and not enough clothes. He decided when he was very young that when he grew up the first thing he would do was to buy a good house for his mother, not just so that she would have some electricity and indoor plumbing, but so that when it stormed the lightning and thunder would not seem to be right there inside the house. Of the nine children he was the next to the youngest. When he was about ten years old he told his mother what he intended. "We'll see, we'll see," she had said.

Sometime after he had reached Portland and become an instant success, reporters would wait in the locker room and ask him how it had all happened so quickly, the meteoric rise to the highest level of professional success from nowhere, and Billy Ray Bates would answer, not a bit surprised or perplexed by the question, no bravado in his voice, "I was born to play basketball." Perhaps he was. He had one of the most powerful bodies of any guard in the NBA, a huge barrel chest, immense hands, strong legs that sprang from thick thighs. He had done some hard physical work as a boy, but he believed the body had been given to him; almost everyone else in his family, uncles, aunts, cousins, had bodies something like his. The talent had always been there. No one had ever taught him to jump, he could simply do it from the first day he tried. He could dunk the ball from his sophomore year in high school and he lived for those moments, sailing above the rim, and then slamming the ball *down;* in that instant, back in Mississippi, he felt all-powerful; he was up and everyone else was down. Dunking was outlawed in Mississippi high school play, deemed illegal by white men writing white rules. But sometimes when his team was up by fifteen points he would risk a technical foul and he would take off and soar in the air, every split second to be remembered and savored.

Billy Ray Bates was in some ways much luckier than many black Mississippians of his generation. He was born in 1956, two years after the Supreme Court had ordered the nation to integrate its schools with all deliberate speed. Mississippi, the state with the highest percentage of blacks, resisted integration the most fiercely and its speed was more deliberate than anywhere else in the South. For years after the ruling, black children continued to attend the tattered rural schools which the state had deeded over to its less favored citizens. But by the time Billy Ray Bates had arrived at McAdams High School in 1970, the courts had finally pressured Mississippi into integration. He arrived at the once all-white school to find riots and signs that said NIGGERS GET OUT, NIGGERS GO HOME. Police were everywhere and no one knew which side the police were on, including themselves. Thus was he welcomed to the white world of Attala County. For a week the school shut down. When it reopened what had been a white high school had turned into a predominantly black school. Whites departed for their own new instant private schools. But they left behind for the young blacks of Mississippi something previously unattainable—first-rate facilities, gyms built by white school boards for white children, athletic budgets set by white boards for white players, and a tradition of white newspapers covering local high school sports events. That was important, it kept these same teams, now black, still a point of community focus. His coach, Wilson Jackson, then twenty-seven, was a black Mississippi native who had grown up with far less in the way of state-supplied facilities.

Even in the seventh and eighth grades he had always been hanging around the gym trying to get on the basketball team. No matter that he was smaller than the other kids and too young to be on the team. Finally, when he was a high school freshman, Jackson allowed him to join the team. "You that little boy I always used to chase out of here?" Jackson asked. Billy nodded his assent. His shooting eye was exceptional and his body was growing and filling out quickly. He loved shooting the ball and regrettably had a good deal less interest in playing defense. But whenever McAdams was behind, Jackson sent him in. Once in a game, Billy refused to look his coach in the eye in the event of a time-out—he was afraid Jackson might pull him. Jackson would see him out there, always scrupulously looking down, checking to see whether or not his sneakers were properly tied.

By the time he was a sophomore he was the strongest player on the team. He already had a powerful body and great jumping ability. Jackson sensed immediately that he was of college or pro caliber. The problem basic to the entire region was how to ward off the sense of hopelessness and defeat that destroyed so many young blacks early in their lives. Mississippi was Jackson's home and he had no great desire to go anywhere else, but he also knew what it did to young people. The signs of defeat, he knew, came early. The boys would start dropping out of class, and then slipping out of school. Then they would start drinking. The drinking was the big move. It was just a way of showing off at first, he thought, of being big men. But once a boy started, he rarely stopped. Jackson was sure Billy could play college ball. The problem was going to be getting him that far in school. The moment that basketball season was over, Billy simply disappeared. School was a gym, it had no other attraction. Billy Ray Bates, like countless other young black kids in America, was going to be a professional basketball player or he was going to be nothing. (Harry Edwards, the black sociologist who disliked the singular attraction of professional athletics for black youths, once estimated that there were some 3 million blacks between thirteen and twenty-two planning to be professional athletes; the odds, Edwards figured, were worse than 20,000 to 1 against their making it.) When Billy disappeared Wilson Jackson simply went to Billy's cousin's house, deep in the backcountry. There would be the two of them, Billy and his cousin, playing basketball. Coach and player resumed their ongoing argument.

"*Boy*, what are you going to do with yourself after school?"

"I'm going to play pro ball, Coach. I *know* I can make it."

"Boy, before you turn pro you got to turn college first, and before you go to college you got to finish this school right here."

Finally, in desperation, Jackson prevailed on the school authorities to add an extra period of gym to the school schedule, right at the end of the day. The pot sweetened, Billy stayed in school. But the pull of defeat was always there. He slept through classes, he missed others, and Jackson had to force him to study. Sometimes the hopelessness around them was so great that Jackson was afraid it was going to pull all of them down. Jackson would give the students his lectures on hard work, on staying in school, on what the future might be. But then when they were gone, he often at night had his own doubts. He knew their families, he knew how many fathers were gone, and how many fathers were not able to make a living. Above all, he knew the odds against them. Mostly he knew in his heart what they could *not* be. What could he tell them to be—doctors, lawyers, architects? Who would listen to him? Maybe if he found a few students a year with strength and character, they might be able to become teachers and nurses. In Billy's junior and senior years, Jackson, worried about the drinking, took his star home with him on the day of games so that he would not drink. Billy, Jackson believed, didn't drink all that much, it was just that he wanted people to *think* he had been drinking, and that he was a big man. In his senior year Billy stayed away from booze and averaged forty-five points and twenty-one rebounds. In the end, in his senior year, an astonishing number of once all-white colleges, including Ole Miss, applied for his services. Ole Miss would take him as a football player *or* a basketball player. Billy seemed to be gravitating towards Jackson State, which was a black sports power only sixty miles away. Wilson Jackson fought the decision. He knew what would happen if Billy went to Jackson State: it was too near McAdams and Billy would play basketball, drift back in the off-season to his old haunts, start drinking and hanging around. Wilson Jackson thought his best chance was if he got out of Mississippi and he pushed him towards Kentucky State, where he finally enrolled.

He played well at Kentucky State, a sure scorer, a powerful exciting presence on the court, but by the mid-seventies black schools like Kentucky State, once a prime producer of talent for the NBA, were no longer considered a very good source of athletic talent. The revolution had come so quickly in black athletics, so many once all-white schools had opened up to blacks, the scouts had become so much better at foraging through the high school circuit, that by the early seventies the finest black southern talent was already being spotted in high school, and the better players were now going to the best state schools in the Midwest and the South. States like Alabama and Tennessee and Kentucky, which had once allowed their indigenous blacks to play in the Big Ten, now fought to keep them in state, not at some small black school but at the main university. White fans now cheered for blacks, players they had once tried to bar from their colleges, finding in them lesser racial qualities only when they lost. The world of black colleges was now worked by the second and third tier of scouts looking for fourth-, fifth- and sixth-round draft choices. Indeed if a player was with an all-black college, there was already an unstated judgment against him: the presumption was that he would have been picked up at the high school level if he were really any good. That presumption worked against Billy Ray Bates at Kentucky State. Scouts watching him saw the powerful body and the natural instinct for the game. But they looked at his annual statistics and then they asked themselves: Why hadn't he been picked by a better college? Was he a bad kid? Was he a head problem? As for the points, who did he get them against? Above all, was he smart enough to learn plays and be part of a disciplined system? By going to a black college he had at the age of seventeen already damaged his reputation in the professional basketball world. But then he had looked good in the Portsmouth All-Star game, and he was drafted for the NBA in the fourth round by an interested but wary Houston. Given the growing odds against him, it wasn't bad. Yet since in America it is largely true that the rich get richer, the converse is surely true, that the poor get poorer, and at this juncture Billy Ray Bates, who desperately needed good advice, signed with an agent who gave him what Bates later concluded had been the worst kind of advice imaginable.

The agent, who had been brought to Billy by his college coach, told him to hold out for guaranteed money from Houston, and not to report without it. This made little sense. In the first place, fourth-round draft choices did not get guaranteed money, and even more important, Billy Ray Bates's best chance was simply to go to the camp and *play*, letting his game be his best advertisement. The last thing wanted by any team already ensnarled in tedious negotiations with its first- and second-round draft choices, as Houston was, was problems with its fourth-round picks. So he arrived late to the camp, a camp he could have dominated, and found the place filled with guards holding no-cut contracts. He immediately showed raw skill but had trouble with the plays. Tom Nissalke, the coach, was already furious with Billy's agent, and the anger reached over to Billy. Soon he was cut. He was hurt but not yet bitter. He was sure he was better than some of the players they kept. Deciding that somehow he would be back, he went to Bangor, Maine, to play for the Maine Lumberjacks of the Continental Basketball Association.

Within limits Billy Ray Bates enjoyed playing in the Continental league. The Maine Lumberjacks were not the Boston Celtics but it *was* professional basketball, and the dream was still on, just one step away. Sometimes in those games he would go against a player who had once played in the NBA and then he turned it on; inevitably he was the stronger player, and the experience encouraged him to believe that he still had a chance. There were, of course, almost always rumors of scouts in the crowd, and when the rumors circulated, the Continental game, not very much given to structure anyway, completely degenerated. *No one* passed the ball. It wasn't just Billy Ray Bates who was desperate to get to the top, it was everyone in that league. He was Rookie of the Year in the Continental, and won a slam-dunk contest in the All-Star game. In the summer he returned to Mississippi, played some ball, worked some construction. He had a car and he often drove his mother around town. Every day he would pick her up and they would go to a cousin's house, or to a store. She bought less and less at the stores so that she would have more reason to drive back the next day, he noticed. She loved the power and the freedom that the car gave her.

While he was doing this, a young man named Don Leventhal, a Philadelphia basketball junkie who had worked as a publicity man for the Continental Association, was in his spare time trying to put together a team for Philly's summer circuit, the Baker League. Leventhal in his own way was as anxious to get into the NBA as any Continental player. He wanted to get into player personnel, and become, he hoped, the next Stu Inman. The Baker was comparable to the other outdoor summer leagues, an almost perfect showplace of black playground play. Pros, college stars, high school stars and of course playground wizards were all blended together. No one really knew on a given night which famous player might show up. It was the kind of wild, exciting game which made a purist like Jack Ramsay nervous. Individual artistry triumphed over teamwork. Nor was there a lot of defense. Almost all of the players were from the Philadelphia area. Leventhal, putting together his team, sent out letters to a number of players he knew. Then, almost as a joke, because he had handled Billy Bates's statistics so often in his Continental league job, though of course he had never seen him play, Leventhal sent a letter to Billy Ray Bates in Goodman, Mississippi, asking if he would like to play in the Baker League. The letter included a form which asked a prospective player to check off which month he preferred to play—June, July or August. In a week Billy Bates returned the form, checking off all three months. Soon they were talking on the phone. Billy said he needed money for the bus ride to get up there, and Leventhal somewhat nervously lent him $85 for a ticket. At the same time Billy went to Wilson Jackson and borrowed bus money from him as well. Thus well-armed he set off for Philly. The Philadelphia bus station at 3 a.m. is not the most hospitable place in the world, but Leventhal was there to meet him. Out came the bus riders of America, a few elderly people, a few young people, a few servicemen and then a tall powerfully built young black man. His cream-colored pants were adorned with his own handwritten graffiti. BILLY RAY "DUNK" BATES they read. Oh my god, thought Leventhal, what kind of a cowboy have I got? Leventhal and a young lawyer named Steve Kauffman took him in, and tried to explain the complexities of a city to him, how to use a bank, how to lease an apartment. The thing that staggered Billy, Leventhal thought, was how many young women Philadelphia had. "You know," he kept saying, "Kosciusko is a *small* town, and it's only got one or two girls, but *this* town, there's *thousands,* man, *thousands.*"

The night after he arrived, Billy Bates scored twenty-nine points in a game. Some of his opponents were professional players. Leventhal and Kauffman worked to get him a professional tryout. Soon Jack McMahon, a veteran white basketball man and former player-coach, now a Philly scout, showed up. "Billy, this is Mister Jack McMahon of the Sixers," Leventhal had said. "Mister McMahon, it's very nice to meet you and I'll try not to disappoint you, sir," Billy had answered. Then he had hit his first nine shots and scored thirty-eight points. McMahon, who had signed Darryl Dawkins out of high school, loved him. "I've scouted all year and that's the best game by a guard I've seen yet," he told Leventhal. Philly held a secret predraft camp where they let some of the players they were thinking of drafting work out. Billy Bates went, was the best player there and, without drafting him, Philly gave him a $10,000 bonus and a $60,000 guaranteed contract for one year. Billy Bates was sure he made it. So was Leventhal. A week later the draft was held and in the first round Philadelphia drafted Jim Spanarkel, a tall white guard from Duke. Leventhal became immediately suspicious. Billy Bates did well in the early drills and there were favorable articles about him in the Philly papers. He wrote back to Mississippi to tell Coach Jackson that he was going to make it. Could they now retire his jersey? he asked. Then he began to struggle. No one doubted his talent. Jack McMahon was for him but Chuck Daly, an assistant who had coached at Penn, was dubious. Philadelphia, an assemblage of great raw talent, was still smarting from the defeat by Portland two years earlier, and trying to change the freewheeling nature of its team. The last thing it needed was another one-on-one superstar; it had, after all, just gotten rid of Lloyd Free and no one in the league had been particularly anxious to pick Free up. In the camp Billy Bates looked at Jim Spanarkel, who was white and slow, and he thought that there was never a day that the sun had come out that he could not take Spanarkel anywhere he wanted on the court and do with him what he wanted. But Spanarkel was a first-round draft choice, he knew, and professional teams were reluctant to admit that they had made mistakes with their firsts. In the end Billy was cut. The last day he had looked long and carefully at Spanarkel, a quiet reserved young man, and he had thought, *I know I'm better than you. I know there are lots of things that you can do better than me, all kinds of things. But this is one thing I know I can do better than you.*

Cut, but still signed to a Philly contract, he went back to Bangor. He was very bitter now, he had failed twice. He had been given a chance without being given a chance. He was also shrewd enough to know that in the NBA being cut a second time was more serious, that by then it became part of your reputation, there was always a *they* in life and the *they* in professional basketball would believe now that he had had his chance. He felt terribly cheated; he knew it was not because he lacked talent. It was, he believed, because he was a poor black from Mississippi. It was as if people were telling him he was a nigger without actually using the word. The others, the ones who made it, were *blacks*, but he was still somehow because of Mississippi a *nigger*. When he had been a boy he had always thought that sports was his way out, and now he felt beaten because sports seemed to be just another dead end like everything else. His coach in Bangor was Mike Uporsky, who had spent the previous season scouting for Seattle, had tried to sell the Sonics on Calvin Natt and had been let loose by the Sonics. He was himself unhappy about being back in the minor leagues.

"Billy, can you play here?" Uporsky asked him.

"I don't know yet," Bates had answered, "my head's so far down it hasn't caught up with my body yet. I don't know if I can spend the rest of my life in the Continental league."

Uporsky had expected Billy Bates to be a smart-ass, a difficult kid who thought he knew more than the coach, an attitude which frequently accompanied such raw skills, but the reverse turned out to be true. He was a child of Mississippi poverty, untouched and uncorrupted still, a great favorite in Bangor where he spent the entire winter wrapped in a huge sheepskin coat out of which only his eyes seemed to appear. He could, Uporsky thought, have run for mayor of Bangor, he was so good and kind with people, so much loved. At one point, wary of tampering with this natural force, Uporsky asked Billy to shoot less and go for six assists a game. "When you're on the court I want you to think only of sacrificing. We know you can score. Can you do it?" "I don't know if I can handle it," he had answered. "There's something in me that's just got to go. I don't know if I can control it." But he tried, and became a good passer.

The Continental league, Uporsky thought, with its dinky gyms and tiny $12-a-night motels and cold franchise-food hamburgers was like prison for Billy. The team traveled back and forth to games in a huge Winnebago motor home. Midway during the year there was a call from Gene Shue at San Diego. The Clippers were looking for a small forward. Billy Ray Bates went down to Philadelphia for a tryout with them. Uporsky warned him not to get his hopes up. He did not even play in a full scrimmage, just three-on-three. He never heard from the Clippers again, something which was to haunt Shue later in that same season.

By mid-February the Portland guard situation was desperate. Lionel Hollins was gone, Dave Twardzik, the other lead guard, was playing with a body exhausted by injuries. His legs, Ron Culp told Ramsay, were dead. Anytime Twardzik played more than twenty minutes in a game, he paid for it the next two or three days. Ramsay seemed to be losing confidence in T. R. Dunn. Ron Brewer, who had started the season so strongly, was apparently losing confidence in himself. Jim Paxson, the first-round draft choice from Dayton whom Inman had been so high on, was playing erratically, a disappointment to himself and to Ramsay. His court vision and intelligence were excellent, but he had been drafted as a shooter and the team needed points and he was shooting poorly. He was playing tight. Because of all the other injuries he was getting an exceptional chance to play and he was doing very little with it. Midway through the season, Ramsay had begun to wonder if Paxson, product of a secure middle-class home, son of a former professional player who had given up the sport to take over a successful life insurance business, was tough enough to play in the NBA. He never contested referees' calls on the floor, never seemed to fight back. Rather he accepted things. Ramsay was convinced that one thing common to all superior professional athletes was a certain meanness or toughness, whichever you wanted to call it, a desire to leave their mark on opponents. Possibly Paxson, so fine and intelligent and secure a young man, lacked that. He might, Culp thought, be too stable for the league. In early February, before Buckwalter began to push for Bates, Inman was scouting the Continental league looking for a big man. But he was also looking at guards. Inman, onetime star of the San Jose Spartans and a connoisseur of offbeat team nicknames, loved the idea of the Maine *Lumberjacks*. He went to Hawaii to watch the Hawaiian *Volcanoes* against the *Lumberjacks*. That way he could see Stan Eckwood, whom he had liked from the previous draft, and Billy Bates, whom Buckwalter and others had talked of. By the time Inman caught up with the Lumberjacks in Hawaii, Uporsky had been fired, replaced by the owner's son, who coached only home games. That fact, the flakiness of it, excited Inman even more. "What kind of plays do you run?" Inman had asked Bates and Eckwood before the game. "Oh, we don't run plays," Bates had answered, "we just take the ball down and shake and bake a little." "Well," said Inman, "what do you talk about before a game?" "Where we're going to go after the game," said Eckwood. Inman watched Bates and liked him, the power in the body was self-evident, the hands were huge, and Bates could, in Inman's coach-talk, "pass for profit in heavy traffic. A big plus." But there was something extra Billy Bates had, something that could neither be studied, nor taught, and that was an essential instinct for the game. It was something you were born with, and Billy Ray Bates had it. Intrigued, Inman located Uporsky in Arizona. They had similar tastes. As scouts both had wanted Calvin Natt. Uporsky had even coveted Seattle's other first-round draft pick that year, Jimmy Paxson. "Mike, is he the best in your league?" Inman asked.

"Stu, he may be the best in *your* league. Only Westphal has more natural ability. I'd get him on a plane before anyone else finds out," Uporsky said.

Inman watched two games in Honolulu and then followed the Lumberjacks to Alaska to watch them against the Anchorage Northern Knights, another perfectly delightful name. He had taken Bates to lunch. When he had arrived Bates was surrounded by kids, signing autographs, asking each of them if he was or she was going to the game that night. Inman liked that—score more points for Billy Bates. "If I were your best friend," Inman told Bates at lunch, "I would tell you that what you're in now is the worst environment I can imagine for you. No coaching, no plays, no discipline. You're blessed with great skills, Billy, and you've got a great body. No one can teach you to shoot like that or jump like that. But there's a thousand players like you all over the country in the Rucker and the Baker and a hundred other leagues. Every city has them and they're talented and they watch some pro game and they think, 'Hey, I'm better than the pros.' Maybe they can do one little thing better, go to the hoop, dunk. But that's not basketball. Can they play in a team? Can they play in harmony with four other players? I think you can but you've got to be able to want to do it. We want to sign you, Billy. Do you know who Coach Ramsay is?"

"I've seen him. Gets angry at referees a lot."

"He can teach you how to see your teammates, he can help you. Do you want to try it?"

"Yes, sir," said Billy Ray Bates. "I want to play in the NBA more than anything else in the world."

So it was that Billy Ray Bates, in February 1980, the season three-quarters gone, joined the Portland Trail Blazers. The signing was not without its acrimony. Bates was represented by Steve Kauffman, the young Philadelphia lawyer who had befriended him and was still trying to get him loose from his unfortunate first contract. Portland wanted a five-year contract, with only the first full season guaranteed. The money, if it ever came through, was acceptable but not particularly good by NBA standards. Kauffman was dubious; it put all the burden on Billy and implied little responsibility on the part of the Portland franchise. If Billy was convenient to them then they had him for a very long time. If he failed then they were out free. Kauffman believed that it was an unfortunate pattern, that they used their maximum leverage at a player's greatest moment of vulnerability, and that there was a dangerous payback. He wanted a two-year contract if possible and a three-year one at most. "You're squeezing my kid and it's wrong," he said. Portland finally came down to four years. Kauffman advised Billy Bates not to sign it. "We've got to sign it," Billy Bates said. "I've got to get my chance to play. I can't fail again." "Go ahead then," Kauffman said, but he did not like the contract; he wished there were more generosity of spirit shown in it.

Among those in Portland who did not seem especially elated by the arrival of Billy Ray Bates was Jack Ramsay. He had not been impressed by Buckwalter's original recommendation and he had no great yearning for a player whose skills were apparently so different from those he sought. The last thing he wanted this late in the season was a raw, untutored kid who had never played in a system. When he talked of Billy Ray Bates it was as if he were talking of an outsider, someone who was not really on the team. Among other NBA coaches and general managers, most of whom knew a good deal about Billy Bates's reputation and even more about Jack Ramsay's system, there was a good deal of amusement at the idea of Dr. Jack Ramsay trying to coach Billy Ray Bates.

But the Blazers had already changed. The treasured Calvin Natt had come at a high price and one day he might be an exceptional player for Ramsay's system, but he was not ready yet. It was clear that Natt was in his own way a project. He was a rookie and more, a rookie with his second team in one year. He did not know the plays. There was even a question of whether he was the right man for the position. He was an immensely powerful young man, perhaps the strongest player at small forward in the league, but was he a small forward—quick, deft, good passer—for the Ramsay system? Or was he a slightly shorter power forward, a hardworking player, but not supple enough for the position? He was not as good a passer as Bobby Gross, and his game was one of power, and one-on-one moves. When the ball came to him it rarely went to anyone else; his presence altered the ball flow, sometimes stopped it. Calvin Natt, it soon became clear, was not exactly the player they had needed. If he was to be effective it would be on a very different team.

When Billy Ray Bates arrived in Portland there was something touchingly innocent about him, uncorrupted. But no one knew what was just beneath the surface, and that was troubling; if he became successful, would he change? Would he start arguing with Ramsay for more minutes, talking about being traded? Would he swagger? Would he demand to renegotiate his contract? For the moment he was completely unspoiled and grateful to be there. "He still calls everyone 'sir,'" said an amused Herm Gilliam. "Young and innocent, isn't he?" In his first road game he dressed for the game Lumberjack style, that is, changing at the hotel. He arrived for the bus in his warmup clothes, while the others were still in their civilian finery. That amused them. Back in Portland he drove to practice on the first day with Ron Culp. In the background, as they drove, stood the majestic Mount Hood. "There's no snow here, right?" he said to Culp, pointing to the Portland streets they were driving through. "That's right, Billy," said Culp. Billy pointed to Mount Hood. "How come there's snow up there?" Culp began a long explanation of elevation, temperature and snow. It was not, he realized, very successful. In the end he had not just confused Billy, he had confused himself. The next day they drove by the Willamette River. "There any fish in there?" Billy asked. "Yes," said Culp. "You ever caught any?" Billy asked. "No," said Culp. "Why not?" asked Billy, absolutely perplexed, such a grand opportunity passed by. I don't know, Billy, thought Culp, I just don't know.

At first Ramsay did not use him very much. Perhaps for a few minutes late in games already gone. But word about him spread throughout the league and crowds began to gather around the baseline when the Blazers came to watch his dunks. Finally Ramsay used him because he had no one else and because his team was playing so poorly. They were struggling for the last spot in the Western conference playoffs, slightly behind San Diego, and they were playing listlessly. They went to Milwaukee with only nine games left in the season, with the competition for the last playoff spot more and more heated.

On the morning of the Milwaukee game, Jack Ramsay, physical fitness freak, devoted exerciser of the Ramsay body, went swimming in the pool of the Pfister Hotel. He tried to swim every day, some twenty laps if possible on good days, many more on bad ones, swimming on the good days to keep in shape, swimming farther on bad ones to exorcise demons and burn off the anger and frustration. On this morning Ramsay was preoccupied with the faltering nature of his own team, and with a new burden, the news that the great center Bob Lanier had managed to trade himself from Detroit, where his presence meant little because the team was so bad, to the Milwaukee Bucks, a rising and aggressively talented team, where he might help create a championship. Ramsay was dissatisfied with his own center lately; Tom Owens was, in the phrase Ramsay used to friends, playing soft. Angry about games past, worried about games to come, especially today's, he dove in and swam as hard as he could, forgetting that the Pfister did not offer an Olympic-size pool, and soon smashed his head against the far end, splitting his scalp badly. Blood began to pour out.

He called Ron Culp in his room. "Do you have something to close up a wound?" he asked.

An odd request, Culp thought, something to close up a wound. "Jack, what kind of wound?" Culp asked, slightly puzzled.

"Well, I've hurt myself, I've got a wound," Ramsay answered.

That's odd, Culp thought. Ramsay, usually so candid, was being unusually evasive. "What kind of injury, Jack?" he asked, intrigued now.

"Well, it's an injury to my head," he said. "An unusual one. You better come up here." So Culp with his kit went up to Ramsay's room where he found the coach with a bloodsoaked cloth around his head. At first Culp was alarmed: was this the denouement of all those Ramsay late-night walks? "Jack, for god's sake, what happened?" the trainer asked.

"You know," said Ramsay, "it's an old hotel and they have a very small pool here." He sounded, Culp thought, very sheepish.

Lanier's play was strong; midway into the third quarter the Bucks were up 85–59. At that point Ramsay went to Bates and Jeelani, the one a very recent veteran of the Continental league, the other of the Italian league. Both of them were, at their best, freelancers, clumsy in a system, strong in games where nothing else worked. They quickly brought Portland back. Bates had 14 points in 15 minutes, Jeelani 16 points in 15 minutes. They closed the score to 98–93 with 7:49 left. Ramsay sent in his regular lineup. The Blazers collapsed.

The next night in Chicago it was even more dramatic. It was a slow, heavy game—everyone, it seemed, worn out by the long season. Bodies moved slowly. Watching his team play against Artis Gilmore, knowing exactly what it should be doing, Ramsay was enraged to see the Blazers walking through their assignments, giving Gilmore position close to the basket again and again. His players looked like sleepwalkers. With four and a half minutes left in the third quarter, Chicago was ahead by 17 points. In came Bates and Jeelani. In the final 17 minutes, the two of them, freelancing and gunning, playing with enthusiasm and excitement, combined for 43 points. Billy more than anyone else simply took over the game. When he had the ball it was as if everyone on the court stopped to watch him. He drove to the basket and scored, then did it again. Chicago changed defensive guards and still he did it. Then they began to drop off him, conceding the jump shot to stop the drive. Immediately he started hitting jump shots. With Portland behind by two points everyone cleared out so he could drive on the immense Artis Gilmore. He took off, drove, jumped, faked, brought Gilmore up with him, pumped again, still held the ball and then, at the last second, dunked. The Chicago arena broke into spontaneous applause. In the end Portland, playing sloppy defense, let Gilmore hit two easy shots from the inside and Chicago won. As Bates walked off the court, the Chicago announcer said: "Billy Ray Bates scored points." He paused. The Chicago crowd began to roar. "Sixteen of them in the last quarter." The noise was deafening.

The locker room, except for a crowd of reporters around Billy, was grim. They had done a terrible job on Gilmore. "You don't stop Artis once he has the ball," Buckwalter was saying, "you prevent him from getting it where he wants. Otherwise he'll score all night. He's too damn strong." Gilmore had eleven of fourteen, all short, easy shots. The coaches had diagrammed exactly what they had wanted done, and nothing had happened. Ramsay was trying to deal with the Chicago reporters. He hated losing so close a game after so exceptional a comeback. Right now it didn't matter that it was an un-Ramsay-like manner of play that had brought them back.

IN A CORNER a Chicago reporter was interviewing Billy Ray. "Billy, how would *you* play defense against *Billy Ray Bates?*" "Well, you know," said Billy, "I can go to the hoop and I can shoot outside. 'How do you play defense against me?' Hard to say, hard to say."

Bobby Gross, the last survivor of the classic team—Twardzik had flown home earlier with a sore neck—was talking about how good a passer Bates was, how he could with those huge hands and his great strength hold on to the ball until the very last split second and then still pass. "I don't know if he can play in a pattern," Gross was saying, "but he's good, isn't he? Something special." Gross felt disconnected from the new team. He was a part, he said, that no longer fit. There was no resonance, no rhythm to this team. He was sure he was going to be traded. He had become a $300,000 a year benchwarmer. Weinberg, he said, would not like that. The trade of Lionel had been the final straw. He had badly needed Lionel for his game; they had always understood each other, and knew what they were going to do as if they had their own secret radar. With Lionel on the court, said Gross, if you gave up the ball, you always knew you might get it back. On this team he tried to pass and because the others were not good passers themselves they were rarely ready to take it. The key to passing was anticipation, two men sensing that the same thing *would* happen, not that it *had* happened. Anything in the past tense, indeed the *present* tense, in this game was already too late. Ramsay was pushing Gross to take his shot. But that was alien to him, his instinct was always to look for the pass first. The night before, in Milwaukee, the Bucks had doubled a Blazer guard and the ball had come to Gross, who was wide open for a shot. He had looked at the basket, looked for a pass, hesitated that fraction of a second and by the time he was ready to shoot the defender was back. Two days later, Ramsay was still angry. *"Can you imagine that!"* he said. *"Can you imagine that! They double us, we beat the double and he waits until his man returns!"* In the Chicago game his line was dispiriting. He played eighteen minutes, shot zero for six, shot no fouls and had one assist. It was a line for a player on his way out of the league.

Several days later Ramsay was still annoyed at Gross. Gross was talking openly with other players of his discontent and the fact that he would probably be with another team the next year. He had been quoted in the *Oregonian* recently saying that basketball was not the only thing in his life, that he had a new baby daughter and that his family was also important. Ramsay, reading the story, had not liked it. That was one of the things wrong with this team. Too many interests outside of basketball. No one was single-minded enough. To Ramsay an athlete was someone consumed by his sport, who in-season during his brief career thought of virtually nothing else. The game was first. Only later, if there was time left over, should there be anything else. Ramsay's own life was organized perilously close to that idea.

He took Gross aside and told him there would be a new team the next year. It would resemble the team of the past and would need Gross's skills. But he also said that Gross must stop living in the past. The championship season was over. There were new strong teams in the league and the accomplishments of the past quickly became meaningless. Gross, listening to Ramsay, was not so sure that he would be back, nor that he wanted to be.

Two nights later they went to Oakland for an important game with Golden State. There were only six games left in the season after this. San Diego was faltering now too. The Portland bus reached the Oakland Coliseum around 5 p.m. While the other players waited in the locker room taking their time getting dressed—there was after all always too much time before a game—Billy dressed and walked out into the empty arena and began shooting baskets. Bucky Buckwalter, walking through the arena, saw him there, a distant lonely figure practicing in a huge darkened room before empty seats. He stopped and watched Billy for a few minutes, suddenly realizing that this moment was devoted not so much to improving Billy

Bates's touch but rather to reconnecting him to reality, to prove to himself that it really was all true, that he was finally playing in the NBA. That night Ramsay went to Billy much earlier than usual. He scored twenty-two points and helped send the game into overtime, which Portland won. Afterwards reporters were asking him about a key play in which he had driven to the basket and scored.

"Well, I knew I could beat the old guy," he said.

"What old guy?" a reporter asked.

"You know, the old guy who used to play for Boston," he said. Thus did Billy Ray Bates describe Jo Jo White, one of basketball's great stars, then all of thirty-three years old.

He was a star now. The NBA made him its Player of the Week. People wanted him to endorse their sneakers. Writers continued to seek him out. On the flight home from Golden State he took aside a writer who had interviewed him two weeks earlier when he had first arrived in the league. "You going to write all of that, aren't you?" he said. "Write all of what?" the reporter asked. "All of what I told you about growing up, about how we had no electricity and no indoor plumbing." The writer said yes, he was going to write it. "That means everywhere I go in the NBA and every time I'm on television, people going to look at me and think of me going to the bathroom outdoors and growing up without electricity. They're going to think about it." He thought for a moment. "They're going to think about Billy Bates out there in that old shack."

Stu Inman invited both Calvin Natt and Billy Bates to dinner at his home. Billy, having been named NBA Player of the Week, was swaggering a little. "I guess you grew up like me, Calvin," Billy said. "You had plenty of meat at home." Calvin, also a southern black of reasonably impoverished origins, looked at Billy quizzically. "We always had two kinds of meat at our house," Billy continued. *Two kinds of meat,* Inman thought, in a sharecropper's house? It just didn't sound right. "What kind of meat, Billy?" Inman asked. "Oh," he said, "you know, coon, possum, rabbit, squirrel. But always two kinds." Calvin Natt started to break into laughter. Billy Ray Bates looked at him, wondering what was funny.

On the seventy-eighth game of the season the San Diego Clippers came to Portland for the first of two games that would decide which of the two struggling teams would make the bottom rung of the playoff ladder. Both were exhausted. San Diego, which had been playing well in midseason, had tailed off badly in the final third. Earlier in the season Nater had been the only Clipper center and he had played with strength and confidence. Then Walton had readied himself to play, and even before he actually returned, Nater's confidence seemed to waver, and his game slipped. When Walton finally reappeared the team became erratic, some good games, some bad ones; it had become a schizophrenic team, unsure whether it was to build its game around the lumbering Nater—which meant that the guards could shoot away—or around the deft Walton, which meant that the ball was to be passed. At one point San Diego had been 27–23; then it had lost 20 of its last 28 games. Now Walton was hurt again. Players were bickering again. "Everyone on this team has a fucking ego problem," Lloyd Free, one of the game's great egos, told reporters. "Everyone wants to shoot. No one wants to pass." By the time San Diego arrived in Portland the players were openly bickering on the court, and Free had apparently removed himself for the rest of the season because of a lingering contract dispute with Irv Levin.

Nater continued to play long minutes. He played like a plowhorse, physical, relentless. The more minutes he got now, the more he liked it, because it helped his statistics. He was in a race with Moses Malone for the NBA rebounding title. As the teams went on the court, Nater turned to his close friend Kermit Washington, Portland's best rebounder. "Hey, Kermit, go easy tonight on the boards. I need a bunch of rebounds to get ahead of Moses. He's right up there with me, you know." Kermit nodded his head. Whatever you say, Swen, he thought. That night Portland simply wore San Diego out. In the third quarter the Blazers were up by twenty points. Ramsay clearly was still not sure about Billy Bates and how to integrate him into the team. As long as Portland was ahead, Billy did not play. In the fourth quarter San Diego made a run, closed to two points. So with five minutes left, Ramsay sent Billy in the game. He hit jumpers, dunked and soon had Portland up by five points. In the last minute, with Portland ahead, and holding the ball, San Diego coach Gene Shue was yelling instructions to Nater: "Swen, Swen, play up on Owens. . . ." Nater seemed not to hear him. Shue turned to the bench and kicked the floor in disgust. "What the hell," he said. "He doesn't know what's going on anyway."

After the game Steve Kelley went in to interview Billy Bates. He had scored eleven points in nine minutes. "What were you thinking when Ramsay put you in?" Kelley asked.

"I was thinking it was the fourth quarter and I wasn't playing," he said.

"How did you decide that you should go to the basket?"

"Well, their guards weren't hulking up on defense . . ." Billy began.

"Weren't doing *what* on defense?" Kelley asked.

"You know, *hulking* up," Billy explained. "Me and Tee [T. R. Dunn], we were hulking them when we were on defense. If they had turned around they would have kissed one of us. Hulking up." *Hulking up,* Kelley thought and wrote it down in his notebook. Hulking up, new in the lexicon of basketball. To hulk. That meant to have a strong body and use it tightly in defense. Not bad. The players, after all, called T. R. Dunn, with his powerful body, The Incredible Hulk.

KERMIT WASHINGTON STAYED in his own home when the team arrived in San Diego. This was his real home. Still, because he was so popular, it was not easy to get very much rest. The neighborhood kids knew he was back and wanted to play pickup games with him at his basket. The kids were thirteen and fourteen years old and they played games of thirty points. When they had first started playing, Kermit, good citizen, had spotted them twenty-eight points, and all too often they would make a lucky shot and beat him. He was losing far too often that way, so he adjusted the rules. Now he spotted them twenty points. This day he had to tell them that no, he couldn't play a pickup game. He was just too tired. His body was absolutely exhausted. Every day he could rest was like a vacation. A few minutes later Swen Nater came by with his basketball and wanted to play a game of twenty-one. Kermit could not believe it. One of the most important games of the year that night, the season already too long, and Swen wanted a pickup game. "No, Swen," he said, "not today. I'm just not up to it." Swen seemed surprised. "You sure, Kerm?" he said. "Just a light game?"

Steve Jones had decided that, the season being almost over, the game being important, it was time to bust Ramsay. A soft bust, of course. "I've held off on that big guy too long," he said. "His time has come." He had announced this to several people before the team boarded its bus. A few minutes later Ramsay joined the players. Jones eyed him carefully and began to smile. He could hardly believe his good luck. Ramsay, the meticulous man who did everything properly, who organized every minute of practice and games, who before important playoff games when he had strong rebounders even made sure to remind the refs to inflate the ball fully, which helped his team, had shown up for practice wearing sneakers which did not match. One was an Adidas, one was a Nike. "I'm going to bust him on those sneakers. Oh, how sweet," Jones said. "Now watch—timing is important." Jones let Ramsay walk on the court with the players, group them in a circle, and then he moved. "What kind of attention to detail do we have on this team? How can we get our act together when the coach cannot even get his sneakers right?" Jones asked. The players began to laugh. Ramsay seemed delighted. Later, the practice over, the players began free throws, and Ramsay joined them, practicing himself. Twardzik immediately got on him. Twardzik began mimicking Ramsay at a free-throw regimen: "Now see the ball through the hoop before you shoot it. If you see it through, you're going to make it. See what you want, see the ball going through. There, that's better."

Larry Steele, his knee still sore, his walk almost a limp, made the last trip. He had been out for several months and during this time had not traveled with the team. Now, he said, he wanted to get out of Portland because the winter rain was so depressing. He had begun to think he was going crazy. "All those years my wife kept telling me how bad it was," he said, "and I never believed her. Now I believe her." Steele wanted to play for one more season, but that was doubtful now, given the history of his knees. He would miss the friendship, and the camaraderie. While it was there, he said, you took it for granted. Only when it was gone and you were almost gone did you miss it. The early years at Portland he thought had been the most fun, the adversity of those losing seasons had bound them together. He remembered how Walton used to ride a teammate named Barry Clemens. One time when they were in a game with Cleveland Walton had turned to Clemens and said, "Just what is it you do here anyway, B.C.?" At that moment Clemens had been sent into the game and he hit his first nine shots. A few minutes later he was pulled out again. As he passed the bench Clemens, who had a bad stutter, turned to Walton and said, "Th-th-that's wh-wh-what I d-d-do, Big Fella." They were all younger then, Steele thought, and basketball was more central to their lives. Soon they became older, tired of all the traveling, and there were children and family pulls. He would miss it all, more perhaps the bad days than the good ones. As he talked, Sidney Wicks was shooting baskets as part of the San Diego practice. I'll even miss Sidney, he said. Wicks had been at the center of the storm of those years, a player who had never really lived up to his potential and who had been seen by Portland coaches and finally management as a divisive force. Sidney, Steele mused, was too caught up in the ego of being a superstar, all that reputation preceding him—it was as if every time he went on the court, all the people in the stands, thirteen or fourteen thousand, were there just to see Sidney Wicks. Steele and Wicks had arrived in Portland together, Wicks a superstar already and a big salary, Steele always just on the edge of being cut. I probably played more games with Sidney Wicks, Steele said, than anyone in history. Maybe three hundred fifty, three hundred seventy-five games with him. How's that for a record. I'll miss Sidney, he said. There was all that ego, but Sidney could be fun, he knew the words to hundreds of songs, and Sidney was always singing. Always talking. I'll miss him. Funny, I never thought I would say that.

FEBRUARY HAD BEEN a good month for Bill Walton, but then the euphoria ended. There was a game against Chicago and as the evening wore on, his left foot began to hurt. By the end of the game running was an effort. For the first time since he had resumed play there was a considerable amount of postgame pain. He kept trying to play during the next two weeks but the pain became steadily worse. What was as bad was the return of all his old anxieties, not just about the coming week, but about the rest of his career. Soon he was trying to push through the pain. Coaches were always telling athletes that, *push through the pain.* A bromide, he thought, and he had always been wary of it, but he tried anyway. Instead the pain simply grew worse. He began to limp on the court. Then he began to look for situations where he would not have to move himself, but where he could anticipate the flow of the ball and have it come to him with as little movement as possible. That was not his game at all. On March 11 he played against the Lakers in San Diego. It was his fourteenth game of the season. He played 31 minutes and had 10 points and 10 rebounds. The game was pure misery for him. Kareem, against whom he loved to play, absolutely dominated the game, scoring 28 points. The Lakers won by almost 20 points. For the next forty-eight hours Walton could barely move and when he did he limped badly. Two local sportswriters who had become friends during the year and who had always been impressed, even in the bad times, by his resilience and his optimism, called and found him barely able to talk, on the verge of tears. "Ask me about anything, but don't ask me about my foot," he told them. He was twenty-seven years old, in the league six years. In that time his teams had played 492 regularly scheduled games. He had been able to play in only 223 of them. The future did not look very much better.

By late March, when Portland arrived, Walton was trying desperately to fight off boredom. About the only thing the doctors permitted him to do was work on the Nautilus and swim. Even long walks were hard on his feet. He was not supposed to go to receptions where he might have to stand around. The doctors were trying to build new devices for his sneakers, to cushion his feet. But given the size of his body and the intensity of his game, the collision of his foot with the floor was so violent that no artificial cushion was likely to help. A stress fracture, Walton said, was especially rough; it was so subtle that it did not even show up on X-rays. A reporter asked how a stress fracture differed from other fractures. "A stress fracture," he said, "is different because it comes not from one violent collision, but from constant repeated stress and strain. Systematic strain. Write that down, *systematic,* that's the right word," he added. "See? I'm good at my medical terms."

GENE SHUE HAD been coach of the Philadelphia 76ers when they had lost to Portland in the 1977 championship. That still rankled, not so much the loss but what had been written about the loss, that good basketball had beaten bad basketball, white hats had beaten black hats. The corollary bothered him as well, that Ramsay was a good basketball coach, who taught the right kind of basketball, and Shue was a bad basketball coach, who preferred playground players and did not discipline them. Ramsay, though careful in what he said—one of the cardinal rules of the coaches' club was that a coach did not criticize another coach—clearly had his reservations about Shue. On occasion he did imitations of him involving his hair, once short and crew cut, now long and styled. In the Ramsay imitation, Shue was constantly checking to be sure that his hair was in place and sufficiently mod. Shue still liked to contest the 1977 championship. He and Walton argued about it constantly. "You had the refs," Shue kept claiming. To others he launched into a litany of what had happened: Lloyd Free had bad ribs, Steve Mix had a bad ankle, George McGinnis had a bad slump.

Now, TWO GAMES away from finishing this season, it was clear that Shue was about to be fired. San Diego was not playing well, not drawing well, and someone had to pay. Most basketball people were surprised at how competitive Shue had made this strange assemblage of players. At breakfast he was talking about Marvin Barnes. "Everyone thought I was crazy taking him on. I've got nothing to lose. If he ever gets himself in shape it's the equal of a first-round pick. I don't know if there's anything left in him. The skills go quicker in this game than most. Powerful athletes in baseball last into their mid-thirties. That's not true here. We wear the body harder. Marvin put a lot of crap in his body over the years. He never had to work for it, you know. Always had the speed and the body. Someone like Kermit had to work for everything he has, but Marvin was given it. I tell him now, 'Look, you're a rookie right before the last cut, think of yourself as a sixth-round draft pick.' Then Marvin smiles that nice smile and he agrees. But I don't know what he's thinking and I don't even know if *he* knows what he's thinking. But he always agrees. It's hard for a man like me who had to work for *everything* to deal with someone who has so many problems and yet had it so easy in this one area. But that's coaching. There's no skill to coaching a Kermit Washington. That's easy. It's coaching Marvin Barnes or Joe Bryant that's work." He got up from the breakfast table. He performed a little light pat on his hair reminiscent of Ramsay imitating him. "I hear," he said, "that Portland's made it back playing a lot of one-on-one basketball these days. How's Doctor Jack doing with Billy Ray?" The idea seemed to delight him and for the first time that morning Gene Shue smiled.

THE DAY PORTLAND was to play San Diego, Walton spent resting according to his doctors' orders. His wife, Susan, was expecting their third child, perhaps that day. In the morning the phone rang and it was the midwife. She was very busy. Three deliveries that day. Could Susan Walton possibly wait until the next day? "Midwives are much harder to find down here than up in Portland," he said, hanging up. His friend Arthur Hartfelt was on hand, trying to borrow Grateful Dead tapes. The two of them drove to practice. This was the biggest game of the year and the Clipper practice was a shambles. Gene Shue was late. When he finally arrived he stood around and talked to his players for a few minutes. Then he departed. The players started shooting baskets. Freeman Williams and Marvin Barnes played HORSE, a game in which they matched shots. It was a schoolyard game of ancient origins. Every time a player missed, he picked up a letter. Most of their shots came from out of bounds behind the basket, as they tried to shoot over it. At the other end of the court, Arthur Hartfelt was playing a game of one-on-one with Lloyd (All-World, or simply, to his friends, *World*) Free. Arthur, short, heavy and balding, quite obviously not a pro basketball player, had gone to Harvard where, even on that school's dreadful teams, he had not played. Free, in a game of ten, was up 9–2. "Drive on him, Arthur," Walton yelled. Arthur drove and scored. The final score was 10–3. They drove back to Walton's house—Hartfelt was euphoric. "Three points off World, you see that, Bill?" he asked. Walton nodded. "I drove on him and scored. What a practice!"

"Yeah," said Walton without rancor, "great practice. Well, Arthur, you're in the bigtime now."

PORTLAND BEAT SAN Diego again. Tom Owens had a good game. When the two teams had played in Portland four days earlier, Swen Nater, 240 pounds, all of it muscle, had accused Tom Owens, 210, very little of it muscle, of being a dirty player. It had become an obsession and during the game he had kept shouting at Owens to watch out. "Swen," Owens had tried to reply, "I can't play dirty against you—I'm too weak." That had not mollified Nater who, much like a bush-circuit wrestler, had gone on San Diego television after the game to invite all of San Diego to come out and see him get his revenge on Owens. Everyone had teased Owens since then, and when Portland arrived at the San Diego airport there had been an abortive attempt to page him in the name of Swen Nater: Would Mr. Tom Owens please meet Mr. Nater? Ramsay had told him not to be nervous, and Kermit had assured him that Swen was really gentle, a little person in a big man's body. Nater had not demolished Owens, who played a crafty game, using Nater's strength against him, throwing Nater small deft fakes which gave Owens just enough of an angle for the shot and the foul. Portland had led by one point with nine seconds left and the ball had gone to Lloyd Free as everyone knew it would and Kermit had come out to double him. That was too much defense, even for Free, and he had passed the ball off to Marvin Barnes. Marvin had launched an airball. There was a sense, watching it die in midair, its trajectory collapse, that it was quite possibly Marvin Barnes's last shot in the NBA. The game was over, Portland won, and was now in the playoffs.

"Did you want Marvin to take that last shot?" Steve Kelley had asked Shue after the game.

"I didn't hear the question," Shue said, and turned to another reporter.

* * *

THEY HAD MADE the playoffs and they were exhausted. Only the fact that Billy Bates had been fresh and strong when everyone else was tired had carried them that far. After the San Diego victory there was no rest, simply an early morning wakeup, an early morning flight to Phoenix and a game that night. On the flight to Phoenix, Tom Owens, his body sapped from the evening with Swen Nater, had asked Ron Culp if Ramsay would rest the players in the two remaining games. Abdul Jeelani chimed in: will he rest us? *Abdul,* thought Culp, you're a rookie playing under twenty minutes, there's an expansion team coming in, and if there's one player on this team who needs every minute, it's you. Well, Abdul, he thought, you're really an NBA player now.

They were absolutely demolished in the last two games. Phoenix led by twenty-two at the half. The rest of the game was a wipeout. Two nights later they were in Seattle for the final regular-season game. Again they were listless, and Seattle, coming together now for the playoffs, looked sharp and coherent; it led by seventeen points at the half. The plane ride home from Seattle was depressing. It hardly looked like a playoff team, it was tired and the fatigue, mental as well as physical, showed. Before the season Ramsay had wanted a record of 45–37. Now he had made the playoffs and the record was 38–44. Seattle, with whom Portland would vie in the three-game mini-series, had won 56 games. The integrity of the regular season had in effect been sacrificed by the owners in order to expand the gate and television revenues of the playoffs. The idea of a team like this, with a record of 38–44, stumbling into the playoffs, offended more than just purists. Of the 22 teams in the league, only 10 were now excluded from playoff competition, and of the 12 that made the playoffs, only 8 had winning records. It was one more example of the league's cheapening of a product in order to get instant revenues. Ramsay knew that, knew the regular season was too long and that the playoffs were too long. But after a season with so many injuries and contract problems he was delighted to be included. He bridled when friends suggested that Portland was not really a playoff team. He bridled again when Harry Glickman, the general manager, came up and congratulated him on making the playoffs and suggested that if they won one game he would consider the season a success. As far as Ramsay was concerned, getting into the playoffs made the season a success, particularly in view of all the contract problems—which were, it was left unsaid, the fault of the front office. The players felt the same way. The next day Steve Kelley mentioned casually to Tom Owens that this did not seem like a playoff team of the past. "I'm tired of hearing that crap," Owens said and walked away from him.

In the first game, played in Seattle, the Sonics—a team marked by dissension in the last month of the season (Lenny Wilkens, exhausted by Dennis Johnson, had told him simply to choose whatever team he wanted to be traded to)—seemed stronger and quicker. Seattle clearly looked like a team with fifty-six wins playing a team with thirty-eight wins. The Sonic guards were just too quick for the Portland guards. The Portland ballhandling was terrible. The final score was Seattle 120, Portland 110. The only thing close was the score. That meant the second game, in Portland, might be the last one of the season. Tickets were easy to get. Season ticketholders had to buy new tickets for these games, and they clearly lacked enthusiasm. Until the last minute nearly a third of the seats were available. The 12,666 was obviously getting soft. CBS was there for the game, mostly, it seemed, because of Billy Ray Bates. They were doing a minispecial on him. They had staked out his locker with cameras and they showed him arriving for the game, dressing and practicing dunks. Even more remarkable, for this was the true sign of NBA status, Brent Musburger, the broadcaster, already had a nickname for him. He was, in honor of how quickly he had become a celebrity, dubbed The Legend. Not every player in the past had liked his Musburgerian nickname. Walton had refused to do postgame interviews until Musburger stopped calling him The Mountain Man, but status it was nevertheless. The Portland fans, knowing the game was going to be on national television, had brought their signs along to the Coliseum. The signs were mostly about Billy Bates, and they had been brought not so much to increase Billy's fame as to get the fans themselves on national television.

In Goodman, Mississippi, Pat Smithson, owner of two thousand acres of good cotton and soybean land, turned on his television set. Friends had told him that Shack Bates's boy was going to be on the TV in some kind of game someplace up north. Amazing, he thought, that a boy off his own land was going to play on TV. It was a team called the Trail Blazers. When he first heard about it, Pat Smithson thought they were talking about a motorcycle gang. Pat Smithson was seventy-nine and he still worked the land himself every day but Sunday. He had spent his whole life there and he had known Billy's grandfather Davis Bates, who had worked that land, and his father, Shack Bates, who had been born on it, and Billy, who had been born on it too. Shack was a difficult man. He was strong but could be a lot of trouble. There had been a lot of children in the family, and he had a vague memory of Billy being the laziest. That memory was of a skinny little boy with a big smile slipping off from work. Now that boy was on the TV. Amazing. Times had changed. Once, just a few years ago, there had been a lot of sharecroppers on his place, forty-two of them if he rightly recalled, and now there were none. They were all gone. He didn't need them anymore with the new machinery. The sharecroppers had been there when they still had the mules. Now it was all machines. He wasn't sure which time was better, then or now. On the TV Billy Bates was playing for a city named Portland. It suddenly struck him that Billy Bates had been to cities that he had never visited. Pat Smithson watched him play and was impressed. That boy could sure jump. They could all jump, he thought, but Billy could jump a little better than the others. He felt a certain stirring of pride watching him, a boy off his own place. It certainly was different these days, he thought.

That night Ramsay started Billy Bates for the first time. He did not want to put him under too much pressure, but he needed his energy and his power. Pressure? Billy said to a reporter who asked him about it. Pressure was *not* playing. There was no pressure in playing. What pressure was there in doing what you loved to do? he asked. "The Seattle guards," a reporter was asking, "some say they're the best in the league. Gus and DJ." "Oh, they're the best," Billy said. "I agree with that, but I can score off them. No way I'm not going to score."

It was a good game. Portland played well this night. It was helped of course by the 12,666, more passionate than ever, since many of them were people who normally could not get regular seats and went to the Paramount instead. Portland played with more discipline: it took fewer poor shots, and there were fewer long rebounds leading to Seattle fast breaks. Thus Seattle's speed became less of a factor. It was a physical game, bodies banging all night—Jim Brewer, Kermit Washington, Calvin Natt for Portland, Lonnie Shelton, Jack Sikma, Paul Silas for Seattle. There was simply too much muscle and power in too small a space; basketball players, with the exception perhaps of Wes Unseld, always looked slim, even skinny, on television, but up close the bodies were awesome. That night, it sometimes seemed the referees would have to call fouls on every play or on no plays. Silas and Washington, teacher and student, two men with deliberately created skills, had gone at it, a swirl of bodies and angles, and above all elbows, the elbow crucial for leverage, for position, for intimidation. It was all physical and grim and somehow amicable.

"Hey, Paul," Kermit said at one point as they were running down the court. "Watch the elbow. Watch it, damnit, Paul."

"But you just chopped me, Kermit," Silas protested.

"Yeah, Paul, but below the neck. *Below the neck, Paul.*"

Seattle was ahead 87–82 on a Sikma free throw with only 2:57 left in the game and thus perhaps in the season. Ramsay, watching, kneeling, loved Sikma, coveted him probably more than any other player in the league, had been surprised that Seattle had drafted him; Portland had been ready to do so (Buckwalter had seen him playing for Illinois Wesleyan, a tall strong white kid playing in a league where everyone else was black, where the crowds were black, where there was a lot of intimidation and where, when they knocked him down, he simply got back up and knocked them down). Then, with the game in hand, Seattle tightened. Ramsay, still kneeling, talked to Billy, telling him not to be afraid to take it to the hoop, to play by instinct, just be himself. Ramsay sweated heavily now, anxiety sweat, not just through his shirt, but through his jacket and even his shoes. Earlier in his career he had been self-conscious about it, and about the telltale stains. Once in college, in a desperate attempt to hide the signs of so delicate a nervous system, he had taped sweat socks to his armpits. That had worked for a time, but as the evening wore on the tape had given out, the sweat socks had slipped and had started coming out his sleeves, flapping in the air as he moved his arms. That ended the sweat socks, and he had decided to go to Pampers instead, which had worked admirably for a time, protecting him as they had protected the finer sensibilities of millions of mothers and fathers. But the Pampers were clumsy, or at least a whole Pamper was, and so he had gotten crafty, and he had cut a Pamper in half, placing a half in each armpit. That had worked well for a time, until during a game in Buffalo the Pampers had started to unravel. Buffalo fans in those days were accustomed to seeing almost anything, but that night they were treated to the sight of the Buffalo Braves coach shedding damp Pamper pellets all over the floor. That was his last night in Pampers. Since then he had gone to games au naturel. Now in this game he was soaked, his shoes, once light, had turned dark. Portland in the final two minutes edged up. With five seconds left Billy Bates hit an eighteen-foot jumper which tied the score, and sent the game into overtime. The script demanded that Portland win in overtime, and that it did, easily.

Ramsay in the locker room was jubilant. "That was one of the best wins I've ever been involved with. Coming from behind like that, making the big plays." But there was still a score to settle. He was angry at writers who suggested that perhaps this team did not deserve to be in the playoffs. "I know this is a disappointment to those of you who thought we should have ended our season tonight, but it just goes to show how little you know about athletics. Athletes never give up on a situation and are privileged to engage in competition at this level. Those of you who've never played any sports would have a hard time understanding that. You only write it. . . ." Later Steve Kelley shook his head. Hell, he said, I didn't write anything about them that Ramsay didn't say and feel himself.

Two days later they went back to Seattle for the third game of the series. In the storybook the good guys always win, but in real life it is much harder to know who the good guys are. Some high school and college coaches make their teams pray before the game, but what if *both* coaches make their teams pray? The Seattle fans clearly thought their players were the good guys. "Are you going to win?" a Seattle reporter asked John Johnson the day before the game. "Are we going to win?" Johnson repeated rhetorically. He was ten years in the league, he played a game which was sheer delight to watch in its economy and intelligence, and he had become, through his seniority and his skill in handling reporters, the designated Seattle press spokesman. "Let's see," he said, "tomorrow's game is . . . Easter Sunday, and it's an afternoon game. We'll win so quickly that they'll be able to get back to Portland and still go to church." It turned out to be a fairly accurate prophecy. Again Seattle played disciplined basketball and this time Portland was shakier, the long jump shots did not go in and the rebounds ignited Seattle fast breaks. It was not a close game or a good game. On the way to the locker room afterwards, score, Seattle 103, Portland, 86, Bobby Gross (who had played 19 minutes and scored 6 points; and seemed like a missing person both on and off the court) was shaking his head. "Live by the jump shot, die by it," he said. "That's not basketball." He was sure he would be gone next year. In the Seattle dressing room other players were standing around shaking hands, saying farewell. Jim Brewer had played a strong three-game series, and his cubicle was surrounded by reporters. It was the first time he had drawn a crowd all season. He was pleased with the way the season had ended. Bill Russell, commenting for CBS, had said that Portland often seemed to play better when Brewer was in the lineup; Buckwalter quietly had been saying much the same thing to Ramsay all year. Brewer was sure he would be back in the league next season. Larry Steele was not sure and his money was not guaranteed. He was going to spend the summer rehabilitating his knee. Twardzik was dubious about the future. But his money at least was guaranteed. The players continued shaking hands with each other, sorry to have the season end, and yet in their own way glad it ended too. It was, after all, a long season for a troubled team in a troubled league.

4

Epilogue

MAURICE LUCAS AROSE VERY LATE IN THE MORNING AFTER WATCHING the last championship playoff game between Philadelphia and Los Angeles and drove off to his meeting with The Monster Man. The Monster Man was a slim young physical therapist named Evan Jones who worked at a Portland hospital and operated a machine called the Cybex, a heartless piece of modern machinery which seemed on that morning designed in equal part to give strength to Maurice Lucas's legs and to draw sweat from his brow. Luke was some eleven inches taller and a hundred pounds heavier than Evan Jones, but the machine was Jones's and Luke, normally a master of territory, was on Jones's turf. The exercises began. "Come on, Maurice," commanded Jones, "you can do more. Come on, Maurice! I want *more!*" Luke's legs drove against the machine and signs of strain appeared on his face. He reached for a towel. Evan Jones slapped it away. "The towel is for later, Maurice. Now come on," he said, watching his machine. "That's twelve . . . thirteen . . . that's good . . . fourteen . . . fifteen, that's better. . . . I can live with that, Maurice." Lucas smiled in relief. Famous for his frown, he dared not inflict it on Evan Jones.

Luke was, after a disappointing season, determined to arrive in the New Jersey camp in the best shape of his life, anxious to be spoken of one day as one of the greatest power forwards ever. (Like Elgin Baylor? someone suggested. No, said Luke, Elgin was really a small forward, not a power forward.) He was strengthening his legs; there had already been corrective surgery to fix a broken finger on his shooting hand. All in all Luke was in a benign mood. In a few days he would fly to Milwaukee to collect his degree from Marquette, and he was proud of that, proud that he had had the character to stick with his studies even after he had left school and turned professional. His wife, Rita, who had attended the Kennedy School of Government at Harvard, was studying law and would probably transfer to Rutgers or some other school in the New York area. Bill and Susan Walton had just named their third son, Luke, after him and he was very proud of that, too. "Stereotypes falling around here right and left," he said. He was pleased with the New Jersey situation; the Nets had almost immediately increased his salary to $400,000 a year. In a year the team would have a handsome new multimillion-dollar arena to call home, within the very gaze of Manhattan and its masters of pub.

There was on this day very little to be angry about. Everywhere he went in Portland he was still hailed with affection, a tall handsome young black man of infinite charm, should the mood suit him. He was still dispensing T-shirts from the Maurice Lucas Basketball Camp to young admirers. The only thing that gnawed on him was CBS. He was angry at the network for the way it had treated the world championship of professional basketball. In the Portland area, basketball fans who watched and suffered through the entire season had not been able to watch the Philly-Lakers games except by staying up until all the regular programming was over at 11:30 p.m. Then they could watch a taped rebroadcast. In some parts of the country, fans were not even that lucky. "Can you imagine?" Luke was saying. "They cover the whole season. They even get the matchups they want. Kareem and Magic against Julius. And then they do this to us. I mean they would never do it to football or baseball. 'Sports fans, we want you to watch the whole season but maybe we'll let you have a midnight replay of the World Series,'" Luke said, imitating a sports announcer. "Can you imagine, *Kareem* and *Magic* and *Julius,* and we're still second-class citizens?"

WHO WAS TO explain to Luke about sweeps, a word from the world of television, the thrice-yearly periods when the networks got their report cards on ratings? Or the unfortunate fact, for professional basketball players and fans, that one of the sweeps fell in May? Since basketball's ratings were very low, it meant that CBS would prefer not to broadcast the games during its regular hours, since they would thus emerge with a smaller share of the pie than NBC and ABC. "Stayed up until two o'clock in the morning, thanks to those television people," Luke said. "Why do you think CBS didn't carry it?" a reporter asked him. "I know why," said Luke, "but I'm not saying. You know what it is. The same thing that it always is." The implication was clear. It was race, basketball was the blackest of the sports.

So it was that in the middle of its massive contract with the NBA, CBS bailed out of the playoffs. The implication of this was clear enough to any-one on either side of the marriage, sports or broadcast: if CBS did not think the playoffs, the denouement of the season, worthy of prime-time coverage, how much longer would it even bother with the regular season? So on that day Maurice Lucas was angry, but the owners were scared.

STU INMAN, Jack Ramsay and Bucky Buckwalter debated for hours which eight players they would protect from Dallas, a new expansion team just coming in the league. If they protected eight, they had to make available three. They had already decided to protect Billy Ray Bates, a decision which just two months ago would have struck both Inman and Ramsay as unlikely. The first five on the protected list were easy to decide: Kermit Washington, Calvin Natt, Tom Owens, Ron Brewer and Mychal Thompson. Then Bates. That was six. For the seventh and eighth it was a choice between Jimmy Pax-son, Kevin Kunnert and Bobby Gross. Again they postulated their own needs against Dallas's likely choice. Paxson had had a disappointing rookie year, but he was seemingly a solid player and a solid person and there were repeated flashes of talent. As a first-round choice he deserved more of a look; if he went on the list, Dallas would certainly pick him. Kunnert was a backup center coming off a serious knee injury and bearing a relatively high salary, $225,000. Gross was the most intriguing, a very talented player but valuable only on a refined, highly sophisticated team, which Dallas, brand new in the league with everyone's leftovers, was unlikely to be. Gross also had a very big salary, some $300,000. Considering who his teammates were likely to be, Gross was almost sure to become frustrated and disillusioned in that envi-ronment. The wild card was that Dallas might pick Gross and then trade him to a better team for a draft choice. Based on what they knew, the Port-land people believed Dallas would go for young players with low salaries.

Portland decided to protect Paxson and Kunnert, and risk Gross. Privately, Inman believed that Dallas would pick T. R. Dunn, a solid defensive player with a small salary, roughly $75,000. Somewhat to his surprise, Dallas took Abdul Jeelani, better offense, less disciplined overall game, and smaller salary, $57,000. For its entrance into the league, and the rights to Abdul Jeelani, Dallas paid Portland more than $500,000.

The change wasn't simple for Jeelani. Dallas was an expansion team and expansion teams were traditionally unsettled. Of the twenty-two players who wore the Dallas uniform at one time or another that year, only four made it all the way from the start of the camp to the end of the season. One of the four was Abdul. He had been told by management not to buy housing in the city, which of course increased his insecurity; at times he wished he was back in Portland, where he knew exactly what was wanted of him. Still, the year was not bad for him; in July a daughter, Kareema, named after the Laker star and fellow Muslim, was born, and gradually as the season wore on Abdul showed that he could score points. In several games he played the entire fourth quarter, scoring in one game more points in the final quarter than the whole New York Knicks team. The fans began to call for him— *"Abdul! Abdul! Abdul!"*—and that pleased him. Dallas was a tough town, you wouldn't expect people to cheer somebody named Abdul there in the year 1981. And he was pleased that he had finally made it in the NBA. By the end of the season his value was even greater than it had been before, because he was now an established league player. He was wanted. For a salary reportedly twice that of his NBA pay, he went back to Europe to play in the Italian league.

THE DRAFT WAS a problem for Inman. It was the center of his world. Ramsay's world was built around the season and the playoffs, but Inman's world was the draft, getting the right players for Ramsay's system, minimizing his own mistakes, preying if possible on weaker franchises to get a little better position. His reputation rose or fell with the draft.

He believed that two good years of drafting back-to-back—the 1975 draft with Hollins in the first round and Gross in the second was a great one—could make a team competitive. Two poor draft years and the team would slip and he might be out of a job. He was still a little angry over what had happened the year before when he had worked out a brilliant trade, Lucas for the Chicago pick, number two in the entire draft, and Weinberg had foiled that.

In this draft Portland badly needed a center but was not very likely to obtain one. The talent pool was generally weak in centers, even if Portland picked higher. Its other need was for a quick playmaking guard to control the offense and showcase the talents of the other players. There were twenty-three teams in the league, including Dallas, and Portland picked tenth among them. The very best players, including the best guards, would be gone in the first five or six picks. Darnell Valentine, who had interested Inman earlier, was a college junior and had decided not to come out. Kelvin Ransey, the Ohio State playmaker whom Inman considered the best player available for Portland, would, he was sure, go fourth. There was one other player who interested him—a quick guard named Ronnie Lester from Iowa. But Lester already had a history of knee injuries and Portland was wary of choosing a player already damaged; it had had enough medical problems in recent years without seeking more. Because of the Walton compensation and other deals, Portland was at the moment relatively rich in first-round draft choices. Inman believed that most middle-level picks in the draft, say, numbers ten to twenty, usually were able to make the team but rarely improved it; he regarded one player from the first four or five picks to be worth two from the middle. So in the weeks before the draft he began working the phone, trying to cut a deal with Chicago, picking fourth, or Denver, picking fifth, offering various deals, the Portland pick plus T. R. Dunn for a switch, or finally, an additional future Portland first. He felt reasonably strong about the makeup of his team. Center was likely to be a constant problem, and Portland would eventually have to do something there; but its forwards, he believed, were the strongest in the league, and he regarded Billy Bates at this moment as the equivalent of a high first-round pick, "say number eight or nine in this draft." Finally, on the eve of the draft, after endless calls he worked out a convoluted deal with Chicago. The Bulls would pick Ransey, and if Ronnie Lester was still available when Portland chose, the Blazers would pick him. Then, with the Blazers throwing in a future first, they would switch players. The pot was sweet for Chicago because Lester had been a popular local schoolboy star. It worked. Portland picked the player it wanted without giving up very much, and the deal was considered one of Inman's most artful. A few months later, when, after only a couple of games, Ronnie Lester had to go into the hospital for further knee surgery, it looked even better. There was one problem with Ransey: his agent was the dreaded Howard Slusher. That meant signing him would take time.

* * *

Tom Owens almost decided to trade himself to Seattle after the season. His contract with Portland was finished, he was affronted by the fact that the negotiations for a new one had taken so long, and he was bothered by the fact that Jack Ramsay in the final days of the season had talked of how the Blazers were *soft* at the center. Owens liked the idea of Seattle, it was nearby, the Sonics wanted him badly and were ready to pay the money he wanted. He also liked the idea of playing for Lenny Wilkens, who was popular with active players. The deed was virtually done, compensation between Seattle and Portland very handsome indeed, even agreed upon, when at the last moment Portland, chary of going into the next season with both Kunnert and Mychal Thompson coming off injuries, pushed Owens to re-sign. In the end he signed again with Portland for three years, at roughly $300,000 a year. His agent, John Lizzo, who thought he had a deal with Seattle, was furious and was heard to say flatly: "I no longer represent Tom Owens." Lenny Wilkens was also furious. But Owens was pleased. Three hundred thousand was about $75,000 a year more than he would have received signing a year earlier, and it was a far, far cry from what Bill Owens had made at the Lotos Club.

In late June Jack Ramsay went to the rookie camp in Portland, liked what he saw there, and then returned to his summer home in Ocean City, New Jersey, to spend the Fourth of July with his family and some old friends. He was in exceptionally good spirits, the darkness of the season was behind him, a new season beckoned, filled with wins, perhaps forty-five, perhaps more, and plays well executed. He found himself, much to his own surprise, enamored of Billy Ray Bates. It was the singularity of Billy's love of basketball which had captivated him. In contrast to so many other modern basketball players, Billy was obsessed by basketball, just as Jack Ramsay himself was. In addition, Kelvin Ransey, as yet unsigned, had also played in the camp, through a special arrangement worked out between Weinberg and Slusher, and Ramsay was very pleased by what he had seen: Ransey was quick, confident, purposeful with the ball. Jack Ramsay was sure that his problems at guard had ended. For the moment basketball was done, a season completed, a season not yet started, and Jack Ramsay was the other Jack Ramsay, no longer the driven basketball coach but momentarily at least the kind, somewhat old-fashioned gentleman, a little shy, who loved and catered to his family, and seemed to blush in the presence of women. Four of his five children were home, and the house was filled with Ramsay grandchildren. It was, like the others on this street near the Jersey shore, a three-decker house, built in a time when families were much larger, and when family life revolved around a discussion of that day's events, not what the television set presented. The Ramsay house was adorned with little basketball memorabilia; instead it seemed a great repository of children's toys.

This day, the Fourth, had become a traditional celebration, with the Ramsays and their neighbors and various old friends sharing the dinner, with Ramsay as the chief barbecue cook. Some of the old friends were men he had known for thirty years, successful, in their mid-fifties now with high-ranking jobs in large regional companies. Much of the talk was lively and affectionate, filled with recollections of similar evenings and follies and disasters past, when they were all younger, of midnight swims, and too many drinks imbibed. Then as the evening progressed Ramsay had startled—and somewhat offended—some of his old friends, suggesting that they lived in protected environments, that it was almost impossible for them to fail, barring, of course, bizarre and unnatural behavior. No one in their world, he suggested, ever lost a job. By contrast, it was not that way in coaching. He was out there alone. Perhaps 30 percent of the NBA coaches who started the next season would be fired. Larry Weinberg was a principled man and he got along rather well with Weinberg. But if he did not coach well, if he did not work well with his players, if his team failed, he would be gone. It was for Ramsay, such a closed man normally, particularly with his friends, a rare outburst. His friends spoke of their own vulnerability, but Ramsay had remained adamant, it was worse for a coach. He was in the most competitive part of American society and they were not. Look at Red Holzman, he had said angrily. One of the best coaches in the league. When New York was winning all those years, everyone applauded. Two or three years later they stocked up on the wrong kind of players, paid them millions of dollars and the team was a flop. But no one blamed the players, no one blamed management. They blamed the coach. It was Holzman who got canned. The players, he said, can always hide their inadequacies by blaming the coach. Ramsay's friends finally accepted his argument, but he had cooled the evening.

IF KELVIN RANSEY was difficult to draft, he was even more difficult to sign. The job of signing him was immediately taken over by Weinberg and his attorney, Alan Rothenberg. Inman, who had engineered the deal, was quickly eased out of the picture. Clearly, if big money was at stake, then a line had been crossed, from basketball expertise, which was Inman's territory, to financial expertise, which Weinberg was not about to concede to anyone.

Immediately after the draft Weinberg had called Howard Slusher. "Are you really representing Ransey?" Weinberg asked. Slusher said he was. "I'd rather have you as a friend than deal with you," said Weinberg. "So would I with you, Larry," said Slusher. In the next sentence the negotiations began. "Our people," said Weinberg, "say he's not the best guard in the draft, that a kid named Andrew Toney is, but that he's what we need." Here we go again, thought Slusher. They've just given up two first-round picks for this man, their own people are quoted as saying he's the best player in the draft for them, and now his value is starting to go down. Maybe we deserve each other, he thought.

The negotiations took weeks, and then months. At one point, frustrated by the slow pace, Slusher had exploded. "You're just trying to squeeze down a poor black kid from the ghetto," he told Rothenberg. The moment he said it, Slusher knew it was a mistake; it might be true of other owners but not of Weinberg. Within minutes his phone rang. It was Weinberg. "Did you really say it? That's all I want to know. *Did you say it?*" "I did and it was a mistake and I apologize," Slusher said. "I've never been so wounded—and coming from you. You're my friend! If it came from another agent I could understand it." Slusher apologized again: "Larry, I made a mistake. You have to forgive me." He had never heard Larry Weinberg, he thought, so close to tears. Still the negotiations dragged on. In the exhibition season Portland played poorly. The guards were slow. Everyone was waiting for Kelvin Ransey, and every other guard was playing out of position because the lead guard-to-be was hidden away at Howard Slusher's house in Palos Verdes. Finally, with the season nearing its start, Ransey still the invisible man, Jack Ramsay, angry that his training camp had been disrupted again, fearing that the new season might be a repeat of the previous one, began to push Weinberg to expedite the signing. Too much rested on Ransey. Slusher's ploy of permitting Ransey to play in the Portland rookie camp, a calculated risk, had worked; he had played brilliantly. Jack Ramsay, however unconsciously, had become Slusher's ally. On the very eve of the season, Weinberg and Slusher had reached essential accord—roughly $240,000 a year.

For the final signing Slusher and Ransey went to Weinberg's office in Los Angeles. The contrast in culture was wonderful. There was Weinberg—the immensely successful Jewish businessman, serious, intense, not entirely comfortable in his public role, yet anxious to dispel the tensions caused by the prolonged negotiations—about to sign Ransey, poor black youth of Toledo, Ohio, son of a truckdriver, one of six children. Weinberg's father was there and, anxious to find some connection between his world and that of Kelvin Ransey, Weinberg had begun to talk about him. "My father is my life," he had said. "I have never heard anyone say an unkind thing about my father. Everyone who knows him loves him." He told about how his father had worked his way up from pushing a cart in Brooklyn. "Kelvin, I will give you some advice. My father always told me never to loan money to anyone—always give it. Otherwise they'll always resent you." Ransey wanted to build a house for his parents, and Weinberg praised him for that; in addition Ransey was creating trust funds for his nine nieces and nephews and Weinberg praised him for that. A sense of family was important, he said. Still the meeting remained stilted. Weinberg did not know how to make small talk, and Ransey, in the presence of so rich a man, remained virtually silent, unsure of what his role should be. The pauses between the words were becoming larger. "Would you like two candy bars?" asked Weinberg, pointing to a Trail Blazer candy bar, part of the team's new promotion. "Can my lawyer have one too?" asked Ransey. One was duly handed to Slusher. Still the atmosphere remained uncomfortable. Weinberg began to talk about his father again and tried to connect this to Ransey's own parents. "Kelvin," he said, "I would like to invite your mother and father to fly out and see a Blazer game this year, at my expense. Would they like that?" "My father would," said Ransey, "but my mother wouldn't like getting on a plane. She won't do it." That produced a long pause, for another connection had failed. "Well," said Weinberg, for this was the last chance, "we play in both Cleveland and Detroit and those places aren't very far from Toledo. Perhaps they'd like to come and be my guests at one of those games."

"They'd like that," said Ransey. Everyone in the room heaved a sigh of relief.

The deal was done. Leaving the office, Ransey turned to Slusher. The agent prepared himself for some complicated judgment about the owner. "Nice man," said Kelvin Ransey, who had just signed for $240,000 a year, and they went to Slusher's car.

* * *

IN THE SUMMER of 1980, while the Blazers were still negotiating with Kelvin Ransey, LaRue Martin, their number-one pick from eight years before, wrote a letter to Jack McKinney, Ramsay's former assistant who had just taken the coaching job in Indianapolis. In it, LaRue described what good shape he was in, how hard he worked out, and asked for a tryout. He was sure, he wrote McKinney, that he could still play. Both McKinney and Dick Vertlieb, the Pacers' general manager, were fond of Martin, they thought him an exceptional young man and they immediately wrote back and invited him to the camp. They did this partly because they thought he was a particularly attractive human being and, at a more pragmatic level, because in training camp you could never have enough centers. That summer LaRue Martin worked even harder building himself up in the Jewish Community Center weight room, and working on his wind, and when he showed up, Vertlieb was impressed. No player was in better shape, and no one worked harder. But soon LaRue pulled a leg muscle and tried to continue playing; McKinney begged him to rest and sit out a day. But LaRue was convinced that this was his last shot. He continued to play, terrified of losing any opportunity to impress his coaches, and pulled another muscle; despite McKinney's request he still refused to stop. McKinney and Vertlieb at length decided sadly that the talent was simply not there. Whether it had ever been there was an intriguing question, but LaRue Martin was older now and he had been away from the game for four years, which in a sport so demanding was the equivalent of a lifetime. Midway through the exhibition season they cut him from the team as gently as they could. They both hoped that, no matter how painful it was at the moment, they had helped LaRue to answer questions about himself. When he was cut LaRue Martin, convinced finally that his career was over, returned to Portland where he went to work for a title insurance company.

IN SEATTLE, LENNY Wilkens's problems were multiplying. That franchise, whose star had been on the rise at precisely the moment that Portland's was on the decline, now, for many of the same reasons, seemed to be on the decline itself. In the final weeks of the season Wilkens could no longer contain his anger over the way Dennis Johnson was playing, and worse, what he was doing to the team. The moment the season was over, calling DJ "a cancer on his team," unusually harsh words for someone as controlled as he liked to be, Wilkens traded him to Phoenix for Paul Westphal. That, however, did not end Seattle's difficulties. Gus Williams, the other talented Seattle guard, considered by many basketball players the fastest guard in the league, was in his option year, and his agent turned out to be, of course, the redoubtable Howard Slusher. Slusher, the toughest negotiator in the game, decided to hold Gus Williams out until a settlement was reached. At one time there was talk of $900,000 a year. Soon it came down to the $600,000–$700,000 level. But Sam Schulman, the owner who had pioneered a decade earlier in paying huge salaries to superstars, now decided to hold the line. So Gus Williams simply sat out the season, believing that when it was over he could enter the first class of players to sign with whatever team they wanted without the burden of compensation. In court, Seattle was challenging that right. In the meantime Gus Williams did not play. That meant Westphal, who had looked forward to teaming with Williams and creating perhaps the fastest pair of guards in basketball history, was suddenly without the man he needed. When he then fractured a bone in his foot he was able to play less and with less freedom. The Seattle fans resented this and Westphal and his wife were surprised by the local animosity which now greeted them. In addition Lonnie Shelton, the young power forward who was an integral part of Seattle's physical game, began having personal problems and missing practices. Then there were confrontations with Wilkens, and Shelton was briefly suspended. Shortly after that he suffered a chronic dislocation of his left wrist and was out for the season. Just two years earlier Seattle, like Portland before it, had been the league champion, young, cohesive and strong, the envy of all other teams. Now it was coming apart. It ended the season with a record of 34–48, its fall from grace sudden and painful.

PAUL SILAS, in many ways the symbol of the Seattle championship team, retired from active playing and took the job of head coach in San Diego. One day right after the championship playoffs, Silas's close friend Bob Ryan, the sportswriter for the *Boston Globe*, called to ask what he thought about Magic Johnson. Magic Johnson had played brilliantly in the championship series against Philadelphia, even—in the final game with Kareem out—playing center and dominating the game. Those games had showcased with a kind of final authority the breadth and originality of his talents. He was more, it seemed, than just a joyous young face. "Magic Johnson," said Silas, "not bad, not bad." He paused. "That young man is *authentic.*" With that Magic was finally and completely welcomed into the game by his peers.

In the summer of 1980, Bill Walton's left foot gradually began to feel better. He had kept his weight off it and favored it for a long time, and believed that it was finally returning to health. One night a San Diego sportswriter, covering a bicycle race at a local arena because Olympic skater Eric Heiden was supposed to be competing, was astounded to see Bill Walton there, careening around the track at breakneck speed. Irv Levin, the Clippers' owner, was furious at the news; but Walton convinced everybody that bicycle racing was just the way for him to get his wind back without putting stress on the foot. In mid-July, in an atmosphere that smacked of hype (and the need to push season-ticket sales), a team of five top orthopedic surgeons under Dr. Tony Daly was brought to Los Angeles to examine him. After doing so they announced that they were optimistic about his playing in the next season. Gradually Walton put more pressure on his foot, playing in pickup games at Balboa Park; in August he went to the Clippers' camp in Yuma, hoping to play again. Paul Silas, the new coach, had his doubts. If Walton could play, of course he wanted him, but he refused to risk a repetition of the year before, when Walton's nonplaying shadow had fallen constantly across the team. There were one or two minor incidents between Silas and Walton, but in the end the men agreed that the practices would be run Silas's way.

In his first exhibition game against the Lakers, Walton played with great skill and almost embarrassed Kareem. That he could be away from the game for so many months and then come back and find his timing and rhythm so quickly was striking. But a few days later, in another game, his left foot began to hurt again and he took himself out. That night a local reporter who was friendly with Walton found him barely able to talk. He had worked so hard at getting in shape and his foot had again so readily betrayed him. By then the Clippers were moving towards a lawsuit with a recalcitrant Lloyd's of London for the insurance money over Walton's absence for the previous season (they later settled out of court). Irv Levin was no longer talking positively about having signed Walton. He admitted he might have been remiss in not having him checked out more carefully before the signing. A local doctor named Richard Gilbert, podiatrist for the San Diego Chargers and a consultant for the Clippers, had not seen Walton's feet until long after the signing. His feet were so bad, Gilbert told friends, that they did not have to be fractured for him to be out. What was amazing about Walton, Gilbert told colleagues, was that he had been able to play at all and have so remarkable a career. During all of this Walton was terribly subdued. He was aware of the increasing odds against his playing the way he wanted to, or even playing at all. Daly had mentioned one possibility to him, a rare operation designed to give him more flex in his foot and perhaps reduce some of the pain as well. Skilled surgeons would cut into the soft tissue of the sole, taking out some bone and some flesh. It was an operation which had been performed successfully before, but only with very young children. Never had it been done, Walton believed, on a grown man who made his living in large part by running. There was a danger that he might end up with his feet in still worse shape than before. Walton was interested but wary. After all these years he was tired of doctors and diagnoses and coun-terdiagnoses, of operations and cures promised and cures failed. He was exhausted by it, hesitant to raise his hopes once again, hesitant also to miss trying something that might work.

He was not in any way a part of the San Diego team. Lloyd Free, whom he had liked, was gone; Marvin Barnes, who had been his closest friend, was out of the league and trying to hold on in Italy. Even Italy looked like it was over for Marvin. There had been a wire service story a few days earlier about Marvin being let go by his Italian team and almost immediately picked up by Italian police on drug charges. "Marvin's the last innocent," Walton said. "If there were six people in a car and they had drugs and Mar-vin had met them all only a few hours earlier and the police came after the car, Marvin would tell them to give him the coke and the gun so that he could hold them when the cops arrived."

At the beginning of the season Walton had shown up at games wearing civvies, and Silas had asked him to sit in the stands instead of on the bench. Silas did not want the other players tantalized as they had been last year. Walton could understand that, it was only a minor wound. Another eve-ning had been much worse. On Halloween night the Clippers held a com-petition for the best costume worn by a fan. A man in red hair wearing a basketball uniform and with his leg in a cast had arrived on crutches. Be-side him was someone dressed as a witch doctor, carrying a sign saying BILL WALTON'S DOCTOR. The cheering had been deafening and the man had won the contest. Walton had felt humiliated and had wanted to leave. It was a moment, he felt, of unusual cruelty, and it reinforced his skepticism about fan loyalty. He knew the Clippers were distancing themselves from him. A reporter asked Hal Childs, the Clipper public relations man, how Walton was doing. "Bill Walton's not on this team," Childs had answered.

If he played, he would play for the love of the game, and for his teammates, Walton told friends. He kept a small piece of paper stuck on the icebox in his kitchen. On it was a quotation that someone had sent him from Arnold Schwarzenegger, the weightlifter: "The mind is the limit. We know now that it's not the body. As long as you can envision the fact that you can do something, you can do it—as long as you believe 100%. It's all mind over matter."

LARRY STEELE, AFTER playing his last game for Portland in early November 1979, had spent most of his time trying to rehabilitate his knees. There had been an arthroscopy on his right knee in late November, a quick shaving of cartilage, but the knee did not respond quickly. Dr. Cook had sent him to other doctors and in late February 1980, Steele had his right knee done again. Then in early May he had his *left* knee done as well. None of these was major knee surgery, but still, it was three knee operations within six months. He was anxious to play one more season, which would give him ten years in the league—all, he hoped, with one team. In addition he had one other problem, which was that his salary for the coming year—roughly $110,000—was not guaranteed. If he made the team, it would have to be behind both Calvin Natt and Bobby Gross.

For a time that summer there was less pain and Steele took it very easy, though teaching at several basketball camps. He was aware that his legs lacked both the strength and the flex he needed for the coming season. He went to a medical clinic and worked out on the Cybex machine which registered virtually no increase in the strength of his knee. That was disquieting. In early September Steele went to see Harry Glickman to tell him that he thought he would not be able to start the season but that he wanted to give it one more shot, and try another operation. This time he went to Dr. Lanny Johnson in East Lansing, Michigan, an expert knee surgeon, who on September 17 made another attempt to smooth down the rough cartilage on the underside of his knee. Dr. Johnson told him to do nothing for two months. Just to be sure that he would be ready, on October 10 Steele had his left knee done again. That made five knee operations in one year, and by then the season had begun. When he returned to Portland and limped into the locker room his friend Bobby Gross had looked up, grinned and said, "Out a week to ten days, huh, Larry?"

It soon became very clear to Steele that the team wanted him to retire. He was told that Portland planned to put him on waivers, which meant that any team in the league could pick him up without paying compensation to Portland. Given his physical condition, it was of course highly unlikely that any team would. It also meant that Portland, having cut him from its roster, would not be required to pay him his salary for the coming year. Steele was stunned by the news; there was, he thought, nothing colder or uglier than being put on waivers, a used barely warm body unwanted by those who knew it best. Steele had always believed that professional sports was a business, that loyalties were minimal, but considering the length of his career, all of it with this team, and considering the fact that he had never drawn big money, he believed he was entitled to more courtesy and more generosity. All he wanted was a chance to recover from surgery and see if he could play again, even if that meant drawing part of his salary. His relations with the team became touchy; he was doing some broadcasting for Portland, and trying to state his case to the front office. The discussions between him and Harry Glickman and Stu Inman were acrimonious. They told him that by putting him on waivers they were doing him a favor; he did not see it that way. For a time it appeared that his case might go to arbitration, which he also considered an unseemly way to end a career.

In the end the club waived him but agreed to pay him for roughly a quarter of the season. It also agreed to help him in his claim against the insurance company for his disability pay. Thus did Larry Steele's active career with the Portland Trail Blazers end. He tried not to be bitter about it. It was, he said, just one of the breaks of the game. Friends in business told him that this sort of thing happened all the time in the corporate world, especially when men reached higher career levels where salaries were greater. The only difference between him and other executives, they told him, was that he was more visible. That, and the illusion of team loyalty. Though he had worried about his knees, he now felt confident that he could lead a relatively normal life. He played racquetball regularly; if he played a little too hard, then he had to ease up for several days. But he was sure he was not going to end up a young man with an old man's body, like so many athletes he knew. Steele liked doing the broadcasting and he was hoping soon to go to work for an advertising company, capitalizing on the name that he had spent so many years in Portland building up. A new child had been born and for the first time he really had time to be around the house and enjoy the miracle of a baby's early months. Still, it felt odd having the winters off.

DAVE TWARDZIK'S BACK bothered him all summer. Whenever he played racquetball the pain was terrible and did not last, as in the past, for a day or two. Now it lasted for four or five days. It was, he decided, a payback for all the years when he had used his body to absorb the charges of much bigger, stronger players. Nevertheless, he had wanted to play for one more season and so he worked harder in the summer than he ever had in the past. He ran three and a half miles a day, and he ran hard; his time was consistently under twenty-five minutes. But when he appeared at camp, his back betrayed him. Each time he tried playing, he had to stay out for several days. His career, he realized, was probably coming to an end. His money for the 1980–81 season was guaranteed, so he felt no financial pressure. He did some work for Ramsay at home games, sitting on the bench, keeping statistics, charting plays, and he saw the game differently and more distantly now. The players' mistakes were much more obvious to him. He suddenly wondered how Ramsay managed to control his temper as well as he did. There was some talk of his going to work in the front office on the promotional side, but he regarded the salary offered as insultingly small. Still, he kept in shape, he planned to work hard during the next summer, and if his back held up he would try out for the fall camp in 1981. He would be thirty-one by then, sixteen months out of the game, but the league was going back to a twelve-man roster and there was no telling what might happen. . . .

JIM BREWER KNEW that his chances of making the team were uncertain. He felt that he had proved during the past season that he could play, if not in Portland then at least somewhere in the league. Yet it became clear as the fall camp progressed that he was locked in a struggle for the last remaining forward job with a third-round draft choice named Michael Harper. Harper was a beguiling rookie, taller and younger than Brewer; the coaches were high on him. One day Brewer went to practice and noticed Ramsay and Inman off to one side talking. They were, he realized, looking at him. Brewer felt his heart beating very quickly. He was sure he was going to be given the bad news that he had been cut. As Ramsay talked, players watching saw Brewer's face begin to break into a huge smile. He shook hands with Ramsay and started walking towards the dressing room. "Anything wrong, Brute?" one of the players asked. "Nothing at all, nothing at all," he answered. "They just traded me to L.A." Confident of Kelvin Ransey and Billy Bates, Portland also traded T. R. Dunn to Denver for a second-round draft choice.

BILLY RAY BATES showed up for the regular-season training camp a little early. He had gone on a local radio show and someone asked him about playing in the Continental league. "The Continental league—that's like hanging around a great street corner. Lots of action there, but you can't hang around a street corner all your life." Amazing, thought Steve Kelley, he's even begun to speak Inman-talk.

IN THE FALL and winter of 1980, Stu Inman was a troubled man, puzzled and bothered by his own behavior. His daughter Janice, a student at Oregon State, one of five children, had the previous spring become pregnant and very shortly thereafter married Steve Johnson, a 6'11" All-American center from Oregon State who also happened to be black. The Inmans were stunned by the marriage and did not deal well with it; their welcome to their new son-in-law was minimal. This had been troubling not just to the young couple and to many of Inman's own friends both in and out of basketball, but increasingly painful to Inman himself, who in the months following the marriage often reviewed his behavior and found his lack of warmth and generosity disturbing. The Inmans were serious, churchgoing people and they wanted to do the right thing; they had not been able, Inman realized, to deal with the most basic human situation imaginable. Inman was aware, in addition, that his response was being closely scrutinized by his associates in the game, both black and white, including members of his own team who had been to his home for dinner, liked him and found the episode puzzling. Now as the season progressed he tried to understand why he had not responded better. It was a situation which he had never thought would happen, yet it had, and his initial anger had been followed, to his surprise, by a feeling of self-pity. He was the middle-class son of conservative California parents whose attitudes on matters like these, forged in the early part of this century, were somewhat narrow. But he had tried to grow as a man and to go beyond that background. He was proud of the fact that when he was interviewed for a job at the University of Idaho some twenty years earlier and had been told by one of the University officials, "Stu, out here we only play three of them at a time"—*them* of course meaning blacks—he had quickly answered, "You've got the wrong man." That had ended the interview. His wife, Elinor, came from an even more conservative background; he knew that Janice's marriage had been harder for her. She had, for the first time in their marriage, burst into tears. He tried to be as honest as he could with himself. Certainly the circumstances of the wedding had bothered him. But the more he thought about it, the more he was convinced that if it had been a white boy he would have reacted far differently. That knowledge was painful. For the person he saw as he looked harder and harder at himself was not the person he wanted to be.

As the season progressed Oregon State was ranked for much of the time as the number-one team in the nation with Steve Johnson as its star. Gradually Stu Inman began to build a better relationship with his son-in-law and, with the college draft approaching, began to advise him on various agents. Inman felt that he and his wife were doing better. Both of them were captivated by their grandson, Marcus.

THE TRAIL BLAZERS started their new season poorly. Ramsay had worked all summer to simplify the offense, throwing out most of the old plays, because he thought them too complicated for these players, and adapting new ones to their considerably different talents. But the training camp and exhibition season were not good. Kelvin Ransey, the key player, was not there, and all the other players seemed slightly out of sync and out of position. Ransey had shown up after the first game signed, but not quite in playing trim, about fifteen pounds overweight. ("I know what I'm going to call him," said Mychal Thompson. "Mrs. Butterworth's, because he's thick and rich.")

It became apparent early in the season that this was not a coherent team. There were the finesse players—Owens, Thompson, Gross—and the power players—Washington, Natt and Kunnert—and it was not so easy to blend them; the team was either strong but not fluid, or fluid but lacking in muscle. They stumbled, began to lose, played tight. As the team played tight it lost, and as it lost it played even tighter. No one had ever seen Ramsay so tense. He seemed unreachable, not just to reporters, but to players and friends. Ron Culp joked that when he booked rooms on the road, he had to avoid getting Ramsay a room with a balcony. Gradually the team began to junk its new offense and return to the old one. Still the players remained tight. At one point, almost a third of the way into the season, the record was a dismal 7 and 19. That was especially damaging to Ramsay; unlike the previous season, marked as it was by contract struggles and injuries, this time—except for Ransey's late arrival—there were no exterior problems. Close friends wondered whether Ramsay would stay in Portland after the season, whether he would want to and whether Weinberg would want him. Weinberg, it was said, was beginning to think of alternative coaches.

Then gradually the team began to win. Its improvement was not dramatic, but its record was; where it had once lost close games it now began to win them. It went on a streak where it won 14 and lost 1. Everyone began to play more loosely. Kelvin Ransey was even better than anyone had hoped. Jimmy Paxson, who had had such a tentative rookie year, blossomed and played skilled intelligent basketball, and to the delight of his coaches began to contest turf with opposing players and yell at referees. He had, a year later, joined the NBA. Mychal Thompson seemed recovered from his broken leg. It was a good team, though still, in matchups with the league's powerhouses, somewhat weak at center. Tom Owens was not having a good year. Kevin Kunnert had been hurt again and was playing tentatively. Mychal Thompson, who preferred playing power forward, was playing center on offense, and Kermit Washington was playing it on defense. It was a team just one piece away from becoming powerful. Still, in contrast with a year ago when it had been on the decline, it was now suddenly on the ascent again.

Ramsay began to relax. Soon, Larry Weinberg had re-signed Ramsay for a new three-year contract, with two option years for the club. Ramsay's doubts about staying in Portland seemed to have been wiped away by the success of the team in the second half of the season. The salary was said to be more than $200,000 a year; the big money from the new commercialism of basketball, which had first reached the players, had finally reached their coach.

KERMIT WASHINGTON WAS named captain of the team. His second season in Portland did not begin easily. Because it was not decided in the early days of the season whether Mychal Thompson would play at power forward or at center, Kermit's role was uncertain. Physically he was suffering from a prolonged bout with the flu. What was even more bothersome to the Portland coaches was the word being passed among some of the league's other power forwards that Kermit, because of the Tomjanovich affair, could not respond to escalated pushing and shoving. First Mark Olberding, then Reggie King and Lonnie Shelton, had taken advantage of Kermit's vulnerability and pushed him around. Worse, no one else on the team was stepping in to protect Kermit and draw a line. It was a symbol of something lacking in the team, a spiritual sense of connection. It would not have been a problem, Steve Kelley thought, if Luke were still there. Finally, in a game against Phoenix when Alvan Adams, one of the least physical players in the league, had beaten on Kermit several times, and no one had come to his defense, Ramsay, as Adams ran down the court, had screamed at him. "Do that one more time, Alvan, and I'll take care of you myself." Adams had immediately taken himself out of the game, and the beating on Washington had stopped.

BILLY RAY BATES started the season erratically. There were brilliant games followed by weak ones. The talent remained impressive, but harnessing it a problem. But gradually, as Ransey came into his own, Bates flourished. He and Ransey appeared to play particularly well together, with Ransey supplying the total court vision that Billy so badly needed. The coaches still worried about Billy, whether the *social* stress of playing in the NBA was going to be too much, and whether he might not become a mark for all of the sharks who lurked just a step outside the locker room, promoting their own form of flattery and hope and destruction. The gap between Billy's level of sophistication and that of most of his teammates seemed considerable; there were worries that he simply lacked friends and had to eat alone too often on the road. Teammates tried to help him, but Billy, they soon decided, had a need to be around sycophants, fans and instant friends who would tell him how great he was. That did not bode well.

THE TELEVISION RATINGS for the league were not good. The 1979–80 season had seen a mild improvement because of the arrival of Larry Bird and Magic Johnson. But it was only a small increase, and CBS still treated basketball as a stepchild. A new head of sports, Van Gordon Sauter, appeared at CBS, and the first thing the owners asked was: is he a basketball fan or a golf fan? Sauter turned out to be a basketball fan, committed to the game within limits. He talked with conviction about the problem of selling a sport which he believed genuinely exciting but not yet national, an urban game with certain limited centers of strength in the country. The year 1981–82 was the last one on the big four-year $74 million contract which CBS had signed with the league. In the final year, each team would get roughly one million. There was increasing talk that CBS was disenchanted with professional basketball and might drop the sport. Given the shakiness of several franchises and their inability to generate very much local television money, that might mean several bankruptcies, and the league could be damaged even further.

CBS worked hard to put on its most attractive presentations each Sunday, trying to steal the spotlight back from college basketball, broadcast by NBC. On Sunday, February 22, the two networks went head to head. CBS showed the New York Knicks, a vastly improved young team, against the Los Angeles Lakers. It was, even with Magic Johnson out with a knee injury, a marvelous media package, pitting the two great national markets against one another. Opposite it, NBC arranged a game between Notre Dame—always a great television draw with its national constituency—and Virginia, with the talented and very tall young Ralph Sampson. It was a great day for the Irish and for Mr. Sampson. The ratings showed that Virginia–Notre Dame had a very respectable 8 rating, while what might have been a powerhouse game in another time, New York–Los Angeles, drew a devastating 4. Very shortly thereafter a team of CBS Sports people flew out to meet with the representatives of the NCAA, and bought, starting in 1982, the rights to the college basketball championship playoffs for three years. The cost was a total of $48 million, or $16 million a year. It was a great victory for college basketball, and there were those who felt it might mean that CBS was preparing to drop the professional sport, or at least to curtail its coverage.

THE LEAGUE'S PROBLEMS were not limited to its television ratings. Live attendance was bad too. It had averaged around 11,000 a game the year before and now it was down nearly 10 percent, to about 10,000. Only 6 of 22 teams showed an increase in attendance and 7 of the teams had a decline of more than 2,000 spectators a game.

MAURICE LUCAS, WHO had worked so hard to get into shape, did not enjoy a very good year. Almost from the beginning things started going wrong. His new team, the New Jersey Nets, let their one legitimate center, George

Johnson, slip away and sign with San Antonio. That affected Luke's game, and for part of the season he found himself, much to his annoyance, playing center. In addition he suffered constant problems with both Achilles tendons, the most dangerous kind of problem a basketball player could have. He rarely felt in good condition. In addition the team he was with was young and uncertain, doomed it seemed to regular defeat. His own season was uneven, good games sandwiched between bad games. Two-thirds of the way through the season a deal was arranged which would send Luke to Seattle for the rights to Gus Williams, but at the last minute it fell through. Luke was wounded by all the talk about it and the whole business had underlined how short a stay could be, and how fragile was an athlete's status in a franchise.

In mid-February of 1981, almost three years to the day since he had first seriously injured his foot in the Portland-Seattle playoff game, Bill Walton, after much deliberation, went into the hospital to have his foot operated on. The hope was to gain greater flex. His doctor, Tony Daly, insisted that even if the operation was successful there was virtually no chance that Walton would ever play professional basketball again. The operation was designed merely to allow Walton to walk and participate marginally in informal athletics with minimal pain. Walton at once accepted that judgment, that he would never play basketball again, that, in the doctors' words, if he played sports again it would be as an avocation, not a vocation. At the same time, he continued to believe that if he was lucky and kept himself in shape he might still play. He did some broadcasting for UCLA, and was considered very good at it, albeit quite outspoken. CBS seemed in no rush to have him join any of its broadcast teams. He enrolled in a San Diego law school intending to pursue a career as a lawyer.

Shortly after that, the San Diego Clippers announced that they would accept an out-of-court $1,250,000 settlement from Lloyd's of London in the Bill Walton case. The settlement meant that there was still some $4 million more of their own money that the Clippers were obligated to pay Walton over the next five years.

Irv Levin, who had once referred to his decision to sign Walton, injuries and all, as "crapshooting," something he would never have done had he owned a stable franchise, decided to stop rolling the dice. To no one's particular surprise, he sold the San Diego Clippers to Donald Sterling, a Los

Angeles realtor-lawyer, for $13.5 million, a figure far far greater than the amount he had spent to buy in.

PORTLAND, AS THE season wore on, continued to need a center badly. The shadow of Moses Malone, having another brilliant season, continued to hang over the Blazers. One night the team arrived in Houston several days before a game with the Rockets. The first night, with nothing to do, Ramsay and a few friends went to the Houston–Golden State game to scout. That night Moses tore up the Warriors—fifty-one points and nineteen rebounds. Late in the fourth quarter, with Moses's play already devastating Golden State, Joe Gushue, the referee, went over to Ramsay. "Hey, Jack," he said. "Tell Harry Glickman he's right—Moses will never make it in this league."

The adjustment to Philadelphia was difficult at first for Lionel Hollins. Where Portland was disciplined, its practices intense and, in Hollins's word, rigid, Philadelphia, with so much more natural power, was loose and casual. Portland's players, perhaps less physically talented, were strong in their fundamentals; the Sixer players, awesomely physical, were weaker in their basics, and seemed to believe that their sheer strength could always bail them out. That often proved true during the regular season and untrue in the playoffs. The Blazers built their season around their practices and to an uncommon degree practice was the glue that held the team together; the Sixers did not practice every day, and when they did work out, it was rarely intense or lasted for more than an hour. Hollins, who in his Portland incarnation believed that Ramsay pressed the team too hard at practices during the season, now found himself at the other extreme. When he complained to his teammates about the lack of focus in their practices, pointing out that there were in fact certain plays they needed to work on, they scorned him. "Hey, man, don't come in here with that Portland shit," one of them would say. "This is Philly, we do it our way here, not Portland's way."

In the tail end of the 1979–80 season Lionel Hollins had made the Sixer backcourt more coherent and had played a major role in Philadelphia's five-game destruction of Boston. In his second season, 1980–81, he played more and seemed to make the Sixers a stronger team. The Philadelphia weaknesses were traditionally a lack of effort on defense and an instinct for one-on-one offense. Hollins by contrast was a fine defensive guard and an unselfish player on offense. With him in the lineup Philadelphia seemed

now each season further from the playground basketball of 1977 and closer
to a fine balance between disciplined teamwork, while still maintaining the
special highly individualistic skills of its players. He felt lucky that he had
been traded to Philadelphia and luckier still that in his career he had had a
chance to play on teams with Bill Walton and Julius Erving. Lionel Hollins
thought that all in all the trade had worked out better for him than he had
any reason to expect. He still did not, as befit a professional athlete, know
what his home was; he had a house in Portland and he had bought a condo
in Philadelphia. As for home—perhaps in the end these decisions were
made for you.

WALKING THROUGH DOWNTOWN Phoenix one night, Ramsay and Buckwalter came upon an art gallery. There they saw a small statue of an impassioned naked man, a madman if truth be told, on his knees, face enraged,
arms raised as if to the gods, imploring above all else an end to the injustice
of his life. The two coaches saw it and both, at exactly the same time, began
to laugh. "What's the title?" Ramsay asked. "Portrait of a coach in his last
season," said Buckwalter. "No," said Ramsay, "it's 'Damn it, Jake, make the
call.'" That was in honor of Jake O'Donnell, one of his favorite referees.
Later that day Buckwalter went back and bought the statue for Ramsay and
had a small plaque attached to it. Then he presented the statue to Ramsay.
The plaque said: DAMN IT, JAKE, MAKE THE CALL.

CALVIN NATT, THE player that Portland got for Maurice Lucas, did not have
a good season in 1980–81. He arrived in camp somewhat overweight, and
Ramsay was mildly displeased. Soon he lost his starting place to Bobby
Gross, and when the team finally began to play well, Gross was a key factor.
Natt did not take the demotion well and seemed to sulk. When Ramsay put
him in a game he was deliberately slow to get off the bench and report to the
scorer's table. He complained to teammates and reporters that Ramsay only
treated him decently and talked to him when he was playing well, and that
not enough plays were being run for him. It soon became clear to Ramsay
that Natt was probably playing out of position at small forward; he was
burly and strong and his game was one of bang and shove but he lacked the
overall grace and his shooting eye lacked the fine edge demanded of the
small forward in the Ramsay system. Soon he and Ramsay began to disagree over the amount of time he was getting, and, even more, over how

good a jump shot he had; he told teammates he didn't care what Portland did with him; if Portland chose not to use him properly, some other team would, sooner or later. Inman, who had liked Natt because of his character, and who had been so nakedly enthusiastic about him just a year earlier, now cooled off and spoke vaguely of him as a journeyman player who would have to learn to play within his limits in this league.

WHEN THE 1980–81 season was over, Portland tried desperately to market Calvin Natt, either for another player, or as a means of moving up in the draft to get a center. None of the potential deals was consummated, and on the day of the 1981 draft, Portland, drafting 15 and 16, was still trying to move up, using Natt as the bait in order to switch picks with Utah and se-cure a promising albeit unfinished young center named Danny Schayes. Inman went to Weinberg for the approval of the move and the owner ex-ploded. "My god," he said, "a year ago we gave up Maurice Lucas and two firsts for this guy and now all we're getting back is a chance to move up a few notches in the draft." Soon, however, he calmed down, and approved the move, though Utah then backed off.

JUST BEFORE THE draft, Portland, disappointed with his play, traded Tom Owens to Indiana for a first-round draft choice in 1984. Both Mychal Thompson and Kevin Kunnert had recovered sufficiently from their leg injuries to make Owens available. That was one more change in the Blazer team which had started the 1979–80 season. Gone from that team were Lucas, in New Jersey, Hollins, in Philly, Dunn in Denver, Ron Brewer (traded in the middle of the 1980–81 season for a first-round choice) in San Antonio, and Abdul Jeelani in Dallas.

AT ALMOST THE same time Portland quietly changed Billy Ray Bates's con-tract. Though the deal was called an extension, others familiar with it re-garded it as a renegotiation, for the money in the years already covered by Billy's existing contract immediately grew bigger. Billy was pleased by the contract. Portland was also showing exceptional sensitivity in handling Bates. At the urging of both Inman and Ramsay, Billy was attending a spe-cial remedial reading class in Portland. To the joy of the people who ran the school, Billy, the most celebrated student the school had ever had, was will-ing to talk publicly about his inability to read, about the social problems it caused him and how he had managed to fool people in the past by reading a key word or two from a paper, but never an entire paragraph, or a book. "Now I'm saying to myself, 'Billy Ray, don't play dumb. You gotta wake up and find out who Billy Ray Bates is,'" he said. The root of his problem, he said, was growing up in Mississippi, where black people did not read because they did not need to read, but used a very limited number of words with varying inflections. "People there speak with soul feeling," he said, "soul words. Common words, but used in a very influenced way." His problem, he said, was always with big words. To demonstrate, he picked up a pamphlet and and showed the words he could read, and the longer ones he had trouble with. The pamphlet was the press guide for the Phoenix Suns. "See," he said, "I have trouble with a word like this." He pointed to a big word. The word was "Auerbach."

IN THE LATE spring after the season the Blazers sent out a press release announcing that in the fall they would retire the uniform numbers of Geoff Petrie, David Twardzik and Larry Steele. Steve Kelley picked up the sheet, read it and called the front office. "Hey," he said, "Twardzik hasn't retired yet." A few minutes later there was a call back from the office. "We're retiring his number provisionally," the official said.

Acknowledgments

THIS IS A BOOK that I researched by being there. I traveled with the players and coaches, I lived with them throughout the entire season and I talked to them almost continually—in many cases thirty times or more. It was, in the truest sense, a season shared. Living so completely in the world of basketball, I saw countless people who were connected to the game for brief interviews; I must thank them without mentioning their names. What follows here is a list of people who accorded me prolonged interviews, usually sessions that lasted more than an hour or two.

Roone Arledge, Red Auerbach, Marvin Barnes, John Bassett, Billy Ray Bates, Joe Boyland, Senator Bill Bradley, Jim Brewer, Ron Brewer, Irv Brodsky, Morris Buckwalter, Paula Buckwalter, Greg Bunch, Mike Burke, Jim Capers, Hal Childs, Jeff Cohen, Jerry Colangelo, Tray Coleman, Beano Cook, Dr. Robert Cook, David Cowens, Jack Craig, Bobby Cremins, Ron Culp, Billy Cunningham, Dan Donoher, T. R. Dunn, Wayne Embry, John Engstrom, Jack Faust, David Fine, Bill Fitch, Cotton Fitzsimmons, Larry Fleisher, Barry Frank, Les Gelb, Betty Gilliam, Herm Gilliam, Harry Glickman, Mike Granberry, Sihugo Green, Ed Gregory, Bobby Gross, Matty Guokas, Joe Gushue, Les Habegger, Joe Hamelin, Arthur Hartfelt, Mark Heisler, Tom Hohensee, Berlyn Hodges, Lionel Hollins, Rod Hundley, Elinor Inman, Stu Inman, Phil Jackson,

Abdul Jeelani, Wilson Jackson, Dennis Johnson, John Johnson, Jimmy Jones, Steve Jones, Steve Kauffman, Chris Kauffman, Steve Kelley, Bill King, Butch Komives, Bobby Knight, Kevin Kunnert, Steve Leff, Don Leventhal, Kevin Loughery, Maurice Lucas, Rita Lucas, Bob MacKinnon, Pete Maravich, LaRue Martin, Al McGuire, Clare McKinney, Jack McKinney, Ray Melchiorre, Anne Meschery, Tom Meschery, Gail Miller, Calvin Natt, Gordon Nash, Lloyd Neal, Don Nelson, Pete Newell, Bruce Newman, Nick Nichols, Tom Nissalke, Milt Northrup, Rich O'Connor, Bruce Ogilvie, Tom Owens, Senator Bob Packwood, Jimmy Paxson, Geoff Petrie, Carolyn Ramsay, Chris Ramsay, Jack Ramsay, Jean Ramsay, Kelvin Ransey, George Rickles, Jay Rosenstein, Pete Rozelle, Steve Rudman, Bob Ryan, Dr. Paul Saltman, Van Gordon Sauter, Leta Schlosser, Bill Schonely, Jack Scott, Gene Shue, Paul Silas, Howard Slusher, Pat Smithson, Norm Sonjou, Jon Spoelstra, Larry Steele, John Strawn, Mychal Thompson, Wayne Thompson, David Twardzik, Mike Uporsky, Dick Vertlieb, Donnie Walsh, Bill Walton, Gloria Walton, Susan Walton, Ted Walton, Kermit Washington, Pat Washington, Larry Weinberg, Tommy Weinberg, Nancy Welts, Paul Westphal, Kenny Wheeler, Lenny Wilkens, Dave Wohl, Jim Wooten, Bart Wright, Allen Yarnell, Tom Young.

I WANT ALSO to thank the management and the players of the Portland Trail Blazers basketball team for being so cooperative during the time I spent with them, and for making it so pleasant as well as so valuable a year. In particular, in the Blazers' office, I would like to thank Mss. Sandy Chisholm, Gail Miller, Lori Ryan, Kathy Cereghino and Cheri White for all the courtesies offered during a busy season. In addition, certain other people were helpful far beyond the call of duty: Steve Kelley of the *Oregonian,* John Engstrom and Steve Rudman of the *Seattle Post-Intelligencer,* Bob Ryan (the game's ombudsman) and Jack Craig of the *Boston Globe;* and in San Diego, Mike Granberry of the *Los Angeles Times* bureau and Joe Hamelin of the *San Diego Union.* In addition I want to thank Alan Schwartz, my lawyer; my editor, Chuck Elliott, and his assistant, Elizabeth Catenaccio, and Lesley Krauss; Matthew and John Schwartz for their help; Irene Smirnoff for typing the manuscript; John Murphy for helping with the uniquely complicated travel arrangements; Jay Lovinger, Neal Dunlap and Stevie McCarthy for their help; and above all John Strawn and Steve Jones for friendship offered and gratefully accepted.

—DAVID HALBERSTAM